Eat Well
Stay Well

StayWell

More than 250 delicious recipes made with foods that heal and keep you healthy

Reader's Digest, Sydney • Auckland

FOR READER'S DIGEST, AUSTRALIA

Editor
Laraine Newberry

Designer
Kate Finnie

Research Editor
Alistair McDermott

Assistant Editor & Indexer
Françoise Toman

Proofreader
Lynn Cole

Production Controller
Bruce Holden

CONTRIBUTORS

Recipe Consultant & Food Stylist
Janet Mitchell

Food Photographer
John Hollingshead

Nutritional Advisers
Jeanine Barone
Lorraine Endicott

READER'S DIGEST GENERAL BOOKS

Editorial Director
Carol Natsis

Art Director
Phillip Bush

Managing Editor
Elaine Russell

Cover photograph:
Veal Scaloppine with Sage
& Lemon (page 220)

Title page photograph:
Fresh Apricots Poached in Syrup
(page 261)

Eat Well, Stay Well

Published by Reader's Digest (Australia) Pty Limited
26–32 Waterloo Street, Surry Hills, NSW 2010.
http://www.readersdigest.com.au

First Australian and New Zealand edition 2001

Eat Well, Stay Well was created by Rebus, Inc.,
632 Broadway, 11th Floor, New York, NY10012, USA
for The Reader's Digest Association, Inc., of Pleasantville, New York, USA.

National Library of Australia Cataloguing-in-Publication data:

Eat well, stay well: more than 250 delicious recipes made with foods that heal
and keep you healthy.

   Includes index.
   ISBN 1 876689 31 5.

1. Nutrition. 2. Diet therapy. 3. Health. I. Reader's Digest (Australia).

641.563

Colour separations by Rainbow Graphic Arts Co. Ltd, Hong Kong
Printed and bound by Tien Wah Press (Pte) Ltd, Singapore

We are interested in receiving your comments on the content of this book.
Write to: The Editor, General Books Editorial,
Reader's Digest (Australia) Pty Ltd,
26–32 Waterloo Street, Surry Hills, NSW 2010
or e-mail us at bookeditors.au@readersdigest.com

Eating well is the key to good health

Nearly every day, researchers announce another exciting discovery about the foods we eat and how they affect our health. Recent studies have shown that vitamins and minerals are more significant than they were previously thought to be, and that some foods and nutrients can help fight illnesses ranging from heart disease and cancer to high blood pressure and cataracts.

It has been found, for instance, that fruit, vegetables, legumes, grains and seeds are not only rich in vitamins and minerals, but also contain compounds called phytochemicals, which can boost immunity and lower the risk of disease. But you don't need to adopt a vegetarian diet to stay healthy. Meat, poultry, fish, eggs and dairy products also supply nutrients that are important for good health. This book covers all the essential food groups, helping you prepare meals that are always delicious.

At the beginning of *Eat Well, Stay Well* you'll find a comprehensive glossary of nutritional terms and information on the foods that fight illnesses. There is also a special illustrated section of step-by-step techniques for preparing healthy food.

The main part of the book gives you more than 250 mouthwatering recipes for tempting ways to cook foods that are good for you. It also gives you important information about these foods, including guidelines for buying and preparation. And the nutritional analysis for each featured food or recipe provides details of the major nutrients it supplies.

As an added bonus, we've marked all the quick recipes – those that can be prepared, cooked and served in 30 minutes or less – with a special symbol for easy identification.

The Editor

Contents

Nutrition A–Z

A

Alcohol

Ethanol (ethyl alcohol) – the active ingredient of alcoholic drinks – is made by yeast fermentation of starch from grains or potato or from sugars such as sucrose (from cane sugar) or fructose (from fruits). The alcohol content of beverages ranges from a high 40 per cent for liqueurs and spirits to 10 or 15 per cent for wines and 2 to 5 per cent for beer. These drinks are primarily a source of energy (KILOJOULES) and lack most essential nutrients. Cooking will evaporate the alcohol content of the beverage, leaving the flavours to enhance the dish.

Allyl sulphides

These PHYTOCHEMICALS are found in onion-family plants – onions, leeks, chives, shallots, spring onions and garlic. Allyl sulphides are sulphur compounds that seem to suppress the production of CHOLESTEROL and help lower blood pressure; they may also have some cancer-fighting properties in that they may deactivate certain hormones that promote tumour growth.

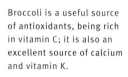

Broccoli is a useful source of antioxidants, being rich in vitamin C; it is also an excellent source of calcium and vitamin K.

Amino acids

The building blocks of PROTEIN. Of the 21 amino acids, nine are *essential*, meaning that they cannot be produced by your body. You must obtain these amino acids from the protein in food. The essential amino acids are histidine, lysine, isoleucine, leucine, methionine, phenylalanine, valine, threonine and tryptophan. Histidine, however, is only an essential amino acid for children as their bodies are unable to make enough to meet the needs for rapid growth.

Anticarcinogens

Substances that fight cancer. Research has shown that many substances in food may be anticarcinogenic. They include VITAMIN C, VITAMIN E and BETA-CAROTENE, and a host of PHYTOCHEMICALS such as ISOFLAVONES, ELLAGIC ACID and SULPHORAPHANE.

Antioxidants

Compounds that deactivate and repair the damage caused by FREE RADICALS, thus preventing the onset of certain diseases. A number of antioxidants are found in food. For instance, BETA-CAROTENE, VITAMIN C and VITAMIN E are known to be antioxidants; scientists are currently researching the antioxidant capabilities of the many different plant compounds called PHYTOCHEMICALS.

Antioxidants are also a class of carefully controlled food additive; they are used in foods containing fats and oils to delay or prevent them from turning rancid or changing in taste, odour and appearance.

Ascorbic acid *see* VITAMIN C

B

Beta-carotene

The most common of the 600 or more CAROTENOIDS, beta-carotene gives colour to carrots, rockmelon and other orange and yellow fruits and vegetables; it's found in dark-green vegetables, too, but its orange colour is obscured by the green colour of chlorophyll. Beta-carotene is a VITAMIN A precursor; that is, the body converts available beta-carotene (from food products) into as much vitamin A as it requires. Beta-carotene is a cancer fighter and may also help prevent cataracts, in both cases partly through its ANTIOXIDANT function. Beta-carotene also seems to enhance immune function.

Beta glucans

The type of soluble DIETARY FIBRE found in barley and oats. Beta glucans have been shown to lower blood CHOLESTEROL levels.

Biotin

One of the B vitamins, biotin is made by the body, so deficiencies of it are virtually unknown. Biotin plays a role in the metabolism of PROTEIN and CARBOHYDRATES. Good food sources include eggs, dairy products, legumes and whole grains.

Boron

A trace MINERAL that possibly works in conjunction with CALCIUM and MAGNESIUM to build strong bones. Boron is found in most foods of plant origin, especially fruits, vegetables and nuts.

Brassica

The cabbage family, which also includes broccoli, Brussels sprouts and cauliflower. These plants are known as CRUCIFEROUS VEGETABLES.

Good Sources of Calcium

Food	Amount	Calcium (mg)
Almonds	50g	118
Broccoli, fresh, cooked	1 serving (150g)	44
Buttermilk	1 cup	372
Cheese, Cheddar	30g	232
Cheese, cottage, low-fat	100g	77
Cheese, mozzarella	30g	262
Cheese, Parmesan	30g	345
Cheese, Swiss	30g	265
Milk, low-fat	1 cup	353
Prawns, king, cooked	6 prawns	131
Salmon, canned, drained, eaten with bones	100g	310
Sardines, canned, eaten with bones	2 sardines	114
Soya drink, calcium-fortified	1 cup	302
Sunflower seeds	20g	20
Tahini (sesame seed paste)	20g	66
Tofu	100g	330
Yoghurt, low-fat flavoured	200g	358
Yoghurt, low-fat plain	200g	420

Caffeine

A natural stimulant found in coffee, tea, colas and, to a lesser extent, chocolate. Caffeine increases the heart rate and enhances mental alertness.

Taken in moderation, caffeine can help wake you up or keep you alert; if you're not accustomed to it, however, it can make you irritable and anxious. Caffeine promotes CALCIUM loss and may increase the risk of osteoporosis. And there is some evidence that it may increase the risk of miscarriage. Pregnant and breast-feeding women should limit their caffeine intake.

Calcium

A major dietary MINERAL that builds and restores bones and teeth and is essential in the prevention of osteoporosis, the 'brittle bone disease' that can cause bone fractures in older people, especially women. An adequate calcium intake is especially important before age 35 – when your body is still building bone – but also after age 35, to maintain strong bones for a lifetime. Another function of calcium is that it helps to regulate muscle contractions, including heartbeat. Some research indicates that an adequate supply of calcium may help to counteract high blood pressure. Many dairy foods, especially milk and yoghurt, are excellent sources of calcium; some dark-green leafy vegetables, such as kale and broccoli, are also good sources, as are the types of canned fatty fish (sardines and salmon) that are eaten bones and all.

Calories

A Calorie (also called a kilocalorie) is a unit used to measure the energy potential in food and the energy used by the body. (Technically, a calorie is the amount of heat required to raise the temperature of 1 gram of water 1°C.) *See also* KILOJOULES.

Capsaicin

A PHYTOCHEMICAL found in chillies and concentrated in the seeds and ribs. Aside from the 'heat' it adds to foods, capsaicin may act as an anticoagulant, preventing blood from

Even with its burning heat, the capsaicin in chillies may help in the treatment of stomach ulcers.

clotting and sticking to blood-vessel walls. Researchers believe that capsaicin may protect DNA from CARCINOGENS, and may help kill *Helicobacter pylori* – the bacteria now known to cause most stomach ulcers. The hotness of capsaicin can also help clear up nasal congestion (think of how a spoonful of super-spicy curry seems to go right through your head) and can be useful when you have a cold. Capsaicin is potent enough to burn skin, so when you are cooking with chillies, wear rubber gloves, or else be sure to wash your hands with soap and water afterwards. Never touch your eyes after handling chillies.

Carbohydrates (sugars or starches)

Along with PROTEIN and FAT, one of the three MACRONUTRIENTS – the major components of foods.

Carbohydrates – which are either sugars or starches – are carbon compounds that the body turns into GLUCOSE, its basic fuel.

Carbohydrates are found in all foods from plant sources – fruits, vegetables, legumes and grains. Foods rich in starchy carbohydrates should make up a large part of your diet: they supply energy and usually also contain other valuable nutrients. Foods that contain large amounts of sugars may supply little else.

Naturally sweet fruits are a notable exception: they contain valuable vitamins and minerals in addition to sugar in the form of fructose or sucrose.

Carcinogen

A substance that causes the growth of cancer.

Carotenoids

These PHYTOCHEMICALS are the yellow, orange and red pigments found in fruits and vegetables. There are 600 or more carotenoids. The body converts some carotenoids, including BETA-CAROTENE, into VITAMIN A. Other carotenoids include LUTEIN, LYCOPENE and ZEAXANTHIN. Scientists are researching the ANTIOXIDANT and other cancer-fighting properties of foods containing carotenoids.

Chloride *see* CHLORINE

Chlorine

An element that in its compound forms (chlorides) is a MINERAL essential to maintaining the water balance in the body's cells. It is supplied in the diet by table salt (sodium chloride) and naturally occuring sources.

Carrots are rich in carotene, a beneficial phytochemical.

Good Sources of Beta-carotene

Food	Amount	Beta-carotene (mg)	Vitamin A equiv. (mcg)
Apricots, dried	½ cup (70g)	1.7	280
Apricots, fresh	1 medium (55g)	0.7	112
Broccoli, fresh, cooked	1 serving (150g)	0.5	88
Capsicum, red, raw	1 medium (90g)	1.3	225
Carrots, raw	2 medium (120g)	12.2	2040
Leeks, cooked	2 medium (170g)	0.7	121
Mango	1 medium (205g)	4.9	820
Pawpaw	1 cup, diced (150g)	1.3	225
Pumpkin, fresh, cooked	1 serving (160g)	4.3	720
Rockmelon	1 cup, diced (170g)	1.4	238
Spinach, fresh, cooked	1 serving (90g)	1.9	333
Sweet potato, orange, cooked	1 serving (150g)	8.6	1440
Tomato	1 large (180g)	0.6	104
Watercress, raw	1 serving (40g)	0.8	136

Cholesterol

A waxy, fatlike substance present in every cell in animals, including humans. Cholesterol is essential to several of the body's functions, including the manufacture of VITAMIN D, hormones and bile salts, so we need a certain amount of cholesterol. But when excess cholesterol circulates in the blood, it adheres to the artery walls, forming a substance called plaque that can limit blood flow and contribute to stiffening of the arteries – a condition called atherosclerosis. This can eventually lead to a heart attack or stroke.

The body produces all the cholesterol it requires, but there is also cholesterol in some foods; this dietary cholesterol does not go directly into your bloodstream. If you do consume a lot of dietary cholesterol, however, it will have the *indirect* effect of elevating your blood cholesterol level; but consumption of saturated fat does more to raise blood cholesterol – especially LDL cholesterol (*see below*) – than does consumption of cholesterol.

Only foods from animal sources (meat, poultry, seafood, eggs and dairy products) contain cholesterol. There is no cholesterol in foods from plant sources – and that includes fatty foods like nuts, avocados and coconuts, as well as vegetable, seed and nut oils.

Cholesterol circulates in the bloodstream in compounds, called lipoproteins, that also contain FAT and PROTEIN. There are two types of lipoprotein:

• *Low-density lipoprotein*, or LDL, carries CHOLESTEROL from the liver to other parts of the body. This is the cholesterol that leaves deposits on blood vessel walls. Sometimes referred to as 'bad' cholesterol.

• *High-density lipoprotein*, or HDL, performs the reverse task, carrying cholesterol from the body's tissues back to the liver – which includes removing some of the cholesterol deposits from the blood vessels. Hence, HDL is sometimes called 'good' cholesterol.

Your goal should be a low *total* blood cholesterol level (under 5.5 millimoles per litre), but the *balance* of lipoproteins is equally important: a high level of HDL (between 1.0 to 2.0 millimoles per litre) and a low level of LDL (below 3.5 millimoles per litre) is desirable. A diet low in total fat and, more important, low in saturated fat, will help you towards this goal. Eating plenty of fibre, especially soluble fibre, is also a good idea. An exercise program can also help lower your blood cholesterol.

Chromium

A trace MINERAL that helps the body turn GLUCOSE into energy, chromium also helps regulate the action of the hormone insulin. Some experts believe that chromium deficiency is fairly common, but it's easy to get an adequate amount of this mineral: it is found in meat, seafood, eggs, nuts, whole grains, dairy products, fruit and potatoes (be sure to eat the skin). Another good source of chromium is brewer's yeast – as found in a glass of beer.

Cobalt

A trace MINERAL, one of the 17 that have been identified as essential for the continuing good health of the body. The need for cobalt, which helps to make up VITAMIN B_{12}, was identified by Australian researchers in the 1920s. The body requires very small quantities and these are readily obtained from dark leafy greens and from meat. If your vitamin B_{12} intake is sufficient (2 mg for an adult female), your cobalt intake will be fine.

Copper

A trace MINERAL that aids in the formation of genetic matter, red blood cells, bones and connective tissue. Copper also supports the functioning of the immune system. Copper deficiencies are rare – but where they do occur, can cause problems in the blood and blood vessels, as well as skeletal defects. Among the best sources of copper are shellfish (especially oysters), sunflower seeds, nuts, lentils and whole grains.

Cruciferous vegetables

The word 'cruciferous', which means 'cross-shaped', describes a family of vegetables with cross-shaped flowers. Cruciferous vegetables – which are members of the cabbage family – are also called brassicas. They include cabbage, broccoli, Brussels sprouts, cauliflower and kale, as well as turnips and swedes. These vegetables contain PHYTOCHEMICALS called INDOLES, which seem to offer protection against some forms of cancer. Cruciferous vegetables are also rich in VITAMIN C, and most are good sources of DIETARY FIBRE. Those that are dark green or yellow, such as broccoli and swede, also contain BETA-CAROTENE.

Cyano-cobalamin *see* VITAMIN B_{12}

An apple a day will help contribute to your intake of dietary fibre – as well as act as a natural toothbrush.

Good Sources of Dietary Fibre

Food	Amount	Dietary Fibre (g)
Apple, with skin	1 medium (155g)	3
Barley, pearl, cooked	1 serving (110g)	4
Beans, baked	1 serving (130g)	6
Beans, kidney, cooked	1 serving (130g)	9
Corn	1 large cob	4
Figs, dried	3 figs	6
Lentils, cooked	1 serving (130g)	5
Oatmeal, cooked	1 serving (180g)	2
Pear, with skin	1 medium (185g)	5
Peas, green, fresh, cooked	1 serving (130g)	8
Peas, split, cooked	1 serving (130g)	5
Potato, peeled, boiled	1 large (185g)	4
Prunes	5 prunes	3
Rice, brown, cooked	1 serving (150g)	2
Wheat bran	2 tablespoons	4
Wheatgerm	1 tablespoon	1

D

Dietary fibre

The parts of foods from plant sources (fruits, vegetables, legumes, grains, nuts and seeds) that we eat but, for the most part, cannot digest in the small intestine. This fibre performs some vital functions in the body. There are two basic types of fibre: insoluble (insoluble in water) and soluble.

Insoluble fibre, which used to be known as roughage, is bulky material that helps move waste through the digestive tract. This promotes regular bowel function and may also reduce the risk of colon cancer. Some good sources of insoluble fibre are wheat bran and whole grains, the skins of apples and pears, and vegetables such as potatoes, carrots and broccoli.

Soluble fibre is found in oats, barley, beans and many fruits and vegetables. Some types of soluble fibre have been found to help lower blood CHOLESTEROL. Soluble fibre also helps control blood-sugar levels.

Many health experts agree that Australians and New Zealanders should increase their fibre consumption to a total of 30 grams a day. In addition to the known benefits of fibre itself, foods that are naturally high in fibre (foods from plant sources) are rich in other important nutrients.

Strawberries – along with raspberries and cranberries – contain ellagic acid, a phytochemical which inactivates carcinogens.

E

Ellagic acid

Found in strawberries, raspberries, cranberries and some other fruits, nuts and vegetables, this PHYTOCHEMICAL shows promise as a cancer preventive through its ability to inactivate CARCINOGENS and inhibit the formation of FREE RADICALS.

Endosperm

The inner kernel of a whole grain, seed or nut, which contains most of the carbohydrate (starch) and protein.

Enriched

The terms 'enriched' and 'fortified' are often used interchangeably. In Australia, enriched is rarely used.

Enrichment of foods was introduced in the 1940s and 1950s when it became economically viable to manufacture vitamins synthetically.

Enriched generally means that some of the nutrients that were lost during processing are replaced. *See also* FORTIFIED.

Fat

One of the three MACRO-NUTRIENTS found in the foods we eat. Dietary fats are vital to many of the body's functions; for instance, vitamins A, D, E and K are fat-soluble, and will not be absorbed by the body in the absence of sufficient dietary fat. And fats are important in cooking: they carry flavour, lock in moisture, and help keep baked goods tender.

Although some dietary fat is necessary, excessive fat intake can lead to obesity and it is known to also increase the risk of heart disease, diabetes and cancer.

Fats are composed of chains of fatty acids, of which there are a number of different types. These fatty acids are classified as either saturated or unsaturated, according to the number of hydrogen atoms they contain.
- *Saturated fatty acids* carry a full complement of hydrogen atoms.
- *Monounsaturated fatty acids* are missing one pair of hydrogen atoms.
- *Polyunsaturated fatty acids* lack two or more pairs of hydrogen atoms.

Fats are classified according to the proportions of fatty acids they contain: highly saturated, highly polyunsaturated, etc. Highly saturated fats are mostly animal fats, such as those found in butter, lard, meat and poultry; palm, palm kernel and coconut oil are also highly saturated. Saturated fats are usually solid at room temperature. Highly polyunsaturated fats include corn, safflower and sesame oils, while olive and canola oils are highly monounsaturated fats.

Hydrogenated fats form another category. These are vegetable oils that have been specially treated with hydrogen to make them solid at room temperature and resistant to rancidity. Hydrogenation creates what are called 'trans fatty acids' by saturating unsaturated fatty acids and changing their structure.

The different types of dietary fat have different effects on the body. Mono- and polyunsaturated fats have been shown to lower total CHOLESTEROL levels. Highly saturated fats raise total blood cholesterol and, in particular, LDL, or 'bad' cholesterol. Trans fats have a similar, and possibly worse, effect: they raise overall cholesterol and LDL, and perhaps also lower HDL. So from a health standpoint, liquid fats (cooking oils) are a better choice than solid fats (butter, lard, shortening or margarine).

Of course, overall fat intake is important, too. Health authorities recommend that adults get no more than 30 per cent of their daily KILOJOULES from fat; some researchers call for an

Peanuts, like all nuts, are high in fat, but it is mostly mono- and polyunsaturated. Their oil is good for cooking,

Comparing Cooking Oils

Type of Oil	% Poly-unsaturated	% Mono-unsaturated	% Saturated
Avocado	14	74	12
Canola	28	61	7
Corn	55	27	13
Olive	9	73	14
Peanut	34	44	18
Safflower	73	14	9
Sesame	42	38	14
Soya bean	62	19	15
Sunflower	60	25	11
Butter (for comparison)	2	22	54

Note: Most percentages do not add up to 100% because water and other substances make up the total composition of the oil.

Good Sources of Folate

Food	Amount	Folate (mcg)
Artichoke, globe, cooked	1 medium (120g)	64
Asparagus, cooked	5 medium spears	110
Bread, wholemeal	2 slices	24
Breakfast cereal	30g	50–100
Broccoli, fresh, cooked	1 serving (150g)	122
Brussels sprouts, fresh, cooked	1 serving (155g)	136
Chickpeas, cooked	1 serving (130g)	61
Grapefruit	1 medium (200g)	50
Leeks, cooked	2 medium (170g)	82
Lentils, cooked	1 serving (130g)	33
Orange juice, freshly squeezed	1 cup	58
Peanuts, raw	30g	34
Peas, green, frozen, cooked	1 serving (130g)	60
Silverbeet, cooked	1 serving (115g)	124
Wheatgerm	1 tablespoon	20
Yeast extract spread	1 teaspoon	69

A diet rich in green vegetables, such as asparagus, will ensure a good supply of folate.

even lower fat intake. (Note that this recommendation applies to food intake over the course of a day or a week, and not to a single dish or meal.) But most of us need to cut down on saturated fat as well: it should account for no more than one-third of your total fat intake. The most effective way to do this is to eat less animal fats. The first step in cutting down on trans fats is to read labels: hydrogenated fats are often used in margarines, biscuits, crackers and potato crisps. Solid vegetable shortening sold for cooking and baking is also a hydrogenated fat; this type of fat is widely used to cook fast-food potato chips (ask before you order).

Fibre *see* DIETARY FIBRE

Flavonoids

These PHYTOCHEMICALS are found mostly in fruits and vegetables, including citrus fruits, cranberries, onions, soya beans, carrots and broccoli, and also in tea and wine. They act as ANTIOXIDANTS. High flavonoid intake has been linked to reduced risk of coronary heart disease; one of the known effects of these phytochemicals is that they keep platelets from clumping together and blocking blood vessels. Flavonoids may also inhibit enzymes responsible for the spread of malignant cells.

Fluoride

This MINERAL contributes to the formation of bones and teeth. Many Australians and New Zealanders get fluoride from their water supply; canned salmon and sardines, which are commonly eaten with their bones, are also a source, as are black and green tea.

Folate

This member of the VITAMIN B COMPLEX – also called folacin or folic acid – is vital to tissue growth and thus plays a role in the prevention of certain birth defects, so it is particularly important that women of childbearing age get enough of this nutrient. Folate is one of three B vitamins that help fight heart disease by lowering levels of HOMOCYSTEINE, an AMINO ACID that may contribute to arterial blockage. Folate is found in leafy vegetables (the word 'folate' is related to 'foliage'), but also in legumes, whole grains, nuts, pork and shellfish. Because of this vitamin's importance, breakfast cereals and other products are now FORTIFIED with folate.

Fortified

The term 'fortified' has a specific meaning that refers to the procedure of adding a vitamin or mineral to a processed food to achieve accepted public health objectives. Fortification may exceed the level of nutrients that would be achieved by restoring the food to pre-processed levels. By law in Australia and New Zealand, margarine must be fortified with VITAMIN A and VITAMIN D.

Free radicals

These are unstable compounds (oxygen compounds, among others) formed in the body during normal metabolic processes. These unstable, highly reactive molecules attempt to bind with other elements, creating even more unstable molecules and setting up a chain reaction that can damage basic genetic material (DNA) as well as other cell structures and tissues. This cellular damage, if uncorrected, can eventually result in cancer and other diseases (free radicals are suspected of playing a role in heart disease, cataracts, arthritis and neurological diseases). External factors can promote the formation of free radicals: these include exposure to heat, radiation, environmental pollutants, including cigarette smoke, and drinking alcohol. The body has its own mechanisms for self-repair, but certain nutrients – which function as ANTIOXIDANTS – can also aid in repairing the damage caused by free radicals. These antioxidant nutrients include VITAMIN C, VITAMIN E and BETA-CAROTENE. Other CAROTENOIDS, such as LYCOPENE, LUTEIN and ZEAXANTHIN, are currently being researched for possible antioxidant effects.

Genistein

This compound belongs to the category of PHYTOCHEMICALS called ISOFLAVONES. Genistein, found in soya beans and soya products (tofu, soya drink, etc), may block the formation of new blood vessels; this in turn slows the growth of tumours.

Glucose

Your body turns most of the CARBOHYDRATES you eat into its basic energy source, glucose. Glucose is carried in the bloodstream to the cells when energy is required, or stored as GLYCOGEN.

Glycogen

Excess GLUCOSE not utilised by the body is converted into glycogen, a form in which it can be stored in the muscles or liver until required.

HDL *see* CHOLESTEROL

Haem iron *see* IRON

Homocysteine

An AMINO ACID that circulates in the blood; people with elevated homocysteine levels are at increased risk of arterial blockage, resulting in a heart attack or stroke. Normally, three of the B vitamins (FOLATE, VITAMIN B_6 and VITAMIN B_{12}) assist in the conversion of homocysteine into other non-damaging amino acids; however, if these vitamins are in short supply (due to dietary deficiency or a genetic problem) the homocysteine in the bloodstream will continue to pose a risk.

Indoles

Nitrogen compounds found in CRUCIFEROUS VEGETABLES. Indoles seem to have the ability to convert the active form of oestrogen (which can promote the growth of breast tumours) into an inactive form. Indoles may be protective against other cancers as well.

Iodine

Required for normal cell metabolism, this MINERAL is essential to the functioning of the thyroid gland, which controls human growth from conception to adulthood. Most of our dietary iodine comes from iodised salt, but the mineral is also found in seafood and dairy products, among other foods.

Iron

This MINERAL plays a key role in the blood's distribution of oxygen to the body. A serious shortage of iron – iron-deficiency anaemia – produces fatigue and impaired immunity. Iron is found in red meat, poultry, fish, egg yolks, legumes, nuts, dried fruits, leafy greens, and foods such as FORTIFIED breakfast cereals, bread and pasta. There are two types of iron in food: haem and non-haem.

Fresh shellfish, including mussels, are a prime source of iodine, which is found in the hormones produced by the thyroid gland.

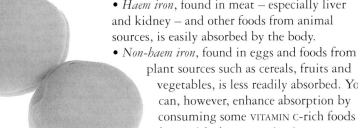

As well as providing beta-carotene, apricots also supply lycopene, a valuable phytochemical.

• *Haem iron*, found in meat – especially liver and kidney – and other foods from animal sources, is easily absorbed by the body.
• *Non-haem iron*, found in eggs and foods from plant sources such as cereals, fruits and vegetables, is less readily absorbed. You can, however, enhance absorption by consuming some VITAMIN C-rich foods along with the vegetarian iron sources. Some examples are beans (non-haem iron) with cabbage (vitamin C); prunes or raisins (non-haem iron) with orange juice (vitamin C); and broccoli (non-haem iron) with tomatoes (vitamin C). Iron absorption is reduced by phytic acid in bran, oxalic acid in spinach and tannin in tea.

Isoflavones
PHYTOCHEMICALS found in legumes, including soya beans. Isoflavones are PHYTO-OESTROGENS – plant substances that mimic oestrogen's action in the body. Some researchers believe that a diet rich in isoflavones may protect against 'hormone sensitive' cancers, such as those of the breast and prostate. Isoflavones also lower total CHOLESTEROL while raising HDL.

Isothiocyanates
The class of PHYTOCHEMICALS, found in CRUCIFEROUS VEGETABLES such as broccoli, cabbage and Brussels sprouts, that includes SULPHORAPHANE. Isothiocyanates are believed to stimulate anticancer enzymes.

Kilojoules
In the metric system, the kilojoule (kJ) is the basic unit used to measure the energy value of foods and the energy requirements of the body. One kilocalorie (usually called a CALORIE) equals 4.2 kJ. We get kilojoules from the CARBOHYDRATES, PROTEIN and FAT in the foods we eat. Carbohydrates have 16 kJ per gram, protein has 17 kJ, while fat supplies 38 kJ per gram.

The basic rule for weight maintenance in terms of kilojoules is that 'kilojoules out' should equal 'kilojoules in': if you consume just the amount of kilojoules that your body needs to maintain itself and to power your daily activities, your weight will remain fairly constant. However, if you consistently consume more kilojoules than you need, they will be stored as fat and you will gain weight.

LDL *see* CHOLESTEROL

Lactose
The type of sugar found in milk. Some people, called lactose-intolerant, have difficulty digesting lactose, but such people can more easily digest cheese (most of the lactose is removed in processing) and cultured dairy products, such as yoghurt and buttermilk. Specially treated milk, in which the lactose is predigested through the addition of lactase (an enzyme), is widely available.

Legumes
A family of plants characterised by the seed-bearing pods that grow on them. All beans and peas, as well as lentils and peanuts, are members of this group of plants. Legumes are nutritious foods, being good sources of IRON, B vitamins and fibre. By themselves, legumes do not provide complete PROTEIN, but they can be made complete by combining them, in the same meal, with whole grains or animal protein.

Limonenes
Compounds found in the peels of citrus fruits that may deactivate certain CARCINOGENS.

Lipoproteins *see* CHOLESTEROL

Lutein
A CAROTENOID found in kale, spinach, parsley, capsicums, avocados and many other fruits and vegetables. This PHYTOCHEMICAL may protect against age-related macular degeneration, the leading cause of blindness in the elderly.

Lycopene
One of the CAROTENOIDS, this PHYTOCHEMICAL is found in tomatoes and tomato products, red capsicums, watermelon, pink grapefruit, apricots and some other fruits and vegetables. Studies have shown that a diet that includes plenty of tomato products can be protective against prostate cancer. (The lycopene is best absorbed by the body if the tomatoes are cooked, as they are in tomato sauce, paste or purée.) Lycopene also seems to have protective effects against other types of cancer, including tumours of the colon, cervix and bladder.

Lysine *see* AMINO ACIDS

Important Minerals at a Glance

Mineral	The Role it Plays	Where to Find it
Calcium	Builds and maintains bone strength and density; helps regulate heartbeat and muscle contraction	Dairy products, sardines and salmon (with bones), dark leafy greens
Chlorine	Helps maintain fluid and acid balance	Table salt
Chromium	Metabolism of carbohydrates and fats	Seafood, whole grains, potato
Copper	Formation of red blood cells; for healthy bones, nerves, immune system	Shellfish, nuts, beans, whole grains, cocoa
Fluoride	Keeps teeth and bones strong	Fluoridated water; sardines and salmon (with bones); black or green tea
Iodine	Necessary for function of the thyroid gland, cell metabolism	Iodized salt; fish; produce grown in iodine-rich soil
Iron	Essential to formation of haemoglobin; component of enzymes and proteins	Red meat, eggs, legumes, nuts, fortified breakfast cereals
Magnesium	Aids in bone growth, nerve and muscle function	Whole grains, leafy greens, nuts, soya beans, bananas, apricots, milk
Manganese	Aids in reproduction and energy production; helps build bones	Nuts, whole grains, beans, coffee, green and black tea
Molybdenum	Helps build strong bones and teeth	Grains, dark leafy greens, beans
Phosphorus	Helps build bones and teeth and form cell membranes and genetic material	Meat, poultry, fish, dairy products, legumes, nuts
Potassium	Helps regulate muscle contraction, nerve impulses, function of heart and kidneys, fluid balance	Bananas, potatoes, avocados, dried fruits, dairy products, beans
Selenium	Component of an enzyme that acts as an antioxidant; detoxifies toxic metals	Brazil nuts, fish, shellfish, red meat, grains, chicken, garlic
Sodium	Helps regulate fluid balance and blood pressure	Table salt, salt and sodium compounds added to prepared foods
Zinc	Involved in activity of enzymes for cell division, growth and repair as well as proper functioning of immune system; maintains taste and smell acuity	Oysters, chicken, meat, eggs, milk

Even though they are high in cholesterol, eggs are still a highly recommended part of a nutritious diet, being rich in protein, B vitamins and minerals.

Macro-minerals *see* MINERALS

Macro-nutrients
The food components – PROTEIN, CARBOHYDRATES and FAT – from which we get energy.

Magnesium
This MINERAL works with its allies – CALCIUM, MOLYBDENUM, POTASSIUM and PHOSPHORUS – to build and maintain bones and teeth; magnesium also contributes to the functioning of the nerves and muscles. Magnesium is found in whole grains, leafy greens, meat, fish, dairy products, nuts, seeds, legumes, avocados and bananas.

Manganese
A trace MINERAL, manganese plays a role in reproduction and in the production of energy. It is also a component of ANTIOXIDANT enzymes. Good sources include whole grains, nuts, beans and egg yolks.

Minerals
Inorganic elements that originate in the soil; some minerals act as essential nutrients. The *macro-minerals* – minerals of which we need to consume relatively large amounts – are CALCIUM, CHLORINE, MAGNESIUM, PHOSPHORUS, POTASSIUM, SODIUM, IRON and SULPHUR. The other minerals, which our bodies require in minute amounts, are called the *trace minerals*. At least 17 have been identified as essential for good health. The most important include ZINC, CHROMIUM, COBALT, COPPER, FLUORIDE, IODINE, MANGANESE, SELENIUM and MOLYBDENUM.

Minerals are required for formation of bones, teeth and nails, as well as other parts of the body. They are components of enzymes and play roles in the regulation of the nervous and digestive systems and in heart function. A diet including a wide variety of foods will usually ensure an intake adequate enough to meet our mineral requirements.

Unlike VITAMINS, minerals cannot be destroyed by overcooking food. But if you boil mineral-rich foods (such as vegetables) for a long time and then discard the cooking liquid, you will be pouring some of the mineral down the drain. To conserve the mineral content when cooking vegetables, steam, stir-fry or microwave them whenever possible; if blanching in a large quantity of water, do it quickly – in a matter of seconds or minutes. *See also* BORON.

While fatty fish is a well-known source of omega-3 fatty acids, gram for gram walnuts provide more than five times as much as canned red salmon (and ten times as much as canned pink salmon).

Molybdenum
This trace MINERAL is a component of various enzymes; it also helps strengthen bones and teeth. Molybdenum deficiency is almost unknown. Milk, legumes and grains, as well as offal, are all good sources.

Monoterpenes
PHYTOCHEMICALS that function as ANTIOXIDANTS and seem to protect against heart disease and cancer. Monoterpenes are found in citrus fruits, berries, parsley, broccoli and cabbage.

Monounsaturated fat *see* FAT

Niacin
One of the B vitamins (VITAMIN B_3), niacin is important in the body's production of energy from food. It is also required for normal growth and the synthesis of DNA (genetic material). In addition, niacin contributes to keeping the skin, nerves and digestive system healthy. Lean meat, poultry and seafood are excellent sources of niacin; milk, legumes and cereals also supply good amounts of this vitamin.

Omega-3
This term describes two types of polyunsaturated fatty acids (*see* FAT). The pre-eminent source of omega-3 fatty acids is seafood. Omega-3s are unique in their ability to lower levels of TRIGLYCERIDES in the blood. In addition, omega-3s function as blood thinners, lessening the likelihood of a heart attack or stroke. (Some researchers believe that omega-3s help lower total CHOLESTEROL and/or LDL, or 'bad' cholesterol, but the studies are inconclusive.) In addition, omega-3s also seem to protect against certain forms of cancer and, because they have anti-inflammatory powers, may be effective against rheumatoid arthritis.

The best sources of omega-3 fatty acids are fish such as salmon, herrings, mackerel, anchovies and sardines; many leaner fish are also good sources, as are linseeds, walnuts and pecans. Omega-enriched eggs are available.

Oxalic acid (oxalates)

A natural compound found in some vegetables, including spinach, beetroot and celery leaves, and rhubarb. Oxalic acid binds with CALCIUM and IRON, thus limiting the body's absorption of these minerals. Vegetarians should not depend on these vegetables for iron and calcium.

Pantothenic acid

This B vitamin (VITAMIN B₅) helps the body convert food into energy; it also plays a role in synthesising hormones and other body chemicals. Good sources are liver and kidneys, whole grains, nuts, watermelon, broad beans and dark-green vegetables. Some pantothenic acid is lost in cooking water, but deficiencies are virtually unknown.

Pectin

A type of soluble DIETARY FIBRE, pectin is found in apples, citrus fruits, berries, bananas and grapes, as well as other fruits, vegetables, legumes and nuts. (Pectin is also sold in powdered form for use in making jams and jellies.) This type of soluble fibre helps reduce CHOLESTEROL, and thus may help prevent heart disease. Pectin also helps regulate intestinal function.

Phosphorus

This bone-building MINERAL is also important for energy production and the formation of cells. Phosphorus is found in a great variety of foods, notably fish, meat, poultry, dairy products, eggs, peas, beans and nuts. Phosphorus deficiencies are rare.

A bunch of grapes not only supplies some potassium and fibre, you'll also benefit from boron, which helps keep bones strong.

Good Sources of Omega-3 Fatty Acids

Food	Fat (g)*	Omega-3(mg)*
Egg, omega-enriched (60g)	5.9	340
Gemfish	7.2	485
Linseeds (flaxseeds) (5g)	3.0	900
Mackerel, blue	5.0	1220
Mackerel, canned in brine	17.9	3075
Mullet, sea	6.0	2359
Oysters, Sydney rock (6)	2.2	1417
Pecans	71.9	1066
Salmon, Atlantic	7.1	2138
Salmon, pink, canned in brine	6.5	1114
Salmon, red, canned in brine	12.0	2738
Sardines, canned in water	10.7	2837
Scallops	0.7	325
Soya beans, canned	5.5	1000
Tailor	5.5	1360
Trevally	2.8	1932
Trout, rainbow	3.8	556
Tuna	5.7	1152
Tuna, canned in brine	2.6	242
Walnuts	69.2	5000
Whiting, King George	0.7	577

*unless otherwise noted, approximate values per 100g edible portion, raw

Phytochemicals

Chemical compounds found in plants; some are produced to protect the plants against natural enemies. Ongoing research, however, demonstrates that some phytochemicals also boost immunity and help fight diseases, including cancer and heart disease. Phytochemicals include ALLYL SULPHIDES, BETA-CAROTENE and other CAROTENOIDS, CAPSAICIN, ELLAGIC ACID, FLAVONOIDS, GENISTEIN, INDOLES, ISOTHIOCYANATES, LIMONENES, LUTEIN, LYCOPENE, RESVERATROL, SAPONINS, SINIGRIN, TRITERPENOIDS and ZEAXANTHIN.

Phyto-oestrogens

These compounds, found in plants, mimic the action of the oestrogen produced by the human body. Phyto-oestrogens may protect against both cancer and heart disease. Soya beans and soya products are rich sources of phyto-oestrogens.

Polyphenols

PHYTOCHEMICALS that show promise as disease-fighters in several different arenas. They act as ANTIOXIDANTS and, in the laboratory, have been shown to have antiviral and anticarcinogenic properties. FLAVONOIDS, ISOFLAVONES and ELLAGIC ACID are all polyphenols.

Polyunsaturated fat *see* FAT

Potassium

This MINERAL is crucial to the regulation of muscle contraction and nerve impulses and thus helps regulate heart contractions (a deficiency can alter the rhythm of the heart). It also helps control fluid balance in the cells as well as blood pressure. Some studies have indicated that a diet rich in potassium may reduce the risk of high blood pressure and stroke. The RECOMMENDED DIETARY INTAKE for adult females is 50–140 millimoles or 1950–5460 mg. Potassium is found in most foods; white and sweet potatoes, bananas, dried apricots, avocados,

Recommended Dietary Intakes*

Nutrient	Amount
Vitamin A	750 mcg
Vitamin C	30 mg
Calcium	800 mg
Iron	12 mg
Vitamin E	7 mg
Thiamin	0.9 mg
Riboflavin	1.4 mg
Niacin	15 mg
Vitamin B_6	0.8–1.1 mg
Folate	200 mcg
Vitamin B_{12}	2 mg
Phosphorus	1000 mg
Potassium	1950–5460 mg
Iodine	120 mcg
Magnesium	270 mg
Zinc	12 mg
Selenium	70 mcg

*For adult females, 19–54 years, with light to moderate activity, not pregnant and not breastfeeding (for both Australia and New Zealand)
mcg = micrograms   mg = milligrams

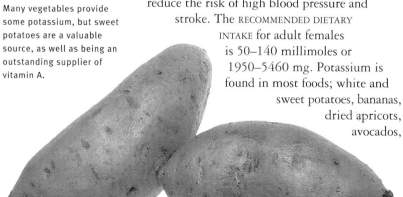

Many vegetables provide some potassium, but sweet potatoes are a valuable source, as well as being an outstanding supplier of vitamin A.

prunes, beef, natural yoghurt and milk are some particularly good sources. Dried beans also supply good amounts of potassium.

Protein

The basic building material of our bodies, protein consists of chains of AMINO ACIDS. They can be combined in many different ways. Some foods provide complete protein; that is, they have a full complement of essential amino acids. Foods from animal sources – meat, poultry, seafood, eggs and dairy products – fall into this category. Among plant-derived foods, only soya beans contain complete protein; all other plant foods are deficient in one or more essential amino acids. Still, even if you are a vegetarian (or eat little meat), you needn't worry about getting complete protein as long as you eat a wide range of foods over the course of each day. For instance, the amino acids that are in short supply in grains are found in legumes, so a combination such as peanut butter on bread, or chilli beans with rice, will help restore the balance. If you consume sufficient protein, you

needn't monitor your amino acid intake; it will take care of itself. For vegetarians, eating whole grains and legumes will increase protein intake, as will eating dairy products.

Pyridoxine *see* VITAMIN B₆

Recommended Dietary Intakes (RDIs)

First issued by the Australian National Health and Medical Research Council in 1954 (and also applicable to New Zealand), the RDIs – also known as Recommended Daily Intakes – suggest the average quantities of essential nutrients and kilojoules that children and adults require daily from their diet to achieve and maintain long-term health. While RDIs consider age and gender, and are revised regularly, they do not take into account any differences in individual nutritional requirements according to occupation, weight or other factors such as emotional needs or illness. Some people may need a little more than the RDI for a nutrient or they may need less. *See chart, at left.*

In addition to those nutrients for which there are RDIs, there are other vitamins and minerals that play an important part in maintaining health and well-being. For example, it is recommended that elderly people confined to nursing homes have 10 mcg of Vitamin D per day – Vitamin D is naturally produced by exposure to sunlight.

Resveratrol

A PHYTOCHEMICAL found in red grapes, grape juice and wine – and also in peanuts. It may lower CHOLESTEROL and seems to protect against coronary artery disease.

Riboflavin

This B vitamin (VITAMIN B₂), found in dairy products, lean meats, eggs, nuts, legumes, leafy greens and FORTIFIED breakfast cereals, plays essential roles in the production of red blood cells, energy production and growth. It is not a stable vitamin and is easily destroyed by light – and also by cooking, if bicarbonate of soda is used. Symptoms of deficiency include skin disorders, especially around the nose and lips; as well, eyes can become very sensitive to light.

Salt *see* SODIUM

Saponins

PHYTOCHEMICALS found in potatoes, onions, garlic and other vegetables, as well as legumes. Saponins reduce blood cholesterol by binding and excreting bile salts, and may fight cancer.

Saturated fat *see* FAT

Selenium

This trace MINERAL may have cancer-fighting properties: it forms a part of an enzyme, glutathione peroxidase, that is an ANTIOXIDANT. Selenium also helps detoxify poisonous metals, such as mercury. Selenium is found in garlic, chicken, fish, prawns, oysters, whole grains, dried beans and Brazil nuts.

Sinigrin

A PHYTOCHEMICAL found in CRUCIFEROUS VEGETABLES that gives them their slightly bitter flavour; Brussels sprouts are especially rich in sinigrin. In the laboratory, sinigrin has been shown to suppress the development of precancerous cells.

Sodium

A MINERAL that is vital for maintaining proper fluid balance in the body. The problem for most people, however, is getting *too much* sodium. This mineral is found not only in table salt, but also (as a part of various chemical compounds) in most processed foods, particularly canned goods, fast foods, cheese and smoked meats. Sodium occurs naturally in fresh foods as well, although usually at moderate levels. Excess sodium elevates blood pressure in many people (however, not everyone with high blood pressure is sodium-sensitive), and it can also contribute to such problems as osteoporosis.

Solanine

A bitter natural compound in potatoes that can rise to mildly toxic levels if the potatoes have been improperly stored (in too warm a place, or exposed to light). Potatoes that have sprouted or taken on a greenish tinge have high levels of solanine; either peel the greenish skin off (solanine only goes about 1–2 mm deep) or discard the potatoes.

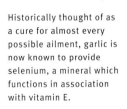

Historically thought of as a cure for almost every possible ailment, garlic is now known to provide selenium, a mineral which functions in association with vitamin E.

High in vitamin C, folate, fibre, potassium and iron, Brussels sprouts also contain sulphoraphane, a beneficial phytochemical.

Starch *see* CARBOHYDRATES

Sterols

PHYTOCHEMICALS found in monounsaturated and polyunsaturated vegetable oils, some vegetables (including cucumbers) and some shellfish. Sterols have a cholesterol-lowering effect.

Sugar *see* CARBOHYDRATES

Sulphoraphane

A PHYTOCHEMICAL found in CRUCIFEROUS VEGETABLES such as broccoli, cabbage and Brussels sprouts. Sulphoraphane stimulates the production of enzymes that rid the body of CARCINOGENS.

Sulphur

One of the MACRO-MINERALS, essential for the formation of cartilage, hair and nails. Major sources of sulphur are three of the amino acids that make up protein, so if your diet has adequate animal protein there will be no sulphur deficiency. And since it is easily obtained from such foods, there is no recommended intake. The sulphur content of vegetable protein varies.

Thiamin

One of the B vitamins (VITAMIN B$_1$), thiamin helps the body transform food into energy. Pork is a leading source of thiamin; fish, sunflower seeds, rice and pasta also supply good amounts, as do liver, nuts, yeast, and yeast and vegetable extracts. Many cereals are FORTIFIED with this delicate vitamin, which is reduced by cooking – either by direct heat or leached into water.

Tocopherol *see* VITAMIN E

Trace minerals *see* MINERALS

Trans fat *see* FAT

Avocados are a good source of fat-soluble vitamin E, which is a powerful antioxidant that helps in the prevention of heart disease.

Triglycerides

Triglycerides are fats that circulate in the bloodstream. Some come from the food we eat, but the body also assembles its own triglycerides. High blood triglyceride levels may accompany low levels of 'good' CHOLESTEROL (HDL) and are often present in people who are overweight. High levels are also thought to indicate an increased risk of diabetes. Blood triglycerides can often be lowered through weight loss, decreased consumption of sugars and ALCOHOL, and exercise. The OMEGA-3 FATTY ACIDS found principally in seafood have also been shown to help lower triglycerides.

Triterpenoids

Found in citrus fruits, grains and cruciferous vegetables, these PHYTOCHEMICALS help deactivate certain hormones that promote tumour growth; they also slow down the rapid cell division that is characteristic of malignant tumours.

Vitamins

These nutrients, required by the body in minute amounts, are organic compounds that regulate reactions taking place in the body. They enable the body to convert food to energy and help the body to protect itself from disease and to heal itself when injured. If we consume a balanced diet, we get most of the vitamins we need from foods; the body also produces a few vitamins.

The B-COMPLEX VITAMINS and VITAMIN C are water soluble; any excess of these vitamins is excreted in urine, rather than stored. So it's important to replenish your body's supply of these vitamins regularly.

Water-soluble vitamins, especially vitamin C, can be lost if foods that contain them – such as vegetables and fruits – are cooked too long, over too high heat, or in too much liquid. Try steaming or microwaving, and always cook these foods as quickly as possible (or eat them raw).

The fat-soluble vitamins – A, D, E and K – are stored in the liver and in body fat, so you don't need to renew your supply as often. These vitamins are less likely to be lost in cooking, although high heat (as used in frying) can destroy some vitamin E in vegetable oils.

Important Vitamins at a Glance

Vitamin	The Role it Plays	Where to Find it
Biotin	Important in the metabolism of protein, carbohydrates and fats	Eggs, dairy products, mushrooms, whole grains
Folate (folacin, folic acid)	Formation of red blood cells; adequate intake reduces risk of birth defects and some cancers	Leafy greens, asparagus, broccoli, beans, orange juice, fortified cereals
Vitamin A	Important for healthy eyes; also maintains health of skin, teeth, bones	As beta-carotene (which the body converts to vitamin A) in yellow, orange and dark-green fruits and vegetables; as preformed vitamin A in eggs, full cream milk, fish
Vitamin B_1 (thiamin)	Conversion of carbohydrates into energy; brain, nerve cell and heart function	Pork, fish, sunflower seeds, rice, breads and fortified cereals
Vitamin B_2 (riboflavin)	Conversion of food to energy; growth; red blood cell production	Dairy products, meat, poultry, fish, leafy greens, nuts
Vitamin B_3 (niacin)	Conversion of food to energy; health of skin, nerves, digestive system	Nuts, meat, fish, poultry, dairy products
Vitamin B_5 (pantothenic acid)	Conversion of food to energy; production of essential body chemicals	Found in nearly all foods
Vitamin B_6 (pyridoxine)	Important in chemical reactions of proteins and amino acids in the body; production of red blood cells	Poultry, beef, fish, bananas, beans, nuts, whole grains
Vitamin B_{12} (cyano-cobalamin)	Essential for development of red blood cells, nervous system function	Meat, poultry, seafood, eggs, dairy products, fortified soya drink
Vitamin C	Antioxidant; helps reduce risk of cancer, cataracts; also essential for healthy gums and teeth, wound healing; enhances iron absorption	Citrus fruit, red capsicums and chillies, strawberries, kiwifruit, rockmelon, broccoli, potatoes
Vitamin D	For strong bones and teeth	Milk, dairy products, fatty fish
Vitamin E	Antioxidant; helps prevent heart disease	Nuts, vegetable oil, avocados, leafy greens, almonds, sunflower and pumpkin seeds
Vitamin K	Essential for normal blood clotting; may aid in calcium absorption	Broccoli, Brussels sprouts, cabbage, leafy greens, milk, soya beans, eggs

Capsicums, especially when red, are an important source of vitamin C, whose antioxidant powers are beneficial to almost all parts of the body.

Good Sources of Vitamin C

Food	Amount	Vitamin C (mg)
Broccoli, fresh, cooked	1 serving (150g)	128
Brussels sprouts, fresh, cooked	1 serving (155g)	136
Cabbage, green, fresh, raw	1 serving (95g)	43
Capsicum, red, raw	1 medium (90g)	153
Cauliflower, fresh, cooked	1 serving (140g)	78
Chilli, red, raw	2 medium (60g)	102
Grapefruit juice, freshly squeezed	1 cup	94
Honeydew melon	1 cup, diced (180g)	32
Kiwifruit	1 medium (80g)	58
Mango	1 medium (205g)	57
Orange juice, freshly squeezed	1 cup	92
Pawpaw	1 cup, diced (150g)	90
Pineapple, fresh	1 slice (110g)	23
Potato, peeled, boiled	1 large (185g)	39
Rockmelon	1 cup, diced (170g)	58
Strawberries, fresh	1 cup (145g)	65
Sweet potato, orange, cooked	1 serving (150g)	35
Tomato, fresh, fully ripe	1 large (180g)	32

Vitamin A

Known as a vision enhancer, vitamin A is also important for healthy skin, teeth and bones. This vitamin may have some anticarcinogenic powers, but many of the disease-fighting properties formerly attributed to it actually belong to BETA-CAROTENE and the other CAROTENOIDS that are precursors of vitamin A (that is, the body converts them from food into vitamin A). The best sources of vitamin A, in the form of beta-carotene, are dark green, orange or yellow fruits and vegetables, such as apricots, mangoes, spinach, kale, carrots, pumpkin and sweet potatoes. Preformed vitamin A is found in egg yolks, dairy products, fish and organ meats.

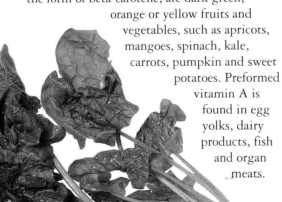

Dark green leafy vegetables, such as spinach, are nutritional powerhouses, supplying beta-carotene, which is converted by the body into vitamin A.

Vitamin B complex

BIOTIN, FOLATE, NIACIN, PANTOTHENIC ACID, RIBOFLAVIN, THIAMIN and VITAMINS B$_6$ and B$_{12}$ are the nutrients that make up this group of essential water-soluble vitamins.

Vitamin B$_1$ *see* THIAMIN

Vitamin B$_2$ *see* RIBOFLAVIN

Vitamin B$_3$ *see* NIACIN

Vitamin B$_5$ *see* PANTOTHENIC ACID

Vitamin B$_6$ (pyridoxine)

This vitamin aids in the body's utilisation of PROTEIN and in the production of red blood cells. Pyridoxine works with other B vitamins to help keep levels of HOMOCYSTEINE low. Vitamin B$_6$ plays a role in antibody production, so an adequate supply of this nutrient strengthens immunity. Many elderly people do not get as much of this vitamin as they should for optimal health. Some good sources of B$_6$ are chicken, rabbit, beef, fish, beans, bananas, avocados, walnuts and FORTIFIED breakfast cereals.

Vitamin B₁₂ (cyano-cobalamin)

Vitamin B_{12} plays a role in the formation of red blood cells and in the functioning of the nervous system. A very important role of vitamin B_{12} is that it enables the body to utilise FOLATE, thus helping to keep HOMOCYSTEINE levels down. This vitamin is plentiful in meat, poultry, fish, eggs and dairy products – that is, foods from animal sources. Strict vegetarians can get B_{12} from soya products, such as soya drinks, that are FORTIFIED with this vitamin.

Vitamin C (ascorbic acid)

This water-soluble vitamin is an important ANTIOXIDANT. It helps the body build new cells and repair damaged ones, and promotes the absorption of dietary IRON. Researchers are investigating vitamin C as a line of defence against many diseases, including several types of cancer, heart disease, cataracts and the common cold. The body does not produce vitamin C and does not retain stores of the vitamin for very long, so you should eat C-rich foods often. Most fruits and vegetables have some vitamin C, and the following are particularly rich in this important nutrient and should be eaten regularly: citrus fruits and juices, strawberries, kiwifruit, melon, capsicums, cabbage, broccoli and potatoes.

Vitamin D

A fat-soluble vitamin, D works in concert with CALCIUM and PHOSPHORUS to build and maintain strong bones and teeth. This makes it a crucial nutrient in the prevention of osteoporosis. Vitamin D is produced by exposure to sunshine. Provided the ultraviolet light is not affected by smog, dust or cloud, about 15 minutes a day or 1 to 2 hours a week will ensure adequate amounts are produced. You can also get vitamin D from dairy foods, including full-cream milk, cheese and cream. This vitamin is also found in fatty fish, such as salmon, mackerel, sardines and herrings, and in eggs, butter and margarine.

Vitamin E (tocopherol)

A potent ANTIOXIDANT, vitamin E is a fat-soluble vitamin. Research indicates that vitamin E helps prevent heart disease, in part by reducing the harmful effects of LDL CHOLESTEROL, and by preventing blood clots. Vitamin E is also under investigation as a treatment for osteoarthritis. It is found in some fatty foods, including vegetable oils, avocados, nuts and seeds, but also in brown rice and dark leafy greens. However, it

is almost impossible to get sufficient vitamin E from food to have an antioxidant effect; where needed, many health authorities now recommend supplements.

Vitamin K

This fat-soluble vitamin facilitates blood clotting; it may also play a role in CALCIUM absorption, thus helping to prevent osteoporosis. The body makes most of the vitamin K it needs, but K is also found in dark leafy greens, broccoli, Brussels sprouts and many other vegetables, as well as in eggs, liver and whole milk.

Water

Although not a nutrient, water plays a vital role in many body processes, making possible the functions of every cell and organ. Water lubricates the joints, rids the body of waste, and regulates body temperature. An adult needs 1.5 to 2.5 litres (8–12 x 200ml glasses) of water just to replace what's lost daily through normal body functions. Of course, you don't need to take in all this liquid by drinking water: you also replenish fluids with other beverages, such as milk or juice, and by eating foods (such as soups and most fruits and vegetables) that have a high water content. Because fibre absorbs water, anyone who eats lots of fibre (adults should aim for 30 g a day) also needs to drink plenty of fluids.

Zeaxanthin

One of the CAROTENOIDS, zeaxanthin, like LUTEIN, may help prevent age-related macular degeneration, the leading cause of blindness in the elderly. Kale and broccoli are two good sources of zeaxanthin.

Zinc

An important MINERAL with many functions, zinc is involved in cell division, repair and growth, as well as immune function, and keeps your senses of taste and smell working properly. A Dutch study suggests that high zinc levels are associated with a reduced risk of cancer. Zinc deficiency is rare, although it is sometimes seen in vegans (vegetarians who eat no animal products at all, including dairy products or eggs). Slight zinc deficiencies have also been noted in elderly people. Good sources of zinc include seafood, meat, eggs and dairy products.

Oranges, and other citrus fruits, are a primary source of vitamin C in most diets. Eat them whole rather than juiced, to gain maximum fibre benefits.

Foods that Fight Illness

Since ancient times, food has been used to prevent and cure disease. Recently, this concept has been seen in a whole new light, thanks to research that has shown that many substances in foods – from vitamins and minerals to fibre and phytochemicals – play roles in disease prevention.

The recommendations in this chart are for foods that have proven or possible disease-fighting qualities. It is not meant as a prescription and not as a list of cures for diseases. Consult your doctor or a dietitian for personal advice before making dramatic changes in your diet.

With its bright orange flesh, the pumpkin (in all its varieties) is an obvious source of beta-carotene – a valuable addition to anyone's diet.

Disorder	Consume plenty of
Acne	Carrots, rockmelon and dark leafy greens for beta-carotene. Poultry and fish for zinc. Yoghurt for its active cultures.
Anaemia (iron deficiency)	Meat, poultry, fish, legumes, dried fruit, dark leafy greens and cereals for iron. Citrus fruit, cabbage, broccoli, red capsicums, kale, Brussels sprouts, strawberries and kiwifruit for vitamin C, which enhances iron absorption.
Arthritis	Seafood for omega-3 fatty acids (for rheumatoid arthritis only). Citrus fruit for vitamin C and flavonoids. Dark leafy greens, orange and yellow fruit and vegetables for beta-carotene.
Cancer	Orange and yellow vegetables, tomatoes, red capsicums, chillies, dark leafy greens, cabbage family vegetables (broccoli, Brussels sprouts, cauliflower), garlic, onions, orange fruit (apricots and nectarines), citrus (including pink grapefruit), berries, grapes, watermelon, whole grains, legumes, nuts, seafood, lean poultry, low-fat dairy products. These foods supply beta-carotene, lycopene, indoles, ellagic acid and other phytochemicals; folate, vitamins C and E, calcium and selenium; and omega-3 fatty acids.
Cataracts and other eye disorders	Broccoli, kale, spinach, parsley, green peas, celery, carrots, sweet potatoes, potatoes, oranges, lemons, limes, grapefruit, mandarins, kiwifruit, bananas; wheatgerm and whole grains; lean meat, poultry and fish. These supply the antioxidants lutein and beta-carotene, as well as vitamins C and E, the B vitamins, zinc and selenium.
Colds	Citrus fruit, strawberries, kiwifruit, red capsicums, broccoli and cabbage for vitamin C. Chillies for capsaicin. Onions and garlic as decongestants. Whole grains, legumes, seafood and meat for zinc.
Constipation and other intestinal ills	Wholegrain breads and cereals, fruit (including prunes, figs and other dried fruit) and vegetables (especially root vegetables) for a high intake of both soluble and insoluble fibre.
Diabetes	Plenty of whole grains, fruit and vegetables (totalling more than 50% of energy intake); moderate portions of lean meat, poultry and fish – these add up to a low-fat, high-fibre diet. Weight control is a prime factor in diabetes prevention.

Foods that Fight Illness

Disorder	Consume plenty of
Heart disease	Fruit (including citrus, berries, apples), vegetables (including dark leafy greens), legumes, wheatgerm, whole grains (including oats), nuts, unsaturated oils, low-fat dairy products, tofu, seafood. These supply the antioxidant vitamins C and E, as well as soluble and insoluble fibre, calcium and omega-3 fatty acids. Garlic, ginger, onions, chillies, grapes and wine supply heart-healthy phytochemicals.
High blood pressure	Low-fat dairy products, dark leafy greens and tofu for calcium. Lots of fruit and vegetables (including bananas, avocados, dried apricots, potatoes and tomatoes) for potassium. Citrus fruit, strawberries, kiwifruit and red capsicums for vitamin C. Garlic, onions and celery for their phytochemicals. Fish and shellfish for omega-3 fatty acids. Follow an overall low-fat diet for weight control and limit added salt.
High cholesterol	Fruit (including citrus fruit – especially grapefruit – apples, blackberries, raspberries, bananas, dried apricots and figs), oat bran, barley, carrots and legumes (especially soya beans) for soluble fibre. A wide variety of other fruit and vegetables for their antioxidant powers. Low-fat dairy products for calcium. Unsaturated vegetable oils (in place of saturated fats). Garlic, onions and their relatives also seem to lower cholesterol. Alcohol – in moderate amounts – raises HDL, or 'good' cholesterol.
High triglycerides	Fish and shellfish, linseeds, walnuts and pecans for omega-3 fatty acids.
Osteoporosis	Dairy products, canned fish with bones, and dark leafy greens for calcium. Grapes, apples and pears for boron. Whole grains and nuts for magnesium and manganese. Milk, fish and fortified cereals for vitamin D and phosphorus. Poultry, lean meat and beans also for phosphorus.
Stroke	Fruit and vegetables for vitamin C and other antioxidants. Fish for omega-3s. Nuts and seeds for vitamin E. Fruit for potassium and soluble fibre. Garlic for its phytochemicals, which lower blood pressure.
Tooth decay and gum disease	Dairy products, leafy greens and canned salmon and sardines (with their bones) for calcium. Citrus fruit and buckwheat for bioflavonoids (phytochemicals). Cheddar cheese, cherries, apples, tea and grape juice help fight decay after you eat sugary foods. Crisp fruit and vegetables act as natural 'toothbrushes' and supply vitamin C.
Urinary tract infection	Cranberries and blueberries contain substances that fight UTIs. Eat other fruit and vegetables for vitamin C. Drink plenty of water.
Weight control	Starchy carbohydrates and fresh fruit and vegetables for energy, vitamins, minerals, and a feeling of fullness without fat. Low-fat dairy products, lean poultry and fish for protein. Drink plenty of water.

Fruit rich in vitamin C – such as kiwifruit – are especially useful in fighting such problems as heart disease and high blood pressure.

Techniq

uTechniques

Roasting Capsicums

1

It's easy to roast and peel capsicums if they are first cut into flat sections. To start, cut off the top and the bottom.

2

Cut the capsicum into flat strips; remove the seeds and ribs from the inside. Place the pieces, skin-side-up, on a griller tray and grill until the skin is well charred.

3

Place the charred capsicums in a bowl and cover with a plate; allow to steam for a few minutes to loosen the skins.

4

After steaming, the charred skin will pull off easily. If not, scrape the capsicum with a knife.

Peeling Tomatoes

1

To peel tomatoes, drop them into a big pot of boiling water; blanch for about 30 seconds, or until the skin splits.

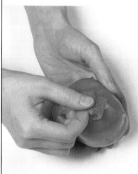

2

Lift the tomatoes out of the boiling water and stand for a minute or so to cool; then peel off the loosened skin with your fingers.

Softening Sun-Dried Tomatoes

1

Reconstitute sun-dried tomatoes by soaking in boiling water. Stand for 5 to 10 minutes, or until softened.

2

Drain the tomatoes; save the liquid for use in the recipe, or in a soup or sauce. Use scissors to snip the tomatoes into strips or dice.

Cutting Carrots into Julienne

1 First cut the carrot (or zucchini, celery, etc) into 5cm lengths.

2 Then cut the 5cm pieces lengthways into 5mm slices.

3 Finally, cut the slices into julienne strips that are about 5mm wide.

Cutting Zucchini into Ribbons

1 Slice zucchini into ribbons with a vegetable peeler. To serve, steam or blanch the ribbons, then sauté briefly.

Steaming Vegetables

1 Steaming is one of the healthier ways to cook most vegetables. This inexpensive collapsible steamer is widely available.

2 This is an Asian bamboo steamer. It comes with its own lid and is used over a wok. Place a shallow layer of vegetables in the bottom of the steamer, don't fill.

Caramelising Onions

1 Cook thinly sliced onions in a little oil, covered, over moderate heat, stirring often, for 10 minutes, or until very soft.

2 Uncover the pan and cook, stirring occasionally, for 10 minutes longer, or until the onions are nicely browned but still soft. Adding a pinch of sugar to the onions will speed the process.

Preparing Asparagus

1 To remove the tough end from an asparagus stalk, bend the stalk not far from the bottom. The tough bit will snap off.

Shredding Cabbage

1 Start by halving the head lengthways, through the core. Then cut each half in half again, lengthways.

2 Core each of the cabbage quarters by cutting a wedge-shaped section from its base.

3 Cut crossways slices from each quarter to produce strips or shreds.

Snipping Herbs

1 It's easier to snip herbs, such as dill or parsley, with scissors than to chop them with a knife.

Peeling Turnips

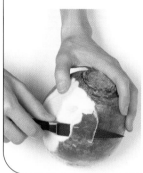

1 Turnips and swedes both have a thick skin. To peel them, cut off the skin with a sturdy paring knife.

Peeling Garlic Cloves

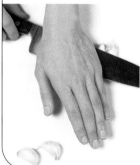

1 To crack the skin, place a clove under the flat side of a knife blade (sharp edge away from you); smack blade with the heel of your hand.

Stringing Snow Peas

1 String snow peas and sugar snap peas by pinching the tips of the pods, then pulling the strings off both front and back.

Paring Citrus Fruit

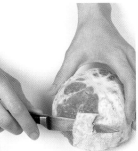

1 When peeling citrus fruits for use in recipes, use a paring knife to remove all of the white pith, which is bitter.

Grating Citrus Zest

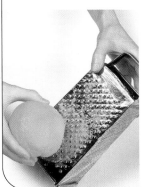

1 Cover the face of the grater with a sheet of plastic wrap before grating the zest; cleaning up will be much easier.

Juicing Citrus

1 You don't need an electrical appliance to squeeze citrus juice. This cheap, practical wooden juicer does the job cleanly and quickly.

2 There are also juicers with a strainer top set into a bowl or cup to catch the juice. The container at the bottom is sometimes conveniently marked as a measuring cup.

Coring and Slicing Apples

1 A timesaver when you need apple wedges, a corer-slicer does two jobs at once. Use it on either a peeled or an unpeeled apple.

Preparing Fresh Pineapple

1 Delicious fresh pineapple is worth the trouble of preparing it. To start, twist off the leafy 'crown' at the top.

2 Stand the pineapple on the work surface and use a chef's knife to slice downwards through the rind; don't cut too deeply or you'll lose a lot of the fruit.

3 The 'eyes' run in a fairly even diagonal pattern around the fruit. Cut long diagonal notches about 5mm deep around the pineapple to remove the eyes.

Preparing Mango

1 A mango has a large, flat stone in the centre. To avoid it, cut away each 'cheek' of the fruit, leaving the centre piece intact.

2 It's hard to peel mango flesh; try this serving method instead. Score the fruit into cubes, cutting to, but not through, the skin.

3 Push the skin side of the mango slice upwards to turn the whole section 'inside out'.

4 Serve as is, or simply slice the mango cubes off the skin. (Finally, slice the remaining strip of flesh off the stone and cube it as well.)

Freezing Berries

1 To freeze berries without crushing them, spread the fruit in a shallow baking tray and freeze rock-hard.

2 Then pour the frozen berries into freezer bags. For many recipes, you can use them without thawing. This method works for any kind of berries.

Adding Cornflour to Fruit Sauce

1 For a glossy sauce, stir cornflour mixed to a paste with a little cold water into cooked fruit. Simmer, stirring gently.

2 In a few minutes the juices will be glossy and thick. Remove the sauce from the heat as soon as it thickens since overcooking can 'break' the sauce.

Baking Bread

1
Dissolve yeast in warm water to which a little sugar has been added. If the yeast is properly 'live', the mixture will foam.

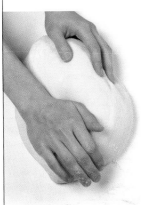

2
To knead dough, push into it with the heel of your hand to stretch it away from you. Fold back the stretched portion, then give the dough a quarter turn. Repeat until the dough is smooth and elastic.

3
Let the dough rise, covered, in a warm, draught-free spot. When the dough is doubled in size and does not spring back when poked with your fingers, punch it down with your fist.

4
If making a conventional loaf, shape the dough into a rectangle whose width matches the pan's length, then fold in the sides and place the loaf in the pan seam-side-down. Put aside to rise.

Transferring Pastry to a Pie Plate

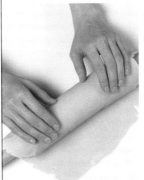

1
When the pie pastry is rolled out to the proper size, roll it partway onto the rolling pin, using a light touch.

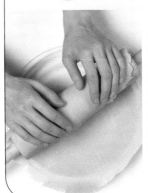

2
Carefully place the rolling pin over the pie plate so that the edge of the pastry hangs over about 2cm. Unroll the pastry, then press it gently into the plate.

Toasting Nuts

1
Toast nuts in a dry pan over moderate heat, stirring and shaking the pan frequently, for 5 to 7 minutes.

2
When the nuts are a light golden colour and fragrant, immediately turn them out of the pan, or they will overcook from the retained heat.

Making Low-Fat Whipped Cream

1 Soften gelatine in water in a heatproof cup. Place the cup in simmering water for 2 minutes to dissolve the gelatine; cool.

2 For maximum volume, pre-chill evaporated milk in a large mixing bowl for 30 minutes in the freezer. Then begin beating at medium speed. Beat until the milk is foamy.

3 Increase the mixer speed to high and beat until the milk holds soft peaks when the beaters are lifted (with mixer turned off). If the recipe requires it, continue beating until stiff peaks form.

4 Fold the cooled gelatine mixture into the milk. Then chill the whipped milk in the refrigerator for 15 minutes, or until you can mound it with a spoon.

Beating Egg Whites

1 Have egg whites at room temperature. Use a clean, dry bowl and beaters. Starting at a medium-low speed, beat until frothy.

2 Increase the mixer speed to medium and continue beating until the whites have become foamy and increased in volume.

3 Continue beating, occasionally tilting the bowl and moving the beaters around to incorporate as much air as possible. Beat until the egg whites are stiff but still moist and glossy.

Making Yoghurt Cheese in a Coffee Filter

1 Drain the whey from yoghurt in a coffee filter. In 2 hours the yoghurt will be slightly thickened; in 12 hours it will be quite firm.

Boning Salmon Fillets

1

Salmon fillets sometimes contain pinbones. Pull them out with large tweezers or use needle-nose pliers.

Debearding Mussels

1

Before cooking mussels, scrub the shells under running water with a stiff brush and pull out the hairlike 'beards'.

Shelling and Deveining Green Prawns

1

Hold the prawn with one hand and twist the head off with the other. Remove the body shell and the legs; the tail shell can be left on or taken off.

2

If you can't get a good grip on the end of the back vein with your fingers, use a small paring knife to help you remove it.

Baking Food in Packets

1

Place the food on one side of a sheet of foil. Fold the foil over and crimp the long edges together, leaving a little breathing space.

2

When the long side is sealed, fold over the short ends and crimp them, again leaving a little space. This seals in the moisture so that the enclosed food will steam in the oven.

Filleting and Skinning Fish

1

Before you start to fillet a round fish (such as a bream or snapper), trim off the pectoral fins. Then cut deeply across one side of the fish, just below the head.

2

Gently slide the knife along the spine towards the tail. Turn the fish over and repeat on the other side. Pick out any loose bones with tweezers.

Crumbing Chicken Breasts

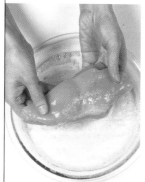

1 Rinse the chicken breasts and pat dry. Lightly beat an egg white in a shallow bowl, then dip the chicken in the egg.

2 Shake off excess egg, then dip both sides of each chicken breast in the breadcrumbs. Gently shake off any excess crumbs.

Roasting Chicken

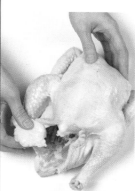

1 Rinse and dry chicken. Remove and discard the pockets of fat from the cavity. Put aside the bag of giblets for use in stocks, if desired.

2 Place the chicken breast-side-down on a rack. The rack lets the fat drain off; starting the chicken breast-side-down keeps the white meat moist (turn the chicken halfway through the cooking time).

Deglazing a Baking Dish

1 After roasting meat or poultry, add liquid (stock, wine, etc) to the pan and stir to scrape the brown bits from the bottom.

2 Pour the juices into a gravy separator. (Or pour the juices into a deep, narrow bowl and place in the freezer for 15 minutes; spoon off the congealed fat.)

3 The gravy separator lets you pour off the juices while leaving the fat behind. To make gravy, pour the pan juices into a medium saucepan.

4 Add a mixture of flour and water to the pan juices, then cook, stirring, over moderate heat until the gravy is thickened.

Removing Fat and Tissue from Meat

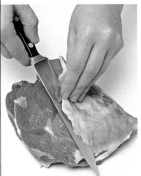

1 When you are preparing meat for a casserole or stir-fry, you may need to trim it further. Using a very sharp knife, first cut and pull the surrounding fat away from the meat.

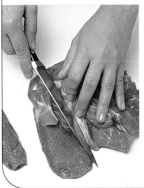

2 Then cut out the connective tissue, membrane and any gristle from each of the smaller pieces of meat. Shown here is boneless lamb.

Cutting Meat for Stir Frying

1 A stir-fry requires meat that's cut into uniform pieces. When the meat is trimmed (shown here is boneless lamb), cut across the grain at right angles.

2 Then cut each piece crossways into strips about 5mm thick.

Making Medallions from Chops

1 You can make boneless pork medallions from loin chops at least 2cm thick. First, carefully cut away the bone.

2 Then trim all the fat from the edges of the chop with a sharp paring knife.

3 If you want thinner medallions, use a large, sharp knife to carefully halve each chop horizontally to make two slices.

4 If the recipe calls for pork escalopes, place the thinner medallions between sheets of plastic wrap and pound with a meat mallet or small, heavy pan to a 5mm thickness.

Vegetal

Vegetables

Artichokes

Actually the bud from a thistle-like plant, globe artichokes are high in fibre, folate and potassium, and supply a surprising amount of vitamin C as well.

Healthy Highlights

1 medium, cooked (120g)		Nutrients % RDI	
Kilojoules	107	Vitamin C	52%
Fibre	1.1g	Folate	32%
Protein	3.7g	Potassium	20%
Carbohydrate	1.7g		
Saturated Fat	0g		
Total Fat	0.2g		
Cholesterol	0mg		
Sodium	7mg		

Shopping & Preparation

At the market Globe artichokes are available from February to November, and are at their peak in August and September.

Look for Select small to medium, compact, bright green globes that look plump and feel heavy for their size. Large artichokes tend to be a little tougher and have less flavour than the smaller ones.

Preparation Pull off the loose lower leaves; trim the stem to about 3cm. Slice about 3cm off the top of the artichoke.

Trimming the top of the artichoke eliminates some of the sharp, inedible leaf tips.

Basic cooking Steam whole artichokes in a steamer basket over boiling water for 20 to 40 minutes or until an inner leaf can easily be pulled out. To microwave, rinse but do not dry 4 artichokes, then wrap individually in plastic wrap and cook for 9 to 15 minutes on high. Let stand; after 3 minutes, check an inner leaf as above.

Artichokes with Sun-Dried Tomatoes

Preparation: 20 minutes / Cooking: 20 minutes / Serves: 4

1 lemon, cut in half

4 medium globe artichokes

Salt

¼ cup olive oil

1 small onion, diced

2 cloves garlic, peeled and chopped

¼ cup chopped flat-leaf parsley

2 teaspoons chopped fresh thyme leaves

8 sun-dried tomatoes in olive oil, cut into strips

Freshly ground pepper

1. Squeeze the juice of half a lemon into a large bowl of water. Use the other lemon half to rub the cut portions of the artichokes as you work. Trim the artichokes with a stainless-steel knife, cut into quarters and cut away the chokes. Squeeze any remaining lemon juice into a large saucepan containing enough water to cover the artichoke quarters.

2. Bring the water to the boil. Add a pinch of salt and the artichokes. Cook for 5 to 8 minutes or until almost tender. Drain well and pat dry.

3. Heat the olive oil in a large nonstick frying pan over medium-low heat and add the onion. Cook gently for 5 minutes until pale golden. Add the garlic, parsley and thyme and cook for 1 minute. Add the artichokes, tomatoes and pepper to taste. Cook over medium-low heat for 5 minutes. If the mixture appears dry, add a few tablespoons of water. Serve the artichokes hot or at room temperature.

Nutrients per serving: Kilojoules 757; Fibre 3g; Protein 5g; Carbohydrate 6g; Saturated Fat 2g; Total Fat 15g; Cholesterol 0mg

Did you know?

When artichokes are first picked, much of their carbohydrate is in the form of inulin, which is an indigestible starch. With time, though, the inulin is converted to sugar. That's why it's hard to be specific about kilojoule counts when it comes to artichokes, but they're always quite low.

Artichoke Dip

Preparation: 8 minutes / Cooking: 20 minutes / Makes: 2 cups

1 can (400g) artichoke hearts, drained and coarsely chopped

½ cup grated Parmesan cheese

½ cup reduced-fat mayonnaise

1 clove garlic, peeled and finely chopped

1 tablespoon lemon juice

1. Preheat the oven to 180°C. Combine the artichokes, cheese, mayonnaise, garlic and lemon juice in a medium-sized mixing bowl. Spoon the mixture into an ungreased small casserole dish and bake, uncovered, for 20 minutes or until bubbly and slightly browned.

2. Serve hot, warm or chilled as a dip with savoury biscuits or toast rounds.

Nutrients per ½ cup: Kilojoules 618; Fibre 2g; Protein 5g; Carbohydrate 8g; Saturated Fat 3g; Total Fat 10g; Cholesterol 18mg

Artichokes with Sun-Dried Tomatoes

Artichokes with Lemon & Herb Mayonnaise

Preparation: 25 minutes / Cooking: 30 minutes / Serves: 6

6 large globe artichokes

6 cloves garlic, peeled

2 tablespoons fresh rosemary leaves

½ cup low-fat mayonnaise

2 tablespoons reduced-fat sour cream

2 teaspoons grated lemon zest

¼ cup lemon juice

½ teaspoon dried tarragon

1. Trim the artichoke stems to about 3 cm with a stainless-steel knife. Snap off any discoloured leaves with your fingers. Cut off 3 cm from the tops of the artichokes. (For a neater presentation, cut off about 1 cm from the tops of all the remaining outer leaves.) Peel the stems.

2. Choose a pot large enough to hold a steamer basket with the whole artichokes comfortably. Fill the pot with water to a depth of 3 cm. Add the garlic and rosemary and bring to the boil. Arrange the artichokes in the steamer basket, put the basket into the saucepan, then cover and bring to the boil. Steam for 30 minutes (adding

water as necessary) or until a heart is tender when pierced with a knife. Turn the artichokes upside-down to drain. Discard the garlic cloves and the rosemary.

3. Meanwhile, combine the mayonnaise, sour cream, lemon zest, lemon juice and tarragon in a small bowl. Serve as a dipping sauce with the hot artichokes.

Nutrients per serving: Kilojoules 401; Fibre 1g; Protein 5g; Carbohydrate 6g; Saturated Fat 2g; Total Fat 5g; Cholesterol 10mg

Asparagus

Asparagus is an impressive source of folate. It also provides vitamin C, as well as some beta-carotene and alpha-carotene.

Healthy Highlights

5 spears, cooked (70g)		Nutrients % RDI	
Kilojoules	55	Folate	55%
Fibre	1g	Vitamin C	28%
Protein	2g	Potassium	10%
Carbohydrate	1.1g		
Saturated Fat	0g		
Total Fat	0.1g		
Cholesterol	0mg		
Sodium	1mg		

Shopping & Preparation

At the market Three varieties of locally grown asparagus – green, white and purple – are available, with the best supplies from September to November.

Look for Asparagus should be a bright, clear colour. Whether fat or skinny, stalks should be full, firm and round, with compact tips and tight scales.

Preparation Hold each stalk with both hands, close to the base, then bend the stalk until it snaps. The stalk should break where the tough part begins. Store the trimmed spears, standing in some cool water and covered with plastic wrap, for up to 2 weeks in the refrigerator.

Snap off the tough ends of each asparagus stalk; discard or use to flavour homemade vegetable stock.

Basic cooking Steam whole stalks for 3 to 5 minutes, or until the thickest part is tender. To microwave 500g asparagus, arrange the stalks in a shallow dish with tips towards the centre. Add ¼ cup water, cover and cook on high for 5 to 7 minutes. Let stand, covered, for 5 minutes.

Asparagus & Chicken Stir-Fry

Preparation: 15 minutes

Cooking: 10 minutes / Serves: 4

3 teaspoons olive oil
3 spring onions, thinly sliced
375g skinless, boneless chicken breasts, cut across the grain into 1cm pieces
750g asparagus, trimmed and cut into 5cm lengths
250g sugar snap peas or snow peas
½ cup chicken stock
½ teaspoon grated lemon zest
1 tablespoon light soy sauce
1 teaspoon cornflour blended with 1 tablespoon water

1. Heat 2 teaspoons of the oil in a large frying pan over moderate heat. Add the spring onions and cook for 1 minute or until wilted. Add the chicken and cook for 3 minutes or until no longer pink.

2. Add the remaining oil and the asparagus and cook for 2 minutes to coat the asparagus.

3. Add the peas, stock, ½ cup water, the lemon zest and soy sauce and bring to the boil. Reduce to a simmer and cook, uncovered, for 2 minutes or until the chicken and asparagus are just cooked through.

4. Stir in the cornflour mixture and cook, stirring, for 1 minute or until the sauce is slightly thickened.

Nutrients per serving: Kilojoules 1074; Fibre 3g; Protein 32g; Carbohydrate 6g; Saturated Fat 3g; Total Fat 11g; Cholesterol 84mg

Did you know?

• If you throw out the water after cooking asparagus, you discard nutrients, too. So try to include the cooking liquid in the dish (as in the Bisque recipe, right).

• If stored at room temperature, fresh asparagus spears will lose as much as half of their vitamin C within two days. The vegetable's texture and its delicate taste will suffer as well.

• Asparagus is one of the few vegetables high in purines. As a high intake of purines is linked to the build-up of uric acid salts in the joints, gout sufferers should avoid this vegetable.

Creamy Asparagus & Sweet Potato Bisque

Preparation: 15 minutes / Cooking: 35 minutes / Serves: 4

750g asparagus, trimmed and cut into 2cm lengths (trimmings reserved)

250g sweet potato, peeled and cut into 1cm cubes

2 teaspoons olive oil

1 onion, halved and thinly sliced

1 cup chicken stock

½ teaspoon dried marjoram

¼ teaspoon cayenne pepper

Salt

¾ cup skim milk

1. Bring 2½ cups water to the boil in a medium saucepan. Add the asparagus tips and cook for 2 minutes to blanch. Remove with a slotted spoon and put aside for garnish.

2. Add the sweet potato to the boiling water and cook for 10 minutes or until just tender. Remove with a strainer or slotted spoon. Add the asparagus trimmings, reduce to a simmer, cover and cook for 10 minutes. Reserving the liquid, strain and discard the trimmings. You should have about 2 cups liquid.

3. Meanwhile, heat the oil in a medium saucepan over moderately low heat. Add the onion and cook for 7 minutes or until light golden. Stir in the reserved cooking liquid, the stock, the remaining asparagus, the marjoram, cayenne pepper and a pinch of salt, and bring to the boil. Reduce to a simmer, cover and cook for 6 minutes or until the asparagus is tender.

4. Transfer the mixture to a food processor, add the sweet potato and process to a smooth purée. Return the purée to the saucepan and stir in the milk. Cook for 2 minutes or until heated through. Serve the soup garnished with the reserved asparagus tips.

Nutrients per serving: Kilojoules 459; Fibre 3g; Protein 7g; Carbohydrate 14g; Saturated Fat 1g; Total Fat 3g; Cholesterol 1mg

Creamy Asparagus & Sweet Potato Bisque

Beans

Delightfully crisp, fresh beans offer useful vitamin C, folate, iron and – in the case of green beans – some beta-carotene.

Healthy Highlights

Green beans
1 serving, cooked (110g)

		Nutrients % RDI	
Kilojoules	76	Vitamin C	47%
Fibre	3.1g	Folate	26%
Protein	1.6g	Vitamin A	11%
Carbohydrate	2.4g	Iron	10%
Saturated Fat	0g		
Total Fat	0.2g		
Cholesterol	0mg		
Sodium	3mg		

Butter beans
1 serving, cooked (110g)

		Nutrients % RDI	
Kilojoules	92	Vitamin C	40%
Fibre	3.4g	Folate	26%
Protein	2.5g	Zinc	13%
Carbohydrate	2.5g	Potassium	12%
Saturated Fat	0g	Niacin	10%
Total Fat	0.2g		
Cholesterol	0mg		
Sodium	3mg		

Shopping & Preparation

At the market Fresh beans are almost always available, although the season peaks in summer.

Look for The beans should snap when you bend them. Choose slender, straight beans with a 'peach fuzz' feel, free of nicks or rusty brown spots. For uniform cooking, choose beans that are of roughly equal size.

Preparation Although they don't need to be 'stringed', most beans (except for young beans) should be topped and tailed – their stem ends and pointed tips removed.

For a more attractive presentation, you can cut beans diagonally.

Basic cooking Steam beans for 3 to 5 minutes; they should remain bright and crisp-tender. Microwave 500g beans with ¼ cup liquid on high for 5 to 6 minutes.

Lemony Beans

Lemony Beans ⓠ

Preparation: 15 minutes / Cooking: 10 minutes / Serves: 4

375g green beans, halved crossways

375g butter beans, halved crossways

2 teaspoons olive oil

3 cloves garlic, crushed

¼ cup chicken stock

1 teaspoon julienned lemon zest

¼ cup lemon juice

Salt

1 tablespoon chopped fresh dill

2 teaspoons unsalted butter

1. Steam the beans in a steamer or colander set over a saucepan of boiling water for 6 minutes or until crisp-tender.

2. Meanwhile, heat the oil in a large nonstick frying pan over moderately low heat. Add the garlic and cook for 2 minutes or until soft. Add the stock, lemon zest, lemon juice and a pinch of salt, and bring to the boil. Add the beans and cook for 2 minutes or until heated through and well coated. Add the dill, remove from the heat, and stir in the butter until melted.

Nutrients per serving: Kilojoules 326; Fibre 6g; Protein 4g; Carbohydrate 5g; Saturated Fat 2g; Total Fat 5g; Cholesterol 6mg

Did you know?

Although most people associate beta-carotene with orange vegetables and fruits, the chlorophyll in green vegetables can mask the orange colour. A surprising fact: green beans have more than five times as much beta-carotene as butter beans.

Bean & Prosciutto Salad @

Preparation: 10 minutes / Cooking: 10 minutes / Serves: 4

250g green beans

1 tablespoon olive oil

6 slices prosciutto (100g)

1 onion, finely diced

1 clove garlic, crushed

1 tablespoon chopped fresh parsley

1 tablespoon chopped fresh basil

1. Cook the beans in a little water in a small saucepan for 4 to 5 minutes or until crisp-tender. Drain and keep warm.

2. Heat the oil in a medium frying pan and fry the prosciutto briefly over moderate heat until crisp. Remove the prosciutto and put aside.

3. Cook the onion and garlic in the same pan for 2 minutes or until translucent. Cut the prosciutto into 2 cm pieces, return to the pan along with the parsley and basil, then pour the dressing over the beans. Tip into a bowl and serve hot or at room temperature.

Nutrients per serving: Kilojoules 375; Fibre 2g; Protein 6g; Carbohydrate 3g; Saturated Fat 1g; Total Fat 6g; Cholesterol 13mg

Beetroot

Deliciously sweet (yet low in kilojoules), beetroot provides significant amounts of folate, vitamin C and potassium. The leafy tops are high in calcium and iron.

Healthy Highlights

3 slices, cooked (90g)		Nutrients % RDI	
Kilojoules	156	Folate	40%
Fibre	2.3g	Potassium	12%
Protein	1.7g	Vitamin C	12%
Carbohydrate	7.6g		
Saturated Fat	0g		
Total Fat	0.1g		
Cholesterol	0mg		
Sodium	46mg		

Shopping & Preparation

At the market You'll find beetroot available all year, but it is at its best from April to August.

Look for The leaves should look fresh and green, and the root should be smooth, firm and unbruised.

Preparation Cut off the stems 1 cm from the roots (no closer). Scrub the roots very gently but thoroughly, being careful not to nick the skin.

Don't cut the stems too close to the root or the colour will bleed as the beetroot cooks.

Basic cooking Bake whole beetroot wrapped in foil at 220°C for 1 to 2 hours (the time will depend on the age and size). Simmer whole beetroot, covered, in boiling water for 40 minutes to 2 hours. Microwave 500g whole beetroot with ¼ cup water, covered, on high for 10 minutes.

Egyptian Beetroot Dip

Preparation: 45 minutes / Cooking: 30–40 minutes / Serves: 4–6

5 medium beetroot (1kg)

300ml plain low-fat yoghurt

2 cloves garlic, crushed

¼ cup lemon juice

2 tablespoons extra virgin olive oil

½ teaspoon ground cumin

½ teaspoon ground coriander

½ teaspoon ground cinnamon

½ teaspoon paprika

Salt

Freshly ground pepper

1. Cut the stems off the beetroot (do not peel the roots, just wash well). Cook in a large pot of simmering, salted water for 30 to 40 minutes until tender. Drain, cool slightly and rub off the skins.

2. Finely chop, grate or process the beetroot in a food processor. Add the yoghurt, garlic, lemon juce, oil, cumin, coriander, cinnamon and paprika and mix well. Season to taste with salt and pepper. Chill until required. Serve with warm, crusty bread.

Nutrients per serving: Kilojoules 719; Fibre 3g; Protein 7g; Carbohydrate 14g; Saturated Fat 1g; Total Fat 9g; Cholesterol 4mg

Egyptian Beetroot Dip

Roasted Baby Beetroot Salad

Roasted Baby Beetroot Salad

Preparation: 10 minutes / Cooking: 45 minutes / Serves: 4

1 large bunch baby beetroot (750g), trimmed and scrubbed

3 cloves garlic, peeled and bruised

2 tablespoons olive oil

2 teaspoons red wine vinegar

1 teaspoon seeded mustard

Salt

Freshly ground pepper

1 orange, rind removed and the flesh cut into segments

100g black olives

1 small red onion, thinly sliced

1 bunch rocket

1. Combine the beetroot, garlic and olive oil in a small baking dish. Cover with foil and roast at 180°C for 45 minutes or until the beetroot is tender. Remove the beetroot from the baking dish, saving any pan juices. Cut the beetroot into quarters and place in a serving bowl.

2. Combine the vinegar and mustard in a small bowl. Add the pan juices and season to taste with salt and pepper.

3. Toss the orange segments, olives, onion and rocket with the beetroot. Pour over the dressing and toss again just before serving.

Nutrients per serving: Kilojoules 678; Fibre 4g; Protein 3g; Carbohydrate 16g; Saturated Fat 1g; Total Fat 10g; Cholesterol 0mg

Did you know?

• If you buy beetroot with nice fresh tops, cook the leaves as you would spinach or silverbeet. They're also rich in beta-carotene.

• Beetroot, like Brussels sprouts, contain a substance that can hinder thiamin absorption – but this won't be a problem for anyone with a well-balanced diet.

Broccoli

Broccoli

One cup of cooked broccoli has more vitamin C than a fresh orange. Vitamin C enhances iron absorption, making lightly cooked broccoli an ideal companion for iron-rich poultry, seafood or meat.

Healthy Highlights

1 serving, cooked (150g)		Nutrients % RDI	
Kilojoules	161	Vitamin C	434%
Fibre	6.3g	Folate	62%
Protein	7.2g	Potassium	26%
Carbohydrate	0.9g	Riboflavin	22%
Saturated Fat	0g	Iron	13%
Total Fat	0.5g	Magnesium	12%
Cholesterol	0mg	Niacin	12%
Sodium	31mg	Vitamin A	12%
		Thiamin	11%

Shopping & Preparation

At the market Available all year, fresh broccoli is tastiest in the cooler months of April to October. Frozen broccoli retains high levels of nutrients.

Look for Broccoli tops should be dark green to bluish- or purplish-green with compact clusters of tightly closed florets; avoid any that are yellowing. The stalks should be tender yet firm (not rubbery).

Preparation Cut off broccoli florets of desired size and put aside. If the stalks are tough, peel before cooking.

If the stalks are long, you may need to peel them. Catch the edge of skin between your thumb and a knife blade and pull smoothly upwards.

Basic cooking Steam broccoli florets for 5 to 8 minutes. To microwave 500g florets, add ¼ cup water, cover and cook on high for 3 to 4 minutes. Let stand for 1 minute.

Creamy Broccoli Soup

Preparation: 15 minutes / Cooking: 25 minutes / Serves: 4

1 onion, chopped
2 teaspoons olive oil
1 packet (300g) frozen broccoli
2 cups chicken stock
1 teaspoon dried oregano
Cayenne pepper
1 cup skim milk

1. Cook the onion in the oil in a medium saucepan until translucent.

2. Add the broccoli, stock, oregano and a pinch of cayenne pepper. Simmer until the broccoli is crisp-tender.

3. Purée the mixture in a blender. Return to the saucepan and add the milk. Gently heat through.

Nutrients per serving: Kilojoules 344; Fibre 3g; Protein 8g; Carbohydrate 6g; Saturated Fat 1g; Total Fat 3g; Cholesterol 2mg

Broccoli & Roasted Capsicum Salad ⓞ

Preparation: 10 minutes / Cooking: 5–6 minutes / Serves: 4

1 cup Roasted Red Capsicums (recipe, page 61)

4 cups broccoli florets (300g)

½ cup olives

¼ cup balsamic vinegar

2 tablespoons olive oil

2 teaspoons Dijon mustard

1 clove garlic, crushed

1. Prepare the Roasted Red Capsicums.

2. Steam the broccoli in a steamer or colander set over a saucepan of boiling water for 5 to 6 minutes or until crisp-tender. Place in a serving bowl with the capsicums and olives.

3. Whisk together the vinegar, oil, mustard and garlic in a small bowl. Pour over the broccoli.

Nutrients per serving: Kilojoules 556; Fibre 4g; Protein 4g; Carbohydrate 7g; Saturated Fat 1g; Total Fat 10g; Cholesterol 0mg

Did you know?

• Broccoli is not only rich in disease-fighting vitamin C, it also contains phytochemicals – including beta-carotene, sulphoraphane and indoles – which protect against or slow the growth of some types of cancer.

• Cooked broccoli offers even more benefits than raw. Cooking the vegetable increases the indole content by freeing a crucial enzyme.

• Broccoli contains dithiolthiones, which trigger the formation of enzymes that may stop carcinogens from damaging DNA.

Prawns with Broccoli, Bok Choy & Basil

Preparation: 20 minutes

Cooking: 20 minutes / Serves: 4

1 cup rice

Salt

1 tablespoon olive oil

4 spring onions, thinly sliced

3 cloves garlic, crushed

1 small red chilli, finely sliced

1 tablespoon minced fresh ginger

6 cups small broccoli florets (500g)

⅓ cup chicken stock

2 tablespoons soy sauce

500g medium green prawns, peeled and deveined

½ cup chopped fresh basil

2 cups sliced bok choy

1. Bring 2¼ cups water to the boil in a medium saucepan. Add the rice and a pinch of salt and reduce to a simmer. Cover and cook for 17 minutes or until the rice is tender.

2. Meanwhile, heat 1 teaspoon of the oil in a large nonstick frying pan over moderate heat. Add the spring onions, garlic, chilli and ginger and cook for 2 minutes or until the spring onions are tender.

3. Add the remaining oil to the pan along with the broccoli, stirring to coat. Add the stock and soy sauce and cook, stirring frequently, for 3 minutes. Add the prawns, basil and bok choy, then cook for a further 3 minutes.

4. Spoon over the rice and serve hot.

Nutrients per serving: Kilojoules 1453; Fibre 7g; Protein 27g; Carbohydrate 44g; Saturated Fat 1g; Total Fat 6g; Cholesterol 116mg

Prawns with Broccoli, Bok Choy & Basil

Thai Beef & Broccoli Salad

Preparation: 25 minutes / Cooking: 10 minutes / Serves: 4

500g rump steak

½ cup salt-reduced soy sauce

2 cloves garlic, crushed

5 tablespoons lime juice

1 cup broccoli florets (75g)

⅓ cup fresh mint leaves

⅓ cup fresh basil leaves

¼ cup fresh coriander leaves

½ cucumber, sliced

2 red chillies, thinly sliced

2 teaspoons light brown sugar

1. Place the steak, half the soy sauce, the garlic and 2 tablespoons of the lime juice in a large bowl and allow to stand for 10 minutes.

2. Cook the steak on a preheated grill pan for 1 to 2 minutes each side. Put aside.

3. Steam the broccoli in a steamer or colander set over a saucepan of boiling water for 5 to 6 minutes or until crisp-tender. Allow to cool for 10 minutes, then combine with the mint, basil, coriander and cucumber.

4. Slice the steak and add to the broccoli mixture. Combine the chillies, sugar and the remaining soy sauce and lime juice. Pour over the steak and broccoli, folding gently. Pile the salad onto serving plates.

Nutrients per serving: Kilojoules 1035; Fibre 2g; Protein 36g; Carbohydrate 5g; Saturated Fat 4g; Total Fat 9g; Cholesterol 78mg

Thai Beef & Broccoli Salad

Farfalle with Broccoli & Anchovy Sauce

Farfalle with Broccoli & Anchovy Sauce

Preparation: 15 minutes / Cooking: 20 minutes / Serves: 4

6 cups broccoli florets (450g)

500g farfalle pasta

¼ cup olive oil

45g anchovies, chopped

3 cloves garlic, chopped

½ teaspoon dried crushed chillies

¼ cup grated Parmesan cheese

1. Cook the broccoli florets in a little water in a medium saucepan for 15 minutes or until soft, then drain.

2. Meanwhile, cook the pasta in a large saucepan of boiling water according to the packet directions, until firm-tender. Drain and keep warm.

3. Heat the oil over gentle heat in a medium saucepan. Add the anchovies, garlic and chilli and cook for 5 minutes. Add the broccoli to the pan and mix well.

4. Stir the sauce through the drained pasta, mixing thoroughly. Serve in individual bowls and sprinkle with the Parmesan.

Nutrients per serving: Kilojoules 2288; Fibre 11g; Protein 23g; Carbohydrate 72g; Saturated Fat 3g; Total Fat 18g; Cholesterol 14mg

Did you know?

• Broccoli is a rich source of zeaxanthin and lutein, two carotenoids. According to a Harvard University study, these substances may protect against macular degeneration, the leading cause of irreversible blindness in adults over the age of 65. Lutein also seems to offer some protection against lung cancer.

• You may soon be eating broccoli sprouts. Scientists have been breeding sprouts with up to 50 times the concentration of cancer-fighting phytochemicals found in regular broccoli.

Cabbages & Brussels Sprouts

Cabbage is a good source of vitamin C and is also rich in indoles. Preliminary studies suggest that these phytochemicals may help prevent breast cancer. And in a test of some common fruits and vegetables for their overall antioxidant power, Brussels sprouts ranked number five.

Healthy Highlights

Green cabbage

1 serving, raw (95g)		Nutrients % RDI	
Kilojoules	68	Vitamin C	141%
Fibre	3.4g	Folate	43%
Protein	1.4g	Potassium	16%
Carbohydrate	2.4g		
Saturated Fat	0g		
Total Fat	0.1g		
Cholesterol	0mg		
Sodium	17mg		

Red cabbage

1 serving, raw (95g)		Nutrients % RDI	
Kilojoules	95	Vitamin C	216%
Fibre	3.7g	Folate	24%
Protein	2.1g	Potassium	22%
Carbohydrate	2.9g		
Saturated Fat	0g		
Total Fat	0.3g		
Cholesterol	0mg		
Sodium	15mg		

Bok choy

1 serving, cooked (110g)		Nutrients % RDI	
Kilojoules	143	Vitamin C	77%
Fibre	1.2g	Folate	30%
Protein	1.1g	Vitamin A	13%
Carbohydrate	1g	Potassium	13%
Saturated Fat	0g	Iron	10%
Total Fat	0.2g		
Cholesterol	0mg		
Sodium	11mg		

Brussels sprouts

1 serving, cooked (155g)		Nutrients % RDI	
Kilojoules	168	Vitamin C	458%
Fibre	5.5g	Folate	69%
Protein	5.5g	Potassium	27%
Carbohydrate	3.3g	Riboflavin	15%
Saturated Fat	0g	Thiamin	13%
Total Fat	0.5g	Iron	12%
Cholesterol	0mg	Niacin	12%
Sodium	45mg	Magnesium	10%

Baby Bok Choy with Chilli Sesame Dressing

Preparation: 10 minutes

Cooking: 1 minute / Serves: 2–4

1 tablespoon fresh ginger, finely chopped
2 red chillies, finely sliced diagonally
2 cloves garlic, finely chopped
1 tablespoon sesame oil
1 tablespoon mirin (Japanese rice wine)
1 tablespoon soy sauce
1 teaspoon sugar
1 bunch baby bok choy (500g)
2 tablespoons toasted sesame seeds

1. Combine the ginger, chilli, garlic, sesame oil, mirin, soy sauce and sugar in a small bowl.

2. Blanch the whole bok choy in boiling water in a large saucepan for 1 minute, then place on a serving plate. Drizzle with the dressing then sprinkle with the sesame seeds.

Nutrients per serving: Kilojoules 1080; Fibre 5g; Protein 6g; Carbohydrate 7g; Saturated Fat 2g; Total Fat 16g; Cholesterol 0mg

Three-Cabbage Slaw with Honey & Mustard Dressing

Preparation: 20 minutes

Chill: 1 hour / Serves: 6

¼ cup cider vinegar
⅓ cup reduced-fat sour cream
1½ tablespoons honey
1½ tablespoons spicy brown mustard
1 teaspoon olive oil
3 cups shredded red cabbage
3 cups shredded green cabbage
2 cups shredded savoy cabbage
4 carrots, grated
2 spring onions, thinly sliced

1. Whisk together the vinegar, sour cream, honey, mustard and oil in a large bowl.

2. Add the cabbages, carrots and spring onions, tossing to combine. Cover and refrigerate for 1 hour or until chilled.

Nutrients per serving: Kilojoules 460; Fibre 6g; Protein 3g; Carbohydrate 12g; Saturated Fat 3g; Total Fat 5g; Cholesterol 13mg

Baby Bok Choy with Chilli Sesame Dressing

At the market Widely grown, green, red and white cabbages are always in good supply. Chinese cabbages, such as bok choy, are best around Easter, and again in the months leading up to Christmas. Brussels sprouts are abundant on the shelves from April to August.

Look for Choose a firm head of cabbage; the outer leaves should be free of tiny holes and the stem should not be woody or split. When buying Chinese cabbages, look for those with fresh, bright green leaves and crisp, pale green stems. And when choosing Brussels sprouts, select small, bright green, firm sprouts with tightly packed leaves and no patches of yellow.

Preparation Remove and discard loose outer leaves of cabbages. For shredded or chopped cabbage, halve or quarter the head through the stem, then cut out the core; if cutting into quarters, do not core. The leaves and stalks of bok choy and similar Asian greens may be cooked together, or the stalks cut off and cooked separately. Brussels sprouts need only a light trim of the stems, but you should pull off any loose or discoloured outer leaves.

Slice most of the stem off each sprout, but leave on a bit of the base.

Basic cooking Steam shredded cabbage for 5 to 8 minutes, and wedges for 12 to 20 minutes. Microwave 500g cabbage wedges in a dish with ¼ cup liquid; cover and cook for 6 to 8 minutes. Cook shredded cabbage or bok choy the same way for 4 to 6 minutes. Steam Brussels sprouts for 6 to 12 minutes, depending on size. To microwave 500g whole sprouts, place in a dish with ¼ cup water, cover and cook on high for 4 to 8 minutes. Let stand for 3 minutes.

Warm Red Cabbage with Pears

Preparation: 15 minutes / Cooking: 10 minutes / Serves: 4

2 teaspoons olive oil

1 small red onion, finely chopped

1 tablespoon minced fresh ginger

2 cloves garlic, crushed

6 cups shredded red cabbage

2 pears, peeled and cut into 1cm slices

Salt

¼ cup balsamic vinegar

1. Heat the oil in a large nonstick frying pan over moderate heat. Add the onion, ginger and garlic, and cook for 5 minutes or until the onion is tender.

2. Add the cabbage, pears and a pinch of salt, and cook for 5 minutes or until the cabbage is crisp-tender. Sprinkle with the vinegar, cook for 1 minute, and serve hot or at room temperature.

Nutrients per serving: Kilojoules 319; Fibre 3g; Protein 1g; Carbohydrate 12g; Saturated Fat 0g; Total Fat 3g; Cholesterol 0mg

Did you know?

• Cabbage contains isothiocyanates, which appear to stimulate the production of cancer-fighting enzymes.

• Red cabbage provides more vitamin C than green; savoy, which has medium-green leaves, has a significant amount of beta-carotene.

• Buy a whole cabbage, rather than a head that has been halved; when cabbage is cut, it loses vitamin C.

• Although plain cabbage (like most vegetables) is virtually fat-free, a one-cup serving of coleslaw dressed with mayonnaise may contain as much as 16 grams of fat.

Stir-Fried Bok Choy with Garlic Sauce

Preparation: 15 minutes / Cooking: 15 minutes / Serves: 4

2 teaspoons peanut oil

10 cloves garlic, crushed

1 tablespoon chopped fresh ginger

¼ cup chicken stock

1 red capsicum, cut into 1cm squares

2 carrots, halved lengthways and thinly sliced

4 cups sliced bok choy or green cabbage

1 teaspoon sugar

2 teaspoons sesame oil

1. Heat the peanut oil in a large nonstick frying pan over moderately low heat. Add the garlic and ginger and cook for 1 minute or until slightly softened. Add the stock and ¼ cup water, cover and cook for 7 minutes or until the garlic and ginger are very soft.

2. Add the capsicum and carrots and cook for 1 minute. Add the bok choy and toss until well coated. Sprinkle with the sugar and a pinch of salt and cook for 4 minutes (6 minutes if using green cabbage) or until tender. Drizzle with the sesame oil and serve hot.

Nutrients per serving: Kilojoules 365; Fibre 3g; Protein 2g; Carbohydrate 6g; Saturated Fat 1g; Total Fat 5g; Cholesterol 0mg

Sprouts with Prosciutto & Almonds

Preparation: 10 minutes / Cooking: 15 minutes / Serves: 4

300g Brussels sprouts, trimmed

2½ tablespoons olive oil

6 slices prosciutto (100g)

½ cup flaked almonds

1 tablespoon lemon juice

1. Preheat the oven to 180°C. Cook the Brussels sprouts in boiling water in a small saucepan for 5 minutes or until crisp-tender. Drain well, cut in half and put aside.

2. Meanwhile, heat 2 teaspoons of the oil in a small frying pan over high heat. Fry the prosciutto until crisp. Cut into bite-sized pieces.

3. Toast the almonds on a baking tray in the oven for 5 to 10 minutes until golden.

4. Pour the remaining oil and the lemon juice over the sprouts and toss well. Sprinkle with the prosciutto and almonds.

Nutrients per serving: Kilojoules 890; Fibre 3g; Protein 9g; Carbohydrate 2g; Saturated Fat 2g; Total Fat 19g; Cholesterol 13mg

Did you know?

• You can avoid the lingering, sulphurous odour of boiled cabbage and Brussels sprouts by cooking them quickly in lots of water, in an uncovered pot.

• The slightly bitter undertone you can sometimes taste in Brussels sprouts comes from sinigrin, a natural compound in the plant that helps keep away insects. The substance is not toxic to humans – in fact, it shows promise in combating the early stages of colon cancer.

• Because of its dark green leaves, bok choy is rich in beta-carotene and also supplies calcium.

Sprouts with Prosciutto & Almonds

Capsicums

Capsicums – especially red ones – are a superb source of vitamin C. These relatives of the chilli also contain flavonoids, which seem to fight cancer in several different ways.

Healthy Highlights

Green capsicum
1 medium, raw
(90g)

Nutrients		% RDI	
Kilojoules	60	Vitamin C	270%
Fibre	0.8g	Folate	15%
Protein	1.4g		
Carbohydrate	2.1g		
Saturated Fat	0g		
Total Fat	0.1g		
Cholesterol	0mg		
Sodium	2mg		

Red capsicum
1 medium, raw
(90g)

Nutrients		% RDI	
Kilojoules	94	Vitamin C	510%
Fibre	1.1g	Vitamin A	30%
Protein	1.5g		
Carbohydrate	3.6g		
Saturated Fat	0g		
Total Fat	0.2g		
Cholesterol	0mg		
Sodium	1mg		

Shopping & Preparation

At the market Red, orange, yellow and green capsicums are commonly available, and there are black, brown and mauve varieties, too. They are available all year, but sweetest from November to May.

Look for Capsicums should be firm, with smooth, unblemished skin, and be bright in colour. Avoid any that are dull-looking or have soft spots.

Preparation If you're slicing or chopping capsicums, halve them lengthways and pull off the stem and cap; pull out the ribs and seeds with your fingers. For roasting, slice the capsicum lengthways into flat strips.

It's easier to peel roasted capsicums if you stem them and then cut into relatively flat pieces instead of roasting them whole.

Bread Salad with Roasted Capsicums

Preparation: 15 minutes / Cooking: 20 minutes / Serves: 4

3 cups Roasted Red Capsicums (recipe, below right)

3 cups Italian or French bread cubes (3cm)

1 large tomato, diced

1½ cups diced (1cm) cucumber

100g feta cheese, crumbled

½ cup Kalamata or other brine-cured olives

1. Prepare the Roasted Red Capsicums as directed, but omit the salt and garlic.

2. Preheat the oven to 190°C. Spread the bread cubes on a baking tray and bake, tossing occasionally, for 7 minutes or until lightly crisped but not browned.

3. Combine the capsicums in a large salad bowl with the toasted bread, tomato, cucumber, feta and olives, tossing well. Serve at room temperature or chilled.

Nutrients per serving: Kilojoules 1176; Fibre 5g; Protein 12g; Carbohydrate 33g; Saturated Fat 4g; Total Fat 11g; Cholesterol 18mg

Did you know?

Both red and yellow capsicums contain about two teaspoons of natural sugar, which makes them seem sweet. Green capsicums have comparatively little sugar, which is why they taste somewhat bitter.

Mixed Capsicum Scramble

Preparation: 20 minutes / Cooking: 15 minutes / Serves: 4

3 teaspoons olive oil

3 red capsicums, cut into 5mm strips

2 green capsicums, cut into 5mm strips

1 onion, halved and thinly sliced

4 cloves garlic, crushed

Salt

1 large tomato, finely chopped

2 eggs

4 egg whites

¼ cup low-fat ricotta cheese

Freshly ground black pepper

1. Heat the oil in a large nonstick frying pan over moderate heat. Add the capsicums, onion, garlic and a pinch of salt, and cook for 5 minutes or until the capsicums are crisp-tender. Add the tomato and cook, stirring, for 7 minutes or until the liquid has evaporated.

2. Meanwhile, combine the whole eggs, egg whites, ricotta cheese, a good grinding of pepper and a pinch of salt in a food processor, and process until smooth.

3. Pour the egg mixture into the frying pan, reduce the heat to low, and cook, stirring, for 3 minutes or until set.

Nutrients per serving: Kilojoules 635; Fibre 3g; Protein 12g; Carbohydrate 8g; Saturated Fat 2g; Total Fat 8g; Cholesterol 114mg

Bread Salad with Roasted Capsicums

Roasted Red Capsicums

Preparation: 10 minutes / Cooking: 12 minutes / Chill: 1 hour / Makes: 3 cups

4 large red capsicums, cut lengthways into flat strips

3 teaspoons olive oil

Salt

1 clove garlic, crushed

1. Preheat the griller. Place the capsicum pieces, skin-side-up, on the griller rack and cook 10 cm from the heat for 12 minutes or until the skin is blackened. When the capsicums are cool enough to handle, peel and cut into 5 cm strips.

2. Combine the oil and a pinch of salt in a medium bowl. Add the garlic and the capsicums, tossing well. Cover and refrigerate for at least 1 hour or up to 3 days. Remove and discard the garlic before serving.

Nutrients per ½ cup: Kilojoules 207; Fibre 2g; Protein 2g; Carbohydrate 5g; Saturated Fat 0g; Total Fat 2g; Cholesterol 0mg

Did you know?

Red, yellow and orange capsicums are higher in antioxidant beta-carotene than green ones, and their vitamin C content makes them a good choice to serve with iron-rich foods.

Penne with Capsicum Sauce

Penne with Capsicum Sauce

Preparation: 10 minutes / Cooking: 20 minutes / Serves: 4

1kg red and yellow capsicums

⅓ cup olive oil

4 cloves garlic, crushed

500g penne

⅓ cup chopped fresh basil

¼ cup grated Parmesan cheese

1. Remove the seeds from the capsicums and cut the flesh into large dice (2 cm).

2. Heat the oil in a large frying pan. Add the capsicums and garlic. Cover and cook over gentle heat for 20 minutes, stirring occasionally.

3. Cook the pasta in a large saucepan of boiling water according to the packet directions, until firm-tender. Drain, then turn into a serving bowl and toss with the capsicums. Stir in the basil.

4. Serve with Parmesan cheese on the side.

Nutrients per serving: Kilojoules 2453; Fibre 8g; Protein 17g; Carbohydrate 79g; Saturated Fat 4g; Total Fat 22g; Cholesterol 5mg

Red Capsicum Soup

Preparation: 10 minutes / Cooking: 40 minutes / Serves: 4–6

1 tablespoon olive oil

4 red capsicums, diced

1 medium onion, diced

2 cloves garlic, crushed

2 cups chicken stock

2 medium tomatoes, skinned, seeded and chopped

1 teaspoon ground coriander

Salt

Freshly ground pepper

2 tablespoons plain low-fat yoghurt

1. Heat the oil in a large saucepan. Add the capsicums, onion and garlic and cook gently for 5 minutes, stirring.

2. Add the stock, tomatoes and coriander. Cover and simmer for 30 minutes.

3. Purée the mixture in a blender. Return to the saucepan and heat through. Season to taste with salt and pepper, pour into serving bowls and swirl a little yoghurt on top.

Nutrients per serving: Kilojoules 455; Fibre 3g; Protein 5g; Carbohydrate 9g; Saturated Fat 1g; Total Fat 5g; Cholesterol 0mg

Did you know?

• The longer a capsicum ripens, the sweeter and more nutritious it becomes. Red capsicums supply eight times the beta-carotene of green – and half again as much vitamin C.

• Gram for gram, a red capsicum contains three times as much vitamin C as an orange.

Red Capsicum Soup

Carrots

Carrots are one of the best sources of beta-carotene. They also contain flavonoids, which are phytochemicals that function as health-giving antioxidants.

Healthy Highlights

2 medium, raw (120g)		Nutrients % RDI	
Kilojoules	129	Vitamin A	277%
Fibre	3.5g	Vitamin C	24%
Protein	1g	Potassium	16%
Carbohydrate	6.5g	Folate	12%
Saturated Fat	0g		
Total Fat	0.1g		
Cholesterol	0mg		
Sodium	52mg		

Shopping & Preparation

At the market Carrots are always in good supply. They're sold 'topped' (minus leaves), and in bunches with the leaves attached. Baby carrots are also available.

Look for The leaves on bunched carrots should be springy and a fresh green.

Preparation Peel carrots with a vegetable peeler, then slice, dice or chop as needed.

Carrot slices cut on a long diagonal are attractive and they cook very quickly.

Basic cooking Steam cut-up carrots (or cook them in a small amount of orange or apple juice) for 3 to 4 minutes. To microwave 500g cut-up carrots, place in a dish, add 1–2 tablespoons water, cover and cook on high for 4 to 6 minutes.

Carrot Cake

Preparation: 15 minutes / Cooking: 30 minutes / Serves: 8

1 cup plain flour

1 teaspoon bicarbonate of soda

1 teaspoon cinnamon

½ teaspoon ground ginger

¼ teaspoon ground cardamom

Salt

2 tablespoons peanut or other vegetable oil

½ cup white sugar

½ cup firmly packed light brown sugar

1 egg

2 egg whites

4 medium carrots, grated

¼ cup sultanas

2 tablespoons sunflower seeds

1. Preheat the oven to 180°C. Spray a 20 cm round cake tin with cooking spray. Line the bottom of the tin with greaseproof paper and spray it with cooking spray.

2. Sift together the flour, bicarbonate of soda, cinnamon, ginger, cardamom and a pinch of salt on a sheet of greaseproof paper. Beat the oil and both sugars with an electric mixer in a large bowl, until light and fluffy. Beat in the whole egg, then beat in the egg whites. Fold in the carrots, sultanas and sunflower seeds. Fold in the flour mixture until just combined.

3. Spoon the batter into the prepared tin. Bake for 30 minutes or until a skewer inserted in the centre comes out clean. Cool in the tin on a rack for 20 minutes, then invert the cake onto the rack to cool completely.

Nutrients per serving: Kilojoules 1067; Fibre 2g; Protein 5g; Carbohydrate 44g; Saturated Fat 1g; Total Fat 7g; Cholesterol 27mg

Did you know?

Carrots really can be good for your eyes: beta-carotene may help prevent cataracts.

Pork Medallions with Roasted Carrot Purée

Preparation: 15 minutes / Cooking: 30 minutes / Serves: 4

500g carrots, thinly sliced

3 cloves garlic, peeled

5 teaspoons olive oil

½ cup chicken stock

3 teaspoons no-added-salt tomato paste

Salt

Cayenne pepper

500g well-trimmed pork fillet, cut into 8 slices

2 tablespoons chopped fresh basil

1. Preheat the oven to 220°C. Toss together the carrots, garlic and 2 teaspoons of the oil in a metal baking dish. Bake, tossing the carrots occasionally, for 20 minutes.

2. Transfer the carrots to a food processor and purée along with the stock, ½ cup water, the tomato paste and a pinch each of salt and cayenne pepper. Put aside.

3. Heat the remaining oil in a large nonstick frying pan over moderately high heat. Cook the pork for 2 minutes each side or until browned and cooked through. Transfer to a plate.

4. Wipe out the pan, add the carrot purée and bring to the boil. Spoon onto 4 plates, top with the pork, then sprinkle with the basil.

Nutrients per serving: Kilojoules 1184; Fibre 4g; Protein 40g; Carbohydrate 7g; Saturated Fat 3g; Total Fat 10g; Cholesterol 160mg

Creamy Carrot & Mint Soup

Creamy Carrot & Mint Soup

Preparation: 10 minutes / Cooking: 20 minutes/ Serves: 4

500g carrots, thinly sliced

1 tablespoon rice

1 cup chicken stock

1 teaspoon sugar

¼ teaspoon cayenne pepper

Salt

1 cup low-fat milk

⅓ cup chopped fresh mint

1. Combine the carrots, rice, stock, 1 cup water, sugar, cayenne pepper and a pinch of salt in a large saucepan. Simmer, covered, for 17 minutes or until the rice is tender.

2. Purée in a food processor along with the milk, then return the soup to the saucepan to reheat. Stir in the mint just before serving.

Nutrients per serving: Kilojoules 366; Fibre 4g; Protein 5g; Carbohydrate 14g; Saturated Fat 1g; Total Fat 1g; Cholesterol 4mg

Did you know?

• Raw carrots are a nutritious snack but you should eat cooked carrots, too: cooking breaks down the vegetable's tough cell walls, releasing more beta-carotene. Cooking also brings out the natural sweetness of the vegetable.

• If you eat lots of carrots, the palms of your hands (and the soles of your feet) may turn yellow-orange. This is quite harmless – just an accumulation of carotenoids – and the colour will fade with time . . . and it's no reason to cut down on your carrot intake.

Moroccan-Style Carrot Salad

Preparation: 25 minutes / Cooking: 8 minutes / Serves: 4

500g carrots, peeled and cut into thick slices

2 teaspoons vegetable oil

1 teaspoon ground coriander

1 teaspoon ground cumin

¼ teaspoon ground ginger

Salt

2 teaspoons honey

2 tablespoons lemon juice

1 tablespoon orange juice

⅓ cup finely chopped fresh coriander

1. Lightly boil the carrots in a little water in a medium saucepan for 5 minutes or until slightly softened then pulse in a food processor with a little of the cooking liquid until roughly chopped.

2. Heat a medium nonstick frying pan and add the oil, ground coriander, cumin, ginger and a pinch of salt. Cook for 2 to 3 minutes or until aromatic, then remove from the heat. Toss the carrots with the spices in the pan. Add the honey and toss again.

3. Transfer the mixture to a serving bowl and mix with the lemon juice, orange juice and the fresh coriander.

Nutrients per serving: Kilojoules 274; Fibre 3g; Protein 1g; Carbohydrate 10g; Saturated Fat 0g; Total Fat 2g; Cholesterol 0mg

Carrot & Apricot Muffins with Pecans

Preparation: 22 minutes / Cooking: 30 minutes / Makes: 12 muffins

¼ cup pecans

2 cups plain flour

1¾ teaspoons baking powder

¾ teaspoon cinnamon

Salt

½ cup unsweetened puréed cooked apple

¼ cup white sugar

¼ cup firmly packed light brown sugar

2 tablespoons vegetable oil

1 egg

1 egg white

2 cups firmly packed grated carrots

⅓ cup coarsely chopped dried apricots

1. Preheat the oven to 190°C. Spray a 12-hole tray of 6 cm muffin cups with cooking spray or line with paper liners; put aside.

2. Toast the pecans on a small baking tray for 5 minutes or until lightly fragrant. When cool enough to handle, chop coarsely.

3. Combine the flour, baking powder, cinnamon and a pinch of salt in a medium bowl. Combine the apple, both sugars, the oil, whole egg and egg white in a separate bowl. Stir in the pecans, carrots and apricots.

4. Make a well in the centre of the flour. Stir in the carrot mixture until just moistened. Spoon into the prepared muffin cups and bake for 30 minutes or until a skewer inserted in the centre of a muffin comes out just clean.

Nutrients per muffin: Kilojoules 763; Fibre 2g; Protein 4g; Carbohydrate 29g; Saturated Fat 1g; Total Fat 6g; Cholesterol 18mg

Did you know?

• Flavonoids, found in carrots, may inhibit enzymes responsible for the spread of malignant cells. Research indicates that they may also fight heart disease.

• Calcium pectate, a type of soluble fibre found in carrots, has a cholesterol-lowering effect.

Carrot & Apricot Muffins with Pecans

Cauliflower

A good source of folate and vitamin C, cauliflower shares the health benefit of all brassica (cabbage family) vegetables: that of cancer-fighting phytochemicals.

Healthy Highlights

1 serving, cooked (140g)		Nutrients % RDI	
Kilojoules	114	Vitamin C	260%
Fibre	2.5g	Folate	33%
Protein	3.1g	Potassium	22%
Carbohydrate	2.9g	Riboflavin	10%
Saturated Fat	0g	Thiamin	10%
Total Fat	0.3g		
Cholesterol	0mg		
Sodium	19mg		

Shopping & Preparation

At the market Available all year round, cauliflower is at its best in the cooler months of May to November.

Look for The florets should be firm, compact and creamy white, free of brown or soft spots (a yellow tinge indicates that the vegetable is over-mature). The leaves should be bright green and crisp.

Preparation Pull off the leaves and cut off the stem, then cut around the core to free the branched florets. Cut the florets apart, if you wish.

Use a small, sharp knife to cut the cauliflower florets from the stem.

Basic cooking Steam cauliflower florets for 3 to 5 minutes, and a whole head, cored, for 15 to 20 minutes. Microwave 500g florets with ¼ cup water; cover and cook on high for 4 to 7 minutes; let stand for 3 minutes.

Vegetable Antipasto

Preparation: 20 minutes / Cooking: 15 minutes
Marinate: 4 hours / Serves: 4

1 cup vegetable or chicken stock
½ cup dry white wine
½ teaspoon dried oregano
½ teaspoon dried crushed chilli
500g carrots, diagonally sliced
2 cups cauliflower florets (200g)
125g green beans, halved crossways
2 tablespoons white wine vinegar
1 teaspoon olive oil
Salt
½ cup cubed mozzarella cheese
½ cup chopped fresh basil

1. Bring the stock, wine, oregano and chilli to a simmer in a large frying pan. Add the carrots, then cover and cook for 6 minutes. Add the cauliflower and beans, return to a simmer, and cook for 8 minutes.

2. Transfer the vegetables and liquid to a medium bowl, stir in the vinegar, oil and a pinch of salt. Cover and put aside for at least 4 hours. Just before serving, stir in the mozzarella and basil.

Nutrients per serving: Kilojoules 521; Fibre 5g; Protein 8g; Carbohydrate 9g; Saturated Fat 3g; Total Fat 6g; Cholesterol 11mg

Did you know?

• Cauliflower quickly loses its folacin to the cooking water when boiled. When possible, steam, braise or roast it.

• Broccoflower, a new cross between cauliflower and broccoli, has been developed overseas and is more nutritious than cauliflower. It has green florets rather than white, has more vitamin C and also some beta-carotene.

Roasted Cauliflower with Tomatoes & Garlic

Preparation: 10 minutes / Cooking: 45 minutes / Serves: 4

1½ tablespoons olive oil
8 cloves garlic, unpeeled
2 teaspoons fresh rosemary leaves
1 head cauliflower (600g), cut into florets
1½ cups chopped egg tomatoes (about 4)
Salt

1. Preheat the oven to 210°C. Combine the oil, garlic and rosemary in a 33 x 23 cm glass baking dish. Place in the oven and, when the oil is hot but not smoking, add the cauliflower. Roast, turning the cauliflower occasionally, for 20 minutes or until lightly browned.

2. Add the tomatoes and salt to taste, tossing well. Roast for 20 minutes or until the tomatoes are hot and the cauliflower is tender.

Nutrients per serving: Kilojoules 381; Fibre 3g; Protein 3g; Carbohydrate 4g; Saturated Fat 1g; Total Fat 7g; Cholesterol 0mg

Cauliflower Soup with Chive Cream

Cauliflower Soup with Chive Cream

Preparation: 10 minutes / Cooking: 40 minutes / Serves: 4

1 onion, chopped

1 tablespoon butter

1 head cauliflower
(600g), cut into florets

Nutmeg

2 cups low-fat milk

Salt

White pepper

2 tablespoons cream

2 tablespoons chopped
fresh chives

1. Sweat the onion in the butter in a large saucepan for 5 minutes, making sure it does not brown. Add the cauliflower and a pinch of nutmeg and sweat for a further 5 minutes over moderately low heat.

2. Cover with the milk, bring to the boil and simmer for about 20 to 30 minutes until the cauliflower is soft.

3. Purée the soup in a blender, then pass through a fine sieve. Pour into a clean saucepan

and gently reheat. Season to taste with salt and pepper.

4. Mix the cream and chives together. Ladle the soup into individual serving bowls and top with the chive cream.

Nutrients per serving: Kilojoules 682; Fibre 2g; Protein 8g; Carbohydrate 10g; Saturated Fat 7g; Total Fat 10g; Cholesterol 35mg

Chillies

Capsaicin, which makes chillies hot, is an antioxidant; it may protect the DNA from carcinogens. It may also help kill the bacteria that cause most stomach ulcers.

Healthy Highlights

Hot chillies

2 medium (60g)		Nutrients % RDI	
Kilojoules	61	Vitamin C	346%
Fibre	1.6g	Vitamin A	15%
Protein	1.2g	Niacin	12%
Carbohydrate	1.8g		
Saturated Fat	0g		
Total Fat	0.2g		
Cholesterol	0mg		
Sodium	2mg		

Banana chillies

1 medium (60g)		Nutrients % RDI	
Kilojoules	35	Vitamin C	305%
Fibre	0.8g		
Protein	0.5g		
Carbohydrate	1.3g		
Saturated Fat	0g		
Total Fat	0.1g		
Cholesterol	0mg		
Sodium	2mg		

Shopping & Preparation

At the market Fresh red, yellow and green chillies are available all year but are best from February to April. They range from mild (usually the larger ones, such as banana chillies) to extremely hot (the small ones). Canned and pickled chillies are also available, but they have virtually no vitamin C.

Look for Fresh chillies should be glossy, colourful, plump and unwrinkled.

Preparation The capsaicin in chillies is in the seeds and ribs; if you wish to cool the heat, you can remove them. And to avoid burning your skin and eyes, wear rubber gloves when handling chillies, or wash your hands well with soap and water afterwards.

Rubber gloves protect you from the capsaicin as you scrape out the seeds and the ribs.

Spaghetti with Chilli, Lemon & Rocket

Spaghetti with Chilli, Lemon & Rocket

Preparation: 15 minutes / Cooking: 15 minutes / Serves: 4

500g spaghetti or linguine

⅓ cup olive oil

2 cloves garlic, crushed

3 fresh red chillies, seeded and finely sliced, or 1½ teaspoons dried crushed chilli

6 anchovy fillets, chopped

2 teaspoons grated lemon zest

¼ cup lemon juice

3 cups coarsely chopped rocket

⅓ cup fresh mint leaves, shredded

¼ cup grated Parmesan cheese

1. Cook the pasta in a large saucepan of boiling water according to the packet directions, until firm-tender.

2. While the pasta is cooking, heat the oil in a large frying pan over medium heat. Add the garlic and cook for 1 minute. Add the chillies, anchovies, lemon zest and lemon juice and cook for 1 minute.

3. Drain the pasta and combine with the garlic mixture, the rocket and mint in a large bowl. Toss well and top with the Parmesan.

Nutrients per serving: Kilojoules 2366; Fibre 7g; Protein 17g; Carbohydrate 73g; Saturated Fat 4g; Total Fat 22g; Cholesterol 10mg

Did you know?

Chillies can be mild or fiery hot, so before you cook, taste a tiny sliver; add a pinch of dried crushed chilli to the dish if the fresh is too bland.

Thai Sour Prawn Soup

Preparation: 15 minutes / Cooking: 15 minutes / Serves: 4

- 6 cups fish stock or water
- 3 stalks lemon grass, tender white part only, crushed and cut into 2cm slices
- 5 kaffir lime leaves
- 150g small mushrooms, halved
- 2 tablespoons Thai fish sauce
- 4–6 fresh red chillies, seeded and sliced
- 8 large or 16 medium green prawns (about 500g), cleaned and deveined, with tails left attached
- 4 spring onions, sliced
- ½ cup lime juice
- 2 teaspoons Thai red curry paste
- 1 tablespoon brown sugar
- 1 cup coriander leaves

1. Bring the stock to the boil in a large saucepan and add the lemon grass, lime leaves, mushrooms, fish sauce and chillies. Boil for 2 minutes.

2. Add the prawns, spring onions, lime juice, curry paste and sugar to the saucepan and cook for 2 minutes or until the prawns turn pink. Add the coriander just before serving.

Nutrients per serving: Kilojoules 647; Fibre 2g; Protein 22g; Carbohydrate 8g; Saturated Fat 1g; Total Fat 3g; Cholesterol 121mg

Did you know?

- Chillies are a leading source of vitamin C. They're not usually eaten in large quantities – but the more, the healthier.

- Red chillies contain more than ten times the beta-carotene of green chillies.

- Capsaicin acts as an anticoagulant and thus may help prevent heart attacks.

Thai Sour Prawn Soup

Eggplants

Eggplants – closely related to potatoes and tomatoes – belong to the deadly nightshade family, but are safe and delicious to eat. They are a good source of dietary fibre, as well as offering some potassium and vitamin C.

Healthy Highlights

I serving, cooked (145g)		Nutrients % RDI	
Kilojoules	117	Potassium	11%
Fibre	3.6g	Folate	11%
Protein	1.7g	Vitamin C	10%
Carbohydrate	4.2g		
Saturated Fat	0g		
Total Fat	0.4g		
Cholesterol	0mg		
Sodium	7mg		

Shopping & Preparation

At the market Eggplants, also known as aubergines or brinjals, come in a range of shapes and colours. Although most are purple and oval- to pear-shaped, they can also be white, lavender or red-striped – and either long, or small and round. Thai eggplants, commonly called pea eggplants, are small, green, pea-like fruit which cluster at the end of small branches. Generally, eggplants are available year round, but they are at their best from January to July.

Look for Select eggplants with smooth, firm, glossy skin; avoid any with brown or soft spots and a dull skin. The bigger eggplants should feel heavy for their size.

Preparation Keep eggplants in the vegetable crisper or in an unsealed plastic bag in the refrigerator; use within 5 days.

Basic cooking It is no longer considered necessary to salt eggplant before frying it, but if you wish to do so, slice or dice the unpeeled eggplant, sprinkle with cooking salt and leave for at least 30 minutes. Rinse and pat dry with paper towel. To cook eggplant slices, shallow-fry in a little vegetable oil for 5 minutes until golden brown, or brush with a little oil and place under a hot griller for 4 minutes each side.

Eggplant & Bean Casserole

Preparation: 45 minutes / Cooking: 1 hour 20 minutes
Standing: 5 minutes / Serves: 8

1½ cups Roasted Red Capsicums (recipe, page 61)

4 medium eggplants (1.2kg total)

Salt

⅓ cup olive oil

2 large onions, finely sliced

4 cloves garlic, crushed

3 cans Italian plum tomatoes (400g each)

1 bunch fresh sage, chopped

1 teaspoon fresh thyme leaves

2 cups cooked kidney beans

2 cups cooked chickpeas

8 sprigs fresh flat-leaf parsley

1. Prepare the Roasted Red Capsicums as directed, but omit the oil, salt and garlic.

2. Dice 2 of the eggplants and slice the others. Salt lightly, if you wish, and put aside for 30 minutes.

3. Warm half the oil in a large saucepan and add the onion and garlic. Cook slowly for 5 minutes or until golden. Add the diced eggplant to the onions and cook for 20 minutes until softened. Add the tomatoes and their juice, cover and cook for 20 minutes, then stir in the sage and thyme. Add the kidney beans and chickpeas to the tomato mixture and combine. (Add a spoonful or two of vegetable stock or water if the mixture seems a little dry.)

4. Rinse the sliced eggplant and pat dry. Lightly fry the slices in the remaining oil for 5 minutes or until golden.

5. Preheat the oven to 180°C. Place a layer of the bean and tomato mixture in a large shallow casserole dish. Cover with a layer of the eggplant slices and a few strips of capsicum. Add another layer of beans then cover with alternate slices of eggplant and capsicum. Bake for 30 minutes, then stand the casserole for 5 minutes before serving garnished with the flat-leaf parsley.

Nutrients per serving: Kilojoules 1023; Fibre 12g; Protein 11g; Carbohydrate 24g; Saturated Fat 2g; Total Fat 12g; Cholesterol 0mg

Baked Tomato & Eggplant

Preparation: 30 minutes / Cooking: 1 hour 50 minutes / Serves: 4

3 teaspoons olive oil

1 clove garlic, peeled and crushed

1 large eggplant (450g), thinly sliced

500g ripe tomatoes, thinly sliced

2 tablespoons chopped fresh oregano

2 tablespoons chopped fresh basil

1 large onion, thinly sliced

Freshly ground black pepper

1. Combine 1 teaspoon of the oil with the garlic and spread inside a medium-sized baking dish.

2. Preheat the oven to 190°C. Layer half the eggplant and tomato slices in the dish. Sprinkle with half the oregano and basil, then top with half the onion. Season with pepper and sprinkle with 1 teaspoon of the oil. Repeat with the remaining vegetables, herbs and oil.

3. Cover the dish tightly with foil and bake for 1½ hours. Serve hot or at room temperature.

Nutrients per serving: Kilojoules 336; Fibre 5g; Protein 3g; Carbohydrate 8g; Saturated Fat 0g; Total Fat 4g; Cholesterol 0mg

Eggplant & Bean Casserole

Eggplant & Spinach Salad

Preparation: 5 minutes / Cooking: 6 minutes / Serves: 4

1 large eggplant (450g), thinly sliced

⅓ cup olive oil

150g baby spinach leaves

1 cup cooked chickpeas

200g feta cheese, crumbled

1 small Spanish onion, thinly sliced

¼ cup fresh mint leaves, shredded

2 tablespoons lemon juice

1. Brush the eggplant with half the oil. Place in a large nonstick frying pan over medium-high heat and cook for 2 to 3 minutes on each side until golden.

2. Place the spinach on a serving platter and top with the eggplant, chickpeas, feta cheese, onion and mint.

3. Combine the remaining oil with the lemon juice. Pour the dressing over the salad and serve at room temperature.

Nutrients per serving: Kilojoules 1623; Fibre 6g; Protein 14g; Carbohydrate 10g; Saturated Fat 10g; Total Fat 32g; Cholesterol 34mg

Did you know?

Eggplants are really a fruit but are always treated as a vegetable. Like many other plant foods, they are a good source of dietary fibre.

As long as minimum quantities of salt or oil are used in the preliminary cooking, eggplants can be comfortably low in kilojoules.

Fennel

Along with its unique flavour, this favourite Italian vegetable offers fibre, vitamin C and potassium, as well as a respectable amount of calcium and a little iron.

Healthy Highlights

½ medium, raw (110g)		Nutrients % RDI	
Kilojoules	84	Vitamin C	32%
Fibre	3.1g	Folate	28%
Protein	1.1g	Potassium	16%
Carbohydrate	3.6g		
Saturated Fat	0g		
Total Fat	0.1g		
Cholesterol	0mg		
Sodium	41mg		

Shopping & Preparation

At the market   Fennel – also known as Florence fennel to distinguish it from the feathery-leaved herb – has a bulbous fleshy base with a distinct liquorice flavour. It is tastiest from April to August.

Look for   The bulb should be smooth and glossy, not dry or brown. Stalks and fronds, if attached, should be fresh and green. Our recipes call for medium fennel bulbs (about 400g each). If you have any left over, sliver the fennel and add to salads or serve as part of a crudité platter.

Preparation   Trim and discard the stalks; save the fronds for garnishing and flavouring.

Basic cooking   Steam sliced or chopped fennel for 10 to 15 minutes. Cook halved fennel bulbs (or sliced fennel) in a frying pan with just enough boiling liquid to cover; cook for 25 to 40 minutes or until tender.

Don't discard the fronds of fennel – they're rich in flavour and vitamin C, and are a pretty garnish as well as a tasty salad ingredient.

Fennel & Potato Hash with Caramelised Onions

Preparation: 25 minutes / Cooking: 40 minutes / Serves: 4

500g all-purpose potatoes
2 bulbs fennel (800g total)
3 teaspoons olive oil
2 large onions, finely chopped
2 cloves garlic, crushed
Salt
Pepper

1. Cook the potatoes in a large saucepan of boiling water for 30 minutes or until tender. Drain and, when cool enough to handle, peel and thinly slice.

2. Meanwhile, cut off the fennel stalks and fronds. Finely chop ¼ cup of the fronds and reserve; discard the stalks. Cut the bulb in half lengthways and thinly slice crossways. Put aside.

3. Heat the oil in a large nonstick frying pan over moderate heat. Add the onions and garlic, and cook for 12 minutes or until the onions are golden brown.

4. Add the sliced fennel to the pan and cook, stirring, for 10 minutes or until crisp-tender. Add the potatoes, sprinkle with salt and pepper, and cook, stirring frequently, for 10 minutes or until the potatoes and fennel are tender. Stir in the chopped fennel fronds and serve.

Nutrients per serving: Kilojoules 606; Fibre 8g; Protein 5g; Carbohydrate 22g; Saturated Fat 0g; Total Fat 4g; Cholesterol 0mg

Did you know?

Recipes that call for fennel sometimes suggest celery as an alternative, but the nutritional difference is significant. Although they're similar in texture, fennel has considerably more fibre. Fennel also provides more potassium, vitamin C and folate than celery. And, of course, there's that wonderful liquorice-like flavour.

Fresh Fennel Salad with Lemon

Preparation: 10 minutes / Serves: 4

¼ cup lemon juice
1 tablespoon olive oil
Salt
2 bulbs fennel (800g total)
¼ cup shaved Parmesan cheese

1. Whisk together the lemon juice, oil, a pinch of salt and 2 tablespoons water in a medium bowl.

2. Cut off the fennel stalks and fronds. Finely chop ¼ cup of the fronds and add to the bowl of dressing; discard the stalks. Cut the bulb in half lengthways and thinly slice crossways. Add the fennel to the bowl and toss well to combine. Scatter the Parmesan over the salad before serving.

Nutrients per serving: Kilojoules 372; Fibre 3g; Protein 3g; Carbohydrate 4g; Saturated Fat 2g; Total Fat 6g; Cholesterol 5mg

Fennel & Potato Hash with Caramelised Onions

Garlic

Used medicinally since ancient times, garlic is now being studied by scientists. While not high in individual nutrients, it appears that garlic may fight cancer and heart disease, and lower blood pressure.

Healthy Highlights

2 cloves, raw (6g)		Nutrients % RDI
Kilojoules	23	*Standard serve has*
Fibre	1g	*less than 10% of*
Protein	0.4g	*RDI for individual*
Carbohydrate	0.6g	*nutrients*
Saturated Fat	0g	
Total Fat	0.2g	
Cholesterol	0mg	
Sodium	0mg	

Shopping & Preparation

At the market A kitchen staple, garlic is always in good supply.

Look for Choose a full, plump head of garlic with taut, unbroken outer skin. Pass up heads with shrivelled cloves or green shoots sprouting from the top.

Preparation Separate the cloves from the head; avoid piercing the skin on the remaining cloves. To peel, place each clove under the flat side of a broad knife blade; strike the blade with your fist. This will crack and loosen the skin, making it easy to remove.

Basic cooking Blanching whole, unpeeled garlic cloves for just a few minutes tempers the pungent flavour a bit and makes the garlic easier to peel. Roasting a whole head of garlic, wrapped in foil, renders it sweet and spreadable. Roast at 220°C for about 45 minutes.

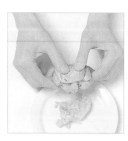

After roasting, garlic pulp can be squeezed out of the skin – no peeling is required.

Chicken Breasts with Roasted Garlic Sauce

Preparation: 10 minutes

Cooking: 1 hour / Serves: 4

2 heads garlic (150g total)

2 teaspoons olive oil

4 skinless, boneless chicken breast halves (125g each)

½ cup chicken stock

2 tablespoons fresh rosemary leaves

1 teaspoon grated lemon zest

Salt

White pepper

3 teaspoons lemon juice

2 tablespoons chopped fresh parsley

1. Preheat the oven to 220°C. Wrap each head of garlic in foil. Bake for 45 minutes or until very soft when squeezed. When cool enough to handle, cut off the stem end from each head, squeeze the garlic pulp into a small bowl and mash with a fork.

2. Heat the oil in a large nonstick frying pan over moderate heat. Add the chicken breasts and cook for 8 minutes or until lightly browned on both sides.

3. Add the mashed garlic, the stock, ½ cup water, the rosemary, lemon zest and a pinch each of salt and pepper, and bring to the boil. Reduce to a simmer, then cover and cook, stirring occasionally, for 4 minutes or until the sauce coats the chicken and the chicken is cooked through. Stir the lemon juice and parsley into the sauce. Serve the chicken topped with the sauce.

Nutrients per serving: Kilojoules 1000; Fibre 6g; Protein 30g; Carbohydrate 4g; Saturated Fat 3g; Total Fat 11g; Cholesterol 89mg

Did you know?

• A study in China's Shandong province showed that the more garlic people ate, the less likely they were to develop stomach cancer.

• Garlic has been shown to lower high blood pressure and blood cholesterol, and to inhibit blood clotting.

White Bean Garlic Dip

White Bean Garlic Dip ⓐ

Preparation: 10 minutes / Cooking: 5 minutes / Makes: 2 cups

10 cloves garlic

2 cans (375g each) cannellini beans, rinsed and drained

⅓ cup olive oil

2 tablespoons lemon juice

1 teaspoon ground coriander

Salt

2 tablespoons chopped fresh mint

2 tablespoons chopped fresh parsley

1 teaspoon paprika (optional)

1. Cook the garlic in a small saucepan of boiling water for 3 minutes to blanch. Drain, reserving 2 tablespoons of the cooking liquid. Peel the garlic cloves.

2. Combine the garlic, reserved cooking liquid and beans in a food processor and process to a smooth purée. Add the oil, lemon juice, coriander and a pinch of salt, and process briefly to blend. Fold in the mint and parsley.

3. Transfer the mixture to a small serving bowl. Serve sprinkled with the paprika, if liked.

Nutrients per ¼ cup: Kilojoules 677; Fibre 6g; Protein 7g; Carbohydrate 12g; Saturated Fat 1g; Total Fat 10g; Cholesterol 0mg

Did you know?

Garlic contains sulphur compounds that may speed the breakdown of carcinogens, which are cancer-causing substances.

Ginger

Revered in Asia for being both a stimulant and a calmative, ginger shows promise as a remedy for seasickness, morning sickness, and other stomach ills.

Healthy Highlights

10g, raw		Nutrients % RDI
Kilojoules	11	*Standard serve has*
Fibre	0.3g	*less than 10% of*
Protein	0.1g	*RDI for individual*
Carbohydrate	0.5g	*nutrients*
Saturated Fat	0g	
Total Fat	0g	
Cholesterol	0mg	
Sodium	1mg	

Shopping & Preparation

At the market You'll find fresh ginger all year round in the fresh produce section of most supermarkets, and at greengrocers and Asian markets.

Look for Ginger should be smooth and very firm, with glossy, pinkish-tan skin. Fresh ginger should not look dry or shrivelled.

Preparation Cut off a knob of ginger as required; pare with a vegetable peeler then grate, chop, sliver or crush as needed. To make ginger juice, see below.

To make ginger juice, first grate the desired amount of ginger (a 5cm piece will yield about 2 teaspoons juice). To extract the juice, squeeze the grated ginger with your fingers, press in a tea strainer, or wring tightly in a square of muslin.

Homemade Ginger Ale

Homemade Ginger Ale

Preparation: 5 minutes / Cooking: 30 minutes / Serves: 8

¾ cup thinly sliced unpeeled fresh ginger

1 cup sugar

3 strips (5 x 1cm) lemon zest

⅛ teaspoon whole black peppercorns

⅛ teaspoon allspice berries (optional)

Soda water

8 mint sprigs

1. Bring 2 cups of water and the ginger to the boil in a medium saucepan over moderate heat. Reduce the heat to low, cover and simmer for 25 minutes. Reserving the liquid, strain and discard the ginger.

2. Combine the ginger liquid, sugar, lemon zest, peppercorns and allspice, if using, in the same saucepan over low heat. Bring to the boil and cook for 2 minutes. Cover the syrup and let stand until cooled to room temperature. Strain the ginger syrup and refrigerate.

3. To serve, pour ¼ cup of the syrup into a tall glass. Add ¾ cup cold soda water; top with ice and garnish with mint.

Nutrients per serving: Kilojoules 437; Fibre 0g; Protein 0g; Carbohydrate 27g; Saturated Fat 0g; Total Fat 0g; Cholesterol 0mg

Did you know?

One teaspoon ground ginger contains 0.5mg of manganese – a trace mineral that is involved in energy production and helps build strong bones.

Gingerbread Cupcakes with Ginger Glaze

Preparation: 15 minutes / Cooking: 20 minutes / Makes: 12 cupcakes

1⅓ cups plain flour

3 teaspoons ground ginger

1 teaspoon mustard powder

1 teaspoon bicarbonate of soda

½ teaspoon cinnamon

Salt

Ground cloves

½ cup firmly packed dark brown sugar

¼ cup treacle

2 tablespoons vegetable oil

2 egg whites

½ cup buttermilk

1 piece (5cm) fresh ginger

½ cup icing sugar

2 tablespoons chopped crystallised ginger

1. Preheat the oven to 180°C. Line a 12-hole tray of 6 cm muffin cups with paper liners; put aside. Combine the flour, ginger, mustard, bicarbonate of soda, cinnamon and a pinch each of salt and cloves on a sheet of greaseproof paper.

2. Beat the brown sugar, treacle and oil with an electric mixer until well combined. Beat in the egg whites, one at a time, until incorporated and light in texture. Alternately fold the flour mixture and the buttermilk into the sugar mixture, beginning and ending with the flour mixture. Spoon into the prepared muffin cups and bake for 20 minutes or until a skewer inserted in the centre of a cupcake comes out clean. Cool in the tray on a wire rack.

3. Grate the fresh ginger finely. Squeeze the ginger to extract the juice and measure out 2 teaspoons. Combine the icing sugar and ginger juice in a small bowl. Spread the tops of the cooled cupcakes with the ginger glaze. Sprinkle with the crystallised ginger.

Nutrients per cupcake: Kilojoules 765; Fibre 1g; Protein 3g; Carbohydrate 36g; Saturated Fat 1g; Total Fat 3g; Cholesterol 1mg

Did you know?

For centuries, various forms of ginger have been used to quell nausea. Several studies have investigated this effect and, in Germany, ginger is approved as a medical treatment for motion sickness and also for heartburn.

Gingerbread Cupcakes with Ginger Glaze

Greens

Dark, leafy greens have such a lot to offer: disease-fighting carotenoids, indoles and isothiocyanates, as well as quantities of vitamin C, calcium and iron.

Healthy Highlights

Spinach

1 serving, cooked (90g)

Nutrient	Amount	Nutrients	% RDI
Kilojoules	70	Vitamin C	48%
Fibre	5.7g	Vitamin A	44%
Protein	2.7g	Folate	41%
Carbohydrate	0.7g	Potassium	24%
Saturated Fat	0g	Iron	23%
Total Fat	0.4g	Magnesium	22%
Cholesterol	0mg		
Sodium	18mg		

Silverbeet

1 serving, cooked (115g)

Nutrient	Amount	Nutrients	% RDI
Kilojoules	71	Folate	62%
Fibre	3.8g	Vitamin C	50%
Protein	2.2g	Iron	21%
Carbohydrate	1.5g	Potassium	14%
Saturated Fat	0g	Vitamin A	11%
Total Fat	0.4g	Calcium	10%
Cholesterol	0mg	Magnesium	10%
Sodium	213mg		

Kale

1 serving, cooked (100g)

Nutrient	Amount	Nutrients	% RDI
Kilojoules	80	Vitamin C	283%
Fibre	3.6g	Vitamin A	69%
Protein	3.1g	Folate	42%
Carbohydrate	1.1g	Iron	25%
Saturated Fat	0g	Calcium	19%
Total Fat	0.3g	Potassium	17%
Cholesterol	0mg	Magnesium	10%
Sodium	17mg		

Broccolini

1 serving, cooked (120g)

Nutrient	Amount	Nutrients	% RDI
Kilojoules	220	Vitamin C	195%
Fibre	1.5g	Folate	50%
Protein	4.5g	Potassium	21%
Carbohydrate	3g	Riboflavin	18%
Saturated Fat	0g	Magnesium	10%
Total Fat	0g	Vitamin A	10%
Cholesterol	0mg		
Sodium	37mg		

Silverbeet with Bacon & Chilli

Preparation: 15 minutes / Cooking: 20 minutes / Serves: 4

- 1 bunch silverbeet (500g), tough stems removed
- 2 rashers bacon, cut crossways into 5mm strips
- 1 large red onion, finely chopped
- 4 cloves garlic, crushed
- ½ teaspoon dried crushed chilli

1. Bring a large saucepan of water to the boil. Add the silverbeet in batches and cook for 30 seconds to wilt. Drain the silverbeet, reserving ¼ cup of the cooking liquid,

2. Cook the bacon in the reserved cooking liquid in a large nonstick frying pan over moderate heat for 4 minutes or until the bacon has rendered its fat. Remove the bacon with a slotted spoon. Add the onion and garlic to the pan and cook for 7 minutes or until the onion is soft. Stir in the chilli.

3. Add the silverbeet and bacon. Heat through.

Nutrients per serving: Kilojoules 358; Fibre 5g; Protein 8g; Carbohydrate 4g; Saturated Fat 1g; Total Fat 4g; Cholesterol 14mg

Did you know?

The Popeye myth of spinach being high in iron stems from a mathematical misprint. In the 1950s a food analyst put the decimal point in the wrong place ... thus implying that spinach had ten times the iron it really does.

Wilted Spinach Salad with Croutons

Preparation: 15 minutes / Cooking: 15 minutes / Serves: 4

- 125g Italian bread, cut into 1cm slices
- 1 clove garlic, peeled and halved
- 1½ tablespoons olive oil
- 1 large red onion, cut into 1cm chunks
- 250g mushrooms, thinly sliced
- 1kg spinach (2–3 bunches), torn into bite-sized pieces
- ⅔ cup chicken stock
- 1 tablespoon balsamic vinegar
- Salt

1. Preheat the oven to 180°C. Place the bread on a baking tray and bake for 5 minutes or until golden brown and crisp. Rub the toast lightly with the cut garlic (discard the garlic). Cut the toast into cubes.

2. Meanwhile, heat 2 teaspoons of the oil in a large nonstick frying pan over moderate heat. Add the onion and cook for 4 minutes or until crisp-tender. Add the mushrooms and cook, stirring occasionally, for 4 minutes or until the mushrooms are softened. Transfer to a large bowl. Add the spinach and toasted bread cubes, tossing to combine.

3. Add the remaining oil to the pan along with the stock, vinegar and a pinch of salt. Bring to a rolling boil and cook for 1 minute. Pour the hot dressing over the spinach mixture and toss. Serve immediately.

Nutrients per serving: Kilojoules 865; Fibre 9g; Protein 11g; Carbohydrate 19g; Saturated Fat 1g; Total Fat 8g; Cholesterol 0mg

Mixed Greens Frittata

Mixed Greens Frittata

Preparation: 15 minutes / Cooking: 20 minutes / Serves: 4

1 tablespoon olive oil

1 onion, chopped

2 cloves garlic, crushed

500g mixed greens, such as kale, silverbeet and spinach, torn into bite-sized pieces

2 eggs

4 egg whites

¼ cup low-fat ricotta cheese

¼ cup grated Parmesan cheese

3 teaspoons plain flour

Salt

1. Heat 2 teaspoons of the oil in a large grillproof nonstick frying pan over moderate heat. Add the onion and garlic and cook for 2 minutes. Add the greens and cook, stirring often, for 7 minutes or until very tender. Transfer the greens to a plate and wipe out the frying pan.

2. Combine the whole eggs, egg whites, ricotta cheese, Parmesan, flour and a pinch of salt in a food processor. Add the remaining oil to the frying pan and heat over moderate heat. Add the greens and the egg mixture, then cook without stirring for 10 minutes or until the edges of the frittata are set and the centre is slightly wobbly.

3. Preheat the griller. Grill the frittata 15 cm from the heat for 1 minute or just until the centre is set. Serve immediately.

Nutrients per serving: Kilojoules 748; Fibre 5g; Protein 14g; Carbohydrate 5g; Saturated Fat 4g; Total Fat 12g; Cholesterol 137mg

Did you know?

Some types of greens (such as spinach and silverbeet) contain compounds that interfere with the body's absorption of minerals. For the greatest benefits, eat a variety of greens.

Shopping & Preparation

At the market Kale has a fairly short season, being freshest around July. Silverbeet is in best supply from March to October, while the season for fresh spinach (which is sold in bunches or, when very young, as loose leaves) extends from March to November, peaking in midwinter. Broccolini (also known as flowering broccoli) is available all year, but is also best during winter.

Look for All greens should have fresh, vivid colour. The stalks should be plump and moist; the leaves should be crisp and free of holes or spots. Avoid any that are wilted or yellow. Small leaves are usually more tender than large ones.

Preparation Wash greens well as they can be gritty. Trim silverbeet stems with a knife (the stems are edible, too, but require longer cooking than the leaves).

Basic cooking Steam washed leaves in their own moisture: tender young leaves for about 2 minutes, sturdier greens for up to 15 minutes. Microwave washed greens, covered, for 2 to 7 minutes. (Cooking times depend on the type of greens; 250g spinach, for example, takes 2 to 3 minutes on high.)

Be sure to squeeze the excess liquid out of frozen spinach after thawing it.

Pasta with Broccolini & Sun-Dried Tomatoes

Preparation: 15 minutes

Cooking: 25 minutes / Serves: 4

½ cup sun-dried tomatoes (not oil-packed)

1 large bunch broccolini (650g), cut into 3cm lengths

3 teaspoons olive oil

4 cloves garlic, crushed

1–1½ teaspoons dried crushed chilli

2 tablespoons no-added-salt tomato paste

Salt

Black pepper

⅓ cup sultanas (optional)

250g fusilli pasta

⅓ cup grated Parmesan cheese

1. Add the sun-dried tomatoes to a large saucepan of boiling water; cook for 5 minutes or until softened. Remove with a slotted spoon and when cool enough to handle, chop coarsely.

2. Add the broccolini to the boiling water and cook for 4 minutes or until crisp-tender. Transfer with a slotted spoon to a colander.

3. Meanwhile, heat the oil in a large frying pan over low heat. Add the garlic and chilli and cook for 3 minutes. Add the tomatoes, broccolini, tomato paste, a pinch each of salt and pepper, the sultanas, if using, and the reserved cooking liquid. Cook, stirring, for 4 minutes or until heated through and tender.

4. Cook the pasta in a large saucepan of boiling water according to the packet directions, until firm-tender. Drain, then turn into a large serving bowl. Stir in the sauce and serve with the Parmesan cheese.

Nutrients per serving: Kilojoules 1465; Fibre 8g; Protein 17g; Carbohydrate 46g; Saturated Fat 2g; Total Fat 7g; Cholesterol 7mg

Did you know?

• Spinach is loaded with beta-carotene, folate, vitamin C and lutein, the phytochemical that helps keep your eyes healthy.

• Other greens that are nutrition powerhouses include beetroot and turnip leaves, which are considerably more nutritious than their roots when it comes to vitamin C, beta-carotene, calcium, iron and folate.

Pasta with Broccolini & Sun-Dried Tomatoes

Mushrooms

Very low in kilojoules, yet packed with meaty flavour, mushrooms also contain substances that may enhance the immune system and slow tumour growth. Cooking mushrooms breaks down their fibrous cell walls, making some of their nutrients more available to the body.

Healthy Highlights

6 medium, raw (70g)		Nutrients % RDI	
Kilojoules	71	Riboflavin	20%
Fibre	1.8g	Niacin	19%
Protein	2.6g	Folate	18%
Carbohydrate	1.1g	Potassium	11%
Saturated Fat	0g	Phosphorus	10%
Total Fat	0.2g		
Cholesterol	0mg		
Sodium	5mg		

Shopping & Preparation

At the market Cultivated mushrooms are available all year round. If you can't find shiitake or other 'exotic' mushrooms at the supermarket, try a specialist greengrocer.

Look for Fresh mushrooms should look clean, plump and moist; pass up those that are dry or darkening. The gills (under the caps) should be tightly closed.

Preparation Trim the stem bases of flat and button mushrooms; trim the entire stem from shiitakes. Wipe fresh mushrooms with a damp paper towel, if necessary. Soak dried mushrooms in boiling water to soften, then drain. If using the soaking liquid in the dish, strain through a coffee filter or paper towel to remove any grit.

Shiitake stems are too tough to eat. Trim them close to the base of the cap.

Cooking tip Simmer mushrooms in a little stock to give them extra flavour with no added fat. Cook for 3 to 5 minutes.

Penne with Creamy Mushroom Sauce

Preparation: 25 minutes / Cooking: 25 minutes / Serves: 4

2 teaspoons vegetable oil

5 spring onions, thinly sliced

4 cloves garlic, crushed

250g fresh shiitake mushrooms, trimmed, halved and thinly sliced

500g button mushrooms, halved and thinly sliced

Salt

1½ tablespoons plain flour

2 cups low-fat milk

White pepper

375g penne

1 teaspoon unsalted butter

¼ cup grated Parmesan cheese

1. Heat the oil in a large nonstick frying pan over moderate heat. Add the spring onions and garlic and sauté for 2 minutes. Add the shiitakes, cover and cook, stirring occasionally, for 5 minutes or until tender.

2. Add the button mushrooms and sprinkle with salt to taste. Cover and cook, stirring occasionally, for 5 minutes. Increase the heat to high, uncover and cook for 4 minutes or until the liquid has evaporated. Sprinkle with the flour, stirring until absorbed. Gradually add the milk and cook, stirring, for 5 minutes or until slightly thickened. Stir in pepper to taste.

3. Cook the pasta in a large saucepan of boiling water according to the packet directions, until firm-tender. Drain well and transfer to a large serving bowl.

4. Add the sauce, butter and Parmesan to the hot pasta, tossing well to coat, then top with another grinding of pepper.

Nutrients per serving: Kilojoules 2007; Fibre 10g; Protein 24g; Carbohydrate 74g; Saturated Fat 3g; Total Fat 8g; Cholesterol 17mg

Fresh & Dried Mushroom Soup

Preparation: 20 minutes / Cooking: 30 minutes / Serves: 4

½ cup (20g) porcini or other dried mushrooms

1 cup boiling water

2 teaspoons vegetable oil

1 large onion, finely chopped

4 cloves garlic, crushed

250g fresh shiitake mushrooms, trimmed, halved and thinly sliced

500g button mushrooms, thinly sliced

¼ cup dry sherry

1½ cups chicken stock

1 large tomato, finely chopped

½ teaspoon dried tarragon

½ teaspoon pepper

1. Combine the dried mushrooms and boiling water in a small bowl and stand for 10 minutes or until softened. Reserving the liquid, scoop out the dried mushrooms and chop coarsely. Strain the soaking liquid through a coffee filter or a paper towel-lined sieve.

2. Heat the oil in a large saucepan over moderate heat. Add the onion and garlic and cook for 5 minutes or until the onion has softened. Stir in the dried mushrooms. Add the shiitakes and cook for 5 minutes. Add the button mushrooms and cook, stirring frequently, for 5 minutes.

3. Add the reserved soaking liquid and bring to the boil. Add the sherry and cook for 5 minutes or until reduced by half. Add the stock, tomato, tarragon, pepper and 1½ cups water. Bring to the boil, reduce to a simmer, cover and cook for 10 minutes or until the soup is richly flavoured.

Nutrients per serving: Kilojoules 651; Fibre 8g; Protein 10g; Carbohydrate 15g; Saturated Fat 1g; Total Fat 3g; Cholesterol 0mg

Penne with Creamy Mushroom Sauce

Onions & Leeks

Onion-family vegetables offer cancer-fighting compounds and antioxidant flavonoids; they also seem to help lower blood pressure and levels of cholesterol.

Healthy Highlights

Onions
1 large, cooked
(170g)

		Nutrients % RDI	
Kilojoules	232	Vitamin C	28%
Fibre	2.9g	Folate	11%
Protein	3g	Potassium	11%
Carbohydrate	10.4g		
Saturated Fat	0g		
Total Fat	0.2g		
Cholesterol	0mg		
Sodium	20mg		

Spring onions
2 medium, raw
(30g)

		Nutrients % RDI	
Kilojoules	34	Vitamin C	32%
Fibre	0.7g	Folate	10%
Protein	0.5g		
Carbohydrate	1.4g		
Saturated Fat	0g		
Total Fat	0.1g		
Cholesterol	0mg		
Sodium	4mg		

Leeks
2 medium, cooked
(170g)

		Nutrients % RDI	
Kilojoules	185	Vitamin C	134%
Fibre	4.9g	Folate	40%
Protein	3.2g	Potassium	20%
Carbohydrate	6.4g	Vitamin A	16%
Saturated Fat	0g	Iron	10%
Total Fat	0.7g		
Cholesterol	0mg		
Sodium	27mg		

Penne with Golden Onion Sauce

Penne with Golden Onion Sauce

Preparation: 25 minutes

Cooking: 30 minutes / Serves: 4

2 teaspoons vegetable oil

750g brown onions, finely sliced

3 cloves garlic, crushed

I teaspoon sugar

Salt

375g penne

2 tablespoons Marsala or water

¾ cup chicken stock

2 teaspoons unsalted butter

¼ cup chopped parsley

1. Heat the oil in a large nonstick frying pan over moderate heat. Add the onions and garlic and sprinkle with the sugar and a pinch of salt. Cover and cook, stirring frequently, for 20 minutes or until the onion is very soft.

2. Meanwhile, cook the pasta in a large saucepan of boiling water according to the packet directions, until firm-tender. Drain the pasta, reserving ¾ cup of the cooking liquid, and transfer to a large serving bowl.

3. Stir the Marsala into the onions and cook for 1 minute or until evaporated. Add the stock and the reserved cooking liquid, and cook, stirring frequently, for 5 minutes or until the liquid is reduced by half.

4. Add the onions, butter and parsley to the hot pasta, tossing well to combine.

Nutrients per serving: Kilojoules 1558; Fibre 7g; Protein 12g; Carbohydrate 65g; Saturated Fat 2g; Total Fat 5g; Cholesterol 6mg

Did you know?

A study of Dutch men and their intake of flavonoids (antioxidants found in fresh produce, tea and wine) showed that those who consumed the most flavonoids had the lowest heart-disease risk. Onions, apples and tea were the main flavonoid sources in the subjects' diets.

Braised Leeks with Tomato & Olives

Braised Leeks with Tomato & Olives

Preparation: 20 minutes / Cooking: 20 minutes / Serves: 4

4 medium leeks (750g total), roots and dark green ends trimmed

3 teaspoons olive oil

3 cloves garlic, minced

2 large tomatoes, diced

½ cup Kalamata olives

2 tablespoons chopped fresh parsley

2 tablespoons chopped fresh basil

1. Make 4 lengthways cuts in each leek with a sharp paring knife, starting 3 cm above the root end. Soak the leeks in several changes of warm water until thoroughly clean. Pat dry.

2. Heat the oil in a large nonstick frying pan over moderate heat. Add the leeks, turning until well coated. Add the garlic and cook for 1 minute or until tender.

3. Add the tomatoes, ½ cup water, the olives, parsley and basil, and bring to the boil. Reduce to a simmer, cover and cook for 10 minutes or until the leeks are fork-tender. Serve warm or at room temperature.

Nutrients per serving: Kilojoules 361; Fibre 4g; Protein 3g; Carbohydrate 9g; Saturated Fat 1g; Total Fat 4g; Cholesterol 0mg

Red Onion & Capsicum Relish

Preparation: 10 minutes / Cooking: 32 minutes / Makes: 2 cups

2 teaspoons olive oil
3 cups diced red onions
1 red capsicum, diced
2 cloves garlic, crushed
¼ cup red wine vinegar
3 teaspoons no-added-salt tomato paste
2 teaspoons honey

1. Heat the oil in a large nonstick frying pan over low heat. Cook the onions, capsicum and garlic gently for 30 minutes until tender.

2. Add the vinegar, tomato paste and honey. Simmer for 2 minutes, then remove from the heat. Serve at room temperature.

Nutrients per ¼ cup: Kilojoules 162; Fibre 1g; Protein 1g; Carbohydrate 5g; Saturated Fat 0g; Total Fat 1g; Cholesterol 0mg

Onion & Orzo Pilaf

Preparation: 15 minutes / Cooking: 35 minutes / Serves: 6

2 teaspoons vegetable oil
750g onions, finely chopped
6 spring onions, thinly sliced
2 cloves garlic, crushed
¾ cup orzo (rice-shaped pasta)
1 cup chicken stock
⅓ cup grated Parmesan cheese

1. Heat the oil in a medium-sized nonstick saucepan over moderate heat. Add the onions, spring onions and garlic. Cover and cook for 7 minutes or until the onions are soft. Uncover and cook, stirring occasionally, for 5 minutes.

2. Stir in the orzo. Add the stock and 1 cup water. Bring to the boil, cover and simmer for 20 minutes. Stir in the Parmesan.

Nutrients per serve: Kilojoules 595; Fibre 3g; Protein 7g; Carbohydrate 20g; Saturated Fat 1g; Total Fat 3g; Cholesterol 4mg

Double-Onion Pizza

Preparation: 25 minutes / Cooking: 30 minutes / Serves: 4

1 tablespoon olive oil
2 red onions (250g total), halved and cut into 5mm slices
2 brown onions (250g total), halved and cut into 5mm slices
2 cloves garlic, minced
½ teaspoon sugar
White pepper
1 purchased pizza base (30cm)
¼ cup tomato pasta sauce
⅓ cup sliced bocconcini cheese
10 fresh sage leaves

1. Heat 2 teaspoons of the oil in a large nonstick frying pan over moderate heat. Add the onions and garlic, and sprinkle with the sugar. Cover and cook, stirring occasionally, for 7 minutes or until the onions are soft. Uncover and cook, stirring frequently, for 5 minutes or until golden brown. Stir in pepper to taste.

2. Preheat the oven to 240°C. Spray a baking tray with cooking spray. Place the pizza base on the prepared tray.

3. Stir together the pasta sauce and the remaining oil in a small bowl. Brush the mixture over the base, spread the onion mixture on top, then add the bocconcini and the sage leaves. Bake for 10 minutes or until the dough is crisp and the onions are piping hot.

Nutrients per serving: Kilojoules 1951; Fibre 7g; Protein 15g; Carbohydrate 76g; Saturated Fat 2g; Total Fat 11g; Cholesterol 5mg

Creamy Onion Soup

Preparation: 5 minutes / Cooking: 15 minutes / Serves: 4

2 teaspoons olive oil

3 cups diced onions

6 spring onions, sliced

3 cloves garlic, crushed

1 teaspoon sugar

2 teaspoons fresh
   thyme leaves

Salt

¾ cup chicken stock

1 cup low-fat milk

1. Heat the oil in a large nonstick saucepan over low heat. Add the onions, spring onions, garlic, sugar, thyme and a pinch of salt, and cook gently for 10 minutes or until tender.

2. Add the stock and ¾ cup water and simmer, covered, for 5 minutes. Purée with the milk, then heat through to serve.

Nutrients per serving: Kilojoules 423; Fibre 2g; Protein 5g; Carbohydrate 11g; Saturated Fat 1g; Total Fat 3g; Cholesterol 4mg

Did you know?

Saponins, as well as sulphur compounds called allyl sulphides, are cancer-fighting substances found in onions, leeks and spring onions. Saponins also have a heart-protective effect.

Double-Onion Pizza

Parsnips & Turnips

Parsnips and turnips are high in fibre and also provide folate, while turnips contain cancer-fighting indoles. Both supply vitamin C.

Healthy Highlights

Parsnips
1 large, cooked (130g)

		Nutrients % RDI	
Kilojoules	270	Vitamin C	35%
Fibre	3.2g	Potassium	25%
Protein	2.3g	Folate	24%
Carbohydrate	13g	Niacin	13%
Saturated Fat	0g	Magnesium	11%
Total Fat	0.3g		
Cholesterol	0mg		
Sodium	23mg		

Turnips
1 large, cooked (150g)

		Nutrients % RDI	
Kilojoules	133	Vitamin C	80%
Fibre	4.6g	Potassium	22%
Protein	2.1g	Folate	10%
Carbohydrate	5.7g	Niacin	10%
Saturated Fat	0g		
Total Fat	0g		
Cholesterol	0mg		
Sodium	35mg		

Shopping & Preparation

At the market Parsnips, turnips and swedes (a yellow-fleshed turnip) are available all year, peaking April to September.

Look for Select parsnips that are medium in size, well-shaped with a creamy white, smooth, firm surface (large parsnips tend to be woody). When choosing turnips and swedes, look for those that are firm, feel heavy for their size, and have a sweet smell.

Preparation Peel parsnips and trim the top and bottom. Cook whole or cut up. Remove the skin from turnips and swedes with a sturdy paring knife.

Basic cooking Steam sliced parsnips for 5 to 15 minutes, cut-up turnips for 15 minutes. To microwave 500g cut-up parsnips or turnips, place in a dish with ¼ cup water. Cover and cook on high for 9 to 11 minutes.

Mashed Turnip with Carrots & Potatoes

Preparation: 15 minutes / Cooking: 20 minutes / Serves: 4

875g turnip or swede, peeled, quartered and thinly sliced

250g potatoes, peeled and thinly sliced

250g carrots, thinly sliced

5 cloves garlic, peeled

1 bay leaf

1 teaspoon fresh thyme leaves

Salt

Pepper

2 teaspoons olive oil

¼ cup grated Parmesan cheese

1. Combine the turnips, potatoes, carrots, garlic, bay leaf, thyme, a pinch each of salt and pepper, and 4 cups of water in a large saucepan. Bring to the boil over moderate heat, reduce to a simmer, cover and cook for 15 minutes or until tender. Drain the vegetables and garlic, reserving ½ cup of the cooking liquid. Remove and discard the bay leaf.

2. Mash the vegetables and garlic cloves with a potato masher, adding the reserved cooking liquid and the oil. Stir in the Parmesan just before serving.

Nutrients per serving: Kilojoules 564; Fibre 9g; Protein 7g; Carbohydrate 17g; Saturated Fat 1g; Total Fat 4g; Cholesterol 5mg

Parsnip Patties

Parsnip Patties

Preparation: 20 minutes / Cooking: 15 minutes / Serves: 4

500g parsnips, peeled and grated

1 large carrot, grated

6 spring onions, thinly sliced

3 eggs

½ cup plain flour

1 teaspoon baking powder

Salt

3 teaspoons vegetable oil

1. Preheat the oven to 120°C. Steam the parsnips and carrot in a steamer or colander set over a saucepan of boiling water for 5 minutes or until softened but not mushy. Put aside to cool slightly.

2. Transfer the cooked vegetables to a medium bowl and add the spring onions, eggs, flour, baking powder and a pinch of salt, stirring until well combined.

3. Heat 1½ teaspoons of the oil in a large nonstick frying pan over moderate heat. Using a ¼-cup measure, pour 6 pancakes into the pan, using half the batter. Cook for 2 minutes each side or until golden brown. Transfer the first batch of pancakes to a large baking tray.

4. Repeat with the remaining oil and batter. Bake all the pancakes for 7 minutes or until they are heated through and lightly crisped.

Nutrients per serving: Kilojoules 921; Fibre 4g; Protein 9g; Carbohydrate 25g; Saturated Fat 2g; Total Fat 8g; Cholesterol 161mg

Did you know?

• Try young, tender parsnips raw in salad or slaw. You'll get every bit of their vitamin C.

• Some of a parsnip's starch turns to sugar when the vegetable is chilled (making it tastier), so some growers place parsnips in cold storage for a few weeks. This does not diminish the nutritional value.

Peas

Peas

Fresh peas are a good, low-fat protein source. They are all rich in vitamin C, while green peas also contain folate and thiamin. Pea pods offer measurable potassium.

Healthy Highlights

Green peas
1 serving, cooked
(130g)

		Nutrients % RDI	
Kilojoules	287	Vitamin C	61%
Fibre	8.5g	Thiamin	31%
Protein	6.2g	Niacin	18%
Carbohydrate	9.7g	Folate	12%
Saturated Fat	0g	Iron	12%
Total Fat	0.5g	Vitamin A	12%
Cholesterol	0mg	Phosphorus	11%
Sodium	1mg	Magnesium	10%

Edible-pod peas
1 serving, cooked
(100g)

		Nutrients % RDI	
Kilojoules	183	Vitamin C	117%
Fibre	2.3g	Potassium	20%
Protein	3g	Magnesium	13%
Carbohydrate	4.6g		
Saturated Fat	0g		
Total Fat	0.2g		
Cholesterol	0mg		
Sodium	1mg		

Shopping & Preparation

At the market Green peas are abundant from early spring through July, while sugar snaps have a short season in late spring/early summer. Snow peas are sold all year.

Look for For both green peas and edible-pod peas, choose plump pods that are medium-sized, with satiny skins and a good green colour.

Preparation Crack open green pea pods and push out peas with your thumb. Pinch the tips off snow peas and pull off the strings from snow peas and sugar snap peas.

Basic cooking Cook green peas in a little liquid for 5 to 10 minutes; cook snow peas and sugar snaps for just 1 to 2 minutes. Or, steam snow peas or sugar snaps for 3 to 5 minutes. Microwave 1 cup shelled green peas with 1 tablespoon water. Cook on high for 5 minutes.

Penne with Sugar Snaps & Smoked Salmon

Penne with Sugar Snaps & Smoked Salmon

Preparation: 20 minutes / Cooking: 15 minutes / Serves: 4

- 375g penne or ziti
- 500g sugar snap peas or snow peas, strings removed
- 1 tablespoon chopped fresh dill
- 3 spring onions, thinly sliced
- ¼ cup olive oil
- 1 teaspoon grated lemon zest
- 2 tablespoons lemon juice
- 125g smoked salmon, slivered
- Freshly ground black pepper

1. Cook the pasta in a large saucepan of boiling water according to the packet directions, until firm-tender. Add the peas to the water during the final 1 minute of cooking; drain.

2. Meanwhile, combine the dill, spring onions, oil, lemon zest and lemon juice in a large bowl. Add the hot pasta and the peas, tossing well. Add the smoked salmon and a good grinding of pepper, then toss again.

Nutrients per serving: Kilojoules 2013; Fibre 7g; Protein 20g; Carbohydrate 59g; Saturated Fat 2g; Total Fat 17g; Cholesterol 15mg

Did you know?

- Peas contain lutein, a carotenoid that fights macular degeneration, which is the leading cause of blindness in older people.

- Nutritionally, frozen green peas are very close to fresh, although if salt is added during the processing it does raise the sodium content.

Risi e Bisi

Preparation: 10 minutes / Cooking: 40 minutes / Serves: 4

2 rashers bacon (30g), finely chopped

1 small onion, finely chopped

1 cup rice

1¾ cups chicken stock

½ teaspoon pepper

Salt

3 cups frozen peas

¼ cup chopped parsley

¼ cup grated Parmesan cheese

2 teaspoons unsalted butter

1. Combine the bacon and ¼ cup water in a large nonstick saucepan over moderate heat. Cook, stirring occasionally, for 5 minutes or until the bacon has rendered its fat. Add the onion and cook for 7 minutes or until golden brown and tender.

2. Add the rice, stirring to coat. Add the stock, 1½ cups water, the pepper and a pinch of salt, and bring to the boil. Reduce to a simmer, cover and cook for 15 minutes. Stir in the peas and parsley, cover and cook, stirring occasionally, for 10 minutes or until the rice is tender and the peas are heated through. Stir in the Parmesan and butter.

Nutrients per serving: Kilojoules 1369; Fibre 8g; Protein 15g; Carbohydrate 52g; Saturated Fat 3g; Total Fat 6g; Cholesterol 15mg

Did you know?

• Cooked edible-pod peas contain twice as much vitamin C as green peas. If they are eaten raw or just barely cooked, their vitamin C levels are even higher.

• Sugar snap peas have a thin, edible pod enclosing good-sized peas; both pod and peas are super-sweet. Because their peas are more fully developed, sugar snaps are somewhat higher in protein than snow peas (the figures given on page 92 are an average).

Risi e Bisi

Stir-Fried Lamb & Peas

Preparation: 15 minutes

Cooking: 10 minutes / Serves: 4

2 teaspoons vegetable oil

3 spring onions, thinly sliced

2 cloves garlic, minced

3 teaspoons minced fresh ginger

1 red capsicum, cut into thin strips

500g well-trimmed leg of lamb, cut into
    5 x 1cm strips

500g sugar snap peas or snow peas,
    strings removed

½ cup chicken stock

¼ cup chilli sauce

3 teaspoons reduced-salt soy sauce

2 spring onions, green part only, cut into
    thin strips

1. Heat the oil in a large nonstick frying pan over moderate heat. Add the spring onions, garlic and ginger, and stir-fry for 3 minutes or until the garlic is tender.

2. Add the capsicum and stir-fry for 2 minutes or until crisp-tender. Add the lamb and sugar snaps and stir-fry for 4 minutes or until the lamb is just cooked through.

3. Combine the stock, chilli sauce and soy sauce in a small bowl. Pour into the pan and cook for 1 minute to heat through. Serve garnished with the spring onion strips.

Nutrients per serving: Kilojoules 1239; Fibre 4g; Protein 30g; Carbohydrate 11g; Saturated Fat 6g; Total Fat 13g; Cholesterol 88mg

Snow Peas with Mint

Preparation: 15 minutes

Cooking: 3–5 minutes / Serves: 4

750g snow peas, strings removed

3 teaspoons olive oil

½ cup chopped fresh mint

1. Steam the snow peas in a steamer or colander set over a saucepan of boiling water for 3 to 5 minutes until crisp-tender.

2. Transfer to a large bowl, add the oil and mint. Toss to combine.

Nutrients per serving: Kilojoules 459; Fibre 4g; Protein 5g; Carbohydrate 8g; Saturated Fat 0g; Total Fat 4g; Cholesterol 0mg

Stir-Fried Lamb & Peas

Potatoes

Potatoes combine energy-giving complex carbohydrates with plenty of vitamin C, fibre and potassium. They're filling and, if sensibly prepared, low in fat.

Healthy Highlights

1 large, boiled* (185g)		Nutrients % RDI	
Kilojoules	484	Vitamin C	129%
Fibre	3.5g	Potassium	41%
Protein	4.6g	Folate	17%
Carbohydrate	23.5g	Niacin	17%
Saturated Fat	0g	Thiamin	15%
Total Fat	0.2g	Magnesium	13%
Cholesterol	0mg		
Sodium	13mg	*peeled	

Shopping & Preparation

At the market Potatoes are in good supply all year round; even new potatoes (those that are freshly dug and have not been stored) are available most of the year.

Look for Well-shaped potatoes, free of sprouts and blemishes, are best. Avoid those with green skin, cracks or wrinkles.

Preparation Scrub potatoes under cold running water; use a vegetable brush if it is necessary.

Basic cooking When boiling potatoes, start them in boiling water to preserve vitamin C. Whole small potatoes take 10 to 15 minutes, larger potatoes 20 to 40 minutes, depending on size. Boil cut-up potatoes for 15 to 20 minutes. Before baking or microwaving, pierce whole potatoes in several places. Oven-bake for 45 to 60 minutes at 180°C. Microwave 4 potatoes on high for 13 to 15 minutes.

A potato masher will leave some texture in mashed potatoes. A food processor can turn them gluey.

Cajun Oven Fries

Preparation: 10 minutes / Cooking: 30–45 minutes / Serves: 4

1½ tablespoons vegetable oil

2 teaspoons chilli powder

½ teaspoon dried thyme

½ teaspoon black pepper

¼ teaspoon cayenne pepper

1kg baking potatoes, thinly sliced lengthways

1. Preheat the oven to 210°C. Combine the oil, chilli powder, thyme, black pepper and cayenne pepper in a large bowl.

2. Add the potatoes, tossing to coat. Place on 2 baking trays and bake for 30 to 45 minutes or until browned and crisp.

Nutrients per serving: Kilojoules 979; Fibre 6g; Protein 5g; Carbohydrate 34g; Saturated Fat 1g; Total Fat 7g; Cholesterol 0mg

Did you know?

Starchy potatoes are best for baking, waxy ones are good for boiling and salads.

Cajun Oven Fries

Potato Torte

Potato Torte

Preparation: 10 minutes / Cooking: 50 minutes / Serves: 4

5 teaspoons olive oil

1kg baking potatoes, peeled and very thinly sliced

¾ teaspoon pepper

Salt

¼ cup grated Parmesan cheese

2 spring onions, thinly sliced

2 teaspoons rosemary leaves

1. Preheat the oven to 220°C. Brush the sides and bottom of a 23 cm pie plate with 1 teaspoon of the oil. Cover the bottom of the plate with an overlapping layer of potatoes, using a quarter of the total. Sprinkle with 1 teaspoon of the oil, ¼ teaspoon of the pepper and a pinch of salt, 3 teaspoons of the Parmesan, one third of the spring onions and one third of the rosemary.

2. Repeat for 2 more layers. Top with a final layer of potatoes and the remaining oil and Parmesan. Place an empty pie plate or round baking dish on top of the potatoes and bake in the lower third of the oven for 50 minutes or until the potatoes are crusty on the bottom (lift gently with a spatula to check) and the torte is tender throughout.

3. Cool in the pan for 5 minutes before loosening the bottom and sides with a small spatula and inverting onto a platter.

Nutrients per serving: Kilojoules 950; Fibre 3g; Protein 8g; Carbohydrate 30g; Saturated Fat 2g; Total Fat 8g; Cholesterol 5mg

Did you know?

• Potatoes are the number-one source of vitamin C, simply because they are the most consumed vegetable.

• Plain potatoes are virtually fat-free, but 50g commercial potato chips contain about 12 grams of fat.

Onion & Potato Cakes

Did you know?

• Potatoes and onions should not be stored together. A gas given off by the onions will speed up the spoilage of potatoes (and vice versa).

• 'Baking' potatoes in a microwave is a healthy way to cook them, and a great timesaver, too. But don't forget to pierce them, or the potatoes may explode.

• It's a good idea to eat the skin on whole baked potatoes, as some of the nutrients are concentrated in or just under the skin. You'll also get more dietary fibre by eating the skin.

Onion & Potato Cakes

Preparation: 15 minutes / Cooking: 40 minutes / Serves: 4

750g baking potatoes, peeled and thinly sliced

5 teaspoons vegetable oil

2 onions, finely chopped

2 tablespoons reduced-fat sour cream

Salt

White pepper

Nutmeg

2 tablespoons plain flour

1 cup low-fat yoghurt or reduced-fat sour cream

1 tablespoon snipped chives

1. Cook the potatoes in a saucepan of boiling water for 15 minutes or until tender. Drain and transfer to a large bowl.

2. Meanwhile, heat 1 teaspoon of the oil in a large nonstick frying pan over moderate heat. Add the onions and fry for 7 minutes or until golden brown and tender.

3. Add the sour cream, and a pinch each of salt, pepper and nutmeg, to the potatoes; mash well. Stir in the fried onions and shape into 8 cakes.

4. Heat 2 teaspoons of the oil in a 30 cm frying pan over moderate heat. Dredge the cakes in the flour, shaking off the excess. Fry 4 of the cakes for 3 minutes on each side or until golden brown and crusty. Repeat with the remaining oil and potato cakes. Serve with the yoghurt topped with chives.

Nutrients per serving: Kilojoules 1031; Fibre 4g; Protein 9g; Carbohydrate 30g; Saturated Fat 3g; Total Fat 9g; Cholesterol 13mg

Roasted New Potatoes

Preparation: 5 minutes / Cooking: 55 minutes / Serves: 4

1½ tablespoons
   vegetable oil

4 cloves garlic, unpeeled

1 tablespoon fresh
   rosemary leaves

1kg small red potatoes,
   quartered

Rock salt

1. Preheat the oven to 210°C. Pour the oil into a 23 x 33 cm baking dish. Add the garlic and rosemary. Heat for 5 minutes in the oven.

2. Add the potatoes; cook, tossing occasionally, for 50 minutes or until done. Sprinkle with the salt to taste.

Nutrients per serving: Kilojoules 974; Fibre 6g; Protein 5g; Carbohydrate 34g; Saturated Fat 1g; Total Fat 8g; Cholesterol 0mg

Garlic & Cheddar Mashed Potatoes @

Preparation: 10 minutes / Cooking: 10 minutes / Serves: 6

1kg baking potatoes, peeled and thinly sliced

6 cloves garlic, peeled

⅓ cup buttermilk

¾ cup shredded Cheddar cheese

½ teaspoon paprika

Salt

1. Cook the potatoes and garlic in a saucepan of boiling water for 10 minutes or until tender.

2. Drain and mash with the buttermilk, cheese, paprika and salt to taste. Serve immediately.

Nutrients per serving: Kilojoules 654; Fibre 3g; Protein 8g; Carbohydrate 18g; Saturated Fat 3g; Total Fat 5g; Cholesterol 16mg

Did you know?

A baked potato supplies more than twice as much potassium as a banana.

Garlic & Cheddar Mashed Potatoes

Mixed Potato Chowder

Preparation: 20 minutes

Cooking: 40 minutes / Serves: 4

2 teaspoons vegetable oil

1 onion, finely chopped

3 cloves garlic, crushed

500g baking potatoes, peeled and thinly sliced

375g red potatoes, cut into 1cm chunks

250g sweet potatoes, peeled and cut into 1cm chunks

1 cup chicken stock

1 teaspoon fresh thyme leaves

Salt

1 cup low-fat milk

⅔ cup frozen corn kernels

½ cup chopped parsley

1. Heat the oil in a medium saucepan over moderate heat. Add the onion and garlic and cook for 7 minutes or until the onion is soft.

2. Add the baking potatoes, red potatoes and sweet potatoes, stirring to coat. Add the stock, 2 cups water, the thyme and a pinch of salt, and bring to the boil. Reduce to a simmer, cover and cook for 25 minutes or until the red potatoes and sweet potatoes are tender, and the baking potatoes are soft and creamy.

3. Stir in the milk and corn and simmer for 4 minutes or until the corn is heated through. Stir in the parsley just before serving.

Nutrients per serving: Kilojoules 1088; Fibre 7g; Protein 11g; Carbohydrate 45g; Saturated Fat 1g; Total Fat 4g; Cholesterol 4mg

Did you know?

• Greenish skin – or sprouts – on a potato signal elevated levels of solanine, a bitter-tasting compound that is a natural component of this vegetable. It's best to discard any potatoes that have a greenish tinge or more than one or two sprouts. It would take a lot of solanine to make you ill, but it's best to avoid it.

• To flavour potatoes without adding fat, toss a few garlic cloves, onion slices or fresh herbs into the cooking water.

Mixed Potato Chowder

Pumpkins

Pumpkins

Sweet and meaty, these sturdy members of the squash family boast high levels of beta-carotene. The content is higher if the pumpkin has been stored for several months.

Healthy Highlights

1 serving, cooked (160g)		Nutrients % RDI	
Kilojoules	285	Vitamin A	97%
Fibre	2.3g	Vitamin C	59%
Protein	3.7g	Potassium	26%
Carbohydrate	11.5g	Folate	16%
Saturated Fat	0.5g	Niacin	12%
Total Fat	0.7g		
Cholesterol	0mg		
Sodium	2mg		

Shopping & Preparation

At the market You can buy grey-skinned pumpkin all year, with many varieties available: Queensland Blue is big and heavily ribbed, with a smooth grey skin; others include Jarrahdale and Ironbark. Jap is a squat, ribbed pumpkin with grey-green mottled skin. Butternut is elongated and bell-shaped with smooth, creamy brown skin, and is best from December to January, in April, and from July to August. Smaller pumpkin varieties, such as Golden Nugget and Sweet Dumpling, are compact and round, with sweet yellow flesh.

Look for The skin of a pumpkin should be dry and clean, with a dull looking finish and clear, uniform colour.

Preparation If you're not cooking a pumpkin whole, use a heavy chef's knife to split it (notch the rind first to give the blade a secure hold).

Basic cooking Cut small pumpkins into halves or quarters and bake in a foil-lined baking dish at 200°C for 40 to 45 minutes. Steam peeled pumpkin chunks for 15 to 20 minutes. Microwave chunks, covered, for 7 to 10 minutes on high.

Pumpkin & Bean Soup

Pumpkin & Bean Soup

Preparation: 30 minutes / Cooking: 35 minutes / Serves: 6

⅓ cup olive oil

I small bulb fennel, diced (5mm)

I small brown onion, diced

2 cloves garlic, finely chopped

I stalk celery, diced

5 cups chicken or vegetable stock

300g pumpkin, peeled and cubed

300g silverbeet leaves, coarsely chopped

I ½ cups cooked cannellini beans

3 tablespoons chopped celery leaves

I tablespoon fresh thyme leaves

Salt

Freshly ground pepper

1. Heat the oil in a large saucepan over moderate heat. Add the fennel, onion, garlic and celery and sweat for 3 to 4 minutes, stirring. Add the stock and bring to the boil. Lower the heat and simmer for 15 minutes.

2. Add the pumpkin and simmer for 5 minutes. Then add the silverbeet and the beans and simmer for a further 5 minutes. Add the celery leaves and the thyme and cook for 5 minutes. Season to taste with salt and pepper and serve with a drizzle of olive oil, if liked.

Nutrients per serving: Kilojoules 855; Fibre 7g; Protein 8g; Carbohydrate 12g; Saturated Fat 2g; Total Fat 14g; Cholesterol 0mg

Did you know?

• Pumpkin seeds are high in iron, magnesium, zinc, phosphorus and potassium, all important health-improving minerals.

• The large pumpkins that win prizes at country shows do not make good eating: the flesh is stringy and dry.

Pumpkin & Date Muffins with Almonds

Preparation: 20 minutes / Cooking: 35 minutes / Makes: 12 muffins

I ½ cups plain flour

⅓ cup firmly packed light brown sugar

2 teaspoons baking powder

½ teaspoon bicarbonate of soda

Salt

½ cup chopped dates

¼ cup chopped almonds

I cup cooked puréed pumpkin

2 eggs, lightly beaten

½ cup buttermilk

½ cup reduced-fat sour cream

1. Preheat the oven to 180°C. Line a 12-hole tray of 6 cm muffin cups with paper liners. Stir together the flour, sugar, baking powder, bicarbonate of soda and a pinch of salt in a large bowl. Stir in the dates and almonds.

2. Combine the pumpkin, eggs, buttermilk and sour cream in a medium bowl. Make a well in the centre of the dry ingredients and pour in the pumpkin mixture. Stir just until combined. Spoon into the prepared muffin cups and bake for 30 to 35 minutes or until a skewer inserted in the centre comes out clean.

Nutrients per muffin: Kilojoules 758; Fibre 2g; Protein 5g; Carbohydrate 26g; Saturated Fat 3g; Total Fat 6g; Cholesterol 47mg

Salad Leaves

Since we eat most salad leaves fresh and raw, they're a reliable source of vitamin C. Leafy greens also supply beta-carotene, folate and some minerals.

Healthy Highlights

Cos lettuce

1 serving, raw (80g)		Nutrients % RDI	
Kilojoules	52	Vitamin C	35%
Fibre	1.7g	Folate	24%
Protein	1.1g	Vitamin A	11%
Carbohydrate	1.4g		
Saturated Fat	0g		
Total Fat	0.2g		
Cholesterol	0mg		
Sodium	14mg		

Mignonette lettuce

1 serving, raw (60g)		Nutrients % RDI	
Kilojoules	32	Vitamin C	24%
Fibre	1.3g	Folate	17%
Protein	0.8g		
Carbohydrate	0.7g		
Saturated Fat	0g		
Total Fat	0.2g		
Cholesterol	0mg		
Sodium	10mg		

Watercress

1 serving, raw (40g)		Nutrients % RDI	
Kilojoules	32	Vitamin C	133%
Fibre	1.5g	Vitamin A	18%
Protein	1.2g	Potassium	12%
Carbohydrate	0.3g	Iron	10%
Saturated Fat	0g		
Total Fat	0.2g		
Cholesterol	0mg		
Sodium	19mg		

Rocket

1 serving, raw (60g)		Nutrients % RDI	
Kilojoules	63	Vitamin C	30%
Fibre	0.9g	Folate	29%
Protein	1.6g	Vitamin A	19%
Carbohydrate	1.3g	Calcium	12%
Saturated Fat	0g	Potassium	11%
Total Fat	0.4g	Magnesium	10%
Cholesterol	0mg		
Sodium	17mg		

Greek-Style Cos Salad with Lemon & Fresh Dill

Preparation: 10 minutes / Serves: 4

¼ cup lemon juice

3 teaspoons olive oil

Salt

1 medium cos lettuce, leaves torn

1 teaspoon snipped fresh dill

4 spring onions, thinly sliced

125g feta cheese, crumbled

1. Combine the lemon juice, oil and a pinch of salt in a large bowl, whisking to blend.

2. Add the lettuce, dill and spring onions, tossing well. Add the feta and toss again.

Nutrients per serving: Kilojoules 603; Fibre 3g; Protein 8g; Carbohydrate 3g; Saturated Fat 5g; Total Fat 11g; Cholesterol 22mg

Mixed Leaf Salad with Avocado

Preparation: 5 minutes / Serves: 4

1½ tablespoons lemon juice

2 teaspoons extra virgin olive oil

1 teaspoon Dijon mustard

Salt

350g mixed salad leaves

2 spring onions, thinly sliced

1 small avocado, peeled, seeded and diced

1. Combine the lemon juice, oil, mustard and a pinch of salt in a large bowl, whisking to blend.

2. Add the salad leaves and spring onions, tossing well. Add the avocado and toss gently to combine.

Nutrients per serving: Kilojoules 603; Fibre 3g; Protein 3g; Carbohydrate 2g; Saturated Fat 3g; Total Fat 14g; Cholesterol 0mg

Rocket, Roast Pumpkin & Parmesan Salad

Preparation: 15 minutes / Cooking: 30 minutes / Serves: 4

300g butternut pumpkin, peeled and cut into 5mm slices

5 tablespoons olive oil

1 tablespoon balsamic vinegar

Salt

Freshly ground pepper

250g rocket

½ cup shaved Parmesan cheese

1. Preheat the oven to 180°C. Toss the pumpkin and 1 tablespoon of the oil together in a shallow metal baking dish and roast for 30 minutes or until golden brown. Put aside to cool.

2. Combine the vinegar with the remaining oil and season to taste with salt and pepper.

3. Combine the rocket and the pumpkin then pour over the vinaigrette and toss well. Top the salad with the Parmesan just before serving.

Nutrients per serving: Kilojoules 1149; Fibre 2g; Protein 6g; Carbohydrate 3g; Saturated Fat 5g; Total Fat 27g; Cholesterol 10mg

Rocket, Roast Pumpkin & Parmesan Salad

Shopping & Preparation

At the market Most salad greens are sold all year round. For a wider selection than your supermarket offers, shop at a specialist greengrocer or growers' market. There you're likely to find cos, mignonette and radicchio, as well as the more traditional lettuces such as butterhead and iceberg. Look also for bunches of watercress, rocket and curly endive, as well as a loose-leaf selection often sold as mixed salad leaves.

Look for It's easy to tell when salad greens are fresh: they're crisp, unbrowned, and moist but not wet.

Preparation Don't wash or tear salad greens until shortly before you use them; this helps conserve their vitamin C. Rinse greens lightly but thoroughly in cool water, then shake or spin dry. Blot any excess moisture with a kitchen towel. Tear greens rather than cutting them – contact with a steel knife causes the leaves to brown. The tough lower stems of watercress should be trimmed off. Some recipes call for just the leaves, but this can easily include the more tender upper branches.

Remove the toughest, lower portions of watercress stems and use the rest of the sprigs.

Asian Chicken Salad

Preparation: 10 minutes / Cooking: 7 minutes / Serves: 4

- 1 tablespoon vegetable oil
- 1 tablespoon minced ginger
- 1 stalk lemon grass, chopped
- 2 red chillies, chopped
- 2 cloves garlic, chopped
- 500g minced chicken breast
- ¼ cup fresh lime juice
- 1 tablespoon fish sauce
- 1 teaspoon brown sugar
- 1 red onion, thinly sliced
- 2 tablespoons fresh mint, shredded
- 1 cup coriander leaves
- 1 small cos or ½ small iceberg lettuce, leaves separated and washed

1. Heat the oil in a large nonstick frying pan over medium heat. Add the ginger, lemon grass, chillies and garlic and cook for 1 minute, stirring. Add the chicken and cook, stirring, for 5 minutes or until the chicken is cooked.

2. Remove the chicken mixture from the heat and allow to cool slightly. Combine the lime juice, fish sauce and brown sugar and pour over the chicken.

3. Add the onion, mint, and all but 2 or 3 of the coriander leaves, and toss gently. Serve the salad in bowls, garnished with the remaining coriander, with the lettuce leaves on the side. If you like, you can eat the salad rolled up in the lettuce leaves.

Nutrients per serving: Kilojoules 934; Fibre 3g; Protein 25g; Carbohydrate 5g; Saturated Fat 2g; Total Fat 11g; Cholesterol 71mg

Asian Chicken Salad

Tossed Salad with Pears & Blue Cheese

Tossed Salad with Pears & Blue Cheese

Preparation: 20 minutes / Serves: 6

2 pears, halved, cored and sliced lengthways

¾ cup buttermilk

3 teaspoons white wine vinegar

Salt

Freshly ground pepper

2 tablespoons fresh chives, cut into 3cm pieces

4 cups torn butterhead lettuce

4 cups torn radicchio or other red lettuce

2 cups watercress leaves

1½ cups thinly sliced cucumber, halved

2 tablespoons blue cheese, crumbled

1. Toss the pears with 2 tablespoons of the buttermilk in a small bowl to prevent browning. Whisk together the remaining buttermilk, the vinegar, and a pinch each of salt and pepper in another small bowl. Stir in the chives.

2. Toss together the lettuces, watercress and cucumber in a large bowl. Arrange the greens on plates and top with the blue cheese and the sliced pears. Drizzle the salad with a little of the buttermilk dressing, if you like, and serve the remainder separately.

Nutrients per serving: Kilojoules 460; Fibre 3g; Protein 4g; Carbohydrate 11g; Saturated Fat 2g; Total Fat 6g; Cholesterol 10mg

Did you know?

• A colourful salad mixture called mesclun is sold in many supermarkets. An authentic mesclun consists of young, tender leaves of a variety of lettuces and herbs. Torn leaves of more mature greens are sometimes sold as mesclun, but they'll be less nutritious: tearing causes the leaves to lose water-soluble nutrients, including vitamin C.

• As a rule, the darker the greens the more nutritious the salad. Cos, watercress and rocket, for instance, have more beta-carotene and vitamin C than iceberg or butterhead lettuce. For the same reason, it's a good idea to use – rather than toss out – the outer, darker leaves from a head of lettuce.

Sweet Potatoes

An outstanding source of beta-carotene, orange-fleshed sweet potatoes also have some vitamin C and B vitamins. All sweet potatoes offer dietary fibre.

Healthy Highlights

1 serving*, cooked (150g)		Nutrients % RDI	
Kilojoules	412	Vitamin A	193%
Fibre	3.5g	Vitamin C	116%
Protein	2.9g	Potassium	17%
Carbohydrate	21.3g	Niacin	15%
Saturated Fat	0g		
Total Fat	0.2g	*orange-fleshed	
Cholesterol	0mg		
Sodium	15mg		

Shopping & Preparation

At the market Sweet potatoes are best from March to August, but they can usually be bought all year. There are several types – cream, orange and purple-fleshed. The orange-fleshed varieties are also known as kumara.

Look for Choose firm, well-shaped tubers with smooth skins and a uniform colour: avoid those with nicks, soft spots or bruises.

Preparation Scrub the sweet potatoes gently, being careful not to nick the skin.

Basic cooking To bake, pierce with a fork in several places, then bake for 45 to 60 minutes. Boil whole, unpeeled sweet potatoes for 20 to 40 minutes, cut-up pieces for 10 to 20 minutes. To microwave, pierce 4 whole sweet potatoes and cook on high for 15 to 20 minutes. Remove from the oven, wrap or cover, let stand for 3 minutes.

Candied Sweet Potatoes

Preparation: 15 minutes / Cooking: 25 minutes Serves: 4

1kg sweet potatoes, peeled and thinly sliced

1 tablespoon unsalted butter

¼ cup firmly packed dark brown sugar

¼ cup lime juice

½ teaspoon ground ginger

Salt

1. Steam the sweet potatoes in a steamer or colander set over a saucepan of boiling water for 12 minutes or until tender.

2. Melt the butter in a large frying pan over moderate heat. Add the sugar and lime juice and bring to the boil. Add the cooked sweet potatoes, ginger and a pinch of salt, and cook for a further 10 minutes or until the sweet potatoes are nicely glazed.

Nutrients per serving: Kilojoules 1002; Fibre 5g; Protein 4g; Carbohydrate 46g; Saturated Fat 3g; Total Fat 4g; Cholesterol 12mg

Did you know?

• Their scrumptious flavour and lush texture are misleading: gram for gram, sweet potatoes have about the same number of kilojoules as white potatoes.

• Studies have shown that high doses of beta-carotene supplements may be harmful to smokers, but there's no evidence that a diet rich in sweet potatoes, carrots and other natural beta-carotene sources can be anything other than beneficial.

• In fact, a group of American researchers experimented on themselves by eating a high-carotenoid lunch every day for three weeks. They choose sweet potatoes as their source – and eating just 170g per day raised their plasma levels of beta-carotene by more than 100 per cent.

Oven-Roasted Sweet Potatoes & Garlic

Preparation: 10 minutes / Cooking: 45 minutes / Serves: 4

1½ tablespoons olive oil

8 cloves garlic, unpeeled

2 teaspoons rosemary leaves

1kg sweet potatoes, peeled and sliced

Salt

1. Preheat the oven to 210°C. Combine the oil, garlic and rosemary in a large baking dish. Heat in the oven for 5 minutes.

2. Add the sweet potatoes and bake, turning occasionally, for 40 minutes or until tender. Sprinkle with salt to taste.

Nutrients per serving: Kilojoules 1057; Fibre 6g; Protein 6g; Carbohydrate 41g; Saturated Fat 1g; Total Fat 7g; Cholesterol 0mg

Spiced Sweet Potato Soup

Spiced Sweet Potato Soup

Preparation: 10 minutes / Cooking: 20 minutes / Serves: 4

750g sweet potatoes,
  peeled and sliced

1¾ cups chicken stock

1 teaspoon ground
  coriander

¼ teaspoon dried
  crushed chilli

½ teaspoon sugar

Salt

2 tablespoons lime juice

1 tablespoon chives

1. Combine the sweet potatoes, chicken stock, 1 cup water, coriander, chilli, sugar and a pinch of salt in a large saucepan. Simmer, covered, for 20 minutes until the potatoes are tender.

2. Purée the mixture in a food processor, then stir in the lime juice. Reheat before serving, garnished with the chives.

Nutrients per serving: Kilojoules 530; Fibre 4g; Protein 4g; Carbohydrate 25g; Saturated Fat 0g; Total Fat 1g; Cholesterol 0mg

Did you know?

• Sweet potatoes can be substituted for ordinary potatoes in many recipes. And using the orange-fleshed ones is an excellent way to increase your beta-carotene intake.

• One serving of mashed orange-fleshed sweet potato supplies almost twice the RDI of Vitamin A for an adult.

Tomatoes

Low in kilojoules and very high on flavour, tomatoes are a wonderful food. Along with vitamin C, they offer a tremendous amount of lycopene, a cancer-fighting carotenoid.

Healthy Highlights

1 large, raw (180g)		Nutrients % RDI	
Kilojoules	102	Vitamin C	109%
Fibre	2.2g	Potassium	19%
Protein	1.8g	Vitamin A	14%
Carbohydrate	3.5g	Folate	12%
Saturated Fat	0g		
Total Fat	0.2g		
Cholesterol	0mg		
Sodium	11mg		

Shopping & Preparation

At the market Tomatoes come into season in different parts of the country all year round, but must be ripe when picked or they will not develop their full flavour. Common tomatoes are roundish, flat-topped, with pink to red flesh. Egg tomatoes are normally red and are a firmer-skinned tomato with a sweet, juicy flesh. Cocktail tomatoes are red or yellow, and are sold as cherry or teardrop tomatoes, depending on their shape.

Look for Choose tomatoes that are heavy for their size and unblemished. Ripen at room temperature until they are brightly coloured and slightly soft. They can be refrigerated once ripe but should be at room temperature before using.

Preparation Many recipes call for tomatoes to be peeled. To do this, cut a cross in the bottom of each tomato, cut out the core, then drop the tomato into boiling water for 30 seconds. Transfer to a bowl of cold water, then strip off the skin with a small paring knife. To seed a peeled tomato, simply cut in half and squeeze firmly.

Sun-dried tomatoes that are dry-packed need to be soaked in boiling water to soften them before chopping and using.

Chicken Cacciatore

Preparation: 15 minutes
Cooking: 30 minutes / Serves: 4

3 teaspoons olive oil
4 skinless, bone-in chicken breast halves (250g each)
1 red onion, finely chopped
4 cloves garlic, crushed
1 red capsicum, cut into 1cm squares
250g small mushrooms, quartered
500g tomatoes, finely chopped
¼ cup chicken stock
1 tablespoon fresh rosemary leaves
Salt
Freshly ground black pepper

1. Heat the oil in a large nonstick frying pan over moderate heat. Add the chicken and cook for 3 minutes each side or until golden brown. Transfer the chicken to a plate.

2. Reduce the heat to moderately low, add the onion and garlic, and cook for 7 minutes or until the onion is tender. Add the capsicum and cook for 4 minutes or until crisp-tender. Add the mushrooms and cook, stirring, for 3 minutes or until softened.

3. Add the tomatoes, stock, rosemary, and salt and pepper to taste, and bring to the boil. Return the chicken to the pan, reduce the heat to a simmer, cover and cook, turning the chicken over midway, for 20 minutes or until the chicken is cooked through.

Nutrients per serving: Kilojoules 1804; Fibre 5g; Protein 57g; Carbohydrate 7g; Saturated Fat 5g; Total Fat 19g; Cholesterol 165mg

Did you know?

• A university study indicates that lycopene may fight heart disease as well as cancer. The study results suggest that lycopene offers a greater protective effect than beta-carotene. Based on their findings, the researchers recommend that people eat more cooked tomatoes.

• It takes about 8kg fresh tomatoes to yield 500g sun-dried. In the process, nutrients are greatly concentrated. So 100g sun-dried tomatoes supply 100mg calcium – about 13 times as much as the same weight of fresh tomatoes.

Fresh Tomato Salsa

Preparation: 10 minutes / Standing: 30 minutes / Makes: 3 cups

500g ripe tomatoes

4 spring onions, sliced finely

½ cup chopped fresh coriander

¼ cup chopped fresh mint

1 small red chilli, finely chopped

½ teaspoon ground coriander

½ teaspoon ground cumin

¼ cup lime juice

1. Cut the tomatoes in half and remove the seeds. Dice the flesh and place in a medium bowl along with the spring onions, fresh coriander, mint, chilli, ground coriander, cumin and lime juice.

2. Stir to combine, then stand for 30 minutes to allow the flavours to develop.

Nutrients per ½ cup: Kilojoules 64; Fibre 1g; Protein 1g; Carbohydrate 2g; Saturated Fat 0g; Total Fat 0g; Cholesterol 0mg

Did you know?

Tomatoes in all their forms — fresh, canned, dried and as juice or pasta sauce — are loaded with lycopene. A study done in 1995 revealed that men who ate lots of tomato products had a greatly reduced risk of prostate cancer; the researchers theorised that the lycopene in the tomatoes might be the protective factor.

Fresh Tomato Salsa

Tomato Bruschetta

Preparation: 20 minutes / Cooking: 10 minutes

Standing: 10 minutes / Serves: 4

24 slices (1cm thick) Italian bread (375g total)

1½ tablespoons olive oil

3 cloves garlic, finely chopped

750g egg tomatoes, coarsely chopped

⅓ cup chopped fresh basil

Salt

Freshly ground pepper

1. Preheat the oven to 200°C. Brush the bread slices with half the oil and bake for 10 minutes or until golden brown and crisp.

2. Combine the garlic, tomatoes, basil, the remaining oil, and salt and pepper to taste, in a medium bowl. Put aside for 10 minutes to allow the flavours to develop. Spoon on top of the toasted bread just before serving.

Nutrients per serving: Kilojoules 1303; Fibre 5g; Protein 10g; Carbohydrate 46g; Saturated Fat 1g; Total Fat 9g; Cholesterol 0mg

Three-Tomato Marinara Sauce

Preparation: 15 minutes / Cooking: 40 minutes / Makes: 10 cups

½ cup sun-dried
   tomatoes (not
   oil-packed)

1½ tablespoons olive oil

2 large onions, finely
   chopped

8 cloves garlic, minced

6 cans no-added-salt
   tomatoes (400g each),
   chopped with their
   juice

2 tablespoons
   no-added-salt
   tomato paste

½ teaspoon sugar

Salt

1. Soak the sun-dried tomatoes in a small bowl in boiling water to cover. Stand for 15 minutes or until softened. Drain and chop finely.

2. Meanwhile, heat the oil in a large saucepan over low heat. Add the onions and garlic and cook for 15 minutes or until very soft.

3. Add the sun-dried tomatoes, the tomatoes and their juice, the tomato paste, sugar and salt to taste. Bring to the boil, reduce to a simmer, cover and cook for 20 minutes or until the sauce is well flavoured and slightly thickened.

Nutrients per ½ cup: Kilojoules 209; Fibre 2g; Protein 2g; Carbohydrate 6g; Saturated Fat 0g; Total Fat 2g; Cholesterol 0mg

Did you know?

Studies indicate that the disease-fighting lycopene in tomatoes is best absorbed when the tomatoes have been heat-processed (cooked or canned) using a small amount of oil.

Gazpacho

Preparation: 30 minutes / Chill: 2 hours / Serves: 4

1kg tomatoes, coarsely
   chopped

1 red capsicum, cut into
   5mm dice

1 green capsicum, cut
   into 5mm dice

1 small red onion, finely
   chopped

1 stalk celery, cut into
   5mm dice

¼ cup red wine vinegar

½ teaspoon ground
   coriander

½ teaspoon Tabasco
   sauce

Salt

1. Combine the tomatoes, capsicums, onion, celery, vinegar, coriander, Tabasco sauce and salt to taste in a large bowl. Stir in 1 cup iced water.

2. Refrigerate the gazpacho for 2 hours or until well chilled. Ladle into soup bowls.

Nutrients per serving: Kilojoules 200; Fibre 4g; Protein 3g; Carbohydrate 7g; Saturated Fat 0g; Total Fat 0g; Cholesterol 0mg

Zucchini

Zucchini, along with other squashes and the related marrows, are a good source of vitamin C as well as providing some fibre.

Healthy Highlights

Zucchini
1 serving, cooked (145g)

		Nutrients	% RDI
Kilojoules	96	Vitamin C	82%
Fibre	2.5g	Folate	20%
Protein	1.9g	Potassium	11%
Carbohydrate	2.6g	Vitamin A	10%
Saturated Fat	0g		
Total Fat	0.4g		
Cholesterol	0mg		
Sodium	1mg		

Button squash
1 serving, cooked (145g)

		Nutrients	% RDI
Kilojoules	162	Vitamin C	87%
Fibre	3.8g	Potassium	10%
Protein	4.2g	Vitamin A	10%
Carbohydrate	4.8g		
Saturated Fat	0g		
Total Fat	0.3g		
Cholesterol	0mg		
Sodium	1mg		

Marrow
1 serving, cooked (145g)

		Nutrients	% RDI
Kilojoules	116	Vitamin C	24%
Fibre	0.8g	Folate	22%
Protein	1.2g		
Carbohydrate	5.5g		
Saturated Fat	0g		
Total Fat	0.2g		
Cholesterol	0mg		
Sodium	1mg		

Shopping & Preparation

At the market Zucchini, button or patty pan squash and marrows are all members of the same family, and are available at most times of the year. Peak seasons are generally spring, summer and autumn.

Look for Zucchini and squash should have glossy skins and be free of blemishes; avoid any that are soft. Marrows should feel firm and full. Store in a plastic bag in the refrigerator and use within a few days.

Preparation Zucchini and squash do not need peeling; simply discard the ends if you wish. Marrow is also left unpeeled, and is usually sliced and fried, or halved and stuffed.

Spring Vegetable Stew

Preparation: 15 minutes

Cooking: 40 minutes / Serves: 4

1 bunch asparagus, sliced into 2cm lengths
8 baby zucchini (500g total), trimmed
8 small golden squash (200g total)
1 cup fresh peas
12 baby carrots (100g total), trimmed and peeled
2 tablespoons olive oil
1 small onion, peeled and finely chopped
3 cups vegetable stock
2 medium tomatoes, peeled, seeded and finely diced
Salt
Freshly ground pepper
10 basil leaves, torn

1. Cook the asparagus, zucchini, squash, peas and carrots separately in salted, boiling water for 3 to 5 minutes or until each vegetable is crisp-tender. Drain and refresh under cold running water.

2. Heat the oil in a large nonstick frying pan. Add the onion and cook over low heat for 2 minutes or until tender. Add the stock and reduce by half (about 10 minutes). Then add the tomatoes and simmer for 5 minutes. Finally add the rest of the cooked vegetables and warm through for a further 5 minutes over gentle heat. Season to taste with salt and pepper and sprinkle with the basil.

Nutrients per serving: Kilojoules 724; Fibre 8g; Protein 8g; Carbohydrate 11g; Saturated Fat 2g; Total Fat 11g; Cholesterol 0mg

Did you know?

• A 100g portion of steamed zucchini provides just over half the vitamin C and a seventh of the folate an adult needs daily.

• Zucchini also contain beta-carotene, which the body converts into vitamin A, but they are high in salicylates which may cause food intolerance in some people.

Zucchini & Broccoli Soup

Zucchini & Broccoli Soup

Preparation: 15 minutes / Cooking: 15 minutes / Serves: 6

1 tablespoon olive oil

1 large onion, finely chopped

2 cloves garlic, chopped

750ml chicken or vegetable stock

8 medium zucchini, diced

400g broccoli, cut into florets

½ cup low-fat cream

Freshly ground pepper

1. Heat the oil in a large saucepan over moderate heat. Add the onion and garlic and cook for 3 minutes. Add the stock and zucchini. Cover and simmer for 5 minutes. Remove from the heat and allow to cool.

2. Steam the broccoli in a steamer or colander set over a saucepan of boiling water for 5 to 7 minutes. Allow to cool.

3. Purée the vegetables in a blender. Pour into a saucepan or bowl and stir in the cream. Serve hot or cold, garnished with pepper.

Nutrients per serving: Kilojoules 565; Fibre 4g; Protein 6g; Carbohydrate 6g; Saturated Fat 4g; Total Fat 10g; Cholesterol 16mg

Did you know?

Yellow-skinned spaghetti squash looks more like a melon than a marrow, and the sweet, nutty flesh resembles spaghetti when cooked – with considerably fewer kilojoules.

and Eggs

Firm Cheeses

Cheddar and Swiss-style cheeses – as well as the Italian grating cheeses – are potent flavourings, even in modest amounts, so are especially good for cooking. They offer quality protein and – along with the melting cheeses like mozzarella – are rich in calcium.

Healthy Highlights

Cheddar
30g

Nutrients		% RDI	
Kilojoules	507	Calcium	29%
Fibre	0g	Phosphorus	16%
Protein	7.6g	Vitamin A	16%
Carbohydrate	0g	Niacin	12%
Saturated Fat	6.5g		
Total Fat	10.1g		
Cholesterol	30mg		
Sodium	196mg		

Gruyère or other Swiss-style cheese
30g

Nutrients		% RDI	
Kilojoules	480	Calcium	33%
Fibre	0g	Phosphorus	18%
Protein	8.5g	Niacin	13%
Carbohydrate	0.1g	Riboflavin	11%
Saturated Fat	5.7g	Zinc	11%
Total Fat	9g	Vitamin A	10%
Cholesterol	28mg		
Sodium	102mg		

Mozzarella
30g

Nutrients		% RDI	
Kilojoules	378	Calcium	33%
Fibre	0g	Phosphorus	17%
Protein	7.8g	Niacin	13%
Carbohydrate	0g	Zinc	12%
Saturated Fat	4.2g		
Total Fat	6.6g		
Cholesterol	19mg		
Sodium	112mg		

Bocconcini
30g

Nutrients		% RDI	
Kilojoules	257	Calcium	12%
Fibre	0g	Vitamin A	11%
Protein	5.2g		
Carbohydrate	0g		
Saturated Fat	3g		
Total Fat	4.6g		
Cholesterol	11mg		
Sodium	85mg		

Caprese Salad

Caprese Salad

Preparation: 15 minutes / Serves: 6

300g baby bocconcini, drained and cut in half

2 punnets cherry tomatoes, cut in half

½ cup black olives

½ teaspoon dried crushed chilli

2 tablespoons chopped flat-leaf parsley

12 fresh basil leaves

2 teaspoons extra virgin olive oil

Salt

Freshly ground pepper

1. Place the bocconcini in a shallow serving bowl. Top with the cherry tomatoes and olives.

2. Sprinkle the chilli, parsley and basil over the top. Drizzle over olive oil to lightly moisten the ingredients and season to taste with salt and freshly ground pepper. Toss gently.

Nutrients per serving: Kilojoules 585; Fibre 2g; Protein 9g; Carbohydrate 5g; Saturated Fat 5g; Total Fat 9g; Cholesterol 17mg

Did you know?

A number of studies have shown that cheese – especially Cheddar cheese – is an impressive tooth-cavity fighter.

Dijon Cheese Tart

Preparation: 25 minutes / Standing: 1 hour / Cooking: 1 hour 10 minutes / Serves: 8

1 cup plain flour

½ teaspoon sugar

Salt

Cayenne pepper

60g reduced-fat cream cheese, cut up

1½ tablespoons unsalted butter, cut up

1½ tablespoons reduced-fat sour cream

1 cup low-fat milk

2 whole eggs

2 egg whites

3 teaspoons Dijon mustard

1 bunch fresh chives, chopped

200g Gruyère or other Swiss-style cheese, shredded

1. Combine the flour, sugar, and a pinch each of salt and cayenne pepper in a large bowl. Cut in the cream cheese and butter with a pastry blender or two knives until the mixture resembles coarse crumbs. Combine the sour cream and 1 tablespoon iced water in a small bowl. Stir into the flour mixture until just combined. Flatten into a round, wrap in plastic wrap, and refrigerate for 1 hour or overnight.

2. Preheat the oven to 180°C. Roll the dough out to a 33 cm round on a lightly floured surface. Fit into a 23 cm pie plate with a removable bottom. Prick the bottom of the shell with a fork in several places. Line with foil and weight down with pie weights or dried beans. Bake for 20 minutes or until the crust is beginning to set. Remove the pie weights and foil and bake for a further 15 minutes or until the crust is cooked through. Leave the oven on.

3. Whisk together the milk, whole eggs, egg whites, mustard and chives in a medium bowl. Stir in the Gruyère. Place the pie plate on a baking tray with sides. Pour the cheese mixture into the crust and bake for 35 minutes or until puffed and golden brown. Serve the tart warm or at room temperature.

Nutrients per serving: Kilojoules 1060; Fibre 1g; Protein 14g; Carbohydrate 16g; Saturated Fat 9g; Total Fat 15g; Cholesterol 103mg

Dijon Cheese Tart

Parmesan

30g		Nutrients % RDI	
Kilojoules	555	Calcium	43%
Fibre	0g	Phosphorus	24%
Protein	11.4g	Niacin	18%
Carbohydrate	0g	Zinc	15%
Saturated Fat	6.2g	Vitamin A	14%
Total Fat	9.7g	Riboflavin	10%
Cholesterol	29mg		
Sodium	432mg		

Shopping & Preparation

At the market You'll find firm cheeses in every supermarket; specialist cheese shops offer more options. As well as the cheeses used in our recipes, you'll come across such favourites as Colby, Cheshire, Red Leicester, Lancaster, Provolone, Haloumi and Pepato. Many hard cheeses have very high levels of saturated fat, so choose low-fat varieties whenever possible.

Look for Young Cheddars are moist and easily sliced; well-aged, slightly crumbly Cheddar (at least six months old) is more flavourful. Among Swiss-style cheeses, Emmental and Gruyère are popular. The indispensable Italian cheeses – like mozzarella and bocconcini (a young, fresh mozzarella), ideal for melting – also include hard grating cheeses such as Parmesan, Pecorino and Romano. When choosing firm cheeses, select those with a fresh, clean appearance, without dryness or cracks.

Preparation Remove any rind from firm cheeses before slicing or grating. For use as table cheeses, they are best served at room temperature. Remove from the refrigerator an hour or so before serving.

Cooking tips Grated or shredded and added to hot food, these cheeses will melt quickly and smoothly. When subjected to high or prolonged heat, they will turn tough and rubbery. The softer Italian cheeses are easier to grate or slice if well chilled.

Asparagus & Capsicum Frittata

Preparation: 10 minutes / Cooking: 20 minutes / Serves: 4

250g asparagus, trimmed and cut into 1 cm lengths

1 red capsicum, cut into 1 cm squares

3 eggs

4 egg whites

2 teaspoons plain flour

½ cup grated Parmesan cheese

Salt

Freshly ground black pepper

2 teaspoons olive oil

1 teaspoon unsalted butter

1. Blanch the asparagus and capsicum in boiling water in a medium saucepan for 2 minutes; drain well.

2. Whisk together the whole eggs and egg whites in a medium bowl. Whisk in the flour until well combined. Whisk in the Parmesan and salt and pepper to taste. Stir in the asparagus and capsicum.

3. Heat the oil and butter in a 25 cm cast-iron or other heavy flameproof frying pan over low heat until the butter has melted. Pour in the egg mixture and cook, without stirring, for 15 minutes or until the eggs are set around the edges and almost set in the centre. Meanwhile, preheat the griller.

4. Grill the frittata 15 cm from the heat for 1 to 2 minutes or until the top is just set. Cut into wedges and serve hot, warm or chilled.

Nutrients per serving: Kilojoules 772; Fibre 1g; Protein 15g; Carbohydrate 4g; Saturated Fat 5g; Total Fat 12g; Cholesterol 201mg

Chicken & Cheese Tostadas

Preparation: 15 minutes / Cooking: 15 minutes / Serves: 4

2 teaspoons vegetable oil

4 spring onions, thinly sliced

2 cloves garlic, crushed

300g skinless, boneless chicken breasts, cut into 1cm chunks

1 cup frozen corn kernels, thawed

1 can (113g) chopped mild green chillies

½ cup chopped fresh coriander

1 pickled jalapeño chilli, halved, seeded and finely chopped

1½ tablespoons lime juice

8 corn tortillas (15cm diameter)

200g Cheddar or other mild cheese, grated

1. Heat the oil in a large nonstick frying pan over moderate heat. Add the spring onions and garlic and cook gently for 2 minutes or until the spring onions are tender. Add the chicken and cook for 5 minutes or until just cooked through. Transfer to a large bowl. Add the corn, green chillies, coriander, jalapeño chilli and lime juice, tossing to combine.

2. Meanwhile, preheat the oven to 200°C. Place the tortillas on a baking tray and heat for 2 minutes.

3. Sprinkle half the cheese over the tortillas. Top with the chicken mixture and the remaining cheese. Bake for 5 minutes or until the cheese is melted and bubbling.

Nutrients per serving: Kilojoules 1973; Fibre 4g; Protein 30g; Carbohydrate 32g; Saturated Fat 12g; Total Fat 24g; Cholesterol 93mg

Mushroom & Capsicum Pizza

Mushroom & Capsicum Pizza

Preparation: 20 minutes / Cooking: 30 minutes / Serves: 6

1 teaspoon olive oil

1 red capsicum, thinly sliced

1 green capsicum, thinly sliced

250g mushrooms, sliced

½ teaspoon dried oregano

Salt

1 purchased pizza base (30cm)

¼ cup tomato pasta sauce

250g mozzarella cheese, thinly sliced

Freshly ground black pepper

1. Heat the oil in a large nonstick frying pan over moderate heat. Add the capsicums and cook for 5 minutes or until crisp-tender. Add the mushrooms, oregano and a pinch of salt, then cook for 4 minutes or until the mushroom liquid has evaporated. Put aside.

2. Preheat the oven to 220°C. Spray a baking tray with cooking spray. Place the pizza base on the prepared tray. Spoon the tomato sauce over the pizza base then top with the capsicum mixture, the mozzarella and a little pepper. Bake the pizza for 15 minutes or until the cheese has melted and the crust is browned.

Nutrients per serving: Kilojoules 1687; Fibre 5g; Protein 21g; Carbohydrate 48g; Saturated Fat 7g; Total Fat 14g; Cholesterol 28mg

Did you know?

A high intake of calcium, especially during childhood and adolescence, can reduce the risk of developing osteoporosis, a condition where bones become brittle and weak. The calcium in cheese (and other dairy products) is more easily absorbed than calcium in other foods.

Fresh Cheeses

You get lots of high-quality protein in these delicate-tasting, unripened cheeses and they also make healthy substitutes for cream in many conventional recipes.

Healthy Highlights

Reduced-fat ricotta cheese

100g		Nutrients % RDI	
Kilojoules	530	Calcium	31%
Fibre	0g	Niacin	17%
Protein	10.4g	Phosphorus	17%
Carbohydrate	2.1g	Riboflavin	12%
Saturated Fat	5.6g	Vitamin A	10%
Total Fat	8.7g		
Cholesterol	42mg		
Sodium	186mg		

Low-fat cottage cheese

100g		Nutrients % RDI	
Kilojoules	376	Niacin	29%
Fibre	0g	Phosphorus	20%
Protein	17.7g	Folate	14%
Carbohydrate	1.9g	Calcium	10%
Saturated Fat	0.8g		
Total Fat	1.2g		
Cholesterol	13mg		
Sodium	129mg		

Reduced-fat cream cheese

30g		Nutrients % RDI
Kilojoules	241	*Standard serve has*
Fibre	0g	*less than 10% of*
Protein	2.5g	*RDI for individual*
Carbohydrate	0.9g	*nutrients*
Saturated Fat	3.3g	
Total Fat	5g	
Cholesterol	15mg	
Sodium	104mg	

Gnocchi Verde

Preparation: 25 minutes / Standing: 3–4 hours
Cooking: 15 minutes / Serves: 4

500g spinach or young silverbeet
250g reduced-fat or low-fat ricotta cheese
Nutmeg
Freshly ground pepper
3 eggs
⅓ cup plus 2 tablespoons grated Parmesan cheese
3 tablespoons sifted plain flour
2 tablespoons butter
12 fresh sage leaves

1. Wash the spinach and strip the leaves from the stalks. Place in a large saucepan with a little salted water, bring to the boil, and cook for 5 minutes. Drain and squeeze the spinach and spread on paper towels to dry completely.

2. Chop the spinach finely. Place in a medium bowl with the ricotta, and a pinch each of nutmeg and pepper, and mix thoroughly. Mix in the eggs, ⅓ cup of the grated Parmesan and the flour. Refrigerate the mixture for a few hours or overnight.

3. Dust a chopping board with flour, then roll out portions of the chilled gnocchi mixture to form cylindrical shapes the size of corks.

4. Bring a large saucepan of salted water to the boil, then lower the heat to a gentle simmer. Carefully drop the gnocchi into the water in batches; they will rise to the surface when cooked – about 5 minutes. Lift the gnocchi from the water and drain well. Keep warm.

5. Melt the butter in a small frying pan. Bruise the sage leaves and add to the pan. Heat until the butter bubbles, pour the sauce over the gnocchi and sprinkle with the remaining Parmesan cheese.

Nutrients per serving: Kilojoules 1307; Fibre 6g; Protein 20g; Carbohydrate 8g; Saturated Fat 12g; Total Fat 22g; Cholesterol 248mg

Did you know?

When the fat content of milk is reduced, its calcium content is slightly increased. Thus, 100g low-fat cottage cheese – which is made from low-fat milk – supplies 10% of the RDI for calcium; the same quantity of full-fat cottage cheese supplies only 9%.

Shopping & Preparation

At the market Cottage cheese, cream cheese and ricotta cheese are usually available in full-fat and lower-fat varieties. (We recommend you choose the lowest fat content you can find for use in our recipes, but any reduced-fat version is acceptable.) You can also buy pressed cottage cheese (sometimes called pot cheese), which is firmer and drier than usual. Mascarpone falls into the fresh cheese category, but is higher in fat than the others. Of the fresh cheeses commercially available, cottage cheese has the lowest fat content. It is made from skim milk which has been curdled, the whey (liquid) removed, and then dried. Ricotta cheese is traditionally made from the whey drained off during the production of mozzarella.

Look for Fresh cheeses should be white and moist, with no sign of any discolouring. You should always check the use-by date before selecting any fresh cheeses, and keep them in the refrigerator. Use within a couple of days of purchase (the same day, whenever possible, for ricotta, as it has a very short shelf life).

Preparation Unlike most table cheeses, fresh cheeses are best served cool, straight from the refrigerator, rather than at room temperature. Some recipes may call for cottage cheese and ricotta cheese to be drained before you use them in cooking. Simply place the cheese in a fine-mesh sieve for a few minutes and shake gently to drain off some of the liquid.

Liptauer Cheese

Preparation: 10 minutes / Chill: 1 hour / Makes: 1¾ cups

375g reduced-fat cream cheese

2 tablespoons low-fat milk

½ medium red onion, finely chopped

4 anchovies, rinsed and mashed, or 2 teaspoons anchovy paste

2 tablespoons capers, rinsed and drained

2 tablespoons chopped, rehydrated sun-dried tomatoes

1 teaspoon paprika

¾ teaspoon grated lemon zest

1. Beat together the cream cheese and milk with an electric mixer in a medium bowl. Fold in the onion, anchovies, capers, sun-dried tomatoes, paprika and lemon zest.

2. Spoon into a serving bowl and serve with rye bread and crisp cracker biscuits.

Nutrients per ¼ cup: Kilojoules 495; Fibre 0g; Protein 6g; Carbohydrate 3g; Saturated Fat 6g; Total Fat 9g; Cholesterol 29mg

Did you know?

Sodium content can vary greatly among different brands of cottage cheese. If you're concerned about sodium intake, check the label carefully.

Lemon & Lime Cheesecake

Preparation: 20 minutes / Cooking: 1 hour 5 minutes / Serves: 12

Liptauer Cheese

100g low-fat sweet wafer biscuits

1½ tablespoons unsalted butter, melted

350g low-fat cottage cheese

500g reduced-fat cream cheese

1 cup plus 3 teaspoons sugar

2 eggs

4 egg whites

1½ tablespoons plain flour

1½ teaspoons grated lemon zest

1½ teaspoons grated lime zest

3 teaspoons lemon juice

3 teaspoons lime juice

½ cup reduced-fat sour cream

1. Preheat the oven to 180°C. Process the wafer biscuits in a food processor until finely ground. Add the butter and pulse until the crumbs are moistened. Spoon the mixture into a 23 cm springform tin, patting it into the bottom. Bake for 10 minutes or until lightly browned; put aside. Leave the oven on.

2. Process the cottage cheese in a food processor (you can use the same bowl) for 1 minute or until smooth.

3. Beat the cream cheese and 1 cup of the sugar with an electric mixer in a medium bowl until light and fluffy. Beat in the whole eggs and egg whites, one at a time, beating well after each addition. Beat in the puréed cottage cheese, the flour, lemon zest, lime zest, lemon juice and lime juice until well blended. Pour the mixture into the prepared tin and bake for 50 minutes or until the centre is set and the top is golden.

4. Meanwhile, combine the sour cream and the remaining sugar in a small bowl. Spread over the top of the hot cake and bake for a further 5 minutes. Remove from the oven and place the tin on a wire rack to cool. Refrigerate the cheesecake in the tin until serving time.

Nutrients per serving: Kilojoules 1186; Fibre 0g; Protein 12g; Carbohydrate 28g; Saturated Fat 9g; Total Fat 14g; Cholesterol 82mg

Coeur à la Crème

Preparation: 10 minutes / Drain: 4 to 6 hours / Serves: 6

500g reduced-fat cream cheese

250g low-fat cottage cheese

⅔ cup icing sugar

½ teaspoon vanilla essence

2 cups fresh or frozen strawberries

1½ tablespoons honey

3 teaspoons lime juice

1. Combine the cream cheese and cottage cheese in a food processor and mix until smooth. Add the sugar and vanilla essence, and mix well.

2. Line one large or 6 individual heart-shaped ceramic coeur à la crème moulds (or a 4- to 6-cup sieve set over a bowl) with a double layer of dampened muslin. Spoon the mixture into the moulds, wrap the muslin over the top, and place the moulds on a plate to drain. Refrigerate for 4 to 6 hours or overnight.

3. Before serving, combine the strawberries, honey and lime juice in a food processor or blender. Process until smooth. At serving time, remove the moulds and peel off the muslin. Turn out onto one platter or individual plates and serve with the strawberry sauce alongside.

Nutrients per serving: Kilojoules 1208; Fibre 1g; Protein 15g; Carbohydrate 26g; Saturated Fat 9g; Total Fat 14g; Cholesterol 47mg

Did you know?

A half-cup serving of low-fat cottage cheese supplies about 20g of protein – nearly half an adult female's daily protein requirement. And the protein in fresh cheese is just as good as the protein in meat, poultry or fish.

Goat & Feta Cheeses

Rich in flavour, these tangy soft cheeses are lower in fat than many other similar cheeses. Rinsing feta before use greatly reduces its high sodium content.

Healthy Highlights

Mild goat cheese
30g

		Nutrients % RDI	
Kilojoules	247	Riboflavin	13%
Fibre	0g	Vitamin A	12%
Protein	3.9g		
Carbohydrate	0.3g		
Saturated Fat	3.1g		
Total Fat	4.7g		
Cholesterol	12mg		
Sodium	104mg		

Feta cheese
30g

		Nutrients % RDI	
Kilojoules	351	Calcium	12%
Fibre	0g	Vitamin A	10%
Protein	5.3g		
Carbohydrate	0.1g		
Saturated Fat	4.6g		
Total Fat	7g		
Cholesterol	21mg		
Sodium	321mg		

Shopping & Preparation

At the market For wider variety and better quality, buy goat and feta cheese at a gourmet shop or specialist cheese shop.

Look for Goat cheese – which ranges from gently tangy to sharply pungent – is often sold under its French name, chèvre. It is usually shaped in rounds or logs, sometimes flavoured with herbs, and is often coated with a fine layer of ash. Other coatings include dried herbs or crushed peppercorns. Feta – made either from cow's or goat's milk – is sometimes sold in a brine solution, which helps to prolong its storage life.

Preparation Small goat cheese logs need no preparation, but if you're cooking with a slice from a thicker log, you'll want to remove the rind. Feta should be rinsed under cold running water and drained well.

Crustless Mini-Quiches with Broccoli & Feta

Preparation: 15 minutes / Cooking: 35 minutes / Serves: 4

1 teaspoon olive oil
2 spring onions, thinly sliced
2 cloves garlic, crushed
1 packet (300g) frozen chopped broccoli, thawed and squeezed dry
⅓ cup low-fat cottage cheese
⅔ cup low-fat milk
2 eggs
3 egg whites
2 tablespoons plain flour
White pepper
200g feta cheese or mild goat cheese

1. Preheat the oven to 180°C. Spray four 1-cup ramekins with cooking spray; put aside. Heat the oil in a medium nonstick frying pan over moderate heat. Add the spring onions and garlic and cook for 1 minute. Stir in the broccoli and cook for 1 minute.

2. Process the cottage cheese in a food processor until smooth. Add the milk, whole eggs, egg whites, flour and a pinch of pepper, and process until well combined. Transfer the custard to a large bowl. Add the broccoli mixture and crumble in the feta cheese, stirring to combine.

3. Spoon into the prepared ramekins, place on a baking tray, then bake for 30 minutes or until the quiches are puffy and set.

Nutrients per serving: Kilojoules 1203; Fibre 4g; Protein 25g; Carbohydrate 8g; Saturated Fat 9g; Total Fat 17g; Cholesterol 164mg

Did you know?

Many people who are allergic to cow's milk can tolerate goat's milk with no adverse reaction.

Composed Salad with Grilled Goat Cheese

Preparation: 20 minutes / Cooking: 15 minutes / Serves: 4

1 red capsicum, cut lengthways into strips
1 yellow capsicum, cut lengthways into strips
12 slices (5 x 6cm) Italian bread (150g total)
250g mild goat cheese, cut into 12 slices
2 tablespoons red wine vinegar
3 teaspoons olive oil
1 teaspoon Dijon mustard
½ teaspoon brown sugar
125g mixed salad leaves, torn if large
6 sprigs fresh chervil or parsley

1. Preheat the griller. Place the capsicum pieces, skin-side-up, on the rack. Grill 15 cm from the heat for 10 minutes or until the skin is blackened. When the capsicums are cool enough to handle, peel and cut into 2.5 cm strips.

2. Top each slice of bread with the cheese and grill for 1 minute or until the cheese is slightly melted and the bread is toasted.

3. Whisk together the vinegar, oil, mustard and brown sugar in a small bowl. Place the lettuce on 4 plates and arrange the capsicum on top. Drizzle the dressing over the salads and place 3 cheese toasts on each. Garnish with the chervil.

Nutrients per serving: Kilojoules 1128; Fibre 3g; Protein 13g; Carbohydrate 21g; Saturated Fat 7g; Total Fat 14g; Cholesterol 26mg

Creamy Polenta with Cheese

Preparation: 10 minutes / Cooking: 20 minutes / Serves: 4

1 cup yellow cornmeal
1½ cups low-fat milk
Salt
Cayenne pepper
200g feta cheese or
  mild goat cheese

1. Stir the cornmeal and 1 cup of the milk together in a small bowl until well blended and smooth.

2. Bring 1½ cups water, the remaining milk, and a pinch each of salt and cayenne pepper, to a simmer in a medium, heavy-bottomed saucepan over low heat. Stirring constantly, gradually pour in the cornmeal mixture. Cook over low heat, still stirring constantly, for 10 minutes or until the polenta is thick and creamy.

3. Crumble in the feta and cook, stirring, for 3 to 4 minutes or until the cheese is melted.

Nutrients per serving: Kilojoules 1194; Fibre 1g; Protein 16g; Carbohydrate 28g; Saturated Fat 8g; Total Fat 12g; Cholesterol 38mg

Composed Salad with Grilled Goat Cheese

Milk

Our main calcium source, milk – vital to maintain good health and strong bones – also provides protein and riboflavin.

Healthy Highlights

Low-fat (<1%) milk

1 cup (250ml)		Nutrients % RDI	
Kilojoules	494	Riboflavin	53%
Fibre	0g	Calcium	52%
Protein	12g	Phosphorus	33%
Carbohydrate	16.9g	Potassium	29%
Saturated Fat	0.3g	Niacin	18%
Total Fat	0.5g	Magnesium	14%
Cholesterol	10mg	Zinc	11%
Sodium	150mg		

Buttermilk

1 cup (250ml)		Nutrients % RDI	
Kilojoules	629	Riboflavin	53%
Fibre	0g	Calcium	46%
Protein	10.9g	Phosphorus	34%
Carbohydrate	14g	Potassium	27%
Saturated Fat	3.4g	Niacin	18%
Total Fat	5.2g	Magnesium	13%
Cholesterol	23mg	Folate	12%
Sodium	148mg	Zinc	11%

Evaporated low-fat milk

½ cup (125ml)		Nutrients % RDI	
Kilojoules	507	Riboflavin	46%
Fibre	0g	Calcium	43%
Protein	10.3g	Phosphorus	36%
Carbohydrate	14.3g	Potassium	23%
Saturated Fat	1.9g	Niacin	16%
Total Fat	2.8g	Magnesium	11%
Cholesterol	12mg	Thiamin	11%
Sodium	125mg	Zinc	10%

Shopping & Preparation

At the market The fat content in milk ranges from 3.8% (full cream) to less than 0.15% (skim) with reduced fat (1–2%) and low-fat (less than 1%) varieties in between. Any of the lower-fat milks are suitable for our recipes. You'll also find evaporated and condensed milks available, in both full cream and reduced fat, as well as buttermilk.

Look for Always choose milk products with the longest possible use-by period.

Cooking tip When a recipe says to 'scald' milk, simply heat over low heat just until small bubbles begin to form around the edge.

Chocolate Latte Cotto

Preparation: 15 minutes / Cooking: 10 minutes / Chill: 4 hours / Serves: 6

2 tablespoons cocoa
1 envelope gelatine
3 cups low-fat milk
½ cup firmly packed light brown sugar
30g semisweet chocolate, coarsely chopped
Grated nutmeg
Dark chocolate shavings (optional)

1. Combine the cocoa and 2 tablespoons water in a small bowl, stirring until the cocoa is moistened. Sprinkle the gelatine over 1 cup of the milk in a separate bowl and stand for 5 minutes or until softened.

2. Meanwhile, combine the remaining milk, the brown sugar, chocolate and a good grating of nutmeg in a medium saucepan. Bring to a simmer and cook just until the chocolate has melted. Remove from the heat and stir in the cocoa mixture.

3. Stir in the gelatine, return to the heat, and cook for 3 minutes or just until the gelatine has dissolved. Divide the mixture among six ¾-cup custard cups or ramekins and cool to room temperature. Chill for at least 4 hours. Decorate with shaved chocolate, if you like.

Nutrients per serving: Kilojoules 674; Fibre 0g; Protein 8g; Carbohydrate 29g; Saturated Fat 2g; Total Fat 2g; Cholesterol 5mg

Homemade Fresh Cheese

Preparation: 30 minutes / Drain: 2 hours / Serves: 4

2.5 litres low-fat milk
⅓ cup lemon juice

1. Bring the milk to the boil in a large saucepan over moderate heat. Remove from the heat and stir in the lemon juice. Let stand until the curds and whey separate. Line a sieve with a double layer of muslin. Place the sieve in the sink and pour in the curdled milk, draining off the whey. Place the sieve over a bowl and stand for 20 minutes.

2. Tie the muslin up and gently squeeze to remove any remaining liquid. Flatten the mixture into a round, place a weight on top (such as a heavy can inside a saucepan) and stand at room temperature for 2 hours or until the cheese is firm enough to cut.

Nutrients per serving: Kilojoules 679; Fibre 0g; Protein 26g; Carbohydrate 13g; Saturated Fat 0g; Total Fat 1g; Cholesterol 23mg

Chocolate Latte Cotto

Curried Spinach & Fresh Cheese

Preparation: 15 minutes
Cooking: 30 minutes / Serves: 4

1 tablespoon vegetable oil
1 large onion, finely chopped
4 cloves garlic, crushed
1 teaspoon ground coriander
¾ teaspoon ground turmeric
Salt
1 packet (300g) frozen chopped spinach, thawed
   and squeezed dry
1 cup chicken stock
2 tablespoons no-added-salt tomato paste
1–2 teaspoons Tabasco sauce
Homemade Fresh Cheese (recipe, left)

1. Heat 2 teaspoons of the oil in a large nonstick frying pan over moderate heat. Add the onion and garlic and cook for 7 minutes or until tender. Add the coriander, turmeric and a pinch of salt, stirring to combine. Add the spinach, stock, tomate paste and Tabasco sauce to taste and bring to the boil. Reduce to a simmer, cover and cook for 5 minutes. Transfer the mixture to a bowl and wipe out the frying pan.

2. Cut the cheese into 1 cm chunks. Add the remaining oil to the pan over moderate heat. Add the cheese and cook, stirring frequently, for 4 minutes or until lightly browned and crusty on all sides. Gently stir in the spinach mixture and cook for 4 minutes or until heated through.

Nutrients per serving: Kilojoules 1038; Fibre 5g; Protein 30g; Carbohydrate 18g; Saturated Fat 1g; Total Fat 6g; Cholesterol 23mg

Did you know?

• A study called DASH – Dietary Approaches to Stop Hypertension – found that a diet rich in fruits, vegetables and low-fat dairy products could substantially reduce blood pressure. The same diet, minus the dairy products, was not as effective.

• To appreciate the healthy advantage of evaporated low-fat milk, just compare it with cream. A half cup of pure cream supplies only 10% of the RDI for calcium – and has 55g fat and 173mg cholesterol.

Yoghurt

A top calcium source, and high in protein, yoghurt is a versatile food that you can use to replace high-fat cream and sour cream.

Healthy Highlights

Low-fat plain yoghurt
200g

Nutrients		% RDI	
Kilojoules	446	Calcium	53%
Fibre	0g	Riboflavin	41%
Protein	11.8g	Phosphorus	33%
Carbohydrate	11.6g	Potassium	27%
Saturated Fat	0.2g	Folate	17%
Total Fat	0.4g	Niacin	17%
Cholesterol	10mg	Magnesium	13%
Sodium	140mg	Zinc	10%

Low-fat flavoured yoghurt
200g

Nutrients		% RDI	
Kilojoules	640	Calcium	45%
Fibre	0g	Riboflavin	41%
Protein	10.4g	Phosphorus	29%
Carbohydrate	25.6g	Niacin	26%
Saturated Fat	0.2g	Potassium	24%
Total Fat	0.4g	Folate	16%
Cholesterol	6mg	Magnesium	12%
Sodium	122mg		

Shopping & Preparation

At the market Most supermarkets offer a wide range of full-fat and low-fat yoghurts, both plain and flavoured. Health-food shops may yield varieties such as organic or goat's-milk yoghurt.

Look for For maximum health benefits, look for yoghurt with active cultures listed on the carton.

Preparation If commercial yoghurt is slightly separated, stir the whey (liquid) back in, as it contains nutrients, including calcium. When making yoghurt cheese (see recipe, right), reserve the whey for use in recipes such as muffins or pancakes.

Cooking tip Yoghurt used in cooked dishes will curdle if subjected to high heat. Combining the yoghurt with flour or cornflour before adding it will help, but always keep the heat moderate.

Tandoori-Style Chicken

Preparation: 25 minutes / Marinate: 2 hours

Cooking: 20 minutes / Serves: 4

3 cloves garlic, peeled and crushed

1 teaspoon paprika

¾ teaspoon ground cumin

¾ teaspoon ground coriander

½ teaspoon cinnamon

½ teaspoon chilli powder

½ teaspoon pepper

Salt

2 cups plain low-fat yoghurt

4 skinless, bone-in chicken breast halves (about 1kg total)

1 small red onion, finely chopped

1 cucumber, seeded and diced

½ cup chopped fresh coriander

1. Combine the garlic, paprika, cumin, ground coriander, cinnamon, chilli powder, pepper and a dash of salt in a shallow glass or ceramic baking dish. Stir in 1 cup of the yoghurt until well blended. Make several slashes in the flesh of the chicken with a sharp knife, cutting almost to the bone. Place the chicken, cut-sides-down, in the yoghurt mixture. Cover and refrigerate for at least 2 hours or overnight, turning the chicken several times.

2. Preheat the oven to 270°C. Lift the chicken from its marinade and place in a shallow baking dish; discard any leftover marinade. Bake the chicken for 20 minutes or until cooked through but still juicy.

3. Meanwhile, combine the onion, cucumber, fresh coriander and the remaining yoghurt in a medium bowl. Serve the chicken with the yoghurt mixture on the side.

Nutrients per serving: Kilojoules 1558; Fibre 1g; Protein 52g; Carbohydrate 9g; Saturated Fat 4g; Total Fat 13g; Cholesterol 148mg

Did you know?

• The 'fruit' in most commercial yoghurt is usually jam or preserves – more sugar than fruit. Nutritionally speaking, you're better off stirring your favourite fresh or dried fruit into plain yoghurt. A touch of vanilla or almond essence will enhance the flavour of the fruit.

• Eating yoghurt with active cultures helps maintain a healthy digestive system.

Yoghurt Cheese

Preparation: 5 minutes / Drain: 12 hours / Makes: about 2 cups

5 cups (1.25kg) plain low-fat yoghurt

1. Line a fine-mesh sieve with a double layer of dampened muslin. Spoon the yoghurt into the sieve and position it over a bowl. Place in the refrigerator and let stand overnight.

Nutrients per ¼ cup: Kilojoules 255; Fibre 0g; Protein 8g; Carbohydrate 4g; Saturated Fat 0g; Total Fat 0g; Cholesterol 7mg

Tzatziki

Tzatziki

Preparation: 15 minutes / Standing: 30 minutes / Serves: 4

1 Lebanese or long cucumber, peeled and finely diced

Salt

2 cups plain low-fat yoghurt

2 cloves garlic, finely chopped

¼ cup chopped fresh mint

Freshly ground pepper

Olive oil (optional)

1. Sprinkle the cucumber with a little salt. Leave for 30 minutes, then rinse, drain and squeeze well to remove the excess liquid.

2. Combine the yoghurt and garlic in a large bowl. Stir in the cucumber and mint. Season to taste with pepper. Turn out into a small bowl and drizzle with oil, if liked. Serve with flat breads and crisp wafers for dipping

Nutrients per serving: Kilojoules 311; Fibre 1g; Protein 8g; Carbohydrate 8g; Saturated Fat 0g; Total Fat 0g; Cholesterol 6mg

Did you know?

The bacteria used to culture yoghurt – either *Lactobacillus bulgaricus* or *Streptococcus thermophilus* – are good for your digestive system. They help you digest the milk protein in the yoghurt, and there is good evidence that they help maintain a healthy balance of 'friendly' bacteria in your intestines.

Fruit-Topped Yoghurt Cheese Tart

Fruit-Topped Yoghurt Cheese Tart

Preparation: 25 minutes / Chill: 1 hour / Cooking: 40 minutes / Serves: 8

1 cup plain flour

⅓ cup plus 3 teaspoons sugar

Salt

3 tablespoons unsalted butter, cut up

1½ tablespoons reduced-fat sour cream

2 cups Yoghurt Cheese (recipe, page 130)

¾ teaspoon vanilla essence

2 punnets strawberries, halved

¼ cup apricot jam

1. Combine the flour, 3 teaspoons of the sugar and a pinch of salt in a large bowl. Cut in the butter with a pastry blender or two knives until the mixture resembles coarse crumbs. Combine the sour cream and 2 teaspoons iced water in a small bowl. Stir into the flour mixture until just combined. Flatten the dough into a round, wrap in plastic wrap, and refrigerate for at least 1 hour.

2. Preheat the oven to 180°C. Roll the dough out to a 33 cm round on a lightly floured surface. Fit into a 23 cm pie plate with a removable bottom. Prick the bottom of the shell with a fork in several places. Line with foil and weight down with pie weights or dried beans. Bake for 20 minutes or until the crust is beginning to set. Remove the pie weights and

foil and bake for a further 15 minutes or until the crust is cooked through. Transfer the shell to a wire rack to cool completely.

3. Combine the Yoghurt Cheese, the remaining sugar and the vanilla essence in a medium bowl. Spread in the bottom of the baked and cooled shell. Arrange the strawberries in concentric circles on top of the tart.

4. Melt the jam in a small saucepan over low heat and brush over the fruit. Let cool until set.

Nutrients per serving: Kilojoules 1107; Fibre 2g; Protein 12g; Carbohydrate 36g; Saturated Fat 5g; Total Fat 8g; Cholesterol 29mg

Lemon Yoghurt Cake

Preparation: 20 minutes / Cooking: 45 minutes / Serves: 12

125g unsalted butter

1⅓ cups caster sugar

2 eggs, lightly beaten

1 cup plain low-fat yoghurt

½ cup lemon juice

1 tablespoon grated lemon zest

2½ cups self-raising flour

½ teaspoon bicarbonate of soda

2 tablespoons lemon zest, julienned

1 cup plain low-fat yoghurt (optional)

1. Preheat the oven to 180°C. Spray a 23 cm cake tin with cooking spray. Combine the butter and 1 cup of the sugar in a large bowl. Beat with an electric mixer until light and creamy. Add the eggs and mix well. Stir in the yoghurt, ¼ cup of the lemon juice, the grated lemon zest, flour and bicarbonate of soda and mix well.

2. Spoon the mixture into the prepared tin and bake for 45 minutes or until a skewer inserted in the centre of the cake comes out clean.

3. Meanwhile, combine the remaining sugar and lemon juice, and ½ cup water, in a small saucepan. Cook, stirring, over low heat until the sugar has dissolved, then add the julienned lemon zest and simmer for 4 minutes.

4. Remove the cake from the oven and pour the zest and syrup over the top while the cake is hot and still in the tin. Let the cake stand for at least 5 minutes before serving in slices with some extra yoghurt, if liked.

Nutrients per serving: Kilojoules 1253; Fibre 1g; Protein 6g; Carbohydrate 47g; Saturated Fat 6g; Total Fat 10g; Cholesterol 69mg

Did you know?

In one study, subjects who ate two cups of yoghurt a day for four months had higher levels of interferon, a chemical vital to immune function.

Lemon Yoghurt Cake

Eggs

The protein content is high and the price is right, making eggs a nutritional bargain. While the yolk does contain cholesterol and some fat, you also get valuable quantities of vitamin A, riboflavin, folate and niacin, as well as some iron, B vitamins, phosphorus and vitamin E.

Healthy Highlights

1 large, boiled (59g)		Nutrients % RDI	
Kilojoules	373	Niacin	14%
Fibre	0g	Riboflavin	14%
Protein	7.8g	Folate	12%
Carbohydrate	0.2g	Vitamin A	12%
Saturated Fat	1.9g		
Total Fat	6.4g		
Cholesterol	253mg		
Sodium	73mg		

Shopping & Preparation

At the market Approximately 90 per cent of all eggs produced and sold in Australia and New Zealand are conventional care eggs, commonly known as factory or battery eggs. Also available are free range eggs, barn laid eggs, organic eggs, omega-3 fortified eggs and vegetarian eggs (from hens that have been fed a special feed mix that contains no meat or fish products).

Look for Shops offer eggs in cartons, with the contents ranging in size from small (about 42g per egg) to jumbo (67g per egg). Our recipes use large (59g) eggs, sold in 700g cartons. Check the use-by date, then open the carton to make sure the shells are not cracked or broken. At home, keep the eggs in their carton in the refrigerator.

Preparation The easiest way to separate the white from the yolk is to use an egg separator (see below). Another way is to break the egg cleanly in half and tip the yolk back and forth between the half-shells, letting the white drop into a bowl. Or you can crack the egg into your clean hand, letting the white run between your fingers.

Unless you've had lots of practice, an egg separator is an indispensable tool.

Crème Caramel

Preparation: 15 minutes / Cooking: 50 minutes / Serves: 8

¾ cup plus ⅔ cup sugar
2 cups low-fat milk
1 cup evaporated low-fat milk
6 strips orange zest
4 eggs
2 egg whites
½ teaspoon vanilla essence

1. Combine ¾ cup of the sugar and ½ cup water in a small saucepan. Bring to the boil over moderately high heat and cook for 5 minutes or until amber-coloured. Pour the caramel into eight ¾-cup custard cups or ramekins, tilting to cover the bottom and partway up the sides. Place the cups in a baking dish and put aside.

2. Combine the milk, evaporated milk, ⅓ cup of the sugar and the orange zest in a medium saucepan. Bring to a simmer over moderate heat. Remove from the heat, cover and stand for 30 minutes. Discard the orange zest.

3. Preheat the oven to 160°C. Whisk together the whole eggs, egg whites, vanilla essence and the remaining sugar in a large bowl. Strain the milk into the egg mixture and whisk to combine.

4. Pour the custard into the prepared custard cups and place the baking dish in the oven. Pour boiling water into the dish to come halfway up the sides of the cups. Bake for 45 minutes or until a knife inserted in the centre of a custard comes out clean.

5. Remove the cups from the baking dish and cool on a rack, then refrigerate until ready to serve. Run a knife around the edge of the cups and invert the crème caramel onto dessert plates.

Nutrients per serving: Kilojoules 1066; Fibre 0g; Protein 10g; Carbohydrate 46g; Saturated Fat 2g; Total Fat 4g; Cholesterol 131mg

Rice Frittata

Preparation: 10 minutes / Cooking: 22 minutes / Serves: 4

3 eggs
4 egg whites
2 cups cooked rice
½ cup grated Parmesan cheese
1 tablespoon chopped fresh thyme leaves
Salt
Freshly ground pepper
1 tablespoon olive oil
1 large onion, diced
⅓ cup Roasted Red Capsicum, diced (recipe, page 61)

1. Whisk together the whole eggs and egg whites in a large bowl. Whisk in the rice, Parmesan, thyme and salt and pepper to taste.

2. Heat the oil in a 23 cm flameproof frying pan over moderately high heat. Fry the onion for 5 minutes or until translucent. Pour in the egg mixture and sprinkle with the capsicum. Cook, without stirring, for 15 minutes or until the eggs are set around the edges and almost set in the centre. Meanwhile, preheat the griller.

3. Grill the frittata 15 cm from the heat for 1 to 2 minutes or until the top is set. Serve hot.

Nutrients per serving: Kilojoules 1311; Fibre 1g; Protein 17g; Carbohydrate 30g; Saturated Fat 4g; Total Fat 14g; Cholesterol 198mg

Crème Caramel

Grains
Pasta

and Pasta

Barley

Cholesterol-lowering soluble fibre is barley's biggest feature. The plump, pearly grains are also rich in B vitamins and magnesium.

Healthy Highlights

Pearl barley
1 serving, cooked
(110g)

		Nutrients % RDI	
Kilojoules	490	Thiamin	25%
Fibre	3.9g	Niacin	16%
Protein	3.4g	Magnesium	11%
Carbohydrate	23.2g	Phosphorus	10%
Saturated Fat	0.2g		
Total Fat	1g		
Cholesterol	0mg		
Sodium	9mg		

Shopping & Preparation

At the market Pearl barley is the most common type; it has been milled several times to completely remove the hull, leaving the grain pearly and smooth. Whole (pot) barley has about half the bran left on the grain. Some health food shops also stock barley flakes (sometimes called rolled barley), barley grits and barley flour.

Basic cooking For pearl barley, use three times as much water as grain. Stir the pearl barley into boiling water, then cover and simmer until tender (about 45 to 50 minutes). Barley grits are parboiled, and barley flakes are usually soaked for up to an hour, to soften them before using in recipes. Whole barley, however, needs to be soaked for at least 2 hours before cooking to make it edible.

Barley & Vegetable Salad

Preparation: 20 minutes / Cooking: 45 minutes / Serves: 4

1½ cups pearl barley

Salt

3 teaspoons olive oil

1 yellow or red capsicum, cut into 1cm squares

1 zucchini, cut into 1cm chunks

3 cloves garlic, crushed

⅓ cup chopped fresh mint

¼ cup lemon juice

½ teaspoon black pepper

250g egg tomatoes, cut into thin wedges

1 cucumber, peeled, seeded and cut into 5mm slices

200g mild goat cheese or feta cheese, crumbled

1. Bring 3 cups water to the boil in a large saucepan. Add the barley and a pinch of salt and cook for 45 minutes or until tender. Drain well.

2. Meanwhile, heat 2 teaspoons of the oil in a large nonstick frying pan over moderate heat. Add the capsicum, zucchini and garlic. Cook, stirring frequently, for 5 minutes or until the capsicum is crisp-tender.

3. Whisk together the mint, lemon juice, pepper and the remaining oil in a large bowl. Add the barley, cooked vegetables, the tomatoes and the cucumber, tossing to combine. Add the cheese and toss gently. Serve at room temperature.

Nutrients per serving: Kilojoules 1545; Fibre 9g; Protein 15g; Carbohydrate 46g; Saturated Fat 6g; Total Fat 13g; Cholesterol 20mg

Did you know?

In Australia, barley – in the form of malted barley – is used primarily to make beer. A by-product of malted barley is malt extract, an ingredient in malted drinks and powders.

Spiced Barley & Corn

Preparation: 15 minutes / Cooking: 55 minutes / Serves: 4

4 spring onions, thinly sliced

½ cup firmly packed fresh coriander or flat-leaf parsley sprigs

2 tablespoons chopped fresh ginger

3 cloves garlic, peeled

3 teaspoons olive oil

1 green capsicum, diced

1 cup pearl barley

1 cup chicken stock

1 cup canned no-added-salt chopped tomatoes

½ teaspoon ground coriander

Salt

1¼ cups frozen corn kernels, thawed

1. Combine the spring onions, fresh coriander, ginger, garlic and 2 tablespoons water in a blender and purée.

2. Heat the oil in a large saucepan over moderate heat. Add the capsicum and cook for 4 minutes or until crisp-tender. Add the spring onion purée and cook for 2 minutes. Add the barley, stirring to coat.

3. Add the stock, ½ cup water, the tomatoes, ground coriander and a pinch of salt, and bring to the boil. Reduce to a simmer, cover, then cook for 45 minutes or until the barley is tender. Remove from the heat and stir in the corn.

Nutrients per serving: Kilojoules 1087; Fibre 8g; Protein 8g; Carbohydrate 43g; Saturated Fat 1g; Total Fat 6g; Cholesterol 0mg

Old-Fashioned Mushroom & Barley Soup

Old-Fashioned Mushroom & Barley Soup

Preparation: 20 minutes / Cooking: 1 hour / Serves: 4

2 teaspoons olive oil

1 onion, finely chopped

2 cloves garlic, crushed

2 carrots, diced

375g button mushrooms, sliced

125g shiitake mushrooms, trimmed and thinly sliced

½ cup pearl barley

2 cups chicken stock

1 cup no-added-salt tomato purée

¾ teaspoon ground ginger

½ teaspoon pepper

1 tablespoon chopped fresh parsley

1. Heat the oil in a large saucepan over moderate heat. Add the onion and garlic and cook for 5 minutes or until tender. Add the carrots and cook, stirring frequently, for 4 minutes or until crisp-tender. Add the mushrooms and cook, stirring frequently, for 5 minutes or until tender.

2. Stir in the barley, stock, 2 cups water, the tomato purée, ginger and pepper. Bring to the boil, reduce to a simmer, cover and cook for 45 minutes or until the barley is tender. Sprinkle with the parsley before serving.

Nutrients per serving: Kilojoules 745; Fibre 8g; Protein 9g; Carbohydrate 27g; Saturated Fat 1g; Total Fat 4g; Cholesterol 0mg

Did you know?

Barley contains the same kind of soluble fibre found in oats. One study divided subjects into two groups: one of the groups received daily servings of oats, while the other was given barley. The cholesterol levels in both groups dropped about 5 per cent.

Burghul

Burghul gives you dietary fibre, B vitamins, and a healthy helping of minerals, including good quantities of magnesium.

Healthy Highlights

½ cup, soaked in water (100g)		Nutrients % RDI	
Kilojoules	652	Thiamin	48%
Fibre	6.3g	Niacin	28%
Protein	5.3g	Magnesium	21%
Carbohydrate	31.1g	Iron	14%
Saturated Fat	0.1g	Phosphorus	14%
Total Fat	0.9g		
Cholesterol	0mg		
Sodium	2mg		

Shopping & Preparation

At the market Burghul (which is sometimes known as bulghar or bulgur, as well as cracked wheat) is made from parboiled wheat kernels that have been dried and cracked. It is good for stuffings and pilafs, but is traditionally used for tabbouleh and other salads.

Basic cooking Place 1 cup dry burghul in a heatproof bowl or a saucepan; add 3 cups boiling water and let stand for 1 hour. Drain off any excess liquid and squeeze the burghul dry.

After steeping burghul, pour off any water that remains and then squeeze the burghul with your hands until it is quite dry, transferring the burghul to a clean bowl as you work.

Mushroom & Burghul Pilaf

Preparation: 15 minutes / Cooking: 30 minutes / Serves: 4

3 teaspoons olive oil

4 spring onions, thinly sliced

2 cloves garlic, crushed

1 carrot, diced

1 stalk celery, diced

250g mushrooms, thinly sliced

1 cup burghul

1½ cups chicken stock

1 teaspoon fresh rosemary leaves

Salt

White pepper

1. Preheat the oven to 180°C. Heat the oil in a flameproof casserole over moderate heat. Add the spring onions and garlic and cook for 2 minutes or until the onions are soft. Stir in the carrot and celery and cook for 4 minutes or until the carrot is crisp-tender. Add the mushrooms and cook for 3 minutes or until the mushrooms are softened.

2. Stir in the burghul, stock, 1 cup water, the rosemary, and a pinch each of salt and pepper, and bring to the boil. Cover and bake in the oven for 20 minutes or until the burghul is tender and the liquid has been absorbed.

Nutrients per serving: Kilojoules 896; Fibre 10g; Protein 9g; Carbohydrate 32g; Saturated Fat 1g; Total Fat 5g; Cholesterol 0mg

Did you know?

• The bone-building manganese in burghul helps to prevent osteoporosis.

• Although a small percentage of the fibre-rich bran is removed from burghul during processing, plenty remains. A 1½-cup serving of cooked burghul supplies half the daily fibre recommendation.

Mexican-Style Tabbouleh

Preparation: 15 minutes / Soaking: 1 hour / Standing: 1 hour / Serves: 4

1 cup burghul

3 cups boiling water

¼ cup lime juice

3 teaspoons olive oil

1 teaspoon ground cumin

1 teaspoon dried oregano

Salt

2 cups cherry tomatoes, halved

1 cup frozen corn kernels, thawed

1 green capsicum, diced

3 spring onions, thinly sliced

½ cup chopped fresh coriander or parsley

1. Combine the burghul and boiling water in a large bowl. Stand for 1 hour. Drain and squeeze the burghul dry.

2. Meanwhile, whisk together the lime juice, oil, cumin, oregano and a pinch of salt in a large bowl. Stir in the tomatoes, corn, capsicum, spring onions and coriander. Add the drained burghul and toss to combine. Stand for at least 1 hour. Serve chilled or at room temperature.

Nutrients per serving: Kilojoules 957; Fibre 9g; Protein 7g; Carbohydrate 38g; Saturated Fat 1g; Total Fat 5g; Cholesterol 0mg

Mexican-Style Tabbouleh

Cornmeal

Cornmeal is a good source of B vitamins. The nutrient content of both the white and yellow varieties is similar, but the yellow is higher in beta-carotene.

Healthy Highlights

1 serving, cooked (160g)		Nutrients % RDI	
Kilojoules	275	Thiamin	10%
Fibre	0.6g		
Protein	1.6g		
Carbohydrate	13.8g		
Saturated Fat	0g		
Total Fat	0.3g		
Cholesterol	0mg		
Sodium	1mg		

Shopping & Preparation

At the market Cornmeal – not to be confused with cornflour – can be bought either coarsely ground or highly refined. It is often sold as polenta (although technically, polenta is the name of a popular dish made from cornmeal) and instant polenta – which requires considerably less cooking time – is widely available.

Basic cooking To precook cornmeal for polenta, sprinkle 1 cup coarse cornmeal into 1.25 litres boiling water in a large saucepan, stirring constantly with a wooden spoon until all the cornmeal is incorporated. Cook, uncovered, for 55 to 60 minutes, stirring frequently. The polenta is cooked when it comes away cleanly from the sides of the saucepan. For instant polenta, sprinkle 1 cup into 1.25 litres boiling water, stirring with a wooden spoon for 3 to 4 minutes. Remove from the heat and proceed with your recipe.

Cornmeal Muffins with Fennel & Bacon

Cornmeal Muffins with Fennel & Bacon

Preparation: 10 minutes / Cooking: 30 minutes / Makes: 12 muffins

100g bacon, coarsely chopped

Vegetable oil (optional)

¼ cup firmly packed light brown sugar

1 egg

1 cup yellow cornmeal

1 cup plain flour

3 teaspoons baking powder

1½ teaspoons fennel seeds

Salt

1 cup low-fat milk

½ cup sultanas

1. Cook the bacon in a small frying pan over low heat for 5 minutes or until it is crisp and has rendered its fat. Drain the bacon on paper towels. Pour the bacon fat into a measuring cup. If you don't have ¼ cup, add enough oil to make up the difference.

2. Preheat the oven to 200°C. Line a 12-hole tray of 6 cm muffin cups with paper liners or spray with cooking spray. Beat the bacon fat and brown sugar with an electric mixer in a medium bowl until well combined. Add the egg and beat until well combined.

3. Stir together the cornmeal, flour, baking powder, fennel seeds and a pinch of salt in a medium bowl. Alternately fold the cornmeal mixture and the milk into the egg mixture, beginning and ending with the cornmeal mixture. Fold in the sultanas and the bacon.

4. Spoon the batter into the prepared muffin cups and bake for 25 minutes or until a skewer inserted in the centre of a muffin comes out clean. Cool for 10 minutes in the tray, then transfer the muffins to a rack to cool completely.

Nutrients per muffin: Kilojoules 635; Fibre 1g; Protein 6g; Carbohydrate 27g; Saturated Fat 1g; Total Fat 2g; Cholesterol 27mg

Lemon & Poppyseed Loaf

Preparation: 10 minutes / Cooking: 1 hour / Serves: 12

1½ tablespoons
   poppyseeds

¼ cup vegetable oil

1½ tablespoons
   unsalted butter

1 cup sugar

2 eggs

1 egg white

3 teaspoons grated
   lemon zest

1 teaspoon bicarbonate
   of soda

1 cup plain low-fat
   yoghurt

1 cup yellow cornmeal

1 cup plain flour

1. Preheat the oven to 180°C. Place the poppyseeds in a small baking dish and bake for 5 minutes or until lightly toasted and crunchy. Spray a 20 x 13 cm loaf tin with cooking spray.

2. Blend the oil, butter and sugar with an electric mixer in a medium bowl. Add the whole eggs and the egg white, one at a time, beating well after each addition. Beat in the lemon zest.

3. Stir the bicarbonate of soda into the yoghurt in a small bowl. Stir together the cornmeal and flour. Alternately fold the cornmeal mixture and the yoghurt mixture into the egg mixture, beginning and ending with the cornmeal mixture. Fold in the poppyseeds.

4. Spoon the batter into the prepared tin and bake for 55 minutes or until a skewer inserted in the centre comes out clean. Cool for 10 minutes in the tin on a rack, then turn out onto the rack to cool completely.

Nutrients per serving: Kilojoules 990; Fibre 1g; Protein 5g; Carbohydrate 34g; Saturated Fat 2g; Total Fat 9g; Cholesterol 49mg

Did you know?

The colour of cornmeal (yellow or white) is determined by the type of corn used to make it. There's virtually no nutritional difference between the two, except that yellow cornmeal contains minute amounts of beta-carotene, alpha-carotene, lutein and zeaxanthin, which are all disease-fighting carotenoids.

Lemon & Poppyseed Loaf

Oats

Rich in magnesium, phosphorus, iron and B vitamins, oats are also a renowned source of betaglucan, a type of soluble fibre that helps to lower blood cholesterol.

Healthy Highlights

Rolled oats
1 serving, cooked
(180g)

		Nutrients	% RDI
Kilojoules	364	Magnesium	12%
Fibre	1.6g	Thiamin	11%
Protein	2.5g		
Carbohydrate	14.6g		
Saturated Fat	0.4g		
Total Fat	2g		
Cholesterol	0mg		
Sodium	2mg		

Shopping & Preparation

At the market Oats come in many forms. In addition to the familiar old-fashioned rolled oats (which are oat kernels rolled flat), you can buy quick-cooking and instant oats. Whole oats, which can be cooked like rice, are sold in health food shops. Also available are oat bran, the fibre-rich coarse outer layer of the grain, and oatmeal, which is finely ground grain traditionally used in oat biscuits and as a baby porridge.

Basic cooking For porridge, simply stir ½ cup rolled or quick-cooking oats into 1 cup boiling water in a small saucepan. Simmer rolled oats for 5 minutes; simmer quick-cooking oats for 1 minute, then cover and let stand for a few minutes, until the porridge is the desired consistency.

Oaty Macaroons

Preparation: 15 minutes / Cooking: 25 minutes / Makes: 30

2 cups rolled oats
½ cup chopped dried apples or raisins
⅓ cup flaked almonds
Salt
3 egg whites
¾ cup caster sugar
1 teaspoon vanilla essence

1. Preheat the oven to 180°C. Spray 2 baking trays with cooking spray; put aside. Place the oats in a small baking dish and toast in the oven, stirring occasionally, for 7 minutes. Transfer to a large bowl to cool.

2. Add the apples, almonds and a pinch of salt, stirring to combine. Whisk the egg whites until stiff peaks form, then gradually add the sugar, whisking until dissolved. Whisk in the vanilla essence. Fold into the oats and fruit.

3. Use a tablespoon to drop the mixture onto the prepared baking trays. Bake for 18 minutes or until golden brown and slightly firm. Cool for 5 minutes on the trays, then transfer the macaroons to a wire rack to cool completely.

Nutrients per macaroon: Kilojoules 233; Fibre 1g; Protein 1g; Carbohydrate 10g; Saturated Fat 0g; Total Fat 1g; Cholesterol 0mg

Did you know?

One study compared oat bran with two cholesterol-lowering drugs, and found that the oat bran was just as effective – and far cheaper.

Perfect Muesli ⓐ

Preparation: 5 minutes / Cooking: 21 minutes / Makes: 10 cups

5 cups rolled oats
½ cup flaked almonds
½ cup shredded coconut
¼ cup honey
⅓ cup sunflower seeds
1 cup wheatgerm
1 cup crunchy bran cereal
½ cup sultanas
1 cup sun-dried apricots, chopped

1. Preheat the oven to 200°C. Place 3 cups of the oats on a baking tray and cook for 4 minutes. Stir the oats and cook for a further 4 minutes or until crisp. Put aside in a large bowl.

2. Place the almonds on the baking tray and cook for 1 minute. Add the coconut and continue cooking for 3 minutes or until lightly golden. Add to the toasted oats and put aside.

3. Place the remaining oats on the baking tray, drizzle with honey and bake for 3 minutes. Stir well, then cook for a further 6 minutes, stirring again after 3 minutes. Allow to cool on the tray.

4. Add the honeyed oats, the sunflower kernels, wheatgerm, bran cereal, sultanas and apricots to the oat and nut mixture. Toss well to combine. Store the cooled muesli in an airtight container.

Nutrients per ½ cup: Kilojoules 816; Fibre 5g; Protein 6g; Carbohydrate 28g; Saturated Fat 2g; Total Fat 7g; Cholesterol 0mg

Oaty Macaroons

Pasta & Noodles

The inspiration for countless quick, healthy meals, pasta and noodles are a low-fat source of protein and, made with enriched flour, offer some vitamins and minerals.

Healthy Highlights

Pasta
1 serving, cooked (160g)

		Nutrients % RDI	
Kilojoules	795	Niacin	13%
Fibre	2.9g	Phosphorus	11%
Protein	6.4g		
Carbohydrate	39.4g		
Saturated Fat	0g		
Total Fat	0.5g		
Cholesterol	0mg		
Sodium	3mg		

Wholemeal pasta
1 serving, cooked (160g)

		Nutrients % RDI	
Kilojoules	864	Thiamin	34%
Fibre	9.1g	Niacin	27%
Protein	8.6g	Iron	24%
Carbohydrate	39.4g	Phosphorus	24%
Saturated Fat	0.2g	Magnesium	23%
Total Fat	1.3g		
Cholesterol	0mg		
Sodium	8mg		

Egg noodles/pasta
1 serving, cooked (170g)

		Nutrients % RDI	
Kilojoules	930	Niacin	14%
Fibre	3.1g	Phosphorus	13%
Protein	9g		
Carbohydrate	43.5g		
Saturated Fat	0.2g		
Total Fat	1g		
Cholesterol	0mg		
Sodium	12mg		

Asian noodles
1 serving, cooked (170g)

		Nutrients % RDI	
Kilojoules	1097	Thiamin	17%
Fibre	4.9g	Riboflavin	13%
Protein	6g	Niacin	11%
Carbohydrate	35.7g		
Saturated Fat	5.1g		
Total Fat	10.5g		
Cholesterol	3mg		
Sodium	11mg		

Tortellini with Zesty Tomato Sauce

Tortellini with Zesty Tomato Sauce

Preparation: 15 minutes / Cooking: 15 minutes / Serves: 4

2 teaspoons olive oil

1 small onion, finely chopped

3 cloves garlic, crushed

1 can (400g) no-added-salt chopped tomatoes

1 cup no-added-salt tomato pasta sauce

¼ teaspoon crushed dried chilli

Salt

500g cheese-filled tortellini

1. Heat the oil in a large nonstick frying pan over moderate heat. Cook the onion and garlic for 5 minutes or until soft. Add the tomatoes, tomato pasta sauce, dried chilli and a pinch of salt. Simmer for 10 minutes.

2. Meanwhile, cook the tortellini in a large saucepan of boiling water according to the packet directions, until firm-tender. Drain and toss with the sauce.

Nutrients per serving: Kilojoules 1717; Fibre 6g; Protein 20g; Carbohydrate 42g; Saturated Fat 10g; Total Fat 18g; Cholesterol 45mg

Did you know?

The most nutritious pastas are made from semolina, a coarse flour ground from durum wheat. Durum is a hard grain that has a higher protein content than other types of wheat.

Bow-Ties with Bocconcini & Fresh Tomatoes

Preparation: 10 minutes / Cooking: 10 minutes / Serves: 4

375g bow-tie pasta

1 cup no-added-salt tomato pasta sauce

1 cup chopped fresh tomatoes

¼ cup fresh basil leaves, cut into thin strips

½ teaspoon sugar

Salt

200g bocconcini, diced

1. Cook the pasta in a large saucepan of boiling water according to the packet directions, until firm-tender. Drain.

2. Meanwhile, bring the tomato sauce to the boil in a large frying pan. Add the fresh tomatoes, basil, sugar and a pinch of salt and heat through.

3. Transfer the sauce to a large bowl, add the hot pasta and the bocconcini. Toss well.

Nutrients per serving: Kilojoules 2115; Fibre 6g; Protein 20g; Carbohydrate 86g; Saturated Fat 5g; Total Fat 9g; Cholesterol 20mg

Did you know?

Added flavours – such as spinach or tomato – do little to increase the nutritional value of pasta.

Bow-Ties with Bocconcini & Fresh Tomatoes

Shopping & Preparation

At the market There are hundreds of different pasta shapes, but all dried pastas are very similar in nutritional value. Dried pasta is available from supermarkets, while fresh pasta is available from specialist shops. The range of noodles, both fresh and dried, is also large. Most commonly found are egg noodles, cellophane noodles, soba noodles (made from buckwheat flour), udon noodles, hokkien noodles and somen noodles. Instant noodles are quite often deep fried, making them very high in fat, so always read the label carefully. The best range of fresh noodles is to be found in Asian food shops, while dried noodles are available in all supermarkets.

Look for For the best texture, choose a brand of pasta made from pure semolina. This includes most imported and domestic brands. When buying fresh noodles, choose those that are soft, with no signs of discoloration. Dried noodles should also be free of any discoloration. Store dried pasta and noodles in a cool cupboard for up to 12 months. Use fresh pasta and noodles the same day you buy them, if possible. Otherwise, keep them in the refrigerator. Never exceed the use-by date.

Basic cooking Cook pasta in plenty of boiling water to keep it from sticking together. Add the pasta all at once, stir briefly, and return the water to the boil. Time the cooking from the second boil. Test the pasta a little sooner than the directions recommend (overcooking ruins pasta) and drain it immediately when it is firm-tender (al dente) to the bite. Fresh rice noodles need only to be rinsed in boiling water; fresh egg noodles, udon noodles, somen noodles and cellophane noodles take about 2 to 3 minutes; hokkien noodles need 3 to 4 minutes; soba noodles need 4 to 5 minutes; while rice stick and rice vermicelli need only 1 minute, after soaking in hot water for 10 to 15 minutes.

Salmon & Pasta Salad

Preparation: 10 minutes / Cooking: 10 minutes / Serves: 4

300g penne

½ cup plain low-fat yoghurt

¼ cup low-fat mayonnaise

1 tablespoon snipped fresh dill

2 tablespoons lemon juice

Salt

1 can (415g) salmon, drained

1 cup cooked peas

1. Cook the pasta in a large saucepan of boiling water according to the packet directions, until firm-tender.

2. Meanwhile, combine the yoghurt, mayonnaise, dill, lemon juice and a pinch of salt in a large bowl. Add the salmon and peas.

3. Drain the pasta, add to the bowl, and toss.

Nutrients per serving: Kilojoules 1658; Fibre 5g; Protein 29g; Carbohydrate 51g; Saturated Fat 2g; Total Fat 8g; Cholesterol 67mg

Chicken & Soba Noodle Salad

Preparation: 20 minutes / Cooking: 15 minutes / Serves: 4

¾ cup chicken stock

2 cloves garlic, crushed

½ teaspoon ground ginger

¼ teaspoon dried crushed chilli

375g skinless, boneless chicken breasts

300g soba noodles (buckwheat noodles)

250g green beans, halved

2 carrots, cut into 5cm matchsticks

1½ tablespoons dark brown sugar

3 teaspoons reduced-salt soy sauce

3 teaspoons peanut or other vegetable oil

2 cups finely shredded cabbage

1. Bring the stock, garlic, ginger and chilli to the boil over moderate heat in a large frying pan. Reduce to a simmer, add the chicken, cover and cook, turning the chicken over once, for 10 minutes or until the chicken is cooked through. Transfer the chicken to a plate, reserving the cooking liquid. When it is cool enough to handle, shred the chicken.

2. Meanwhile, cook the noodles in a large saucepan of boiling water according to the packet directions, until firm-tender. Add the beans and carrots for the last minute of cooking time; drain.

3. Whisk together the brown sugar, soy sauce, oil and the reserved cooking liquid in a large bowl. Add the shredded chicken, noodles, beans, carrots and the cabbage, tossing to combine. Serve at room temperature or chilled.

Nutrients per serving: Kilojoules 1710; Fibre 11g; Protein 28g; Carbohydrate 61g; Saturated Fat 2g; Total Fat 8g; Cholesterol 44mg

Did you know?

Buckwheat, from which soba noodles and kaska (roasted buckwheat) are made, is not a true grain; it is the fruit of a rhubarb-like plant. Buckwheat, however, has been found to contain more lysine (an essential amino acid) than do grains, and is also gluten-free.

Chicken & Soba Noodle Salad

Did you know?

• Pasta with tomato sauce is not just a tradition, it's a smart nutritional choice: the vitamin C in the tomatoes helps your body absorb the iron in the pasta.

• People used to think that pasta was fattening, but only the sauce can make it a high-fat dish: one serving of plain cooked pasta contains less than 1g of fat.

Radiatore with Pesto

Preparation: 15 minutes / Cooking: 15 minutes / Serves: 4

375g radiatore pasta

2 cups firmly packed fresh basil leaves

3 cloves garlic, chopped

½ cup chicken or vegetable stock

3 teaspoons olive oil

3 teaspoons reduced-fat cream cheese

Salt

Freshly ground pepper

½ cup grated Parmesan cheese

1. Cook the pasta in a large saucepan of boiling water according to the packet directions, until firm-tender. Drain and transfer to a large bowl.

2. Meanwhile, combine the basil, garlic, stock, oil, cream cheese, and salt and pepper to taste, in a food processor and process to a smooth purée. Add the Parmesan and process briefly, just to combine.

3. Add the mixture to the hot pasta, tossing well.

Nutrients per serving: Kilojoules 1458; Fibre 5g; Protein 14g; Carbohydrate 54g; Saturated Fat 3g; Total Fat 8g; Cholesterol 12mg

Chinese Chicken Noodle Soup @

Preparation: 10 minutes / Cooking: 10 minutes / Serves: 4

2 cups chicken stock

2 teaspoons reduced-salt soy sauce

1 teaspoon sesame oil

1 tablespoon rice vinegar

250g skinless, boneless chicken breast, sliced

200g vermicelli or fresh egg noodles

2 cups chopped bok choy

1 spring onion, chopped

1. Bring the stock, 3 cups water, the soy sauce, sesame oil and rice vinegar to the boil in a large saucepan. Add the chicken and cook for 2 minutes.

2. Add the vermicelli, bok choy and spring onion and cook for a further 2 minutes or until the noodles are done.

Nutrients per serving: Kilojoules 1268; Fibre 3g; Protein 19g; Carbohydrate 42g; Saturated Fat 1g; Total Fat 5g; Cholesterol 29mg

Did you know?

Pasta sold in cardboard boxes retains more riboflavin than pasta packed in plastic bags. At home, store dried pasta in an opaque container rather than a glass jar.

Chinese Chicken Noodle Soup

Pasta with Butternut Sauce

Pasta with Butternut Sauce

Preparation: 10 minutes / Cooking: 55 minutes / Serves: 4

1 butternut pumpkin (about 1 kg), halved lengthways and seeded

375g fusilli or rotelle pasta

12 fresh sage leaves

2 teaspoons olive oil

2 cloves garlic, crushed

⅓ cup blanched almonds

⅓ cup grated Parmesan cheese

1½ teaspoons mild mustard

Salt

Freshly ground black pepper

1. Preheat the oven to 200°C. Place the pumpkin, cut-side-down, in a small baking dish. Add ½ cup water, then cover and bake for 45 minutes or until the pumpkin is tender. When cool enough to handle, scoop the flesh into a food processor.

2. Meanwhile, cook the pasta in a large saucepan of boiling water according to the packet directions, until firm-tender. Drain the pasta, reserving ⅔ cup of the cooking water, and transfer to a large bowl. Reserve three of the sage leaves for a garnish.

3. Heat the oil in a small nonstick frying pan over low heat. Add the garlic and the remaining sage leaves and cook for 2 minutes or until the garlic is softened.

4. Transfer the garlic and sage to the food processor along with the reserved pasta cooking water, the almonds, Parmesan, mustard, and salt and pepper to taste. Process until smooth and add to the pasta, tossing to coat. Top with another grinding of pepper and serve garnished with the reserved sage leaves.

Nutrients per serving: Kilojoules 1747; Fibre 9g; Protein 16g; Carbohydrate 60g; Saturated Fat 2g; Total Fat 12g; Cholesterol 7mg

Did you know?

If you like wholemeal pasta, with its earthy flavour and chewy texture, you reap a nutritious bonus: wholemeal pasta has more fibre than semolina pasta.

Rice & Wild Rice

Half the world's people rely on rice as their staple food. Rice offers B vitamins and some minerals; its protein features a good balance of amino acids. Wild rice – not a true grain but the seed of a wild grass – supplies slightly more protein than brown rice, and is considerably lower in kilojoules.

Healthy Highlights

White rice
1 serving, boiled
(170g)

Kilojoules	887	Nutrients % RDI	
Fibre	0.9g	Niacin	13%
Protein	3.9g		
Carbohydrate	47.6g		
Saturated Fat	0g		
Total Fat	0.3g		
Cholesterol	0mg		
Sodium	9mg		

Brown rice
1 serving, boiled
(150g)

Kilojoules	945	Nutrients % RDI	
Fibre	2.3g	Magnesium	27%
Protein	4.8g	Niacin	23%
Carbohydrate	47.7g	Thiamin	22%
Saturated Fat	0.3g	Phosphorus	20%
Total Fat	1.5g	Zinc	11%
Cholesterol	0mg		
Sodium	3mg		

Wild rice
1 serving, boiled
(130g)

Kilojoules	533	Nutrients % RDI	
Fibre	2.3g	Niacin	18%
Protein	5.2g	Folate	17%
Carbohydrate	25.2g	Magnesium	15%
Saturated Fat	0g	Zinc	14%
Total Fat	0.4g	Phosphorus	11%
Cholesterol	0mg		
Sodium	4mg		

Italian Rice & Cheese Torte

Preparation: 15 minutes / Cooking: 1 hour 5 minutes / Serves: 8

1½ cups rice

⅓ cup sun-dried tomato halves (not oil-packed), chopped

4 cloves garlic, crushed

Salt

¾ cup chopped fresh basil

125g Fontina cheese, shredded

125g mozzarella, shredded

2 tablespoons grated Parmesan cheese

1 egg, lightly beaten

2 egg whites, lightly beaten

1. Bring 3¼ cups water to the boil in a medium saucepan. Add the rice, sun-dried tomatoes, garlic and a pinch of salt. Reduce to a simmer, cover and cook for 17 minutes or until the rice is tender. Transfer the rice to a large bowl.

2. Preheat the oven to 200°C. Spray a 22 cm springform tin with cooking spray. Stir the basil, Fontina, mozzarella and Parmesan into the rice until well combined. Stir in the egg and the egg whites. Transfer to the prepared tin, smoothing the top. Cover with foil and bake for 20 minutes. Uncover and bake for 25 minutes or until the rice is set. Remove the sides of the tin, cut the torte into wedges, and serve hot or at room temperature.

Nutrients per serving: Kilojoules 1185; Fibre 2g; Protein 14g; Carbohydrate 33g; Saturated Fat 6g; Total Fat 11g; Cholesterol 61mg

Did you know?

It's not necessary or desirable to wash rice before or after you cook it; doing so will rinse away vitamins and minerals.

Biryani-Style Rice

Preparation: 10 minutes / Cooking: 30 minutes / Serves: 4

3 teaspoons vegetable oil

½ teaspoon cinnamon

½ teaspoon ground cardamom

½ teaspoon ground turmeric

Ground cloves

1 onion, finely chopped

1 cup basmati rice, well rinsed

2 tablespoons plain low-fat yoghurt

Salt

½ cup sultanas

¼ cup coarsely chopped pistachios

1. Preheat the oven to 180°C. Heat the oil in a flameproof casserole over moderate heat. Add the cinnamon, cardamom, turmeric and a pinch of cloves, and cook for 30 seconds or until the spices are fragrant. Add the onion and cook for 7 minutes or until tender.

2. Stir in the rice, yoghurt, 2½ cups water and a pinch of salt, and bring to the boil. Cover and bake for 25 minutes or until the rice is tender. Stir in the sultanas and pistachios.

Nutrients per serving: Kilojoules 1413; Fibre 3g; Protein 6g; Carbohydrate 60g; Saturated Fat 1g; Total Fat 8g; Cholesterol 0mg

Prawn Jambalaya

Prawn Jambalaya

Preparation: 25 minutes / Cooking: 30 minutes / Serves: 4

3 teaspoons olive oil

5 spring onions, thinly sliced

3 cloves garlic, crushed

1 stalk celery, sliced

1 green capsicum, cut into 1cm squares

1 red capsicum, cut into 1cm squares

125g fresh chorizo sausage, thinly sliced

1¼ cups rice

1 cup chicken stock

1 teaspoon fresh thyme leaves

½ teaspoon black pepper

500g medium green prawns, peeled with tails left attached

1. Heat the oil in a large saucepan over moderate heat. Add the spring onions and garlic and fry for 1 minute or until soft. Add the celery and capsicums and cook for 5 minutes or until the capsicums are crisp-tender. Stir in the chorizo.

2. Add the rice, stirring to coat. Add the stock, 1¾ cups water, the thyme and black pepper, and bring to the boil. Reduce to a simmer, cover and cook for 17 minutes or until the rice is tender. Stir in the prawns, cover and cook for 3 to 4 minutes or until the prawns are firm and pink.

Nutrients per serving: Kilojoules 1939; Fibre 3g; Protein 27g; Carbohydrate 56g; Saturated Fat 4g; Total Fat 14g; Cholesterol 137mg

Did you know?

• When rice kernels are milled to produce white rice, the bran and germ are polished away. The main advantage of brown rice over white is that it retains its bran, which gives brown rice a superior fibre content.

• Soaking brown rice overnight can cut the cooking time in half. The key to conserving the B vitamins is to soak the rice in the measured amount of cold water, and then to cook the rice in the same water.

Shopping & Preparation

At the market In addition to long-grain brown and white rice, try medium- and short-grain types such as Carnaroli and Arborio (traditionally used for risotto), which cook up softer and stickier. Quick-cooking rice is precooked. Fragrant rices, such as basmati and jasmine, have a delicately sweet, nutlike aroma and flavour. Asian rices are becoming increasingly popular, and thus more readily available. You'll find black and white glutinous rices (also known as sticky rice) in all Asian food shops and many larger supermarkets. Health food shops also stock rice bran, ground rice and rice flour. Wild rice is sold at most supermarkets and in specialist food shops. It is dark brown, with a nutty flavour, and is somewhat chewy in texture. A commercially packaged brown and wild rice mixture is also available.

Preparation Unlike regular rice, wild rice must be thoroughly rinsed before cooking to eliminate any chaff or debris that may remain after the rice is hulled. (Wild rice is not milled like regular rice.)

Place raw wild rice in a colander or strainer and rinse under running water until the water runs clear.

Basic cooking Add the rice to boiling water (use two to three times as much water as rice), cover and simmer for 12 to 15 minutes (for white rice), 40 minutes (for brown), or 45 to 50 minutes (for wild rice). You can add more boiling water if the water is absorbed before the rice is done, but be quick about re-covering the pot. One cup of uncooked white rice will yield about 3 cups cooked; 1 cup of brown rice will yield about 2½ cups cooked; 1 cup of wild rice will yield about 4 cups cooked.

Green Rice

Preparation: 5 minutes / Cooking: 15 minutes
Serves: 4

3 teaspoons olive oil
4 spring onions, sliced
2 cloves garlic, crushed
1 cup rice
Salt
½ cup chopped fresh coriander
   or flat-leaf parsley leaves

1. Heat the oil in a medium saucepan over moderate heat. Add the spring onions and garlic and cook for 3 minutes or until soft.

2. Add the rice, 2¼ cups water, and a pinch of salt, and cook for 12 minutes until the rice is tender. Stir in the coriander.

Nutrients per serving: Kilojoules 931; Fibre 2g; Protein 4g; Carbohydrate 42g; Saturated Fat 0g; Total Fat 4g; Cholesterol 0mg

Did you know?

People with multiple food allergies are rarely allergic to rice, which is also gluten-free.

Brown Rice & Nut Pilaf

Preparation: 10 minutes / Cooking: 50 minutes
Serves: 4

3 teaspoons olive oil
1 large onion, chopped
3 cloves garlic, crushed
1 cup brown rice
1¼ cups chicken stock
1 teaspoon fresh rosemary leaves
¼ cup slivered almonds, toasted

1. Heat the oil in a medium saucepan over moderate heat. Add the onion and garlic and cook for 5 minutes or until soft. Add the rice, stock, 1¼ cups water and the rosemary. Bring to the boil. Cover and simmer for 45 minutes.

2. Stir in the almonds before serving.

Nutrients per serving: Kilojoules 1529; Fibre 4g; Protein 9g; Carbohydrate 56g; Saturated Fat 1g; Total Fat 12g; Cholesterol 0mg

Spicy Tomato & Rice Soup

Preparation: 10 minutes / Cooking: 20 minutes / Serves: 4

⅔ cup rice

Salt

1 can (400g) no-added-salt chopped tomatoes

1 cup chicken stock

2 tablespoons tomato paste

¾ teaspoon ground ginger

¼ teaspoon cayenne pepper

1. Bring 3 cups water to the boil in a medium saucepan. Add the rice and a pinch of salt. Reduce to a simmer, cover and cook for 12 minutes or until the rice is tender.

2. Meanwhile, combine the tomatoes, stock, 1 cup water, the tomato paste, ginger and cayenne pepper in a large saucepan. Bring to the boil. Stir in the cooked rice and heat through.

Nutrients per serving: Kilojoules 646; Fibre 2g; Protein 4g; Carbohydrate 32g; Saturated Fat 0g; Total Fat 1g; Cholesterol 0mg

Did you know?

• Several studies have shown rice bran to lower blood cholesterol. It's believed that the oil found in the rice germ (which ends up in the bran when rice is milled) is the key component. Brown rice includes some of the germ, but pure rice bran is a far more concentrated source.

• You can sprinkle rice bran over your breakfast cereal or add it to baked goods.

Brown Rice & Nut Pilaf

Roasted Pumpkin Risotto

Preparation: 15 minutes / Cooking: 35 minutes / Serves: 6

2 tablespoons olive oil

1.2kg pumpkin, peeled and cut into 2.5cm cubes

1 small onion, finely chopped

2 cups Arborio rice

2 teaspoons rosemary leaves

4 cups chicken stock

Salt

Freshly ground black pepper

¼ cup grated Parmesan cheese

1. Preheat the oven to 180°C. Put 1 tablespoon of the oil in a small baking dish and add half the pumpkin. Roast in the oven for 30 minutes. Meanwhile, steam the remaining pumpkin for 15 to 20 minutes, then mash. Keep warm.

2. While the pumpkin is roasting, cook the onion in the remaining oil in a large nonstick frying pan over low heat for 5 minutes or until soft. Add the rice, raise the heat to moderate, and cook for 4 minutes, then add the rosemary.

3. Heat the stock in a large saucepan until it comes to a gentle simmer. Add 1 ladleful stock to the rice, stirring for about 3 minutes until the rice has absorbed almost all of the liquid.

4. Continue adding the stock, 1 ladleful at a time, until it has all been absorbed (about 20 to 25 minutes) and the rice is cooked and creamy.

5. Remove from the heat, season with salt and pepper to taste, then stir in the Parmesan and the mashed pumpkin. Turn the risotto out into a large bowl and serve topped with the cubes of roasted pumpkin.

Nutrients per serving: Kilojoules 1501; Fibre 4g; Protein 9g; Carbohydrate 61g; Saturated Fat 2g; Total Fat 8g; Cholesterol 3mg

Wild Rice & Pecan Stuffing

Wild Rice & Pecan Stuffing

Preparation: 10 minutes / Cooking: 1 hour / Serves: 6

2 teaspoons vegetable oil

1 large onion, finely chopped

3 cloves garlic, crushed

1 carrot, diced

1 stalk celery, diced

1 cup wild rice

1 cup chicken stock

2 teaspoons finely chopped fresh rosemary

Salt

Freshly ground pepper

1 cup canned sliced water chestnuts

⅓ cup chopped pecans

1. Preheat the oven to 180°C. Heat the oil in a flameproof casserole over moderate heat. Add the onion and garlic, and cook for 5 minutes or until soft. Add the carrot and celery and cook for 4 minutes or until the carrot is crisp-tender.

2. Stir in the wild rice, stock, 2 cups water, the rosemary, a pinch of salt and a good grinding of pepper. Bring to the boil. Cover, transfer to the oven, and bake for 50 minutes or until the wild rice is tender. Stir in the water chestnuts and pecans and serve with the poultry of your choice.

Nutrients per serving: Kilojoules 695; Fibre 4g; Protein 5g; Carbohydrate 20g; Saturated Fat 1g; Total Fat 7g; Cholesterol 0mg

Did you know?

Wild rice is a very good source of zinc, which might be called the 'food-lover's mineral' because it keeps your sense of taste working properly. Some studies have also shown that zinc (in the form of lozenges) helps fight the common cold.

Wheat

Wholemeal flour contains the grain's bran and its germ, too. The germ is rich in protein, vitamin E and B vitamins, while wheat bran is packed with fibre.

Healthy Highlights

Plain white flour
¼ cup (35g)

Kilojoules	509	Nutrients	% RDI
Fibre	1.3g	Thiamin	13%
Protein	3.8g	Niacin	10%
Carbohydrate	25.2g		
Saturated Fat	0.1g		
Total Fat	0.4g		
Cholesterol	0mg		
Sodium	1mg		

Wheatgerm
1 tablespoon (6g)

Kilojoules	77	Nutrients	% RDI
Fibre	1.1g	Folate	10%
Protein	1.5g		
Carbohydrate	2.2g		
Saturated Fat	0.1g		
Total Fat	0.4g		
Cholesterol	0mg		
Sodium	1mg		

Unprocessed wheat bran
2 tablespoons (10g)

Kilojoules	76	Nutrients	% RDI
Fibre	4.5g	Magnesium	18%
Protein	1.7g	Niacin	18%
Carbohydrate	1.8g	Folate	13%
Saturated Fat	0.1g	Iron	10%
Total Fat	0.5g	Phosphorus	10%
Cholesterol	0mg		
Sodium	2mg		

Shopping & Preparation

At the market Wheat flour is available as wholemeal flour or white flour (which has most of the nutrients but less fibre than wholemeal). Wheatgerm is the undeveloped grain and is usually eaten as a cereal. Wheat bran is the finely milled outer layers of the grain. Couscous is made from flour-coated semolina, which is the ground endosperm of hard durum wheat. Semolina flour is also available, and is used to make pasta. Whole wheat (sometimes called wheat berries) and wheat flakes (also known as rolled wheat) are available in health food shops. Store all wholemeal products, such as flour, wheat bran and wheatgerm, in tightly covered containers in the refrigerator or freezer.

Crunchy Dessert Topping

Preparation: 5 minutes / Cooking: 25 minutes
Makes: 2 cups (16 servings)

½ cup firmly packed dark brown sugar

2 teaspoons lemon juice

1½ cups toasted wheatgerm

3 teaspoons vegetable oil

¼ cup chopped pecans

1. Combine the brown sugar and lemon juice in a large frying pan. Cook over low heat, stirring frequently, for 2 minutes or until the sugar has melted. Stir in the wheatgerm and oil and cook, stirring frequently, for 9 minutes or until richly browned.

2. Stir in the pecans and cook for 1 minute. Cool the mixture to room temperature and transfer to an airtight container. You can store the topping at room temperature for up to 3 days, or freeze for longer storage.

Nutrients per serving: Kilojoules 293; Fibre 1g; Protein 2g; Carbohydrate 10g; Saturated Fat 0g; Total Fat 3g; Cholesterol 0mg

Crunchy Dessert Topping

Moroccan Couscous

Moroccan Couscous

Preparation: 10 minutes / Cooking: 10 minutes / Serves: 4

1 cup chicken stock

3 teaspoons vegetable oil

1½ teaspoons grated lemon zest

1 teaspoon ground cumin

Salt

300g couscous

2 cans (300g each) chickpeas, drained and rinsed

1 cup raisins

1. Bring the stock, 1¼ cups water, oil, lemon zest, cumin and a pinch of salt to the boil in a large saucepan. Add the couscous, return to the boil, then remove from the heat, cover and stand for 5 minutes.

2. Fluff the couscous with a fork; add the chickpeas and raisins. Toss well.

Nutrients per serving: Kilojoules 1496; Fibre 7g; Protein 11g; Carbohydrate 64g; Saturated Fat 1g; Total Fat 6g; Cholesterol 0mg

Did you know?

You can increase your fibre intake by substituting unprocessed wheat bran for some of the flour in your favourite muffin and loaf recipes. You may need to add a little extra liquid, as bran absorbs more liquid than flour does.

Nuts and Seeds

Beans

The unbeatable bean is a great low-fat, high-fibre protein source that's rich in folate (and other B vitamins) as well as minerals, including iron, potassium and magnesium.

Healthy Highlights

Red kidney beans
1 serving, cooked
(130g)

		Nutrients % RDI	
Kilojoules	399	Folate	23%
Fibre	9.4g	Potassium	19%
Protein	10.3g	Iron	18%
Carbohydrate	13.8g	Magnesium	18%
Saturated Fat	0.1g	Niacin	17%
Total Fat	0.7g	Phosphorus	17%
Cholesterol	0mg	Zinc	11%
Sodium	10mg		

Cannellini beans
1 serving, cooked
(130g)

		Nutrients % RDI	
Kilojoules	480	Folate	36%
Fibre	9.1g	Potassium	26%
Protein	10.8g	Magnesium	24%
Carbohydrate	18.3g	Iron	23%
Saturated Fat	0.1g	Phosphorus	21%
Total Fat	0.5g	Thiamin	21%
Cholesterol	0mg	Niacin	19%
Sodium	10mg	Calcium	11%
		Zinc	10%

Borlotti beans
1 serving, cooked
(130g)

		Nutrients % RDI	
Kilojoules	733	Folate	91%
Fibre	4.7g	Magnesium	28%
Protein	11.3g	Iron	27%
Carbohydrate	34.2g	Thiamin	27%
Saturated Fat	0.3g	Potassium	25%
Total Fat	0.8g	Phosphorus	20%
Cholesterol	0mg	Niacin	18%
Sodium	10mg	Zinc	12%
		Calcium	11%

Soya beans
1 serving, cooked
(130g)

		Nutrients % RDI	
Kilojoules	698	Folate	46%
Fibre	9.4g	Niacin	36%
Protein	17.6g	Magnesium	34%
Carbohydrate	3.1g	Potassium	28%
Saturated Fat	1.4g	Phosphorus	26%
Total Fat	10g	Iron	24%
Cholesterol	0mg	Zinc	17%
Sodium	12mg	Thiamin	13%
		Calcium	12%

Vegetarian Burgers

Preparation: 15 minutes / Cooking: 15 minutes / Serves: 4

2 cloves garlic, chopped

3 cups cooked borlotti beans

1½ tablespoons low-fat mayonnaise

3 teaspoons chilli sauce

2 teaspoons lime juice

2 tablespoons dry breadcrumbs

2 spring onions, thinly sliced

½ teaspoon pepper

Salt

2 tablespoons plain flour

1 tablespoon vegetable oil

4 hamburger buns, toasted

4 iceberg lettuce leaves

4 slices tomato

4 slices red onion

1. Mash the garlic, beans, mayonnaise, chilli sauce and lime juice in a large bowl with a potato masher or fork. Stir in the breadcrumbs, spring onions, pepper and a pinch of salt. Shape into 4 patties.

2. Dredge the patties in the flour, shaking off the excess. Heat the oil in a large nonstick frying pan over moderate heat. Cook the patties for 3 minutes each side or until browned and crisp on the outside and heated through.

3. Place the patties on hamburger buns and top each with lettuce, tomato and onion.

Nutrients per serving: Kilojoules 2256; Fibre 10g; Protein 21g; Carbohydrate 88g; Saturated Fat 2g; Total Fat 12g; Cholesterol 3mg

Did you know?

• Beans provide substantial amounts of both insoluble fibre (the kind that helps to prevent colon cancer) and soluble fibre (that helps lower blood cholesterol, thereby helping to prevent heart disease and stroke).

• To improve the digestibility of beans that are cooked from scratch – and to reduce possible flatulence – discard the soaking water and cook the beans in fresh water.

Tuscan White Bean & Tuna Salad

Preparation: 5 minutes / Serves: 6

2 cans (375g each) cannellini beans, drained and rinsed

1 can (425g) water-packed tuna, drained

1 red onion, sliced

¼ cup olive oil

3 teaspoons lemon juice

1 tablespoon fresh sage leaves

1 tablespoon chopped fresh parsley

1. Toss the beans, tuna, onion, oil, lemon juice and sage leaves together in a large serving bowl.

2. Sprinkle with the chopped parsley just before serving.

Nutrients per serving: Kilojoules 1082; Fibre 8g; Protein 24g; Carbohydrate 16g; Saturated Fat 2g; Total Fat 11g; Cholesterol 31mg

Tuscan White Bean & Tuna Salad

Chickpeas

1 serving, cooked (130g)		Nutrients % RDI	
Kilojoules	676	Folate	31%
Fibre	7.4g	Iron	27%
Protein	10g	Magnesium	18%
Carbohydrate	20.8g	Niacin	18%
Saturated Fat	0.5g	Phosphorus	15%
Total Fat	3.4g	Potassium	13%
Cholesterol	0mg	Zinc	13%
Sodium	31mg		

Shopping & Preparation

At the market Beans, peas and lentils are all members of the legume family, also known as pulses. Beans are widely available, dried or canned, in supermarkets. For an even greater selection, check Italian delicatessens and gourmet food shops. You'll usually find cannellini beans, pinto beans, red kidney beans, haricot beans (also known as navy or white beans, and commonly used in commercially canned baked beans), broad beans, mung beans, lima beans (butter beans), soya beans and chickpeas (garbanzos). Look also for black kidney beans, great northern beans, fava beans, adzuki beans, black-eyed beans and flageolet beans.

Preparation Before cooking dried beans, spread them out and pick through them, removing any dirt or grit, or damaged beans, then rinse the beans in cold water. Canned beans should be drained and rinsed to remove excess sodium.

Basic cooking Soaking dried beans will shorten their cooking time and double their volume. Place beans in a large saucepan and add cold water to cover. Stand for 8 to 12 hours. (For a quicker soak, bring the water slowly to the boil and simmer the beans for 2 minutes. Cover the saucepan, remove from the heat, and stand for 1 to 2 hours.) After soaking, drain the beans, add fresh unsalted water to cover (salt added to the cooking water will prevent the beans from becoming fully tender), bring to the boil, then simmer for about 1 hour or until tender. The beans are cooked when they are soft but not mushy.

Chickpea Soup with Carrots & Greens

Preparation: 10 minutes / Cooking: 15 minutes / Serves: 4

¾ cup chicken stock
2 carrots, diced
3 cloves garlic, crushed
2 tablespoons chopped fresh parsley
Freshly ground pepper
2 cups cooked chickpeas or red kidney beans
2 cups packed, torn spinach leaves
2 cups packed, torn watercress leaves

1. Bring the stock to the boil in a large saucepan over moderate heat. Add the carrots, garlic, parsley and a good grinding of pepper and cook for 5 minutes or until the carrots are tender. Add 1 cup water and the chickpeas and return to the boil. Reduce to a simmer, cover and cook for 7 minutes or until the chickpeas are piping hot.

2. Stir in the spinach and watercress leaves and cook for 1 minute or until the greens are just wilted.

Nutrients per serving: Kilojoules 594; Fibre 8g; Protein 9g; Carbohydrate 16g; Saturated Fat 1g; Total Fat 4g; Cholesterol 0mg

Did you know?

All beans supply some calcium: soya beans, borlotti beans and cannellini beans are among the best sources.

Cassoulet

Preparation: 15 minutes / Chill: 1 hour / Cooking: 50 minutes / Serves: 4

4 skinless, boneless chicken thigh fillets (100g each)
4 cloves garlic, crushed
2 teaspoons fresh thyme leaves
Freshly ground pepper
2 teaspoons olive oil
1 small onion, finely chopped
2 carrots, diced
1 cup canned no-added-salt chopped tomatoes
3 cups cooked cannellini beans
200g kielbasa or other fully cooked garlic sausage, thinly sliced
2 tablespoons dry breadcrumbs

1. Toss the chicken in a large bowl with the garlic, thyme and a good grinding of pepper. Cover and refrigerate for at least 1 hour.

2. Heat the oil in a small flameproof casserole over moderate heat. Add the chicken and cook for 4 minutes or until the chicken is very lightly browned on both sides. Transfer to a plate and put aside.

3. Preheat the oven to 200°C. Meanwhile, add the onion and carrots to the casserole and cook for 7 minutes or until the onion is soft. Add the tomatoes, the beans and kielbasa. Bring to the boil, reduce to a simmer, then return the chicken to the casserole. Cover, transfer to the oven and bake for 20 minutes.

4. Sprinkle the breadcrumbs over the top of the chicken mixture, drizzle with 2 tablespoons of the cooking liquid to moisten the crumbs, and then bake for a further 20 minutes or until the crumbs are golden.

Nutrients per serving: Kilojoules 1880; Fibre 11g; Protein 33g; Carbohydrate 26g; Saturated Fat 8g; Total Fat 24g; Cholesterol 107mg

Hummous

Preparation: 10 minutes / Cooking: 10 minutes / Makes: 2 cups

4 cloves garlic, peeled

2 cans (300g each) chickpeas, drained and rinsed

⅓ cup plain low-fat yoghurt

3 teaspoons lemon juice

1 teaspoon sesame oil

½ teaspoon ground coriander

Cayenne pepper

Salt

1 teaspoon paprika

1. Cook the garlic in a small saucepan of boiling water for 2 minutes to blanch. Drain and transfer to a food processor.

2. Add the chickpeas, yoghurt, lemon juice, oil, coriander, and a pinch each of cayenne pepper and salt, to the processor and purée. Transfer to a serving bowl and sprinkle with the paprika.

Nutrients per ¼ cup: Kilojoules 204; Fibre 2g; Protein 3g; Carbohydrate 6g; Saturated Fat 0g; Total Fat 1g; Cholesterol 1mg

Did you know?

Beans cause a slow, steady rise in blood sugar rather than a rapid, abrupt one – good news for diabetics, who may be able to lower their insulin dosage if they add beans to their diets.

Hummous

Pasta e Fagioli

Pasta e Fagioli

Preparation: 15 minutes / Cooking: 40 minutes / Serves: 4

3 teaspoons olive oil

1 onion, diced

1 carrot, halved lengthways and cut into 5mm slices

1 red capsicum, diced

3 cloves garlic, crushed

1 cup canned no-added-salt chopped tomatoes

½ cup chopped fresh basil

Salt

Freshly ground black pepper

3 cups cooked red kidney beans

1½ cups chicken stock

125g wagon wheel pasta

½ cup grated Parmesan cheese

1. Heat the oil in a medium saucepan over moderate heat. Add the onion, carrot, capsicum and garlic and cook for 7 minutes or until the onion is soft. Stir in the tomatoes, basil, and salt and pepper to taste, and cook for 5 minutes or until some of the tomato liquid has evaporated.

2. Stir in the beans, stock and 3 cups water. Bring to the boil, reduce to a simmer, cover and cook for 15 minutes or until the beans are beginning to break up and thicken the liquid. With the back of a spoon, mash a quarter of the beans against the side of the saucepan.

3. Return to the boil, add the pasta and cook, uncovered, for 10 minutes or until the pasta is firm-tender. Serve topped with Parmesan.

Nutrients per serving: Kilojoules 1274; Fibre 13g; Protein 20g; Carbohydrate 38g; Saturated Fat 3g; Total Fat 8g; Cholesterol 10mg

Did you know?

Beans and other legumes, such as lentils and peas, are considered the best protein sources in the plant kingdom. They are also filling, flavourful and inexpensive.

Did you know?

Home-cooked beans and commercially canned beans have very similar nutritional properties, except that some vitamin C and niacin may leach into the liquid and be lost when the beans are drained and rinsed; this is offset, however, by the loss of some of the sodium added in the canning process.

Chilli Pork & Beans

Preparation: 20 minutes / Cooking: 1 hour / Serves: 4

3 teaspoons vegetable oil

250g well-trimmed lean pork, diced

1 large onion, finely chopped

3 cloves garlic, crushed

1 green capsicum, diced

1 can (400g) no-added-salt chopped tomatoes

1 can (113g) chopped mild green chillies

1½ teaspoons Mexican chilli powder

1 teaspoon dried oregano

Salt

3 cups cooked red kidney beans

3 teaspoons lime juice

1. Heat the oil in a large nonstick frying pan over moderately high heat. Add the pork to the pan and cook for 2 minutes or until lightly browned. Transfer the pork with a slotted spoon to a plate.

2. Add the onion and garlic to the pan and cook for 5 minutes or until soft. Add the capsicum and cook for 4 minutes or until soft.

3. Add ¼ cup water, the tomatoes, green chillies, chilli powder, oregano and a pinch of salt, and bring to the boil. Reduce to a simmer, return the pork to the pan; add the beans, cover and cook for 40 to 45 minutes or until the pork is tender. Stir in the lime juice.

Nutrients per serving: Kilojoules 1067; Fibre 12g; Protein 24g; Carbohydrate 27g; Saturated Fat 1g; Total Fat 6g; Cholesterol 47mg

Lentils

Lentils offer a valuable amount of iron, along with plenty of folate and low-fat protein. They're also a very good source of niacin and potassium.

Healthy Highlights

Brown lentils
1 serving, cooked
(130g)

Nutrient		Nutrients	% RDI
Kilojoules	378	Iron	22%
Fibre	4.8g	Folate	16%
Protein	8.8g	Potassium	15%
Carbohydrate	12.9g	Niacin	13%
Saturated Fat	0.1g	Magnesium	12%
Total Fat	0.5g	Phosphorus	12%
Cholesterol	0mg	Thiamin	11%
Sodium	10mg	Zinc	10%

Red (dhal) lentils
1 serving, cooked
(130g)

Nutrient		Nutrients	% RDI
Kilojoules	549	Iron	27%
Fibre	6.8g	Vitamin C	26%
Protein	11.6g	Potassium	18%
Carbohydrate	18.7g	Niacin	17%
Saturated Fat	0.3g	Phosphorus	16%
Total Fat	1.4g	Thiamin	15%
Cholesterol	0mg	Folate	14%
Sodium	10mg	Magnesium	13%
		Zinc	11%

Shopping & Preparation

At the market Brown lentils (also known as green lentils) are a supermarket staple. In the larger stores you'll also find whole red lentils and split red lentils (sometimes called 'dhals'). Specialty food shops are beginning to stock Puy lentils, which are smaller, darker and plumper than brown lentils.

Preparation Unlike dried beans, lentils do not need to be soaked before cooking. They should, however, be picked over and rinsed to remove any debris.

Basic cooking Lentils can be cooked in water or stock. Using three times as much liquid as lentils, combine the lentils and liquid in a saucepan and bring to the boil. Cover, reduce the heat, and simmer until the lentils are tender but still hold their shape – 20 to 25 minutes for brown lentils, 12 to 15 minutes for whole red lentils, 5 to 6 minutes for split red lentils. Lentils increase in bulk by about 3 times after cooking.

Hearty Chicken & Lentil Stew

Preparation: 20 minutes / Cooking: 1 hour / Serves: 4

3 teaspoons olive oil

4 large skinless, boneless chicken thighs (200g each), quartered

1 large onion, finely chopped

1 yellow or red capsicum, diced

4 cloves garlic, crushed

¾ cup brown lentils

1¼ cups chicken stock

¾ cup canned no-added-salt chopped tomatoes

1 teaspoon ground coriander

1 teaspoon ground ginger

Salt

300g red-skinned potatoes, cut into small chunks

1. Heat the oil in a large nonstick frying pan over moderate heat. Add the chicken and cook for 6 minutes or until browned on both sides. Transfer the chicken to a plate with a slotted spoon; put aside.

2. Add the onion, capsicum and garlic to the pan and cook for 5 minutes or until soft. Add the lentils, stock, ½ cup water, the tomatoes, coriander, ginger and a pinch of salt, and bring to the boil. Reduce to a simmer, cover and cook for 20 minutes or until the lentils are just barely tender.

3. Return the chicken to the pan and add the potatoes. Return to the boil, reduce to a simmer, cover and cook for 25 minutes or until the chicken is cooked through and the potatoes are tender.

Nutrients per serving: Kilojoules 1785; Fibre 6g; Protein 40g; Carbohydrate 21g; Saturated Fat 5g; Total Fat 20g; Cholesterol 168mg

Did you know?

Lentils contain protease inhibitors, a class of compounds that interfere with certain types of enzymatic action and thus may help fight cancer.

Lentils & Peas

Preparation: 5 minutes / Cooking: 35 minutes / Serves: 4

3 teaspoons vegetable oil

1 medium onion, diced

3 cloves garlic, crushed

1 cup brown lentils

2 teaspoons fresh rosemary leaves

Salt

Freshly ground pepper

1½ cups frozen green peas

1. Heat the oil in a medium saucepan over moderately high heat. Add the onion and garlic and cook for 5 minutes or until soft.

2. Add the lentils, 2 cups water, the rosemary, a pinch of salt and a good grinding of pepper. Bring to the boil, reduce to a simmer, then cover and cook for 25 minutes or until the lentils are tender.

3. Add the peas and cook for 2 to 3 minutes or until the peas are heated through.

Nutrients per serving: Kilojoules 578; Fibre 7g; Protein 10g; Carbohydrate 15g; Saturated Fat 1g; Total Fat 4g; Cholesterol 0mg

Red Lentil Soup

Red Lentil Soup @

Preparation: 5 minutes / Cooking: 15 minutes / Serves: 4

4 cups vegetable stock

I cup whole red lentils

3 cloves garlic, sliced

¾ teaspoon ground cumin

Salt

Cayenne pepper

2 red capsicums, finely chopped

1. Combine the stock, lentils, garlic, cumin, and a pinch each of salt and cayenne pepper, in a large saucepan. Reserving some of the capsicum to use as a garnish, add the rest to the saucepan. Cook for 15 minutes until the lentils are soft.

2. Top with the reserved chopped capsicum just before serving.

Nutrients per serving: Kilojoules 446; Fibre 4g; Protein 9g; Carbohydrate 13g; Saturated Fat 1g; Total Fat 2g; Cholesterol 0mg

Did you know?

One serving of brown lentils (130g) supplies 2.6mg of iron – almost as much as in a 100g serving of lean beef. And whereas the beef has nearly 6g of fat, the lentils have less than 1g.

Warm Lentil & Tomato Salad

Warm Lentil & Tomato Salad

Preparation: 10 minutes / Cooking: 30 minutes / Serves: 4

1 cup brown lentils

1 carrot, diced

2 teaspoons fresh
thyme leaves

Salt

Freshly ground pepper

2 tablespoons red wine
vinegar

3 teaspoons olive oil

2 teaspoons Dijon
mustard

2 cups diced egg
tomatoes (about 6)

2 spring onions, finely
sliced

1. Bring 3 cups water to the boil in a large
saucepan. Add the lentils, carrot, thyme, and
salt and pepper to taste. Cover and simmer for
25 minutes or until tender.

2. Drain the lentils, turn into a large bowl and
add the vinegar, oil, mustard, tomatoes and
spring onions. Toss well.

Nutrients per serving: Kilojoules 480; Fibre 5g;
Protein 7g; Carbohydrate 12g; Saturated Fat 1g;
Total Fat 4g; Cholesterol 0mg

Did you know?

• Lentils and other legumes are a good dietary
source of copper, a trace mineral that may help
lower blood cholesterol.

• The iron in lentils is more easily absorbed by
the body if you cook or serve the lentils with
a food rich in vitamin C, such as tomatoes,
capsicums, cabbage, broccoli or citrus juice.

Potato & Lentil Salad

Preparation: 15 minutes / Cooking: 20 minutes / Serves: 6

1kg waxy potatoes, peeled and cut into large chunks

½ cup olive oil

2 tablespoons red wine vinegar

4 cups cooked brown lentils

150g stoned black olives

1 tablespoon capers, chopped

2 cloves garlic, chopped

1 tablespoon lemon juice

⅔ cup roughly chopped flat-leaf parsley

6 spring onions, sliced diagonally

Salt

Freshly ground black pepper

1. Cook the potatoes in a medium saucepan of boiling water for 20 minutes or until tender. Drain and transfer the potatoes to a large bowl.

2. While the potatoes are still hot, add the oil and vinegar and stir through. Then add the lentils, olives, capers, garlic, lemon juice, parsley, spring onions, a pinch of salt and a good grinding of pepper, and toss well to combine. Serve while still warm.

Nutrients per serving: Kilojoules 1564; Fibre 8g; Protein 12g; Carbohydrate 37g; Saturated Fat 3g; Total Fat 20g; Cholesterol 0mg

Did you know?

Lentils are an excellent non-meat source of the disease-fighting B vitamin, folate.

Potato & Lentil Salad

Soya

Soya beans – one of the world's most important sources of dietary protein and polyunsaturated oil (see the nutritional analysis on p162) – are the source of two highly nutritious food products, tofu and soya milk. Tofu – also known as bean curd – is remarkably nutritious, supplying complete protein and important minerals, as well as the cancer-fighting substance genistein. Soya milk is commonly used as a non-dairy substitute, and is a great boon to the lactose-intolerant. It contains high-quality protein but has less saturated fat than dairy milk and no cholesterol.

Healthy Highlights

Firm tofu
100g, cooked

		Nutrients % RDI	
Kilojoules	304	Calcium	41%
Fibre	0.3g	Magnesium	15%
Protein	8.1g	Niacin	11%
Carbohydrate	0.6g	Phosphorus	10%
Saturated Fat	0.6g	Iron	10%
Total Fat	4.2g		
Cholesterol	0mg		
Sodium	7mg		

Silken tofu
100g, raw

		Nutrients % RDI	
Kilojoules	230	Magnesium	11%
Fibre	0.1g	Thiamin	10%
Protein	4.8g		
Carbohydrate	2.9g		
Saturated Fat	0.4g		
Total Fat	2.7g		
Cholesterol	0mg		
Sodium	5mg		

Unfortified soya milk
1 cup (250ml)

		Nutrients % RDI	
Kilojoules	426	Folate	25%
Fibre	1.3g	Magnesium	16%
Protein	6.5g	Niacin	15%
Carbohydrate	6.8g	Potassium	15%
Saturated Fat	0.8g	Phosphorus	14%
Total Fat	5.5g		
Cholesterol	0mg		
Sodium	192mg		

Stir-Fried Vegetables with Tofu

Preparation: 15 minutes / Marinate: 1 hour
Cooking: 10 minutes / Serves: 4

2 tablespoons reduced-salt soy sauce
1 tablespoon brown sugar
2 teaspoons grated fresh ginger
Salt
500g very firm tofu, halved horizontally
¾ cup chicken stock
2 teaspoons cornflour
3 teaspoons vegetable oil
1 large red capsicum, cut into strips
200g green beans, cut into 5cm lengths
2 carrots, sliced
4 cloves garlic, crushed
2 spring onions, thinly sliced

1. Combine the soy sauce, brown sugar, ginger and a pinch of salt in a shallow bowl. Add the tofu, cut-side-down, and put aside to marinate for 1 hour. Reserving the marinade, remove the tofu and cut into 3 cm chunks. Stir the stock and cornflour into the reserved marinade.

2. Heat the oil in a large nonstick frying pan over moderate heat. Add the capsicum, beans, carrots, garlic and spring onions, and cook for 5 minutes or until the capsicum is crisp-tender. Stir the stock mixture well and pour into the frying pan. Add the tofu and bring the mixture to the boil. Reduce to a simmer and cook for 4 minutes or until the sauce is slightly thickened and the tofu is heated through.

Nutrients per serving: Kilojoules 751; Fibre 4g; Protein 13g; Carbohydrate 11g; Saturated Fat 1g; Total Fat 9g; Cholesterol 0mg

Did you know?

• People in Asian countries, who eat soya products on a daily basis, have lower cancer rates than other populations; genistein – a phytochemical found in soya beans – is one likely reason for this.

• Tofu is a good source of calcium, but firm tofu contains more calcium than silken tofu.

Stir-Fried Vegetables with Tofu

At the market Tofu is available in Asian food shops and supermarkets and is almost always sold in sealed packets (tofu, like meat, is susceptible to bacterial contamination). As well as firm tofu and silken tofu – sometimes labelled soft tofu – you'll find fried tofu cubes and puffs, smoked tofu, flavoured tofu (both savoury and sweet) and tofu desserts. Plain tofu, once opened, should be kept in the refrigerator, covered with water, and will keep fresh for up to a week if the water is changed regularly. Soya milk – also known as soy milk or soy drink – is available, both plain and flavoured, in supermarkets, Asian food shops and health food shops.

Look for Choose tofu according to how you plan to use it. Delicate 'silken' tofu can be simmered briefly, but it works best when puréed, in a shake, sauce or dip. Firm and extra-firm tofu can be sliced, cubed or crumbled. Choose unflavoured soya milk for cooking.

Preparation Pressing tofu renders it denser, drier and easier to slice. To press firm tofu, wrap, weight down and drain it as shown below for 30 minutes. To make your own soya milk for drinking (it's too thin for use in recipes), soak 1 cup soya beans in 2 cups cold water for 2 days, covered and refrigerated. Drain. Process the beans in a blender until paste-like; add 1 cup water and process until creamy. Add another 1 cup water and blend. Strain through several thicknesses of fine muslin into a large saucepan. Bring the liquid to a simmer and cook, stirring, for 5 to 10 minutes. Cool; keep refrigerated in a covered container for up to 5 days.

Cut the tofu in half horizontally, then sandwich it between several layers of paper towels. Place on a board, weight down and prop it at a slant near the sink to drain.

Hearty Vegetarian Lasagne

Preparation: 15 minutes / Cooking: 45 minutes / Serves: 6

6 lasagne sheets
2 teaspoons olive oil
1 large onion, finely chopped
3 cloves garlic, crushed
250g mushrooms, thinly sliced
2 packets (250g each) frozen chopped spinach, thawed and squeezed dry
1½ teaspoons grated lemon zest
Salt
Freshly ground pepper
500g silken tofu
½ cup low-fat cottage cheese
½ cup low-fat ricotta cheese
½ cup grated Parmesan cheese
1 cup no-added-salt tomato pasta sauce
3 tablespoons no-added-salt tomato paste
1 egg
2 egg whites

1. Preheat the oven to 180°C. Cook the lasagne sheets in a large saucepan of boiling water according to the packet directions, until firm-tender. Drain.

2. Meanwhile, heat the oil in a large nonstick frying pan over moderate heat. Add the onion and garlic and cook for 5 minutes or until soft. Add the mushrooms and cook for 4 minutes. Add the spinach and cook, stirring, for 5 minutes or until no liquid remains. Transfer to a medium bowl and add the lemon zest, a pinch of salt and a good grinding of pepper. Toss well.

3. Combine the tofu, cottage cheese, ricotta cheese, 4 tablespoons of the Parmesan, the pasta sauce, tomato paste, whole egg and egg whites in a food processor. Process to a smooth purée.

4. Spray an 18 x 28 cm glass baking dish with cooking spray. Line the bottom with 2 of the lasagne sheets. Spoon half the spinach mixture and a third of the tofu mixture over the pasta. Make another layer of pasta, the remaining spinach mixture, and another third of the tofu mixture. Top with the remaining lasagne sheets and the remaining tofu mixture. Sprinkle the remaining Parmesan on top. Bake for 30 minutes or until hot.

Nutrients per serving: Kilojoules 1211; Fibre 8g; Protein 24g; Carbohydrate 25g; Saturated Fat 4g; Total Fat 11g; Cholesterol 62mg

Basil & Parmesan Salad Dressing

Preparation: 5 minutes / Makes: 1 cup

250g silken tofu
¼ cup grated Parmesan cheese
¼ cup fresh basil leaves
3 teaspoons Dijon mustard
1½ tablespoons red wine vinegar

1. Process the tofu, Parmesan and basil in a food processor until well blended.

2. Add the mustard, vinegar and 1 tablespoon water. Purée until smooth.

Nutrients per ¼ cup: Kilojoules 254; Fibre 0g; Protein 5g; Carbohydrate 2g; Saturated Fat 1g; Total Fat 3g; Cholesterol 5mg

Piña Colada Creams

Piña Colada Creams

Preparation: 35 minutes / Cooking: 10 minutes / Standing: 55 minutes / Chill: 1 hour / Serves: 4

3 cups unflavoured soya milk

½ cup sugar

¼ cup shredded coconut

1 envelope gelatine

1 cup canned juice-packed crushed pineapple, well drained

½ teaspoon coconut essence

½ cup flaked fresh coconut (optional)

1. Bring 2¾ cups of the soya milk, the sugar and shredded coconut to the boil in a small saucepan over moderate heat. Remove from the heat, cover and stand for 30 minutes at room temperature. Strain into a medium bowl, pushing on the solids to extract the liquid.

2. Sprinkle the gelatine over the remaining soya milk in a heatproof measuring cup. Let stand for 5 minutes to soften. Place the cup in a small saucepan of simmering water and heat for 2 minutes or until the gelatine is dissolved.

3. Stir the gelatine mixture into the milk mixture. Place the bowl in a larger bowl of ice and water and let stand, stirring occasionally, for 20 minutes or until the mixture begins to set. Fold in the pineapple and coconut essence. Spoon the mixture into 4 dessert glasses or bowls, cover and chill for 1 hour or until set.

4. Meanwhile, lightly toast the flaked coconut, if using, in a small frying pan over moderate heat for about 5 minutes or until golden. Pile on top of the creams just before serving.

Nutrients per serving: Kilojoules 1008; Fibre 3g; Protein 7g; Carbohydrate 38g; Saturated Fat 3g; Total Fat 7g; Cholesterol 0mg

Did you know?

• Soya milk builds bones: in one study, postmenopausal women given calcium-fortified soya milk gained significantly more bone density than women given protein and calcium in the form of milk powder.

• Because it's made from a legume, soya milk – unlike dairy milk – contains some fibre.

Split Peas

An abundant source of fibre and protein, split peas also supply good amounts of minerals, including iron and magnesium, and the disease-fighting B vitamin, folate.

Healthy Highlights

1 serving, cooked (130g)		Nutrients % RDI	
Kilojoules	312	Folate	38%
Fibre	5.1g	Thiamin	15%
Protein	8.6g	Niacin	14%
Carbohydrate	9.5g	Iron	11%
Saturated Fat	0g	Magnesium	11%
Total Fat	0.5g	Phosphorus	10%
Cholesterol	0mg		
Sodium	12mg		

Shopping & Preparation

At the market Dried split peas, both green and yellow, are widely available and are sold in all supermarkets. Some people consider that the yellow peas have a more robust flavour than the green, but they are interchangeable in all recipes.

Preparation Split peas do not require presoaking, but they should be picked over and rinsed before cooking.

Basic cooking Place 1 cup split peas in a saucepan with 2 cups water and bring to the boil. Reduce to a simmer and cook for 30 minutes, or until the peas are tender. One cup dried split peas will yield about 2½ cups cooked.

Pasta with Creamy Green Sauce

Preparation: 15 minutes / Cooking: 40 minutes / Serves: 4

2 teaspoons vegetable oil
4 cloves garlic, peeled
1 cup split peas
1 cup chicken stock
2 teaspoons fresh rosemary leaves
Salt
300g medium-sized pasta shells
½ cup frozen chopped spinach, thawed and squeezed dry
1 cup evaporated low-fat milk
2 tablespoons reduced-fat cream cheese
¼ cup grated Parmesan cheese

1. Heat the oil in a medium saucepan over low heat. Add the garlic and cook for 4 minutes or until the oil is fragrant. Add the split peas, stock, ½ cup water, the rosemary and a pinch of salt. Bring to the boil over moderate heat. Reduce to a simmer, cover and cook for 30 minutes or until the split peas are tender.

2. Meanwhile, cook the pasta in a large saucepan of boiling water according to the packet directions, until firm-tender. Drain the pasta well and tip into a large bowl.

3. Transfer the split-pea mixture to a food processor along with the spinach, evaporated milk and cream cheese, and purée. Return the sauce to the saucepan and cook for 3 minutes or until heated through and creamy. Add the sauce to the pasta along with the Parmesan, tossing well to combine.

Nutrients per serving: Kilojoules 1776; Fibre 10g; Protein 26g; Carbohydrate 61g; Saturated Fat 3g; Total Fat 9g; Cholesterol 16mg

Did you know?

One cup of cooked split peas supplies more fibre than two slices of wholemeal bread.

Mexican Split Pea Salsa

Preparation: 20 minutes / Cooking: 35 minutes / Makes: 6 cups

1 cup split peas
3 cloves garlic, crushed
¼ cup fresh mint sprigs
Salt
3 teaspoons vegetable oil
¾ teaspoon ground coriander
½ teaspoon ground cumin
Cayenne pepper
⅓ cup lime juice
½ cup chopped fresh coriander
1 large tomato, diced

1. Combine the split peas, garlic, mint and a pinch of salt in a medium saucepan of water. Bring to the boil, reduce to a simmer and cook, stirring occasionally, for 30 minutes or until the split peas are tender. Drain; discard the mint.

2. Meanwhile, heat the oil in a small frying pan over low heat. Add the ground coriander, cumin and a pinch of cayenne pepper, and cook for 30 seconds or until fragrant.

3. Transfer the spiced oil to a medium bowl and whisk in the lime juice. Add the hot split peas, the chopped coriander and tomato, tossing well. Serve warm or chilled.

Nutrients per ¼ cup: Kilojoules 87; Fibre 1g; Protein 2g; Carbohydrate 2g; Saturated Fat 0g; Total Fat 1g; Cholesterol 0mg

Split Pea & Green Pea Soup

Split Pea & Green Pea Soup

Preparation: 15 minutes / Cooking: 35 minutes / Serves: 4

2 teaspoons vegetable oil

6 spring onions, sliced

3 cloves garlic, crushed

4 cups chicken or vegetable stock

1¼ cups split peas

⅓ cup fresh mint leaves

1 teaspoon fresh marjoram leaves

Salt

1½ cups frozen green peas

1 tablespoon plain low-fat yoghurt

Freshly ground pepper

1. Heat the oil in a large saucepan over moderate heat. Add the spring onions and garlic and cook for 2 minutes or until the spring onions are tender. Add the stock, the split peas, mint, marjoram, and a pinch of salt, and bring to the boil. Reduce to a simmer, cover and cook for 25 minutes.

2. Stir in the green peas and cook for a further 5 minutes or until both the split peas and the green peas are tender.

3. Transfer the mixture to a food processor and purée. Return the soup to the saucepan and gently cook for 3 minutes or until heated through. Swirl 1 teaspoon yogurt into each serving and top with a grinding of pepper.

Nutrients per serving: Kilojoules 836; Fibre 11g; Protein 19g; Carbohydrate 21g; Saturated Fat 1g; Total Fat 4g; Cholesterol 0mg

Did you know?

Split peas are a good dietary choice for diabetics, as their complex carbohydrates (starches) are metabolised relatively slowly into glucose (sugar).

Nuts

Of all the nuts commonly available, four are featured in this book. Almonds, walnuts and pecans supply good amounts of fibre and minerals. Almonds also supply plenty of vitamin E, while walnuts have omega-3 fatty acids, which lower triglycerides. Peanuts, which are legumes, provide more protein than any other nut. They also supply good amounts of fibre, vitamin E and B vitamins.

Healthy Highlights

Almonds
30g, raw

		Nutrients % RDI	
Kilojoules	737	Magnesium	29%
Fibre	2.6g	Riboflavin	24%
Protein	6g	Niacin	15%
Carbohydrate	1.3g	Phosphorus	14%
Saturated Fat	1.1g	Potassium	11%
Total Fat	16.6g		
Cholesterol	0mg		
Sodium	2mg		

Walnuts
30g, raw

		Nutrients % RDI	
Kilojoules	855	Magnesium	17%
Fibre	1.9g	Phosphorus	11%
Protein	4.3g	Folate	10%
Carbohydrate	0.9g	Niacin	10%
Saturated Fat	1.3g	Thiamin	10%
Total Fat	20.8g		
Cholesterol	0mg		
Sodium	1mg		

Peanuts
30g, dry-roasted, unsalted

		Nutrients % RDI	
Kilojoules	697	Niacin	37%
Fibre	2.5g	Thiamin	21%
Protein	7.4g	Magnesium	18%
Carbohydrate	2.7g	Folate	14%
Saturated Fat	1.6g		
Total Fat	14.2g		
Cholesterol	0mg		
Sodium	2mg		

Pecans
30g, raw

		Nutrients % RDI	
Kilojoules	873	Thiamin	13%
Fibre	2.5g	Magnesium	12%
Protein	2.9g	Zinc	10%
Carbohydrate	1.5g		
Saturated Fat	1.4g		
Total Fat	21.6g		
Cholesterol	0mg		
Sodium	1mg		

Spiced Walnuts

Preparation: 2 minutes / Cooking: 10 minutes / Serves: 12

3 teaspoons vegetable oil
2 cups walnut halves
2 tablespoons sugar
½ teaspoon cayenne pepper
Salt

1. Heat the oil in large heavy nonstick frying pan over moderate heat. Add the walnut halves, tossing to coat.

2. Add the sugar, cayenne pepper and a pinch of salt and cook, stirring constantly, for 8 minutes or until the sugar has caramelised and the nuts are well coated. Serve the walnuts hot or at room temperature.

Nutrients per serving: Kilojoules 591; Fibre 1g; Protein 3g; Carbohydrate 3g; Saturated Fat 1g; Total Fat 13g; Cholesterol 0mg

Chinese Walnut Chicken

Preparation: 20 minutes / Cooking: 20 minutes

Serves: 4

3 teaspoons vegetable oil

2 tablespoons sugar

1 cup walnut halves

1 red capsicum, cut into strips

4 spring onions, sliced diagonally

2 cloves garlic, crushed

1 tablespoon grated fresh ginger

500g skinless, boneless chicken breasts, cut into cubes

1 cup chicken stock

3 teaspoons reduced-salt soy sauce

1 teaspoon sesame oil

1½ teaspoons cornflour

1. Heat 1 teaspoon of the vegetable oil in a medium frying pan over moderate heat. Add 1½ tablespoons of the sugar, stirring to combine. Add the walnuts and cook, stirring constantly, for 7 minutes or until the walnuts are nicely coated and lightly crisped; put aside.

2. Heat the remaining vegetable oil in a large nonstick frying pan over moderately high heat. Add the capsicum and cook for 2 minutes or until crisp-tender. Add the spring onions, garlic and ginger and cook for 2 minutes. Add the chicken and cook for 4 minutes.

3. Combine the stock, soy sauce, sesame oil and the remaining sugar in a small bowl. Add the cornflour and mix well. Add the mixture to the frying pan, bring to the boil, then cook for 3 minutes or until the sauce is slightly thickened and the chicken is cooked. Stir in the walnuts.

Nutrients per serving: Kilojoules 1786; Fibre 3g; Protein 28g; Carbohydrate 13g; Saturated Fat 4g; Total Fat 30g; Cholesterol 71mg

Did you know?

• Peanuts and walnuts are a fair source of folate.

• Although walnuts and almonds are high in fat, most of it is unsaturated. Almonds are rich in monounsaturates; walnuts are beneficially high in polyunsaturates.

• Gram for gram, walnuts contain more potassium than bananas.

• Research subjects who ate nuts frequently were found to have lowered their risk of heart disease.

Chinese Walnut Chicken

Chicken Salad with Almond Dressing

Preparation: 15 minutes / Serves: 4

⅓ cup whole blanched almonds

¼ cup low-fat mayonnaise

1½ tablespoons lemon juice

Salt

2 cups diced cooked chicken

2 celery stalks, sliced

1 cup halved seedless red or green grapes

2 cups shredded lettuce

2 tablespoons flaked almonds

1. Purée the whole almonds, the mayonnaise, lemon juice and a pinch of salt in a food processor. Transfer to a large bowl.

2. Add the chicken, celery and grapes; toss well to coat with the dressing. Serve the salad on a bed of shredded lettuce and garnish with the flaked almonds.

Nutrients per serving: Kilojoules 1164; Fibre 3g; Protein 21g; Carbohydrate 11g; Saturated Fat 3g; Total Fat 17g; Cholesterol 68mg

Shopping & Preparation

At the market Almonds, walnuts and pecans are sold both in the shell and shelled. Shelled almonds are sold whole, either raw, roasted or blanched; blanched almonds are also available slivered or flaked. It is also possible to buy ground almonds, usually sold as almond meal. Walnuts are always available in the shell. Shelled, they are available whole, in halves, or chopped. Pecans are also sold in the shell, as well as shelled and roasted, and sometimes salted. The ever-popular peanut is available in the shell or shelled, unroasted, oil-roasted or dry-roasted, salted or unsalted.

Look for When buying nuts in the shell, look for clean, uncracked shells. When buying shelled nuts in bulk, check for a pleasant smell; if they are too old, nuts will turn rancid. Instead of oil-roasted nuts, which are very high in fat, use either unroasted or dry-roasted nuts for these recipes. To prepare raw nuts at home, see below. Storing nuts in the freezer, in an airtight container, will keep them fresh.

Basic cooking To blanch almonds, cover with boiling water and let stand for 5 minutes; the skins should slip off easily. Toasting almonds, walnuts and pecans brings out their best flavour. Toast in a heavy, ungreased frying pan on top of the stove (or on a shallow baking tray in the oven) for 5 to 7 minutes, shaking the pan frequently. As soon as the nuts are lightly browned and fragrant, turn out of the pan or they will overcook. Shelled peanuts can be toasted on top of the stove in a heavy, ungreased frying pan, or on a shallow baking tray in a 180°C oven for 7 minutes, shaking the pan frequently. Raw peanuts in their shells can be roasted on a shallow baking tray in a 180°C oven for about 15 minutes.

Pasta with Almond & Basil Pesto

Pasta with Almond & Basil Pesto

Preparation: 10 minutes / Cooking: 15 minutes / Serves: 4

300g fusilli, radiatore or wagon wheel pasta

4 cloves garlic, peeled

2 cups packed fresh basil leaves

⅔ cup chicken stock

½ cup whole almonds, toasted

⅓ cup grated Parmesan cheese

1. Cook the pasta in a large saucepan of boiling water according to the packet directions, until firm-tender. Drain.

2. Meanwhile, put the garlic, basil, stock and almonds in a food processor and purée. Transfer to a large bowl and stir in the Parmesan. Add the hot pasta to the bowl, tossing to combine.

Nutrients per serving: Kilojoules 1573; Fibre 6g; Protein 14g; Carbohydrate 44g; Saturated Fat 2g; Total Fat 16g; Cholesterol 7mg

Did you know?

Researchers recently discovered that peanuts, like red wine, contain an antioxidant called resveratrol – a compound that has been associated with a lowered risk of heart disease. The red skin of the peanut (which most people usually discard) has a higher concentration of resveratrol than the nut itself.

Chicken Satay with Peanut Sauce

Preparation: 25 minutes / Cooking: 10 minutes / Serves: 4

2 tablespoons rice vinegar (mirin)

2 teaspoons sesame oil

2 teaspoons sugar

½ teaspoon dried crushed chilli

2 large cucumbers, cut into 5mm dice

1 small red capsicum, diced

500g skinless, boneless chicken breasts, cut into 3cm cubes

½ teaspoon ground coriander

½ teaspoon black pepper

Salt

2 cloves garlic, crushed

½ cup dry-roasted peanuts

⅓ cup packed fresh coriander sprigs

½ cup chicken stock

2 tablespoons lime juice

1 lemon, cut into wedges

1. Whisk together the vinegar, sesame oil, 1 teaspoon of the sugar and the chilli in a medium bowl. Add the cucumbers and capsicum, tossing to combine. Refrigerate until serving time.

2. Preheat the griller. Toss the chicken with the ground coriander, pepper and a pinch of salt in a medium bowl; put aside.

3. Purée the garlic, peanuts, fresh coriander, stock, lime juice and the remaining sugar in a food processor.

4. Thread the chicken pieces onto 8 skewers. (If using bamboo skewers, soak in water for 30 minutes beforehand, so that they won't burn.) Grill 15 cm from the heat, turning the skewers once, for 5 minutes or until the chicken is cooked through. Serve the satay skewers with the peanut sauce, the cucumber salad and the lemon wedges alongside.

Nutrients per serving: Kilojoules 1287; Fibre 3g; Protein 28g; Carbohydrate 7g; Saturated Fat 3g; Total Fat 18g; Cholesterol 71mg

Chicken Satay with Peanut Sauce

Seeds

Most seeds are nutritious and many are used in cooking. Two in particular – sunflower seeds and pumpkin seeds – offer valuable benefits. Packed with vitamin E, sunflower seeds also supply folate, a possible cancer-fighter. Pumpkin seeds are rich in zinc, an immune-system booster.

Healthy Highlights

Sunflower seeds

20g, raw		Nutrients % RDI	
Kilojoules	462	Thiamin	35%
Fibre	2.2g	Magnesium	27%
Protein	4.5g	Niacin	26%
Carbohydrate	0.4g	Folate	23%
Saturated Fat	0.9g	Phosphorus	17%
Total Fat	10.2g	Zinc	11%
Cholesterol	0mg		
Sodium	0mg		

Pumpkin seeds

20g, raw		Nutrients % RDI	
Kilojoules	467	Magnesium	20%
Fibre	2g	Iron	17%
Protein	4.9g	Phosphorus	17%
Carbohydrate	2.7g	Niacin	11%
Saturated Fat	1.4g	Zinc	11%
Total Fat	9.1g		
Cholesterol	0mg		
Sodium	4mg		

Shopping & Preparation

At the market Pumpkin and sunflower seeds are sold in and out of their shells, plain or roasted.

Look for When buying pumpkin and sunflower seeds in their shells, look for clean, unbroken shells. The seeds should be plump and meaty, not dry or shrivelled.

Preparation When carving a pumpkin, don't throw out the seeds: scoop them out, rinse and let dry. Then toast the seeds in a 180°C oven for 8 to 10 minutes or until crisp. To enhance their flavour, toast shelled pumpkin seeds in an ungreased frying pan over very low heat for 3 minutes or until they begin to pop.

Crispy Seed-Topped Flatbreads

Preparation: 1 hour 10 minutes / Cooking: 15 minutes / Serves: 12

2¼ cups plain flour

¼ teaspoon cayenne pepper

Salt

3 teaspoons unsalted butter

3 teaspoons solid vegetable shortening

1 egg white lightly beaten with 2 teaspoons water

¼ cup shelled pumpkin seeds

¼ cup shelled, dry-roasted sunflower seeds

2 tablespoons grated Parmesan cheese

1. Combine the flour, cayenne pepper and a pinch of salt in a medium bowl. Cut in the butter and shortening with a pastry blender or two knives until the mixture resembles coarse crumbs. Gradually add ⅔ cup water to make a soft, smooth dough. Knead for 5 minutes or until smooth and elastic. Transfer to a bowl that has been sprayed with cooking spray, cover and rest for 1 hour.

2. Preheat the oven to 210°C. Spray 2 large baking trays with cooking spray (or use nonstick trays); put aside. Cut the dough into 4 pieces. Roll each piece out to a 23 cm round (about 1.5 mm thick). Transfer to the prepared baking trays. Brush the dough with the egg-white mixture. Sprinkle the pumpkin and sunflower seeds over the dough. Sprinkle each dough round with 2 teaspoons of the Parmesan. Bake for 12 minutes or until the bread is lightly puffed, golden brown and crisp.

Nutrients per serving: Kilojoules 623; Fibre 2g; Protein 5g; Carbohydrate 19g; Saturated Fat 2g; Total Fat 6g; Cholesterol 4mg

Crispy Seed-Topped Flatbreads

Sunflower Drop Scones

Sunflower Drop Scones ⓐ

Preparation: 10 minutes / Cooking: 15 minutes / Makes: 1 dozen

1½ cups plain flour

1¾ teaspoons baking powder

½ teaspoon bicarbonate of soda

Salt

Cayenne pepper

1½ tablespoons unsalted butter

1½ tablespoons solid vegetable shortening

½ cup dry-roasted sunflower seeds

¾ cup buttermilk

1. Preheat the oven to 220°C. Spray a large baking tray with nonstick cooking spray; put aside.

2. Combine the flour, baking powder, bicarbonate of soda, and a pinch each of salt and cayenne pepper, in a large bowl. Cut in the butter and shortening with a pastry blender or two knives until the mixture resembles coarse crumbs. Stir in the sunflower seeds. Stir in the buttermilk until the mixture forms a soft dough. Do not overmix.

3. Drop the dough by heaped tablespoons 5 cm apart onto the prepared baking tray. Bake

for 12 minutes or until the scones are golden brown and crusty.

Nutrients per scone: Kilojoules 585; Fibre 1g; Protein 4g; Carbohydrate 14g; Saturated Fat 3g; Total Fat 8g; Cholesterol 7mg

Did you know?

As well as being used in the production of polyunsaturated oil and margarine, sunflower seeds are also roasted and ground to make a flour, which is available from health food shops.

Fish and She

Shellfish

Crab & Lobster

Crab and lobster are a delectable, low-fat protein source and are rich in zinc. Crab also supplies phosphorus and calcium, while lobster is high in niacin.

Healthy Highlights

Crab
1 serving, cooked
(125g)

		Nutrients	% RDI
Kilojoules	318	Zinc	95%
Fibre	0g	Calcium	27%
Protein	15.8g	Phosphorus	27%
Carbohydrate	1.5g	Niacin	17%
Saturated Fat	0.1g	Folate	13%
Total Fat	0.8g	Magnesium	13%
Cholesterol	105mg	Iron	10%
Sodium	486mg		

Lobster
1 serving, cooked
(125g)

		Nutrients	% RDI
Kilojoules	509	Niacin	47%
Fibre	0g	Zinc	35%
Protein	27.5g	Phosphorus	33%
Carbohydrate	0g	Potassium	20%
Saturated Fat	0.3g	Magnesium	19%
Total Fat	1.1g		
Cholesterol	145mg		
Sodium	494mg		

Shopping & Preparation

At the market You're most likely to find live crabs and lobsters in markets near the coast; cooked crab and lobster can be bought fresh or frozen, while crab is also available canned.

Look for Whole crabs and lobsters should feel heavy for their size, there should be no discoloration around the claws and the meat should be white and fresh-smelling.

Preparation The most humane way to kill a live crab or lobster is to place it in the freezer for several hours. You can then plunge it into a large saucepan of cold water, which is slowly brought to the boil. Reduce the heat and simmer for 5 minutes for the first 500g, then 3 minutes for each additional 500g. Crab and lobster bought cooked are ready to eat, although crab meat out of the shell may still need to be picked over to remove any stray bits of cartilage.

Soft Crab Rolls

Preparation: 20 minutes / Cooking: 17 minutes / Serves: 4

⅓ cup rice

Salt

2 tablespoons rice vinegar (mirin)

1½ teaspoons sugar

8 rice paper wrappers

8 iceberg lettuce leaves

500g cooked crab meat

½ cucumber, peeled, halved lengthways, seeded and cut into 1cm strips

½ avocado, cut lengthways into 8 pieces

½ cup Roasted Red Capsicums (recipe, page 61)

2 tablespoons lemon juice

1. Bring 1 cup of water to the boil in a small saucepan. Add the rice and a pinch of salt, cover and simmer for 15 minutes or until tender. Sprinkle the vinegar and sugar over the rice and stir to combine. Put aside to cool to room temperature.

2. Place 1 wrapper at a time in a large bowl of hot water for about 30 seconds or until softened. Top each wrapper with a lettuce leaf. Pile the rice in the centre of the lettuce, continue with the crab, then place a cucumber strip, an avocado slice and a capsicum strip on top. Sprinkle each with 1 teaspoon of the lemon juice. Fold the sides of the wrapper over the filling, then roll the wrapper up tightly around the filling.

Nutrients per serving: Kilojoules 1027; Fibre 2g; Protein 19g; Carbohydrate 22g; Saturated Fat 2g; Total Fat 9g; Cholesterol 105mg

Did you know?

The omego-3 fatty acids in shellfish help to reduce high blood pressure.

Crab Cakes with Tomato & Avocado Relish

Preparation: 25 minutes / Cooking: 10 minutes / Serves: 4

1 large tomato, cut into small dice

⅓ cup diced avocado

2 tablespoons chopped fresh coriander or flat-leaf parsley

1½ tablespoons grated red onion

3 teaspoons lime juice

¼ teaspoon Tabasco sauce

Salt

1 slice firm white sandwich bread, crumbled

¼ cup low-fat milk

500g cooked crab meat

1½ tablespoons low-fat mayonnaise

⅓ cup dry breadcrumbs

1 tablespoon vegetable oil

1. Combine the tomato, avocado, coriander, onion, lime juice, Tabasco sauce and a pinch of salt in a medium bowl. Cover and refrigerate while you prepare the crab cakes.

2. Combine the bread and milk in a medium bowl. Add the crab and mayonnaise, stirring to combine. Shape into 8 cakes and dredge in the breadcrumbs.

3. Preheat the oven to 200°C. Heat the oil in a large nonstick frying pan over moderate heat. Fry the crab cakes for 2 minutes on each side or until golden brown. Transfer to a baking tray and bake for 5 minutes or until heated through. Serve the cakes with the relish.

Nutrients per serving: Kilojoules 949; Fibre 2g; Protein 19g; Carbohydrate 15g; Saturated Fat 2g; Total Fat 10g; Cholesterol 107mg

Linguine with Lobster & Asparagus *(l)*

Preparation: 10 minutes / Cooking: 15 minutes / Serves: 6

400g linguine

250g asparagus spears, blanched and cut into 5cm lengths

2 cooked lobster tails (about 200g each), shells removed, or 200g crab meat

2½ tablespoons olive oil

1 red chilli, seeded and thinly sliced

3 tablespoons snipped fresh chives

3 tablespoons chopped fresh parsley

Freshly ground pepper

1. Cook the pasta in a large saucepan of boiling water according to the packet directions, until firm-tender. Drain and return the linguine to the saucepan.

2. Add the asparagus, lobster, oil, chilli, chives and parsley to the saucepan and toss gently over low heat for 3 minutes. Season to taste with freshly ground pepper.

Nutrients per serving: Kilojoules 1211; Fibre 3g; Protein 15g; Carbohydrate 38g; Saturated Fat 1g; Total Fat 8g; Cholesterol 40mg

Did you know?

A Dutch study suggests that high zinc levels are associated with a reduced risk of cancer. One serving of crab provides 95 per cent of your daily zinc requirement, while lobster supplies more than one-third of the RDI.

Linguine with Lobster & Asparagus

Mussels, Oysters & Scallops

Mussels, oysters and scallops are prime sources of vitamin B_{12}, which your body needs in order to utilise folate. They are also rich in minerals, including zinc and iron.

Healthy Highlights

Mussels

12 mussels, steamed (95g)

		Nutrients % RDI	
Kilojoules	541	Iron	119%
Fibre	0g	Magnesium	43%
Protein	18.4g	Zinc	33%
Carbohydrate	7.4g	Niacin	28%
Saturated Fat	0.8g	Phosphorus	26%
Total Fat	2.8g	Vitamin C	26%
Cholesterol	63mg	Folate	23%
Sodium	168mg	Potassium	17%
		Riboflavin	17%
		Calcium	15%
		Vitamin A	10%

Oysters

6 oysters, raw

		Nutrients % RDI	
Kilojoules	277	Zinc	492%
Fibre	0g	Phosphorus	34%
Protein	11g	Iron	29%
Carbohydrate	0.6g	Niacin	23%
Saturated Fat	0.8g	Riboflavin	23%
Total Fat	2.2g	Calcium	15%
Cholesterol	73mg	Magnesium	17%
Sodium	283mg	Potassium	11%

Scallops

6 scallops, grilled (80g)

		Nutrients % RDI	
Kilojoules	303	Zinc	29%
Fibre	0g	Phosphorus	23%
Protein	15.1g	Thiamin	23%
Carbohydrate	0.8g	Niacin	22%
Saturated Fat	0.2g	Magnesium	11%
Total Fat	0.9g		
Cholesterol	43mg		
Sodium	115mg		

Mussels in a Red Chilli Broth

Preparation: 10 minutes

Cooking: 1 hour 10 minutes / Serves: 4

4 medium tomatoes, halved
2 cloves garlic
2 dried chillies, seeded
1¼ cups fish stock
1 tablespoon olive oil
1kg mussels, scrubbed and debearded
2 tablespoons chopped fresh parsley

1. Preheat the oven to 150°C. Spray a baking tray with cooking spray. Arrange the tomato halves and the garlic in a single layer on the tray and roast for 1 hour.

2. Meanwhile, combine the chillies, the stock and ½ cup water in a medium bowl. Put aside for 1 hour or until the chillies are softened.

3. Combine the chillies and their liquid with the tomatoes and garlic in a food processor. Process until puréed.

4. Heat the oil in a large saucepan. Add the mussels, cover with a lid and steam for 3 to 4 minutes or until the mussels have opened. Remove from the saucepan and discard any that have remained closed.

5. Add the puréed tomato mixture to the saucepan and heat until simmering. Return the mussels to the saucepan and gently reheat for 2 to 3 minutes. Sprinkle with the parsley just before serving.

Nutrients per serving: Kilojoules 958; Fibre 2g; Protein 25g; Carbohydrate 12g; Saturated Fat 2g; Total Fat 8g; Cholesterol 79mg

Did you know?

Because they are very low in fat, mussels can be enjoyed by everyone, and are particularly beneficial for people on low-cholesterol diets.

Mussels in a Red Chilli Broth

Shopping & Preparation

At the market Mussels – both the Australian mussel and the green-lipped variety from New Zealand – are available year-round. Oysters are commercially farmed and several varieties are available at different times of the year. Farmed scallops are also available year-round, while wild scallops are at their peak from May to December.

Look for Mussels are usually sold live in the shell; the shells should be tightly closed (discard any that are open), they should have a pleasant fresh smell and look bright and shiny. Oysters should be plump, have a fresh smell, a creamy colour and be free of any shell-grit. Shucked oysters are packed in jars in their 'liquor', which should be clear, not milky. Scallops are becoming more commonly available in the shell, but are generally sold shucked; they should be plump and shiny, and smell sweetly fresh, not fishy. Try to buy them fresh rather than frozen, as frozen scallops retain enormous amounts of water when thawed.

Preparation To clean mussels, pull out the 'beards' (see below) and then scrub under running water. To shuck oysters, use an oyster knife, which has a short, sturdy blade. Protect your hands with a potholder or kitchen towel. Insert the knife at the hinge and twist to break the hinge; work the knife around to sever the muscle, then cut the meat from the shell. Scallops sometimes have a small piece of tough connective tissue along one side. Pull this off and discard. As a general rule, you should eat mussels, oysters and scallops as soon as possible after buying.

To clean a mussel, grab the 'beard' and pull out with a quick, firm tug.

Pasta & Scallops Provençale

Preparation: 20 minutes / Cooking: 20 minutes / Serves: 4

375g ziti, macaroni or penne

3 teaspoons olive oil

2 small leeks, white and tender green parts only, halved lengthways, well washed and cut crossways into 1cm slices

4 cloves garlic, crushed

1 red capsicum, cut into 1cm squares

½ teaspoon fennel seeds

½ teaspoon dried tarragon

⅓ cup chicken stock

1½ cups canned no-added-salt chopped tomatoes

½ teaspoon grated orange zest

Salt

500g shelled scallops

1. Cook the pasta in a large saucepan of boiling water according to the packet directions, until firm-tender; drain.

2. Meanwhile, heat 2 teaspoons of the oil in a large nonstick frying pan over low heat. Add the leeks and garlic and fry for 4 minutes or until the leeks are tender. Add the remaining oil, the capsicum, fennel seeds and tarragon, and cook for 5 minutes or until the capsicum is tender.

3. Add the stock, increase the heat to high, and cook for 2 minutes or until the liquid has evaporated. Add the tomatoes, orange zest and a pinch of salt; reduce the heat to low and cook for 5 minutes.

4. Add the scallops, cover and cook for 3 to 4 minutes or until the scallops are just cooked through. Transfer to a large bowl, add the pasta and toss to combine.

Nutrients per serving: Kilojoules 1854 Fibre 7g; Protein 35g; Carbohydrate 61g; Saturated Fat 1g; Total Fat 6g; Cholesterol 69mg

Did you know?

• Six oysters contain six times more omega-3 fatty acids than 100g water-packed light tuna.

• The cholesterol content of most shellfish is fairly low – lower than that of lean meat and poultry. Among shellfish, mussels are the second lowest in cholesterol content – only scallops contain less.

Oysters with Tomato Salsa

Preparation: 7 minutes / Serves: 4

1 large ripe tomato, seeded and diced

½ red onion, finely chopped

2 tablespoons chopped fresh parsley

2 tablespoons lime juice

Freshly ground pepper

Salt

2 dozen oysters, freshly opened

1. Combine the tomato, onion, parsley, lime juice, a good grinding of pepper and a pinch of salt in a medium bowl. To serve, top each oyster with 1 teaspoon of the salsa.

Nutrients per serving: Kilojoules 328; Fibre 1g; Protein 12g; Carbohydrate 2g; Saturated Fat 1g; Total Fat 2g; Cholesterol 73mg

Oysters with Tomato Salsa

Spaghetti with Mussels in Marinara Sauce

Preparation: 15 minutes / Cooking: 20 minutes / Serves: 4

375g spaghetti

2 teaspoons olive oil

1 small onion, finely chopped

5 cloves garlic, crushed

2 cans (400g each) no-added-salt chopped tomatoes

750g mussels, scrubbed and debearded

⅓ cup chopped fresh basil

¼ cup chopped fresh parsley

Salt

Freshly ground pepper

1. Cook the pasta in a large saucepan of boiling water according to the packet directions, until firm-tender. Drain and transfer to a large bowl.

2. Meanwhile, heat the oil in a large frying pan over low heat. Add the onion and garlic and cook for 5 minutes or until soft. Add the tomatoes and cook, stirring occasionally, for 5 minutes or until the sauce is richly flavoured.

3. Add the mussels, cover and cook for 4 to 5 minutes or until the mussels have opened. Remove from the pan and discard any that have remained closed.

4. Return the opened mussels to the pan. Add the basil, parsley, and salt and pepper to taste,

and cook for 1 minute. Add the mussels and sauce to the pasta, tossing gently to combine.

Nutrients per serving: Kilojoules 1851; Fibre 7g; Protein 28g; Carbohydrate 67g; Saturated Fat 1g; Total Fat 6g; Cholesterol 61mg

Did you know?

Oysters have almost no fat and little cholesterol, and are one of the best sources of minerals, especially zinc, phosphorus and iron.

Octopus & Squid

Both octopus and squid are high in protein and very low in fat. Octopus supplies an impressive range of vitamins and minerals, including a large quantity of iron, as well as lots of niacin. Squid also offers valuable amounts of niacin, as well as phosphorus.

Healthy Highlights

Octopus
1 serving, cooked
(125g)

		Nutrients	% RDI
Kilojoules	644	Iron	90%
Fibre	0g	Niacin	65%
Protein	31.8g	Potassium	36%
Carbohydrate	1.3g	Phosphorus	33%
Saturated Fat	0.5g	Zinc	30%
Total Fat	2.3g	Vitamin C	29%
Cholesterol	103mg	Magnesium	22%
Sodium	575mg	Calcium	14%
		Folate	13%
		Vitamin A	12%

Squid
1 serving, grilled
(125g)

		Nutrients	% RDI
Kilojoules	684	Niacin	48%
Fibre	0g	Phosphorus	48%
Protein	34.8g	Magnesium	28%
Carbohydrate	0g	Iron	23%
Saturated Fat	0.9g	Zinc	23%
Total Fat	2.5g	Thiamin	18%
Cholesterol	415mg	Potassium	17%
Sodium	400mg	Folate	13%

Shopping & Preparation

At the market Fresh octopus and squid, which is also known as calamari, are available year-round. They can both be found frozen.

Look for Small to medium-sized whole octopus are best for cooking; look for firm flesh and a pleasant smell. Squid are sold whole or cut into rings or in tubes. Whole squid should have an intact head and tentacles, and a fresh smell. Tubes and rings should be white and unblemished.

Preparation Octopus and squid should be cleaned and gutted (if not already done before purchase). Use as soon as possible or store in plastic wrap or a sealed container in the refrigerator for 2 to 3 days. They can be frozen for 3 months.

Chargrilled Baby Octopus

Preparation: 15 minutes / Marinate: 4 hours
Cooking: 6 minutes / Serves: 4

500g baby octopus, cleaned, with heads and beaks removed

2 cloves garlic, chopped

2 tablespoons chopped fresh parsley

2 small red chillies, seeded and finely chopped

½ kiwifruit, peeled and roughly chopped

⅓ cup olive oil

2 tablespoons lemon juice

1. Combine the octopus, garlic, parsley, chillies and kiwifruit in a large bowl. Pour over the oil and lemon juice and toss well. Cover and refrigerate for 4 hours (no more or the octopus will start to break down).

2. Preheat a ridged, iron grill pan or a heavy-based frying pan. Reserving the marinade, remove the octopus and drain well. Arrange the octopus in a single layer on the grill pan and sprinkle with marinade. Cook for 3 minutes over high heat, turn, then cook for a further 3 minutes or until the octopus is cooked.

Nutrients per serving: Kilojoules 1343; Fibre 1g; Protein 30g; Carbohydrate 3g; Saturated Fat 3g; Total Fat 21g; Cholesterol 95mg

Did you know?

Squid is very high in cholesterol but because it does not contain much fat, the consumption of squid will have no bearing on the level of cholesterol in your blood.

Warm Squid & Noodle Salad

Preparation: 15 minutes / Cooking: 1 minute / Serves: 4

3 red chillies, seeded and finely chopped

1 teaspoon freshly ground black pepper

Salt

500g small squid, cleaned and halved

1 tablespoon vegetable oil

100g rice vermicelli

3 tablespoons reduced-salt soy sauce

2 tablespoons lime juice

¼ cup fresh coriander leaves

½ red onion, finely sliced

2 teaspoons grated fresh ginger

2 teaspoons brown sugar

2 teaspoons fish sauce

1. Combine the chillies, pepper and a pinch of salt in a medium bowl. Brush the squid with the oil and press in the chilli mix to coat both sides; put aside.

2. Place the vermicelli in another medium bowl and cover with boiling water. Allow to stand for 5 minutes or until tender, then drain.

3. Toss the vermicelli with the soy sauce, lime juice, coriander, onion, ginger, brown sugar and fish sauce in a serving bowl.

4. Meanwhile, preheat a ridged, iron grill pan or heavy-based frying pan. Cook the squid on the grill pan over high heat for 10 to 15 seconds on each side. Serve on top of the noodles.

Nutrients per serving: Kilojoules 1174; Fibre 1g; Protein 33g; Carbohydrate 19g; Saturated Fat 1g; Total Fat 7g; Cholesterol 361mg

Grilled Squid with Catalan Sauce

Preparation: 45 minutes / Cooking: 40 minutes / Serves: 4

1 red chilli, split open and seeded

250g ripe tomatoes

3 red capsicums

3 cloves garlic

⅓ cup blanched almonds

⅓ cup olive oil

750g baby squid, cleaned and split open

⅓ cup white wine

½ tablespoon lemon juice

Freshly ground pepper

4 sprigs fresh basil

1. Preheat the griller. Place the chilli, tomatoes, capsicums, garlic and almonds on a large baking tray. Sprinkle with 1 tablespoon of the oil and place under the griller. Remove the almonds after 5 minutes or as soon as they start to brown; remove the chilli, garlic and tomatoes after 10 to 15 minutes when they have softened; turn the capsicums occasionally and grill for about 25 minutes until the skins are black and blistered.

2. Grind the almonds in a food processor. Then peel the capsicums, tomatoes and garlic. Seed the capsicums and chop finely, along with the chilli, tomatoes and garlic.

3. Spread the squid out on a baking tray and sprinkle with 2 tablespoons of oil and the white wine. Grill the squid 8 cm from the heat for 5 minutes, turn, then cook for a further 5 minutes.

4. While the squid are cooking, combine the almonds, chilli, capsicums, tomatoes and garlic in a large saucepan, then stir in the remaining oil and the lemon juice. Season to taste with pepper. Warm the sauce for 3 to 4 minutes over a gentle heat. When the squid is cooked, garnish with the basil and serve with the sauce.

Nutrients per serving: Kilojoules 2118; Fibre 4g; Protein 50g; Carbohydrate 6g; Saturated Fat 4g; Total Fat 29g; Cholesterol 539mg

Warm Squid & Noodle Salad

Prawns

A low-fat protein source, prawns provide a good amount of B vitamins. They're also mineral-rich, supplying valuable amounts of phosphorus and magnesium.

Healthy Highlights

King prawns*
6 prawns, cooked (100g)

		Nutrients % RDI	
Kilojoules	446	Niacin	35%
Fibre	0g	Phosphorus	31%
Protein	23.8g	Magnesium	23%
Carbohydrate	0g	Calcium	17%
Saturated Fat	0.3g	Zinc	15%
Total Fat	1.2g	Potassium	11%
Cholesterol	188mg		
Sodium	485mg	*peeled	

School prawns*
1 serving, cooked (100g)

		Nutrients % RDI	
Kilojoules	355	Phosphorus	24%
Fibre	0g	Niacin	20%
Protein	18g	Magnesium	14%
Carbohydrate	0g	Calcium	13%
Saturated Fat	0.3g	Zinc	13%
Total Fat	1.3g	Iron	10%
Cholesterol	188mg		
Sodium	315mg	*peeled	

Shopping & Preparation

At the market Prawns come in a range of sizes, from tiny school prawns to large king prawns, and are widely available. They are sold either whole in the shell, or peeled and deveined, both green or cooked, fresh or frozen. They are harvested all year round; farmed prawns are also available all year.

Look for When buying both green or cooked prawns, look for firm bodies with moist flesh and tight, intact shells. There should be a pleasant fresh smell and no sign of black discoloration. Frozen prawns should be solidly frozen; thawed prawns should smell fresh and have firm, glossy shells.

Preparation Prawns cooked in their shells need to be peeled and deveined for some recipes (see page 39), but should be left unpeeled – either refrigerated or frozen – until the last possible moment, to keep in moisture and flavour. Green prawns are best kept covered in cold water to prevent blackening. To freeze, cover prawns with water in a plastic container; they can be kept for up to 3 months.

Prawns Oreganata

Preparation: 30 minutes / Cooking: 5 minutes / Serves: 4

¼ cup chopped fresh parsley

¼ cup chopped fresh mint

½ teaspoons grated lemon zest

3 teaspoons lemon juice

2 teaspoons olive oil

1½ teaspoons dried oregano

Cayenne pepper

500g large green prawns, peeled and deveined

1 large tomato, finely chopped

100g feta cheese, crumbled

1. Combine the parsley, mint, lemon zest, lemon juice, oil, oregano and a pinch of cayenne pepper in a large bowl. Add the prawns, tossing well to coat.

2. Preheat the oven to 220°C. Place the prawns on a large baking tray. Top with the tomato and feta cheese. Bake for 4 minutes, without turning, or until the prawns are cooked through and the feta is melted.

Nutrients per serving: Kilojoules 701; Fibre 1g; Protein 20g; Carbohydrate 1g; Saturated Fat 4g; Total Fat 9g; Cholesterol 137mg

Did you know?

Prawns are rich in zinc, and school prawns also provide some iron. Many adults, especially women and the elderly, consume less of both these minerals than their bodies require. Eating more prawns is a tasty way to get adequate amounts.

Asian Stuffed Prawns

Preparation: 30 minutes / Cooking: 10 minutes / Serves: 4

16 green king prawns (about 750g), peeled and deveined

⅓ cup chopped fresh coriander

1 clove garlic, crushed

3 teaspoons olive oil

1 small carrot, julienned

2 spring onions, cut into 5cm x 5mm strips

3 teaspoons grated fresh ginger

1½ tablespoons reduced-salt soy sauce

1½ tablespoons chilli sauce

1 tablespoon lime juice

1 medium cos lettuce, leaves roughly torn

1 cucumber, peeled, halved lengthways, seeded and sliced

2 tablespoons chopped fresh mint

1. Make a cut along the back of the prawns with a paring knife until you have cut almost, but not quite through, to the other side. Toss together the prawns, coriander, garlic and 1 teaspoon of the oil in a large bowl; put aside.

2. Heat the remaining oil in a large nonstick frying pan over moderate heat. Add the carrot and spring onions and cook for 2 minutes. Add the ginger and cook for 2 minutes. Cool the vegetable mixture to room temperature.

3. Preheat the griller. Place the prawns, cut-side-up, on the griller tray, pressing them down to flatten slightly. Spoon the vegetable mixture onto the prawns and grill 15 cm from the heat for 4 minutes or until the prawns are just cooked through.

4. Meanwhile, combine the soy sauce, chilli sauce and lime juice in a large bowl. Add the lettuce, cucumber and mint, tossing to combine. Serve the grilled prawns on a bed of the salad mixture.

Nutrients per serving: Kilojoules 679; Fibre 2g; Protein 24g; Carbohydrate 4g; Saturated Fat 1g; Total Fat 5g; Cholesterol 180mg

Prawn Cocktail

Preparation: 10 minutes / Serves: 4

½ cup no-added-salt tomato sauce

2 tablespoons Worcestershire sauce

2 tablespoons reduced-fat sour cream

1 tablespoon lemon juice

½ teaspoon Tabasco sauce

375g cooked prawns, peeled with tails left attached

12 baby cos lettuce leaves

4 sprigs fresh dill

1. Combine the tomato sauce, Worcestershire sauce, sour cream, lemon juice and Tabasco sauce in a small bowl.

2. Thread the prawns onto 4 small bamboo skewers. Spoon the sauce into serving dishes, arrange a prawn skewer in each, and garnish with the cos and the dill sprigs.

Nutrients per serving: Kilojoules 637 Fibre 1g; Protein 18g; Carbohydrate 11g; Saturated Fat 2g; Total Fat 4g; Cholesterol 141mg

Coriander Prawns with Mango Salad

Coriander Prawns with Mango Salad ⓒ

Preparation: 15 minutes / Marinate: 10 minutes

Cooking: 2 minutes / Serves: 4

16 green king prawns (about 750g), peeled with heads and tails intact

¼ cup chopped fresh coriander

½ cup lime juice

1 green chilli, seeded and finely chopped

2 teaspoons sesame oil

1 teaspoon cumin seeds

1 clove garlic, crushed

2 green mangoes, finely sliced

4 spring onions, sliced

2 red chillies, seeded and sliced

2 teaspoons brown sugar

½ cup fresh mint leaves

½ cup snow pea sprouts

1. Thread the prawns lengthways onto 16 small bamboo skewers (soak the skewers in water for 30 minutes beforehand, so that they won't burn).

2. Combine the coriander, ⅓ cup of the lime juice, the green chilli, sesame oil, cumin seeds and garlic in a small bowl. Brush the marinade thoroughly over the prawns and put aside for 10 minutes.

3. Meanwhile, combine the mangoes, spring onions, red chillies, brown sugar, mint leaves, snow pea sprouts and the remaining lime juice in a medium serving bowl.

4. Preheat a barbecue or a ridged, iron grill pan. Cook the prawns for 1 minute on each side or until cooked through. Serve with bowls of the salad.

Nutrients per serving: Kilojoules 822; Fibre 3g; Protein 24g; Carbohydrate 16g; Saturated Fat 1g; Total Fat 4g; Cholesterol 169mg

Did you know?

The results of traditional cholesterol assays – which measured all sterols (a type of fat) as a group – indicated that prawns were high in cholesterol. But more sophisticated tests now show prawns to have far less cholesterol than previously thought. And, as it turns out, some of the other sterols found in prawns may have beneficial effects.

Prawns Provençale

Preparation: 30 minutes / Cooking: 35 minutes / Serves: 4

1 red capsicum, cut lengthways into flat strips

½ teaspoon Tabasco sauce

3 teaspoons olive oil

1⅓ cups rice

Salt

1 small onion, finely chopped

2 cloves garlic, crushed

1 small bulb fennel (trimmed) or 1 large stalk celery, cut into 1cm pieces

⅔ cup canned no-added-salt chopped tomatoes

½ cup chicken stock

¾ teaspoon grated orange zest

500g medium green prawns, peeled and deveined

Freshly ground black pepper

4 sprigs fresh dill or fennel

1. Preheat the griller. Place the capsicum strips, skin-side-up, on the griller tray and grill 10 cm from the heat for 12 minutes or until the skin is blackened. When the capsicum strips are cool enough to handle, peel and transfer to a food processor or blender. Add the Tabasco sauce and 1 teaspoon of the oil, and purée.

2. Meanwhile, bring 4 cups water to the boil in a large saucepan. Add the rice and a pinch of salt. Reduce to a simmer, cover and cook for 15 minutes or until the rice is tender. Drain and keep warm.

3. Heat the remaining oil in a large nonstick frying pan over moderate heat. Add the onion and garlic and cook for 5 minutes or until soft. Add the fennel and cook for 7 minutes or until tender. Stir in the tomatoes, stock, orange zest and a pinch of salt. Bring to the boil, reduce to a simmer, cover and cook for 5 minutes.

4. Add the prawns to the pan and cook for 4 minutes or until just cooked through. Stir the capsicum purée into the pan. Top with a good grinding of pepper and serve with the rice and a garnish of dill sprigs.

Nutrients per serving: Kilojoules 1563; Fibre 5g; Protein 21g; Carbohydrate 61g; Saturated Fat 1g; Total Fat 5g; Cholesterol 113mg

Did you know?

Prawns contain a considerable amount of omega-3 fatty acids – less than fatty fish such as herring, but more than lean fish like ling, jewfish or john dory. Omega-3s seem to make blood platelets less 'sticky' – that is, less likely to form artery-clogging plaques.

Prawns Provençale

Salmon

Salmon is one of the best sources of omega-3 fatty acids. It also provides valuable minerals, while fresh salmon in particular supplies copious amounts of niacin.

Healthy Highlights

Fresh salmon
1 serving, grilled (120g)

		Nutrients % RDI	
Kilojoules	923	Niacin	111%
Fibre	0g	Phosphorus	35%
Protein	30.2g	Potassium	34%
Carbohydrate	0g	Thiamin	34%
Saturated Fat	2.5g	Riboflavin	28%
Total Fat	11g	Magnesium	16%
Cholesterol	82mg	Folate	11%
Sodium	73mg		

Canned pink salmon*
100g

		Nutrients % RDI	
Kilojoules	615	Niacin	63%
Fibre	0g	Calcium	39%
Protein	21.9g	Phosphorus	24%
Carbohydrate	0g	Riboflavin	17%
Saturated Fat	1.9g	Potassium	13%
Total Fat	6.5g	Magnesium	10%
Cholesterol	78mg		
Sodium	585mg	*in brine	

Shopping & Preparation

At the market Fresh salmon is sold whole, in cutlets and in fillets. It is available nearly all year, with supplies dwindling in May and June. Most canned salmon is pink (humpback) salmon; canned sockeye salmon is deeper in colour, richer in flavour, and more expensive.

Look for Fresh salmon should smell like an ocean breeze, not 'fishy'. Look for bright pink skin, bright bulging eyes and firm, fresh-smelling flesh. Cutlets or fillets should look moist and slightly translucent; the flesh should feel resilient.

Preparation Salmon cutlets and fillets sometimes contain 'pin bones' firmly embedded in the flesh. Run your fingers over the surface of the fish to find them, then remove them with large tweezers (see page 39). Fresh salmon can be kept in plastic wrap or an airtight container in the refrigerator for 2 to 3 days or for up to 6 months in the freezer.

Salmon with Salsa Verde

Preparation: 15 minutes / Cooking: 10 minutes / Serves: 4

- 1 slice firm white sandwich bread, crumbled
- 2 tablespoons low-fat milk
- ½ cup finely chopped fresh flat-leaf parsley
- 1 tablespoon capers, rinsed
- 2 anchovy fillets
- 1 tablespoon lemon juice
- Freshly ground black pepper
- 2 tablespoons olive oil
- 4 salmon fillets, skinned (200g each)
- 1 small bunch rocket (optional)

1. Preheat the oven to 200°C. Combine the bread and milk in a shallow bowl; put aside to soak.

2. Combine the parsley, capers, anchovies, lemon juice and a good grinding of pepper in a food processor. Pulse to combine. Add the soaked bread and process until puréed. With the motor still running, slowly add the oil; process until smooth.

3. Spray a baking tray with cooking spray. Place the salmon, rounded-side-up, on the tray. Bake for 6 to 10 minutes or until the salmon is rare to medium. Serve on a bed of rocket leaves, if using, with the salsa spooned on top.

Nutrients per serving: Kilojoules 1679; Fibre 1g; Protein 42g; Carbohydrate 4g; Saturated Fat 5g; Total Fat 24g; Cholesterol 111mg

Did you know?

Canned salmon is so rich in calcium because, during processing, the bones become soft enough to eat.

Salmon with Salsa Verde

Parchment-Baked Salmon with Baby Peas

Parchment-Baked Salmon with Baby Peas

Preparation: 10 minutes / Cooking: 10 minutes / Serves: 4

2 cups frozen baby peas, thawed

2 spring onions, thinly sliced

¼ cup chopped fresh mint

1½ tablespoons lemon juice

2 teaspoons olive oil

Salt

4 salmon fillets, skinned (200g each)

1. Preheat the oven to 220°C. Combine the peas, spring onions, mint, lemon juice, oil and a pinch of salt in a medium bowl. Toss well and put aside.

2. Spray four 35 cm lengths of parchment paper or foil with cooking spray. Place the salmon fillets, rounded-side-up, on one half of each piece of parchment paper. Top each salmon fillet with the pea and spring onion mixture. Fold the other half of the parchment paper over the salmon and fold the edges over once or twice to seal the packets.

3. Place the packets on a baking tray and bake for 10 minutes or until the packets are puffed and the salmon is rare to medium.

Nutrients per serving: Kilojoules 1539; Fibre 5g; Protein 45g; Carbohydrate 7g; Saturated Fat 4g; Total Fat 18g; Cholesterol 109mg

Did you know?

Salmon is rich in omega-3 fatty acids, which may help fight cancer and reduce inflammation.

Poached Salmon with Herbed Mayonnaise

Preparation: 10 minutes / Cooking: 10 minutes / Serves: 4

1 onion, sliced

1 carrot, thinly sliced

6 whole black peppercorns

750g salmon fillet, in one piece, skin on

¼ cup low-fat mayonnaise

2 tablespoons reduced-fat sour cream

3 teaspoons lime juice

¼ cup chopped fresh basil

2 tablespoons snipped fresh chives

1. Bring 3 cups water to the boil in a large frying pan over moderate heat. Add the onion, carrot and peppercorns and reduce to a simmer. Slip in the fish, skin-side-up; cover and simmer for 8 minutes or until the salmon is just cooked through. Cool in the poaching liquid. Reserving 2 tablespoons of the poaching liquid, lift the fish out, transfer to a platter, cover and put aside. Discard the remaining poaching liquid and the solids.

2. Whisk together the reserved poaching liquid, the mayonnaise, sour cream and lime juice in a medium bowl. When well combined, stir in the basil and chives.

3. Remove the salmon skin and cut the fillet into 4 portions. Serve the salmon with the sauce spooned on top.

Nutrients per serving: Kilojoules 1329; Fibre 0g; Protein 35g; Carbohydrate 3g; Saturated Fat 5g; Total Fat 18g; Cholesterol 107mg

Did you know?

One American study has shown that omega-3s suppressed the growth of breast tumours in laboratory animals.

Salmon & Mango Ceviche

Preparation: 20 minutes / Marinate: 3–4 hours

Chill: 30 minutes / Serves: 4

250g fresh salmon fillet, cubed, or reduced-salt canned salmon

1-2 tablespoons lime juice

Salt

2 teaspoons grated lime zest

1 large firm mango, cubed

1 large avocado, diced

1 green chilli, seeded and chopped

4 spring onions, sliced

¼ cup fresh coriander leaves

1 tablespoon capers, rinsed

½ small cos lettuce

2 whole pita bread, split, cut into quarters and oven-crisped

1. If using fresh salmon, combine with 1 tablespoon lime juice and a pinch of salt in a small bowl. Cover and put aside in a cool place for 3 to 4 hours, then drain. If using canned salmon, drain, break into large chunks and keep refrigerated.

2. Combine the marinated or canned salmon with 1 tablespoon lime juice, the lime zest, mango, avocado, chilli, spring onions, coriander leaves and capers. Fold everything together gently and chill for 30 minutes. Serve with the lettuce leaves and the pita bread.

Nutrients per serving: Kilojoules 1550; Fibre 4g; Protein 18g; Carbohydrate 31g; Saturated Fat 4g; Total Fat 19g; Cholesterol 32mg

Did you know?

Canned salmon – with its calcium-rich bones and omega-3 fatty acids – is particularly valauable in the diet of older people.

Salmon & Mango Ceviche

Did you know?

Many studies have shown that the omega-3 fatty acids (polyunsaturated fats) found in fish such as salmon significantly reduce triglyceride levels. Triglycerides – blood fats – seem to be a contributing factor to heart disease, although the exact relationship is unclear.

Roasted Salmon with Parsley & Lemon Dressing

Preparation: 5 minutes / Cooking: 15 minutes / Serves: 4

750g salmon fillet, in one piece, skin on

1 tablespoon olive oil

⅓ cup chicken stock

1 teaspoon grated lemon zest

¼ cup lemon juice

3 teaspoons Dijon mustard

½ teaspoon dried tarragon

Freshly ground black pepper

1 red capsicum, cut into 5mm dice

¼ cup chopped fresh parsley

1. Preheat the oven to 200°C. Spray a baking tray with cooking spray. Place the salmon, skin-side-down, on the tray. Rub 1 teaspoon of the oil onto the salmon. Bake for 12 minutes or until the salmon is rare to medium.

2. Meanwhile, whisk together the stock, lemon zest, lemon juice, the remaining oil, the mustard, tarragon and a good grinding of black pepper in a medium bowl. Add the capsicum and parsley.

3. Lift the salmon off the baking tray with a large spatula, leaving the skin behind. Divide the fish into 4 portions and serve with the dressing spooned on top.

Nutrients per serving: Kilojoules 1391; Fibre 1g; Protein 39g; Carbohydrate 2g; Saturated Fat 4g; Total Fat 19g; Cholesterol 102mg

Sardines

In your quest for healthy foods, don't overlook the humble sardine, a rich source of protein, calcium (from the bones) and omega-3 fatty acids.

Healthy Highlights

Fresh sardines
1 serving, cooked (120g)

		Nutrients	% RDI
Kilojoules	804	Niacin	110%
Fibre	0g	Phosphorus	62%
Protein	23g	Potassium	40%
Carbohydrate	0g	Magnesium	31%
Saturated Fat	3.6g	Riboflavin	28%
Total Fat	10.8g	Iron	18%
Cholesterol	96mg	Zinc	12%
Sodium	135mg		

Canned sardines*
4 sardines (60g)

		Nutrients	% RDI
Kilojoules	460	Niacin	45%
Fibre	0g	Calcium	29%
Protein	13.1g	Phosphorus	29%
Carbohydrate	0g	Iron	14%
Saturated Fat	1.7g	Magnesium	13%
Total Fat	6.4g	Potassium	10%
Cholesterol	68mg	Riboflavin	10%
Sodium	366mg		

*in water

Shopping & Preparation

At the market Fresh sardines are available year-round from the larger fish markets; they are sometimes referred to as pilchards. Most supermarkets offer a variety of canned sardines. They are sold with the skin on and the soft, edible bones in, or skinless and boneless; and they may be packed in oil, water, tomato sauce or mustard sauce. Canned sardines are sometimes lightly smoked.

Look for Read and compare the nutrition labelling on cans of sardines: fat and sodium content varies considerably among the different types.

Preparation Fresh sardines are usually sold already cleaned, with heads and backbones removed, ready for cooking. Canned sardines are ready to eat.

Barbecued Sardines in Vine Leaves

Preparation: 30 minutes / Cooking: 2 minutes / Serves: 4

2 tablespoons finely chopped fresh coriander

2 tablespoons finely chopped fresh mint

2 cloves garlic, finely chopped

2 tablespoons finely chopped pine nuts

1 tablespoon lemon juice

16 fresh sardines (about 650g), cleaned, with heads and backbones removed

16 fresh or preserved vine leaves, blanched or rinsed

2 tablespoons olive oil

2 lemons, cut into 8 wedges each

1. Preheat the barbecue or griller. Combine the coriander, mint, garlic, pine nuts and lemon juice in a small bowl. Place a small spoonful in each sardine and close the fish over the stuffing.

2. Spread the vine leaves out flat on a board. Roll each sardine in a vine leaf and secure with a toothpick. Drizzle the fish with a little oil and cook over hot coals or grill 8 cm from the heat for 1 minute each side. Serve with the lemon wedges.

Nutrients per serving: Kilojoules 1220; Fibre 1g; Protein 20g; Carbohydrate 1g; Saturated Fat 4g; Total Fat 23g; Cholesterol 77mg

Did you know?

Their edible bones make canned sardines – like canned salmon – a very valuable source of calcium in the diet.

Sicilian Pasta

Preparation: 20 minutes / Cooking: 30 minutes / Serves: 4

2 teaspoons olive oil

1 small onion, finely chopped

3 cloves garlic, crushed

1 small bulb fennel, trimmed and cut into 1cm dice

2 cans (400g each) no-added-salt chopped tomatoes

2 cans (105g each) sardines packed in oil, drained

Salt

Cayenne pepper

300g macaroni or ziti

1 tablespoon pine nuts, toasted

1. Heat the oil in a large nonstick frying pan over moderate heat. Add the onion and garlic and cook for 5 minutes or until soft. Add the fennel and cook for a further 5 minutes or until soft. Add the tomatoes, sardines, and a pinch each of salt and cayenne pepper, and bring to the boil. Reduce to a simmer, cover and cook for 15 minutes or until the sauce is blended and highly flavoured.

2. Meanwhile, cook the pasta in a large saucepan of boiling water according to the packet directions, until firm-tender. Drain well. Toss the hot pasta with the sauce and scatter over the pine nuts.

Nutrients per serving: Kilojoules 1741; Fibre 9g; Protein 21g; Carbohydrate 52g; Saturated Fat 3g; Total Fat 13g; Cholesterol 56mg

Crostini with Marinated Onions & Sardines

Preparation: 15 minutes / Cooking: 4 minutes / Marinate: 1 hour / Serves: 4

1 small red onion, thinly sliced

½ cup white wine

2 tablespoons white wine vinegar

1 bay leaf

Freshly ground black pepper

Salt

4 slices woodfired bread or other crusty firm bread

8 large canned sardines, drained

1 tablespoon finely chopped fresh parsley

½ lemon, cut into quarters and then into thin slices

1. Place the onion rings in a medium bowl. Combine the wine, vinegar, bay leaf and a good grinding of pepper in a small saucepan and bring to the boil. Pour the liquid over the onions and leave to marinate for 1 hour. Drain.

2. Toast the bread. Divide the onions among the bread slices and arrange 2 sardines on top of each. Sprinkle with the parsley and add a thin slice of lemon.

Nutrients per serving: Kilojoules 1606; Fibre 3g; Protein 21g; Carbohydrate 40g; Saturated Fat 4g; Total Fat 13g; Cholesterol 75mg

Did you know?

Rinsing canned sardines (handle them gently to avoid breaking them) will reduce their sodium content, which is often fairly high.

Crostini with Marinated Onions & Sardines

Tuna & Swordfish

Remarkably lean for so tasty a fish, tuna provides good amounts of healthy omega-3 fatty acids. It is also an excellent source of B vitamins. Swordfish has even less fat than tuna, with a good supply of niacin.

Healthy Highlights

Fresh tuna
1 serving, grilled
(120g)

		Nutrients % RDI	
Kilojoules	990	Niacin	165%
Fibre	0g	Phosphorus	43%
Protein	39g	Potassium	32%
Carbohydrate	0g	Thiamin	26%
Saturated Fat	3.5g	Magnesium	22%
Total Fat	8.9g	Iron	19%
Cholesterol	56mg	Folate	11%
Sodium	60mg	Vitamin A	10%

Canned tuna*
100g

		Nutrients % RDI	
Kilojoules	518	Niacin	88%
Fibre	0g	Phosphorus	19%
Protein	24.8g	Potassium	12%
Carbohydrate	0g	Iron	11%
Saturated Fat	1g	Magnesium	10%
Total Fat	2.6g	Riboflavin	10%
Cholesterol	53mg	Zinc	10%
Sodium	415mg		

*in brine

Swordfish
1 serving, cooked
(120g)

		Nutrients % RDI	
Kilojoules	779	Niacin	91%
Fibre	0g	Phosphorus	40%
Protein	30.5g	Potassium	23%
Carbohydrate	0g	Magnesium	15%
Saturated Fat	1.7g	Zinc	15%
Total Fat	6.2g	Iron	10%
Cholesterol	60mg	Riboflavin	10%
Sodium	138mg		

Tuna Salad Niçoise

Preparation: 15 minutes / Cooking: 20 minutes / Serves: 4

3 cloves garlic, peeled

250g green beans, cut in half

375g small red potatoes (about 6), halved

2 tablespoons balsamic or red wine vinegar

1½ tablespoons low-fat mayonnaise

3 teaspoons olive oil

Salt

¼ cup fresh basil leaves

1 punnet cherry tomatoes, halved

1 can (415g) water-packed tuna, drained

3 cups packed torn cos lettuce leaves

¼ cup black olives

1. Cook the garlic in a large saucepan of boiling water for 3 minutes to blanch. Transfer the garlic with a slotted spoon to a food processor or blender; put aside. Add the beans to the boiling water and cook for 4 minutes or until crisp-tender. Remove the beans with a slotted spoon, rinse under cold water, then drain. Add the potatoes to the saucepan and cook for 12 minutes or until tender; drain.

2. Add the vinegar, mayonnaise, oil and a pinch of salt to the garlic in the food processor, and purée. Add the basil and 2 tablespoons of water, and purée.

3. Transfer the dressing to a large bowl. Add the tomatoes, beans, potatoes and tuna, tossing to coat. Add the lettuce and toss again. Top with the olives when serving.

Nutrients per serving: Kilojoules 1001; Fibre 6g; Protein 24g; Carbohydrate 19g; Saturated Fat 2g; Total Fat 7g; Cholesterol 45mg

Did you know?

• Several studies have now indicated that eating fish reduces the risk of heart disease, and many health authorities advise eating fish at least once or twice each week.

• In Japan, where fish forms part of the daily diet, heart disease is remarkably rare.

Grilled Marinated Swordfish Steaks

Preparation: 10 minutes / Marinate: 1 hour

Cooking: 10 minutes / Serves: 4

¼ cup tomato purée

1½ tablespoons balsamic vinegar

2 teaspoons olive oil

1 teaspoon Tabasco sauce

½ teaspoon dried oregano

½ teaspoon ground ginger

Salt

4 swordfish steaks (200g each)

1. Combine the tomato purée, vinegar, oil, Tabasco sauce, oregano, ginger and a pinch of salt in a shallow bowl. Add the swordfish and rub the mixture into both sides. Cover and refrigerate for at least 1 hour.

2. Preheat the griller. Reserving the marinade, grill the swordfish 15 cm from the heat for 4 minutes. Turn the fish over, spoon on the reserved marinade, and grill for 4 minutes or until the fish is just cooked through.

Nutrients per serving: Kilojoules 838; Fibre 0g; Protein 29g; Carbohydrate 1g; Saturated Fat 2g; Total Fat 8g; Cholesterol 56mg

Tuna Salad Niçoise

Shopping & Preparation

At the market Yellowfin is the type of tuna most often available fresh; boneless cutlets or steaks are the most common form sold, but large fillets are also available. Swordfish may be harder to find; while caught all year, it is generally available in the larger fish markets from February to April. Its flesh is similar to tuna but moister. You can substitute tuna or other meaty fish – ask your fishmonger's advice about what's best and freshest. Canned tuna comes in white (albacore) and light versions; white tuna is packed 'solid' (usually a single piece of tuna), while light tuna comes in chunks or flakes.

Look for Fresh tuna looks more like meat than fish: the darker the red, the fresher the fish. The steaks should have a pleasant saltwater smell; they should look moist and dense, and feel springy to the touch. Swordfish cutlets are a pinkish white; they should have firm, pleasant-smelling flesh and look moist. When selecting canned tuna, do not assume that all water-packed varieties are lower in fat than oil-packed; since the fat content of tuna can vary according to when and where it is caught, always check the nutrition panel on the label.

Preparation Tuna and swordfish steaks, cutlets and fillets come ready to cook. They will keep, wrapped in plastic wrap, in the refrigerator for up to 3 days or in the freezer for 3 months. Canned tuna is ready to eat.

Tuna with Capsicum Salsa

Preparation: 25 minutes / Standing: 30 minutes
Cooking: 5 minutes / Serves: 4

I small red capsicum, finely diced
I small yellow capsicum, finely diced
I small red chilli, seeded and finely chopped
⅓ cup red wine vinegar
⅓ cup finely chopped fresh coriander leaves
⅓ cup finely chopped fresh mint leaves
I small onion, finely chopped
2 tablespoons lime juice
¼ cup olive oil
Salt
Freshly ground black pepper
4 tuna steaks (200g each)
½ lemon, cut into 4 wedges

1. Preheat the oven to 180°C. Combine the capsicums, chilli, vinegar, coriander, mint, onion, lime juice, 2 tablespoons of the oil, and salt and pepper to taste, in a medium bowl. Put aside for 30 minutes to allow the flavours to develop.

2. Heat the remaining oil on a griller tray or in a large nonstick frying pan over moderately high heat. Cook the tuna for 2 to 3 minutes each side or until rare to medium. Top with a little more pepper, then serve with the salsa and the lemon wedges alongside.

Nutrients per serving: Kilojoules 1939; Fibre 1g; Protein 53g; Carbohydrate 3g; Saturated Fat 7g; Total Fat 26g; Cholesterol 75mg

Did you know?

• Tuna and billfishes, such as swordfish, have less than half the fat of an equivalent serving of lean beef, so are considered valuable inclusions in a healthy diet.

• Despite the fact that they live in salt water, marine fish are naturally low in sodium. And they are the best dietary source of iodine, a mineral required for proper thyroid function.

• Seafood is also a good source of fluorine, which – in addition to its well-known role in keeping teeth healthy – helps to prevent calcium loss from bones.

Swordfish Kebabs with Lemon & Garlic Sauce

Preparation: 20 minutes / Cooking: 10 minutes / Serves: 4

3 cloves garlic, peeled and finely chopped

¼ cup lemon juice

1 tablespoon olive oil

1 tablespoon chopped fresh parsley

¼ cup chicken stock

Freshly ground pepper

750g swordfish steaks, cut into 24 cubes

16 cherry tomatoes

1 red onion, cut into 8 wedges

1. Combine the garlic, lemon juice, 3 teaspoons of the oil and the parsley in a small bowl; put aside.

2. Preheat the griller. Combine the stock and a good grinding of pepper. Add the swordfish, tomatoes and onion, tossing gently to coat. Reserving the stock, alternately thread the fish, tomatoes and onions onto 8 skewers. (If using bamboo skewers, presoak for 30 minutes beforehand, so that they don't burn.)

3. Add the remaining oil to the reserved stock mixture. Brush on the skewered fish and - vegetables. Grill 15 cm from the heat for 6 minutes, turning the skewers over once, or until the fish is just cooked through and the onion is lightly browned. Spoon the lemon sauce over the kebabs.

Nutrients per serving: Kilojoules 917; Fibre 2g; Protein 27g; Carbohydrate 4g; Saturated Fat 2g; Total Fat 10g; Cholesterol 50mg

Tuna with Capsicum Salsa

White Fish

White fish are low in cholesterol and kilojoules, but high in valuable minerals, including potassium and phosphorus, and have useful quantities of niacin.

Healthy Highlights

Bream
I serving, grilled (120g)

		Nutrients % RDI	
Kilojoules	809	Niacin	65%
Fibre	0g	Phosphorus	54%
Protein	30.5g	Potassium	27%
Carbohydrate	0g	Thiamin	22%
Saturated Fat	2.8g	Magnesium	18%
Total Fat	7.9g	Vitamin C	12%
Cholesterol	115mg		
Sodium	98mg		

Morwong
I serving, grilled (120g)

		Nutrients % RDI	
Kilojoules	634	Niacin	65%
Fibre	0g	Phosphorus	31%
Protein	27.6g	Potassium	23%
Carbohydrate	0g	Magnesium	13%
Saturated Fat	1.7g		
Total Fat	4.4g		
Cholesterol	84mg		
Sodium	103mg		

Snapper
I serving, grilled (120g)

		Nutrients % RDI	
Kilojoules	629	Niacin	86%
Fibre	0g	Phosphorus	54%
Protein	31.6g	Potassium	36%
Carbohydrate	0g	Magnesium	18%
Saturated Fat	1g	Thiamin	17%
Total Fat	2.5g		
Cholesterol	95mg		
Sodium	122mg		

Blue-eye cod
I serving, grilled (120g)

		Nutrients % RDI	
Kilojoules	502	Niacin	48%
Fibre	0g	Potassium	35%
Protein	27.1g	Phosphorus	34%
Carbohydrate	0g	Magnesium	18%
Saturated Fat	0.3g	Vitamin C	12%
Total Fat	1.8g	Iron	11%
Cholesterol	80mg		
Sodium	408mg		

Snapper in Ginger Marinade

Snapper in Ginger Marinade

Preparation: 15 minutes / Marinate: 1 hour

Cooking: 20 minutes / Serves: 4

2 teaspoons cumin
  seeds, toasted

2 teaspoons coriander
  seeds, toasted

1 bunch fresh coriander,
  roughly chopped

1 red chilli, seeded

4 cloves garlic, crushed

2cm piece fresh ginger,
  peeled

3 tablespoons lemon
  juice

1 tablespoon ground
  paprika

1 teaspoon ground
  turmeric

¼ cup olive oil

4 baby snapper (about
  400g each), cleaned

1 lemon, cut into
  8 wedges

Spring onions curls
  (optional)

1. Combine the cumin seeds, coriander seeds, fresh coriander, chilli, garlic, ginger, lemon juice, paprika, turmeric and oil in a food processor. Process to a paste.

2. Preheat the oven to 180°C. Score both sides of each fish diagonally with a small kitchen knife and rub the paste in well. Put aside to marinate for 1 hour.

3. Spray a large baking dish with cooking spray. Place the fish in one layer in the dish and bake for 15 to 20 minutes or until the flesh is opaque. Serve garnished with lemon wedges and the spring onion curls, if using.

Nutrients per serving: Kilojoules 1408; Fibre 1g; Protein 42g; Carbohydrate 1g; Saturated Fat 3g; Total Fat 18g; Cholesterol 125mg

Did you know?

In a study of two African tribes – one totally vegetarian and the other predominantly fish-eaters – the fish-eaters had lower levels of LDL, or 'bad', cholesterol.

Provençale Fish Stew

Preparation: 25 minutes / Cooking: 20 minutes / Serves: 4

3 teaspoons olive oil

1 medium onion, finely
  chopped

4 cloves garlic, crushed

1 red capsicum, diced

1 can (400g)
  no-added-salt
  chopped tomatoes

⅓ cup chicken stock

¼ cup Kalamata olives,
  pitted and chopped

½ teaspoon fennel seeds

Cayenne pepper

Salt

375g snapper, cut into
  2.5cm cubes

375g morwong or
  blue-eye cod, cut into
  2.5cm cubes

⅓ cup chopped fresh
  basil

1. Heat the oil in a large nonstick frying pan over moderate heat. Add the onion and garlic and cook for 5 minutes or until the onion is soft. Add the capsicum and cook for 4 minutes or until crisp-tender.

2. Add the tomatoes, the stock, olives, fennel seeds, and a pinch each of cayenne pepper and salt. Bring to the boil, then reduce to a simmer. Add the snapper and morwong, cover and cook for 7 minutes or until the fish is cooked. Stir in the basil just before serving.

Nutrients per serving: Kilojoules 1080; Fibre 3g; Protein 37g; Carbohydrate 8g; Saturated Fat 2g; Total Fat 8g; Cholesterol 106mg

Shopping & Preparation

Shopping & Preparation

At the market Fresh white fish, either whole or in fillets or cutlets, are available year-round. The many varieties may vary in name from one area to another, but you will generally find some species of snapper, bream, morwong, jewfish, leatherjacket, flounder, dory, whiting, flathead, perch and cod in the markets. Be guided by your fishmonger's advice, as most white fish are interchangeable in recipes. Frozen white fish fillets are always available in good food shops and supermarkets.

Look for Gutted whole fish should have bright, clear, bulging eyes; the gills should be bright red or pink; the flesh should be firm and springy when touched. Fillets and cutlets should appear translucent and glistening fresh. They should smell pleasant, have no discoloration, and not ooze water when touched. The flesh should be shiny and firm.

Preparation Whole fish should be scaled, with gills and gut removed (your fishmonger will do this for you). Wash cleaned whole fish, fillets or cutlets in cold water and dry well; wrap in plastic wrap or foil and keep in the refrigerator for no more than 3 days, or in the freezer for no more than 6 months.

Cooking tip Measure the thickness of the fish with a ruler, then cook it for about 10 minutes each 2.5cm of thickness.

Blue-Eye Cod with Herb Butter

Preparation: 15 minutes / Cooking: 5 minutes / Serves: 4

1½ tablespoons unsalted butter, softened

2 teaspoons reduced-fat cream cheese

3 teaspoons snipped fresh dill

1 teaspoon snipped fresh chives

1 teaspoon drained horseradish

½ teaspoon grated lemon zest

2 tablespoons lemon juice

4 blue-eye cod or thick bream fillets (200g each)

4 sprigs fresh dill

100g mixed salad leaves

1. Preheat the griller. Beat together the butter and cream cheese in a medium bowl until well combined. Stir in the dill, chives, horseradish, lemon zest and lemon juice.

2. Grill the fish 15 cm from the heat for 2 minutes each side or until the fish is just cooked through. Serve topped with the herb butter and garnished with the dill sprigs. Arrange the salad leaves alongside.

Nutrients per serving: Kilojoules 718; Fibre 1g; Protein 25g; Carbohydrate 1g; Saturated Fat 4g; Total Fat 8g; Cholesterol 91mg

Did you know?

• A health study begun in 1957 included a survey of the dietary habits of its 2107 male subjects. A follow-up 30 years later revealed that the men who ate the most fish had the lowest risk of heart disease – nearly 40 per cent lower than those who ate no fish at all.

• A compound called DHA – one of the omega-3 fatty acids found in fish – is vital to brain development in childhood, especially before the age of two. Researchers suspect that a deficit of DHA in adulthood may be a factor in depression.

Baked Fish Fillets with Ginger & Spring Onions

Preparation: 10 minutes / Cooking: 10 minutes / Serves: 4

4 bream, snapper or other firm white fish fillets, skinned (200g each)

1½ tablespoons reduced-salt soy sauce

3 teaspoons dry sherry

1 tablespoon grated fresh ginger

2 teaspoons sesame oil

2 spring onions, thinly sliced

1. Preheat the oven to 190°C. Line a 23 x 33 cm metal baking dish with foil, leaving a 5 cm overhang on both short ends. Spray the foil with cooking spray. Place the fish in the dish in a single layer.

2. Combine the soy sauce, sherry, ginger and sesame oil in a small bowl. Spoon the mixture over the fish then fold the foil across the top to seal loosely. Bake for 8 to 10 minutes or until the fish is just cooked through.

3. Carefully lift the foil-wrapped fish from the baking dish and transfer the fish fillets to individual serving plates. Spoon the pan juices over the fillets, then sprinkle with the sliced spring onions.

Nutrients per serving: Kilojoules 1406; Fibre 0g; Protein 49g; Carbohydrate 1g; Saturated Fat 5g; Total Fat 15g; Cholesterol 182mg

Blue-Eye Cod with Herb Butter

Meat

Beef

Beef is an iron-rich protein source; it also supplies many of the B vitamins as well as zinc. Served in small quantities, with vegetables and grains, lean beef makes a healthy and flavoursome meal.

Healthy Highlights

Lean beef
1 serving, cooked (125g)

		Nutrients % RDI	
Kilojoules	850	Niacin	83%
Fibre	0g	Zinc	52%
Protein	35.1g	Phosphorus	30%
Carbohydrate	0g	Iron	29%
Saturated Fat	3.1g	Potassium	21%
Total Fat	6.8g	Riboflavin	21%
Cholesterol	85mg	Thiamin	13%
Sodium	75mg	Folate	11%
		Magnesium	11%

Beef mince*
1 serving, cooked (125g)

		Nutrients % RDI	
Kilojoules	976	Niacin	71%
Fibre	0g	Zinc	58%
Protein	34.5g	Thiamin	45%
Carbohydrate	0g	Iron	35%
Saturated Fat	4.6g	Phosphorus	24%
Total Fat	10.5g	Potassium	21%
Cholesterol	91mg	Folate	13%
Sodium	71mg		

*lean

Rump steak*
1 serving, grilled (125g)

		Nutrients % RDI	
Kilojoules	956	Niacin	93%
Fibre	0g	Zinc	47%
Protein	35.6g	Iron	35%
Carbohydrate	0g	Phosphorus	30%
Saturated Fat	4.3g	Riboflavin	27%
Total Fat	9.5g	Potassium	20%
Cholesterol	86mg	Thiamin	12%
Sodium	68mg	Folate	11%

* fat trimmed

Thai Red Beef Curry

Preparation: 10 minutes
Cooking: 10 minutes / Serves: 4

500g lean beef strips
2 teaspoons vegetable oil
1 clove garlic, crushed
½ red capsicum, cut in strips
100g button mushrooms, sliced
1 tablespoon red curry paste
1 tablespoon brown sugar
1 tablespoon fish sauce
2 cans (165ml each) fat-reduced coconut milk
100g spinach, chopped
⅓ cup fresh coriander leaves
Steamed rice (optional)

1. Combine the beef, oil and garlic in a small bowl. Heat a wok or a heavy nonstick frying pan over high heat. Add the beef strips in small batches and stir-fry for 1 to 2 minutes. Remove each batch when cooked and allow the pan to reheat before frying the next batch.

2. Add the capsicum and mushrooms to the pan with a sprinkling of water. Steam for 1 to 2 minutes, then return the beef strips.

3. Stir in the curry paste, brown sugar, fish sauce, coconut milk, spinach and coriander. Toss for 1 to 2 minutes or until heated through. Serve with rice, if liked.

Nutrients per serving: Kilojoules 1167; Fibre 5g; Protein 31g; Carbohydrate 8g; Saturated Fat 7g; Total Fat 14g; Cholesterol 65mg

Lemon Peppered Roast Beef

Preparation: 10 minutes / Marinate: 2–3 hours / Cooking: 1–1½ hours
Standing: 20 minutes / Serves: 6

1½ tablespoons vegetable oil
2 teaspoons grated lemon zest
1 tablespoon lemon juice
1½ tablespoons brown sugar
1 teaspoon ground black pepper
2 tablespoons dry sherry
1kg lean beef roast

1. Combine the oil, lemon zest, lemon juice, brown sugar, pepper and sherry in a large dish. Add the beef and marinate for 2 to 3 hours.

2. Preheat the oven to 180°C. Transfer the roast to a baking dish and cook for about 45 minutes for rare, 1 hour for medium and 1¼ hours for well done. When cooked, cover with foil and rest for 20 minutes to allow the juices to settle.

Nutrients per serving: Kilojoules 1410; Fibre 0g; Protein 40g; Carbohydrate 3g; Saturated Fat 6g; Total Fat 17g; Cholesterol 99mg

Thai Red Beef Curry

Mustard Beef Medallions with Tuscan Salad @

Preparation: 10 minutes / Cooking: 6–10 minutes / Serves: 4

50g green beans, sliced

50g butter beans, sliced

2 medium tomatoes, cut into wedges

150g canned artichoke hearts, drained

150g mixed lettuce leaves

½ bunch rocket

4 lean rump medallions

1 tablespoon tarragon or wholegrain mustard

⅓ cup Italian salad dressing

1. Blanch the green beans and butter beans in boiling water in a medium saucepan for 1 minute and then cool under cold running water. Toss with the tomatoes, artichoke hearts, lettuce and rocket leaves in a salad bowl and refrigerate until ready to serve.

2. Preheat a ridged, iron grill pan. Cook the steaks for 3 minutes each side or until done to your liking. Baste on both sides with the mustard towards the end of the cooking time.

3. Toss the salad with the dressing just before serving and arrange on four plates. Serve with the beef medallions alongside.

Nutrients per serving: Kilojoules 1333; Fibre 4g; Protein 38g; Carbohydrate 5g; Saturated Fat 5g; Total Fat 16g; Cholesterol 84mg

Did you know?

• Many older people suffer from an insufficient intake of dietary protein, leading to a loss of muscle strength and impairment of immune function. Including even small amounts of beef in their meals would give these people a big protein bonus.

• Thirty grams of lean beef supplies more protein than two egg whites.

Shopping & Preparation

At the market Butchers and most supermarkets have low-fat cuts of beef on offer. The lean beef cuts approved by the National Heart Foundations of Australia and New Zealand are blade, fillet, skirt, round, rump, sirloin, silverside and topside. These are variously available as roasts, steaks, strips, cubes/dice or mince.

Look for Roasts and steaks should have little or no exterior fat; whatever fat there is should be pale, not yellowish. The meat should be bright red and fresh-looking. There should also be very little marbling of fat through the lean tissue.

Preparation Beef should be refrigerated as soon as possible after purchase. Take it out of its wrapping, place on a non-plastic plate and cover lightly with foil to allow some air flow. Before cooking, trim off any remaining exterior fat. (For the recipes in this book, weigh the meat after trimming.) For the leanest possible beef mince, cut a piece of round steak into chunks (roughly 4cm square) and chop in a food processor.

To make mince, drop the chunks of round steak through the feed tube of a food processor and chop by pulsing on and off.

Cooking tips To test that a steak is done to your liking, press it with tongs rather than cutting into it. Rare steak feels soft when pressed; medium steak has some resistance; and well-done steak feels firm. Cover and rest the steak for about 1 minute before serving to retain the juiciness. And when carving beef roasts, slice very thinly across the grain and on a sharp diagonal. This cuts across the meat's fibres and makes it more tender.

Madras Meatballs with Fresh Herb Dip

Preparation: 20 minutes / Cooking: 10 minutes / Serves: 4

½ cup plain low-fat yoghurt

2 tablespoons chopped fresh mint

2 tablespoons chopped fresh parsley

300g lean beef mince

1 egg, beaten

1 small onion, finely chopped

1 tablespoon Madras curry powder

Salt

Freshly ground black pepper

3 spring onions, cut into 2cm lengths

1 red capsicum, cut into 2cm squares

1 red onion, cut into 2cm squares

1. Combine the yoghurt, mint and 1 tablespoon of the parsley in a small bowl. Cover and refrigerate until ready to serve.

2. Combine the mince, egg, onion, curry powder, the remaining parsley, and salt and pepper to taste, in a medium bowl. Shape the mixture into 5 cm ovals.

3. Preheat the griller. Thread the meatballs lengthways onto 4 skewers, alternating with spring onion, capsicum and red onion pieces. (If using bamboo skewers, soak in water for 30 minutes beforehand, so that they won't burn.)

4. Grill the meatballs 10 cm from the heat for 8 to 10 minutes, turning occasionally. Serve hot with the herb dip.

Nutrients per serving: Kilojoules 695; Fibre 2g; Protein 20g; Carbohydrate 6g; Saturated Fat 3g; Total Fat 7g; Cholesterol 103mg

Did you know?

Iron-deficiency anaemia can result in fatigue, irritability and lowered immunity. Women are especially susceptible to this condition, so should ensure an adequate intake of iron-rich foods.

Spicy Beef with Lime Pickle

Preparation: 10 minutes / Cooking: 2–2½ hours / Serves: 4

1 tablespoon vegetable oil

1 medium onion, chopped

2 cloves garlic, crushed

750g well-trimmed lean beef, diced

1 tablespoon lime pickle

1 tablespoon sambal oelek

1 cup beef stock

Salt

Freshly ground black pepper

1. Heat 1 teaspoon of the oil in a deep-sided frying pan over high heat. Add the onion and garlic and cook for 1 to 2 minutes. Put aside.

2. Heat another teaspoon of the oil in the same pan over high heat. Add the beef in small batches and brown for 3 minutes. Remove each batch when cooked and allow the pan to reheat before frying the next batch.

3. Return the beef and the onion to the pan. Stir in the lime pickle, sambal oelek and stock. Cover and simmer gently for 1½ to 2 hours until the meat is tender, stirring occasionally.

4. Season to taste with salt and pepper. If the sauce needs thickening, boil with the lid off for a further 10 to 15 minutes.

Nutrients per serving: Kilojoules 1257; Fibre 1g; Protein 42g; Carbohydrate 5g; Saturated Fat 4g; Total Fat 13g; Cholesterol 98mg

Beef Strips with Black Bean Sauce

Preparation: 10 minutes / Cooking: 10 minutes / Serves: 4

500g lean beef strips

2 teaspoons vegetable oil

1 teaspoon chopped fresh ginger

1 red capsicum, sliced

2 stalks celery, sliced

200g snow peas, trimmed

¼ cup black bean sauce

2 tablespoons slivered almonds

Steamed rice (optional)

1. Combine the beef, oil and ginger in a small bowl. Heat a wok or a heavy nonstick frying pan over high heat. Add the beef strips in small batches and stir-fry for 1 to 2 minutes. Remove each batch when cooked and allow the pan to reheat before frying the next batch.

2. Add the capsicum, celery and snow peas to the frying pan with a sprinkling of water. Steam for 2 to 3 minutes, then return the beef strips. Stir in the black bean sauce. Heat through for about 1 to 2 minutes. Top with the almonds and serve with rice, if using.

Nutrients per serving: Kilojoules 1137; Fibre 3g; Protein 31g; Carbohydrate 8g; Saturated Fat 3g; Total Fat 13g; Cholesterol 66mg

Did you know?

• Meat is a valuable part of a healthy diet if it is carefully selected and sensibly prepared. Unfortunately, many people eat much of their beef in the form of fast-food hamburgers, which may have up to 28 grams of fat per serving.

• Through scientifically planned breeding and feeding, beef is now much leaner than it was 20 years ago. In addition, butchers now trim far more fat from retail cuts of beef.

Beef Strips with Black Bean Sauce

Moroccan Beef with Couscous

Preparation: 20 minutes / Cooking: 20 minutes / Serves: 4

500g lean beef strips

1 tablespoon vegetable oil

1 clove garlic, crushed

Moroccan Couscous (recipe, page 159)

1 medium onion, chopped

⅓ cup slivered almonds

½ cup sultanas

1 teaspoon ground turmeric

1 teaspoon ground cumin

1 tablespoon sugar

1 can (400g) no-added-salt chopped tomatoes

60g spinach or silverbeet, shredded

1. Combine the beef, 2 teaspoons of the oil and the garlic in a small bowl. Heat a wok or a heavy nonstick frying pan over high heat. Add the beef strips in small batches and stir-fry for 1 to 2 minutes. Remove each batch when cooked and allow the pan to reheat before frying the next batch.

2. Meanwhile, prepare the Moroccan Couscous as directed, but omit the chickpeas and raisins.

3. Heat the remaining oil in the pan. Add the onion, almonds and sultanas and fry for 1 minute, then return the beef strips.

4. Add the turmeric, cumin, sugar, tomatoes and spinach. Toss to heat through, about 1 to 2 minutes. Serve with the couscous.

Nutrients per serving: Kilojoules 2001; Fibre 4g; Protein 34g; Carbohydrate 41g; Saturated Fat 4g; Total Fat 20g; Cholesterol 66mg

Did you know?

Beef is a very good source of potassium, with 100g providing more than one small banana.

Moroccan Beef with Couscous

Salsa Steak

Salsa Steak

Preparation: 10 minutes / Cooking: 10–15 minutes / Serves: 4

1 small cucumber, chopped

1 large tomato, peeled and diced

1 small red onion, diced

½ yellow capsicum, diced

⅓ cup chopped fresh coriander leaves

1 teaspoon seeded mustard

4 lean beef steaks (150g each)

2 teaspoons vegetable oil

Cajun Oven Fries (recipe, page 96) or other oven-cooked potatoes (optional)

1. Combine the cucumber, tomato, onion, capsicum, coriander and mustard in a medium bowl. Put aside.

2. Heat a heavy nonstick frying pan over high heat. Brush the steaks with oil on both sides and add to the pan. Cook for 2 to 3 minutes each side for rare; reduce the heat to moderate and continue cooking for 2 to 3 minutes each side for medium; cook for a further 4 to 6 minutes each side for well done.

3. Serve with the salsa alongside. Accompany with the oven fries, if liked.

Nutrients per serving: Kilojoules 978; Fibre 1g; Protein 31g; Carbohydrate 3g; Saturated Fat 4g; Total Fat 11g; Cholesterol 75mg

Did you know?

• The complete protein in beef helps your body utilise the incomplete protein in vegetables, legumes and grains when you eat these foods along with beef.

• Because beef supplies two kinds of iron (haem and non-haem iron) – while plant foods, such as spinach, contain only non-haem iron – eating a little beef with iron-rich vegetables or legumes will also help you better absorb the non-haem iron from the plant foods.

Veal

Veal is an excellent low-fat source of protein, and also supplies B vitamins and zinc. While it has less iron than beef, it is still a good source of this important mineral.

Healthy Highlights

I serving, cooked* (125g)		Nutrients % RDI	
Kilojoules	745	Niacin	103%
Fibre	0g	Zinc	39%
Protein	39.5g	Riboflavin	35%
Carbohydrate	0g	Phosphorus	33%
Saturated Fat	0.6g	Potassium	21%
Total Fat	2g	Iron	19%
Cholesterol	139mg	Folate	11%
Sodium	100mg	Thiamin	10%

*all cuts, fat trimmed

Shopping & Preparation

At the market Veal is naturally lean. The leanest cuts are the forequarter, leg, loin and fillet. These are variously available as roasts, steaks, chops, osso bucco, strips, cubes/dice or mince. Scaloppine are thin slices from the leg. Veal for stewing may come from any cut; the meat from the leg or the shoulder is the leanest.

Look for Veal may be either milk-fed or grain-fed. Milk-fed veal is a pale pink and exceptionally tender. Grain-fed veal is darker in colour (though not as red as beef) and somewhat less tender than milk-fed.

Preparation Some recipes call for veal scaloppine to be pounded thin. To do this, place each piece of veal between sheets of plastic wrap. Working from the centre out, use a meat pounder to thin the meat to the required thickness.

Veal Scaloppine with Sage & Lemon

Preparation: 10 minutes / Cooking: 15 minutes
Serves: 4

2 tablespoons plain flour
Salt
Freshly ground white pepper
12 sage leaves
4 veal scaloppine (500g), each cut into 3 equal pieces
2 tablespoons olive oil
2 tablespoons lemon juice
1 cup chicken stock
1 tablespoon unsalted butter
2 tablespoons julienned lemon zest
1 lemon, cut into 8 wedges
2 cups cooked saffron rice (optional)

1. Preheat the oven to 120°C. Sprinkle the flour onto a large plate and season with a little salt and freshly ground pepper to taste. Press a sage leaf firmly onto each piece of veal, then turn in the flour until well coated.

2. Heat the oil over moderate heat in a large, heavy-based frying pan. Add the veal to the pan and cook for 2 minutes on each side, then remove and keep warm on a tray in the oven.

3. Add the lemon juice to the pan, then add the stock and stir over moderate heat until the liquid has reduced by half. Add the butter and the lemon zest and continue to swirl the mixture until the butter has been absorbed into the sauce.

4. Return the veal to the pan and cook gently for a few seconds on each side to heat through. Serve with the lemon wedges, and the saffron rice, if using.

Nutrients per serving: Kilojoules 1170; Fibre 1g; Protein 30g; Carbohydrate 5g; Saturated Fat 4g; Total Fat 15g; Cholesterol 113mg

Did you know?

Lower in fat than all but the very leanest beef cuts, veal is an exceptional source of niacin, which helps to keep your skin, your nerves and your digestive system healthy.

Veal Bake with Orange & Basil

Veal Bake with Orange & Basil

Preparation: 20 minutes / Cooking: 1 hour

Serves: 4

2 teaspoons olive oil

500g lean veal, diced

1 tablespoon plain flour

1 large onion, finely chopped

2 cloves garlic, crushed

250g button mushrooms, quartered

1 cup canned no-added-salt chopped tomatoes

1 teaspoon grated orange zest

½ cup orange juice

Salt

1 cup frozen peas

¼ cup chopped fresh basil

Mashed potatoes (optional)

1. Preheat the oven to 180°C. Heat the oil in a flameproof casserole over moderate heat. Dredge the veal in the flour, shaking off any excess. Add the veal to the casserole in small batches and fry for 4 minutes. Remove each batch when cooked and allow the casserole to reheat before frying the next batch. Transfer the veal to a plate.

2. Add the onion and garlic to the casserole and cook for 3 minutes or until the onion is crisp-tender. Add the mushrooms and cook for 5 minutes or until they release their juices.

3. Add the tomatoes and their juice, the orange zest, orange juice and a pinch of salt to the casserole, then cover and bake for 45 minutes or until the veal is tender.

4. Stir in the peas and basil and cook for 5 minutes or until the peas are heated through. Serve with mashed potatoes, if liked.

Nutrients per serving: Kilojoules 988; Fibre 6g; Protein 35g; Carbohydrate 13g; Saturated Fat 1g; Total Fat 4g; Cholesterol 101mg

Lamb

Exceptionally flavourful, lamb is a super source of niacin and zinc. Like all the other types of red meat, it also supplies a useful amount of iron.

Healthy Highlights

1 serving, cooked* (125g)		Nutrients % RDI	
Kilojoules	936	Niacin	112%
Fibre	0g	Iron	56%
Protein	38.1g	Zinc	50%
Carbohydrate	0g	Phosphorus	35%
Saturated Fat	3.4g	Riboflavin	32%
Total Fat	7.8g	Potassium	27%
Cholesterol	115mg	Magnesium	24%
Sodium	100mg	Thiamin	17%

*lean cut, fat trimmed

Shopping & Preparation

At the market Although lamb is generally considered fattier than beef, there are several lean cuts available that carry the National Heart Foundation seal of approval – the 'tick'. These include the fillet, eye of loin, silverside, round, topside and leg (variously available as roasts, steaks, butterfly steaks, schnitzels, strips, cubes/dice or mince) – as well as shanks (drumsticks).

Look for Fresh lamb should be pinkish red and firm; any bones should be reddish at the centre. Whatever external fat remains should be white to cream in colour.

Preparation There shouldn't be much fat left on lamb, but trim off any that you see.

Although the layer of fat on most chops these days is minimal, it's much healthier to trim it to nothing before cooking.

Cooking tip When grilling or roasting lamb, don't cook it beyond medium-rare or it will lose its rich flavour. Lamb cooked by moist-heat methods, such as stewing, can be cooked longer.

Lamb Kofta

Preparation: 30 minutes / Cooking: 25 minutes / Serves: 4

- 500g lean lamb mince
- 1 egg, lightly beaten
- 1 cup fresh breadcrumbs
- 2 teaspoons garam masala
- Salt
- 1 tablespoon vegetable oil
- 2 cloves garlic, crushed
- 1 teaspoon grated fresh ginger
- 2 tablespoons curry powder
- 1 can (400g) no-added-salt chopped tomatoes

1. Combine the lamb mince, egg, breadcrumbs, garam masala and a pinch of salt in a large bowl. Shape the mixture into 24 meatballs.

2. Heat the oil in a large nonstick frying pan over high heat. Add the meatballs and cook for 8 to 10 minutes, turning occasionally. Remove from the pan and keep warm.

3. Add the garlic and ginger to the same pan and cook for 5 minutes over moderate heat. Add the curry powder and cook for 1 minute. Reduce the heat to low, then add the tomatoes. Simmer for 2 to 3 minutes. Return the meatballs to the pan and heat through, about 5 minutes.

Nutrients per serving: Kilojoules 1396; Fibre 3g; Protein 27g; Carbohydrate 15g; Saturated Fat 5g; Total Fat 15g; Cholesterol 135mg

Did you know?

- Lamb is leaner than it used to be, thanks to advances in breeding. And most retail cuts of lamb now carry a minimum of external fat.
- Avoid pre-packaged lamb mince; 100g, cooked, may contain as much as 12g of fat.

Lamb Steaks Provençale

Preparation: 10 minutes / Cooking: 30 minutes / Serves: 4

- 1 tablespoon light olive oil
- 1 medium onion, sliced
- 1 small green capsicum, sliced
- 2 cloves garlic, crushed
- 1 can (400g) no-added-salt chopped tomatoes
- ½ cup pitted black olives
- 3 large marinated artichoke hearts, halved
- Salt
- Freshly ground black pepper
- 8 lean lamb steaks (60g each)

1. Heat the oil in a medium saucepan over medium heat. Add the onion, capsicum and garlic and cook for 5 minutes until softened.

2. Reduce the heat to low. Add the tomatoes, olives and artichokes. Cover and simmer for 15 to 20 minutes, then season the sauce with salt and pepper to taste.

3. Spray a medium nonstick frying pan with cooking spray. Add the steaks and cook over high heat for 3 to 5 minutes or until done to your liking. Serve with the sauce.

Nutrients per serving: Kilojoules 1277; Fibre 3g; Protein 38g; Carbohydrate 10g; Saturated Fat 4g; Total Fat 12g; Cholesterol 109mg

Italian Lamb Roast

Italian Lamb Roast

Preparation: 20 minutes / Cooking: 15–35 minutes / Standing: 5–10 minutes / Serves: 4

1 tablespoon olive oil

1 tablespoon red wine vinegar

1 tablespoon chopped fresh basil

1 teaspoon brown sugar

4 egg tomatoes

2 lamb mini roasts (350g each)

3 tablespoons basil pesto

Cooked fusilli (optional)

1. Preheat the oven to 220°C. Combine the oil, vinegar, basil and brown sugar in a small bowl. Cut the tomatoes in half and place in an ovenproof dish just large enough to fit them in one layer. Sprinkle with the oil mixture.

2. Spray a small baking dish with cooking spray. Coat the roasts with the pesto and place in the baking dish along with about ½ cup water. Roast the lamb for 15 to 18 minutes for rare (the lamb will be pink), 20 to 25 minutes for medium, or 30 to 35 minutes for well done, basting occasionally with the pan juices. You

can add more water to the pan if the juices evaporate too quickly. Roast the tomatoes at the same time.

3. Remove the lamb roasts from the oven and cover with foil. Rest for 5 to 10 minutes to let the juices settle before carving. Serve with the oven-roasted tomatoes along with the cooked fusilli, if desired.

Nutrients per serving: Kilojoules 1943; Fibre 1g; Protein 32g; Carbohydrate 3g; Saturated Fat 14g; Total Fat 37g; Cholesterol 133mg

Greek Lamb Casserole

Preparation: 20 minutes / Cooking: 1½–2 hours / Serves: 4

1 tablespoon vegetable oil

1 large onion, finely chopped

3 cloves garlic, crushed

750g well-trimmed boneless lamb forequarter, diced

1 red capsicum, diced

⅓ cup red wine

⅓ cup vegetable stock

4 bay leaves

125g okra, trimmed, or zucchini, sliced

Salt

Freshly ground black pepper

½ cup Kalamata olives

Steamed rice tossed with chopped parsley (optional)

1. Heat 1 teaspoon of the oil in a deep-sided nonstick frying pan over moderate heat. Add the onion and garlic and cook for 1 to 2 minutes. Remove and put aside.

2. Add the remaining oil to the pan and heat on high. Add the lamb in small batches and fry for 3 minutes. Remove each batch when brown and allow the pan to reheat before frying the next batch.

3. Reduce the heat and return the lamb, onion and garlic to the pan. Add the capsicum, wine, stock and bay leaves. Cover and simmer gently for 1½ to 2 hours or until the lamb is tender.

4. During the last 20 minutes of cooking, add the okra or zucchini and season to taste with salt and pepper. Garnish with the olives and serve with the rice, if using.

Nutrients per serving: Kilojoules 1598; Fibre 3g; Protein 40g; Carbohydrate 9g; Saturated Fat 8g; Total Fat 20g; Cholesterol 134mg

Greek Lamb Casserole

Moroccan Lamb & Sweet Potato Stew

Moroccan Lamb & Sweet Potato Stew

Preparation: 20 minutes / Cooking: 1 hour 15 minutes / Serves: 4

2 teaspoons olive oil

500g well-trimmed
boneless lamb
shoulder, diced

1 large onion, chopped

3 cloves garlic, crushed

1 teaspoon ground
coriander

1 teaspoon ground cumin

¾ teaspoon paprika

Salt

Freshly ground pepper

2 tablespoons
no-added-salt
tomato paste

750g sweet potatoes,
peeled and cut into
2cm chunks

½ cup pitted prunes,
coarsely chopped

4 sprigs fresh parsley

Steamed rice tossed
with chopped parsley
(optional)

1. Preheat the oven to 180°C. Heat the oil in a nonstick flameproof casserole over moderately high heat. Add the lamb and cook for 4 minutes or until lightly browned. Transfer the lamb to a plate and put aside. Add the onion and garlic to the casserole and cook for 5 minutes or until the onion is tender.

2. Return the lamb to the casserole. Add the coriander, cumin, paprika, and salt and pepper to taste, stirring to coat. Add the tomato paste and 1 cup water and bring to the boil. Cover and transfer the casserole to the oven. Bake for 30 minutes.

3. Add the sweet potatoes, prunes and ⅓ cup water. Cover and bake for 30 minutes or until the lamb and potatoes are tender. Top with the parsley and serve with rice, if using.

Nutrients per serving: Kilojoules 1468; Fibre 6g; Protein 32g; Carbohydrate 32g; Saturated Fat 4g; Total Fat 11g; Cholesterol 99mg

Honey-Roasted Rack of Lamb

Honey-Roasted Rack of Lamb

Preparation: 20 minutes / Cooking: 40 minutes – 1 hour

Standing: 10 minutes / Serves: 4

3 tablespoons honey

3 tablespoons lemon juice

3 tablespoons reduced-salt soy sauce

2 cloves garlic, crushed

4 zucchini, cut into strips

4 parsnips, peeled and cut into strips

4 carrots, peeled and cut into strips

1 stalk celery, halved lengthways then cut into 10cm lengths

1 red capsicum, cut into strips

6 sprigs fresh rosemary

2 cups lamb or beef stock

2 well-trimmed (frenched) lamb racks (8 cutlets each)

1. Preheat the oven to 200°C. Combine the honey, lemon juice, soy sauce and garlic in a medium bowl; put aside.

2. Lightly spray a small baking dish with cooking spray. Add the zucchini, parsnips, carrots, celery and capsicum and roast for about 20 minutes or until the vegetables are lightly browned.

3. Top the vegetables with the rosemary and pour over the stock. Arrange the lamb racks on top of the vegetables, baste with the honey sauce, and roast for 20 minutes for rare (lamb will be pink), 30 minutes for medium, or 40 minutes for well done. Continue basting with the sauce occasionally.

4. Remove the baking dish from the oven and put the lamb racks and vegetables aside; cover and rest for 10 minutes before carving the meat.

5. Boil the pan juices until they thicken slightly. Serve the sauce with the lamb and the vegetables.

Nutrients per serving: Kilojoules 1474; Fibre 5g; Protein 33g; Carbohydrate 29g; Saturated Fat 6g; Total Fat 12g; Cholesterol 109mg

Did you know?

You can save 10g of dietary fat by trimming all the external fat from a chop or large cutlet.

Moroccan Stir-Fry

Preparation: 10 minutes / Cooking: 10 minutes / Serves: 4

500g lean lamb strips

2 teaspoons vegetable oil

2 cloves garlic, crushed

2 tablespoons no-added-salt tomato paste

⅓ cup red wine

⅓ cup sultanas

2 teaspoons chopped chillies

1 tablespoon chopped fresh mint

¼ cup slivered almonds, toasted

1 teaspoon ground paprika

1. Combine the lamb strips, oil and garlic in a medium bowl. Heat a wok or a heavy nonstick frying pan over high heat. Add the lamb strips in small batches and stir-fry for 1 to 2 minutes. Remove each batch when cooked and allow the pan to reheat before frying the next batch.

2. Return all the meat to the pan. Add the tomato paste, wine, sultanas, chillies, mint, almonds and paprika. Cook, stirring constantly, for 2 to 3 minutes.

Nutrients per serving: Kilojoules 1310; Fibre 2g; Protein 27g; Carbohydrate 12g; Saturated Fat 6g; Total Fat 17g; Cholesterol 89mg

Pork

Pork is the number-one dietary source of thiamin; it offers impressive amounts of other B vitamins as well. And pork is now far leaner than it used to be.

Healthy Highlights

Lean pork*
1 serving, cooked
(125g)

		Nutrients	% RDI
Kilojoules	925	Thiamin	154%
Fibre	0g	Niacin	98%
Protein	38g	Phosphorus	35%
Carbohydrate	0g	Zinc	31%
Saturated Fat	2.9g	Potassium	30%
Total Fat	7.5g	Riboflavin	21%
Cholesterol	121mg	Magnesium	14%
Sodium	61mg	Iron	13%

*non specific cut, fat trimmed

Pork steak*
1 serving, grilled
(125g)

		Nutrients	% RDI
Kilojoules	869	Thiamin	128%
Fibre	0g	Niacin	97%
Protein	38.1g	Phosphorus	33%
Carbohydrate	0g	Potassium	28%
Saturated Fat	2.3g	Zinc	28%
Total Fat	6g	Magnesium	13%
Cholesterol	108mg	Iron	11%
Sodium	78mg		

* fat trimmed

Shopping & Preparation

At the market The lean pork cuts approved by the National Heart Foundations of Australia and New Zealand are the leg, loin, fillet and rump. These are variously available as roasts, schnitzels, butterfly steaks, steaks, cutlets, chops, cubes/dice and mince.

Look for Pork should be pink in colour, with a fine, velvety texture. If there is bone in the meat, it should be reddish rather than white.

Preparation Pork requires little preparation, except for the removal of any external fat.

Cooking tip Overcooking will toughen lean pork. The meat should reach an internal temperature of 70°C, but you can remove a roast from the oven when the thermometer registers about 68°C. Let stand for 15 minutes before serving; during this time, the temperature will rise to 70°C.

Lemon Grass Pork Skewers

Preparation: 40 minutes / Marinate: 20 minutes
Cooking: 10 minutes / Serves: 4

3 cloves garlic, crushed
2 tablespoons chopped fresh lemon grass
¼ cup finely chopped fresh coriander stalks
2 tablespoons reduced-salt soy sauce
2 tablespoons fish sauce
2 tablespoons sesame oil
1 tablespoon brown sugar
½ teaspoon ground coriander
¼ teaspoon white pepper
500g lean pork strips
½ cup sweet chilli sauce

1. Combine the garlic, lemon grass, fresh coriander, soy sauce, fish sauce, sesame oil, brown sugar, ground coriander, pepper and ⅓ cup water in a large flat dish.

2. Thread 2 pork strips lengthways onto each of 32 small skewers. (If using bamboo skewers, soak in water for 30 minutes beforehand, so that they won't burn.) Add the skewers to the marinade and put aside for at least 20 minutes.

3. Spray a large nonstick frying pan or barbecue plate with cooking spray. Heat over moderate heat and add the skewers. Cook in small batches, basting with the marinade, for 1 to 2 minutes or until just cooked, turning occasionally; don't overcook or the meat will dry out. Keep the first batch warm while cooking the rest. Serve with the sweet chilli sauce.

Nutrients per serving: Kilojoules 1233; Fibre 2g; Protein 28g; Carbohydrate 11g; Saturated Fat 3g; Total Fat 15g; Cholesterol 85mg

Did you know?

Once considered a fatty meat, some cuts of pork actually have less fat than beef fillet.

Butterfly Steak with Fruity Couscous

Preparation: 15 minutes / Cooking: 10 minutes / Serves: 4

½ cup slivered almonds or pine nuts
1 cup chicken stock
½ cup orange juice
¼ cup olive oil
2 cloves garlic, crushed
½ cup mixed dried fruit or sultanas
250g couscous
4 pork butterfly steaks (125g each)
⅓ cup chopped fresh parsley
½ cup sweet chilli sauce

1. Lightly toast the almonds in a small frying pan over moderate heat for about 2 to 3 minutes; put aside.

2. Combine the stock, orange juice, oil and garlic in a deep saucepan. Bring to the boil over moderate heat, then add the dried fruit and couscous and quickly stir with a fork. Remove from the heat, cover and let stand for 5 minutes.

3. Spray a large nonstick frying pan with cooking spray. Heat over high heat, add the pork and cook for 2 to 3 minutes on each side. Let stand for 5 minutes in a warm place.

4. Combine the nuts, couscous mixture and parsley and fluff up with a fork. Serve with the pork topped with a little chilli sauce.

Nutrients per serving: Kilojoules 2387; Fibre 5g; Protein 35g; Carbohydrate 41g; Saturated Fat 5g; Total Fat 30g; Cholesterol 79mg

Pork Butterfly Steak with Fruity Couscous

Pork Cutlets with Potato & Leek Mash

Pork Cutlets with Potato & Leek Mash

Preparation: 25 minutes / Cooking: 15 minutes / Serves: 4

6 medium potatoes, peeled and diced

1 leek, chopped

¼ teaspoon ground nutmeg

2 tablespoons finely chopped fresh parsley

½ cup low-fat milk

Salt

White pepper

4 lean pork cutlets or steaks (125g each)

4 sprigs fresh parsley

Steamed carrots (optional)

1. Cook the potatoes in boiling water in a medium saucepan for 10 minutes, until tender. Add the leeks during the last few minutes of cooking. Drain, mash and add the nutmeg, parsley, milk, and salt and pepper to taste.

2. Spray a large nonstick frying pan or barbecue plate with cooking spray. Heat over high heat, add the pork and cook for 2 to 3 minutes on each side until just done. Serve with the mash garnished with the parsley, and the carrots, if using.

Nutrients per serving: Kilojoules 1290; Fibre 4g; Protein 38g; Carbohydrate 26g; Saturated Fat 2g; Total Fat 5g; Cholesterol 90mg

Did you know?

The fillet is the choicest cut of pork, and also the leanest. One serving has even less fat than a skinless chicken leg.

Pork Steaks with Bean Salsa

Preparation: 20 minutes / Chill: 1 hour / Cooking: 15 minutes / Serves: 4

1 can (290g) three bean mix, drained and rinsed

½ red onion, finely chopped

½ cucumber, peeled and diced

½ tomato, diced

2 tablespoons finely chopped fresh parsley

2 tablespoons olive oil

2 tablespoon apple juice

2 tablespoons wine vinegar or lemon juice

1 teaspoon brown sugar

Salt

Freshly ground pepper

8 lean pork steaks (60g each)

250g lettuce or baby spinach leaves, washed

1 lemon, cut into 4 wedges

1. Combine the beans, onion, cucumber, tomato, parsley, oil, apple juice, vinegar and brown sugar in a medium bowl. Season to taste with salt and pepper and chill for 1 hour in the refrigerator.

2. Spray a large nonstick frying pan or barbecue plate with cooking spray. Heat over high heat, add the pork and cook for 2 to 3 minutes on each side until just done. Let stand for 3 minutes in a warm place.

3. Arrange the lettuce leaves on individual plates. Serve with the pork steaks and the bean salsa alongside. Accompany with the lemon.

Nutrients per serving: Kilojoules 1221; Fibre 5g; Protein 30g; Carbohydrate 12g; Saturated Fat 3g; Total Fat 14g; Cholesterol 72mg

Did you know?

Fresh pork is a healthier choice by far than pork sausages, which may have up to 25g of fat (and sometimes more than 1000mg of sodium) per serving. This is true of frankfurters and salami, as well as fresh pork sausages.

Pork Steaks with Bean Salsa

Ham

A rich source of B vitamins and protein, ham is surprisingly low in fat. The sodium content can be quite high, however, but reduced-sodium hams are available.

Healthy Highlights

3 slices, (60g)

		Nutrients	% RDI
Kilojoules	259		
Fibre	0g		
Protein	10.5g	Niacin	30%
Carbohydrate	0g	Thiamin	22%
Saturated Fat	0.8g	Phosphorus	17%
Total Fat	2.2g	Zinc	11%
Cholesterol	31mg	Riboflavin	10%
Sodium	835mg		

Shopping & Preparation

At the market Cooked whole and half-leg hams, as well as shoulder hams, can be found in the supermarket meat case; you will also find pre-wrapped mini hams available. Delicatessen counters usually offer a variety of ready-to-eat hams already sliced or which you can have sliced to order.

Look for Ham should be pink and finely grained; any exterior fat should be white. Always read the label on cooked hams: reduced-sodium and extra-lean hams are good choices.

Preparation Trim any external fat from ham before cooking or serving.

Basic cooking These recipes call for ready-to-eat ham. However, when serving ham that is labelled 'cook before eating', you'll need to heat the ham to an internal temperature of 70°C. Hams labelled 'fully cooked' may be heated to 60°C to enhance their flavour.

Baked Ham with Fig Glaze

Preparation: 10 minutes / Cooking: 30 minutes
Standing: 15 minutes / Serves: 8

1kg mini ham
1 cup brown sugar
½ cup apple juice
5 tablespoons fig jam
Ground mixed spice
Ground cinnamon

1. Preheat the oven to 180°C. Place the ham in a small baking dish. Combine the brown sugar, apple juice, jam, and a pinch each of mixed spice and cinnamon, in a medium bowl.

2. Brush the ham with the glaze and bake for 30 minutes, brushing the ham with the glaze regularly until golden brown. Test the ham by piercing with a skewer in the thickest part; the juices should be hot.

Bow-Ties with Smoked Ham & Asparagus

Preparation: 25 minutes

Cooking: 25 minutes / Serves: 4

300g bow-tie pasta
375g asparagus, trimmed and cut into 3cm lengths
2 teaspoons olive oil
1 large onion, halved and thinly sliced
2 teaspoons chopped oregano leaves
Freshly ground black pepper
1 large red capsicum, cut into 1cm squares
125g smoked ham, cut into 5mm dice
⅔ cup chicken stock
¾ teaspoon grated lemon zest
Salt
⅓ cup chopped fresh basil
3 teaspoons lemon juice

1. Cook the pasta in a large saucepan of boiling water according to the packet directions, until firm-tender. Add the asparagus for the last 2 minutes of cooking time. Drain.

2. Meanwhile, heat the oil in a large nonstick frying pan over moderate heat. Add the onion, oregano and a good grinding of pepper, and cook for 12 minutes or until the onions are golden and very tender. Add the capsicum and ham and cook for 5 minutes or until the capsicum is crisp-tender.

3. Add the drained pasta and asparagus, the stock, lemon zest and a pinch of salt, and simmer until the pasta is heated through. Remove from the heat and stir in the basil and lemon juice.

Nutrients per serving: Kilojoules 1252; Fibre 5g; Protein 16g; Carbohydrate 48g; Saturated Fat 1g; Total Fat 4g; Cholesterol 16mg

Bow-Ties with Smoked Ham & Asparagus

3. Rest the ham for 15 minutes in a warm place to allow the juices to settle and to make it easier to carve.

Nutrients per serving: Kilojoules 1161; Fibre 0g; Protein 23g; Carbohydrate 32g; Saturated Fat 3g; Total Fat 7g; Cholesterol 65mg

Did you know?

• While some hams can be high in both fat and sodium, the nutritional content is influenced by the cut of meat and the form of processing, so it is worthwhile looking around for low-fat, low-sodium hams. Sugar-cured hams generally have slightly less salt.

• Dry-cured hams, such as prosciutto, are generally more expensive than hams cured in brine, because dry-curing takes longer. After salting, the ham may be smoked and left to age for up to two years.

Poult

Poultry

Chicken Breasts

One of the leanest of all meats, skinless chicken breast is a superlative protein source for the health-conscious. B vitamins are a healthy bonus.

Healthy Highlights

1 serving, grilled* (125g)		Nutrients % RDI	
Kilojoules	968	Niacin	111%
Fibre	0g	Phosphorus	34%
Protein	35.1g	Zinc	15%
Carbohydrate	0g	Magnesium	13%
Saturated Fat	2.9g	Potassium	13%
Total Fat	10g	Riboflavin	11%
Cholesterol	113mg		
Sodium	79mg	*skinless	

Shopping & Preparation

At the market Perennially popular chicken breasts are sold whole or halved and in several forms: bone-in or boneless, and with or without skin. Skinless, boneless half breasts are also sold as breast fillets.

Look for Chicken should look pink and plump, and smell fresh.

Preparation For some recipes, you may need to pound boneless chicken breasts to flatten them to a uniform thickness.

To pound a boneless chicken breast, place between two sheets of plastic wrap and pound gently with the flat side of a meat mallet or a small, heavy frying pan.

Basic cooking To preserve the juiciness of chicken breasts, cook them quickly (especially when grilling or baking), but long enough so that the meat is fully tender and the juices run clear when the meat is pierced.

Creole-Style Chicken

Preparation: 15 minutes / Cooking: 35 minutes / Serves: 4

1 cup rice
Salt
1 tablespoon olive oil
1 teaspoon paprika
4 skinless, bone-in chicken breast halves (250g each)
1 small onion, finely chopped
4 cloves garlic, crushed
1 red capsicum, cut into 5 x 1cm strips
1 green capsicum, cut into 5 x 1cm strips
2 teaspoons fresh thyme leaves
Freshly ground black pepper
Cayenne pepper
1 can (400g) no-added-salt chopped tomatoes
½ cup chicken stock

1. Bring 3 cups water to the boil in a medium saucepan. Add the rice and a pinch of salt, reduce to a simmer, cover and cook for 12 to 15 minutes or until the rice is tender. Drain and keep warm.

2. Meanwhile, heat 2 teaspoons of the oil in a large nonstick frying pan over moderate heat. Add the paprika and stir for 10 seconds. Add the chicken and cook for 2 minutes on each side or until richly browned. Transfer the chicken to a plate. Add the remaining oil, the onion and garlic to the pan and cook for 3 minutes or until the onion is lightly browned.

3. Add the capsicums, thyme, and a pinch each of black pepper and cayenne pepper, to the pan and cook, stirring, for 5 minutes or until the capsicums are crisp-tender. Add the tomatoes and the stock and bring to the boil. Reduce to a simmer, return the chicken to the pan, cover and cook for 20 minutes or until the chicken is just cooked through. Serve over the rice.

Nutrients per serving: Kilojoules 2333; Fibre 3g; Protein 51g; Carbohydrate 47g; Saturated Fat 4g; Total Fat 18g; Cholesterol 144mg

Did you know?

One serving of cooked skinless chicken breast supplies 78 per cent of your daily protein needs.

Wine-Marinated Chicken Breasts

Preparation: 10 minutes / Marinate: 3 hours
Cooking: 15 minutes / Serves: 4

½ cup dry white wine
3 teaspoons olive oil
4 cloves garlic, peeled and lightly crushed
1 tablespoon fresh rosemary leaves
½ teaspoon pepper
3 strips orange zest (8 x 1cm)
Salt
4 skinless, bone-in chicken breast halves (250g each)

1. Combine the wine, oil, garlic, rosemary, pepper, orange zest and a pinch of salt in a shallow dish. Add the chicken, turning to coat. Cover and marinate in the refrigerator for at least 3 hours, turning the chicken several times.

2. Preheat the griller. Reserving the marinade, grill the chicken, bone-side-up, 15 cm from the heat for 8 minutes. Turn the chicken over, brush with the marinade, and grill for 7 minutes or until cooked through.

Nutrients per serving: Kilojoules 1597; Fibre 1g; Protein 52g; Carbohydrate 1g; Saturated Fat 5g; Total Fat 18g; Cholesterol 164mg

Grilled Chicken with Parsley Sauce

Grilled Chicken with Parsley Sauce

Preparation: 10 minutes / Cooking: 12–16 minutes / Serves: 4

½ teaspoon paprika

½ teaspoon ground coriander

4 skinless, boneless chicken breast halves (150g each)

1 cup packed fresh parsley leaves

¼ cup chicken stock

3 teaspoons lemon juice

2 teaspoons olive oil

Mixed salad (optional)

1. Preheat the griller. Combine the paprika and coriander in a small bowl, then rub into the chicken. Grill the chicken 15 cm from the heat for 6 to 8 minutes on each side, until cooked through.

2. Meanwhile, purée the parsley, stock, lemon juice and oil in a food processor. Slice the chicken and spoon over the sauce. Serve with salad, if liked.

Nutrients per serving: Kilojoules 915; Fibre 1g; Protein 30g; Carbohydrate 0g; Saturated Fat 3g; Total Fat 11g; Cholesterol 94mg

Did you know?

• The fat in chicken is mostly monounsaturated, which some researchers believe helps to lower blood cholesterol.

• Chicken is a fairly good source of vital minerals, including phosphorus, potassium, magnesium and zinc.

Baked Moroccan Chicken & Couscous

Preparation: 20 minutes / Cooking: 35 minutes / Serves: 4

1 teaspoon ground cumin

1 teaspoon ground coriander

½ teaspoon ground ginger

½ teaspoon cinnamon

½ teaspoon pepper

Salt

4 skinless, bone-in chicken breast halves (250g each)

2 teaspoons olive oil

1 medium onion, finely chopped

3 cloves garlic, crushed

1 cup couscous

1½ cups boiling chicken stock

¼ cup chopped fresh coriander or parsley

¼ cup chopped dates or raisins

2 tablespoons lemon juice

1 lemon, cut into 8 wedges

1. Combine the cumin, ground coriander, ginger, cinnamon, pepper and a pinch of salt in a small bowl. Rub the spice mixture onto the chicken.

2. Preheat the oven to 190°C. Heat the oil in a large nonstick frying pan over moderate heat. Add the chicken and cook for 3 minutes on each side. Transfer the chicken to a plate.

3. Add the onion and garlic to the pan and cook for 5 minutes. Add the couscous and boiling stock; stir, cover, remove from the heat and let stand for 5 minutes. Gently stir in the chopped coriander and dates with a fork.

4. Make 4 mounds of the couscous mixture in a 23 x 33 cm baking dish and place a chicken breast half on each mound. Sprinkle the chicken with lemon juice, cover with foil, then bake for 10 minutes. Uncover and bake for a further 10 minutes or until the chicken is cooked through. Serve each person a mound of couscous topped with a sliced chicken breast half. Garnish with lemon wedges.

Nutrients per serving: Kilojoules 1795; Fibre 2g; Protein 49g; Carbohydrate 22g; Saturated Fat 4g; Total Fat 16g; Cholesterol 144mg

Baked Moroccan Chicken & Couscous

Chinese Chicken Salad

Chinese Chicken Salad

Preparation: 20 minutes / Cooking: 15 minutes / Serves: 4

250g spaghetti or linguine

2 tablespoons light soy sauce

1½ tablespoons rice vinegar

3 teaspoons sesame oil

¾ teaspoon sugar

¾ teaspoon ground ginger

Salt

375g cooked shredded chicken breast

2 carrots, julienned

1 red capsicum, slivered

2 spring onions, sliced

1. Cook the pasta in a large saucepan of boiling water according to the packet directions, until firm-tender.

2. Meanwhile, combine the soy sauce, vinegar, sesame oil, sugar, ginger and a pinch of salt in a large bowl. Toss with the chicken, carrots, capsicum and spring onions.

3. Drain the pasta well and toss with the chicken mixture.

Nutrients per serving: Kilojoules 1667; Fibre 4g; Protein 33g; Carbohydrate 39g; Saturated Fat 3g; Total Fat 11g; Cholesterol 84mg

Did you know?

• When meat or poultry is grilled, carcinogenic substances can form as fat drips onto the fire; these substances are deposited back on the food in the form of smoke. But one study demonstrated that when chicken is marinated (the researchers used a marinade based on oil, vinegar, lemon juice and mustard), the amount of these substances formed is greatly reduced.

• Chicken can be marinated (in a covered dish in the refrigerator) for up to two days.

Spiced Yoghurt Chicken

Preparation: 20 minutes / Marinate: 2 hours / Cooking: 25 minutes / Serves: 4

4 skinless, boneless chicken breast halves (150g each)

1 clove garlic, crushed

½ cup plain low-fat yoghurt

1 tablespoon no-added-salt tomato paste

2 teaspoons ground cumin

1 teaspoon ground coriander

1 teaspoon ground turmeric

1 teaspoon chilli powder

1 teaspoon garam masala

½ teaspoon ground ginger

1 tablespoon chopped fresh coriander leaves

Salt

Freshly ground black pepper

1. Place the chicken in a shallow dish. Combine the garlic, yoghurt, tomato paste, cumin, ground coriander, turmeric, chilli powder, garam masala, ginger, fresh coriander, a pinch of salt and some freshly ground pepper in a small bowl. Pour over the chicken, then cover the dish and leave to marinate for at least 2 hours.

2. Preheat the oven to 220°C. Place the chicken on a rack in the oven and position a baking dish underneath the rack to catch any juices. Roast for 25 minutes, or until the chicken is cooked through, and serve immediately.

Nutrients per serving: Kilojoules 806; Fibre 0g; Protein 28g; Carbohydrate 3g; Saturated Fat 2g; Total Fat 7g; Cholesterol 84mg

Spiced Yoghurt Chicken

Chicken Parmigiana

Preparation: 10 minutes / Cooking: 20 minutes / Serves: 4

½ cup grated Parmesan cheese

½ cup dry breadcrumbs

2 egg whites

4 skinless, boneless chicken breast halves (150g each)

3 teaspoons olive oil

¼ cup shredded mozzarella cheese

2 tablespoons tomato pasta sauce

1. Preheat the oven to 200°C. Place the Parmesan on a sheet of greaseproof paper and the breadcrumbs on another sheet. Beat the egg white in a shallow bowl with 2 tablespoons water. Dip the chicken into the Parmesan, then into the egg whites, and then into the breadcrumbs.

2. Heat the oil over moderate heat in a large nonstick frying pan. Cook the chicken for 3 minutes each side. Transfer to a baking tray and sprinkle with the mozzarella; spoon the tomato sauce on top. Bake for 10 minutes or until the chicken is cooked through.

Nutrients per serving: Kilojoules 1415; Fibre 1g; Protein 36g; Carbohydrate 11g; Saturated Fat 6g; Total Fat 16g; Cholesterol 98mg

Chicken & White Bean Soup

Preparation: 10 minutes / Cooking: 10 minutes / Serves: 4

1 can (425g) cannellini beans, drained, rinsed and mashed

2½ cups chicken stock

1½ tablespoons no-added-salt tomato paste

1 red capsicum, diced

1 small onion, finely chopped

3 cloves garlic, crushed

Salt

Tabasco sauce

375g skinless, boneless chicken breast fillets, cut into small chunks

2 tablespoons chopped fresh parsley

1. Combine the beans, stock, tomato paste, capsicum, onion, garlic, a pinch of salt and a dash of Tabasco sauce in a medium saucepan. Bring slowly to the boil.

2. Add the chicken and simmer for 6 minutes or until the chicken is cooked through. Serve sprinkled with the parsley.

Nutrients per serving: Kilojoules 845; Fibre 7g; Protein 24g; Carbohydrate 15g; Saturated Fat 2g; Total Fat 5g; Cholesterol 49mg

Chicken Pieces

Although higher in fat than white breast meat, the darker-fleshed chicken pieces – the legs (drumsticks) and thighs – are a more concentrated source of minerals, including zinc and some iron.

Healthy Highlights

Chicken legs*
1 serving, grilled
(125g)

		Nutrients % RDI	
Kilojoules	900	Niacin	90%
Fibre	0g	Zinc	29%
Protein	32.3g	Phosphorus	26%
Carbohydrate	0g	Riboflavin	21%
Saturated Fat	2.8g	Folate	14%
Total Fat	9.5g	Potassium	14%
Cholesterol	168mg	Iron	11%
Sodium	113mg	Magnesium	10%

skinless

Chicken thighs*
1 serving, grilled
(125g)

		Nutrients % RDI	
Kilojoules	1131	Niacin	93%
Fibre	0g	Phosphorus	28%
Protein	31.8g	Riboflavin	25%
Carbohydrate	0g	Zinc	25%
Saturated Fat	4.8g	Potassium	17%
Total Fat	16g	Folate	16%
Cholesterol	170mg	Iron	13%
Sodium	102mg	Magnesium	10%
		Vitamin A	10%

skinless

Shopping & Preparation

At the market Chicken legs and thighs are sold in one piece, as marylands, and separately; the thighs come boneless as well as bone-in, and with and without skin. Thigh fillets have the skin and bone removed.

Look for All chicken pieces should be plump and firm, with unblemished skin.

Cooking tip Chicken legs and thighs can stand up to fairly long cooking in casseroles and other wet dishes. After cooking, the juices should run clear when the meat is pierced with a sharp knife or skewer.

Chicken Rolls with Lemon & Basil Mayonnaise

Preparation: 10 minutes / Cooking: 6 minutes / Serves: 4

½ cup fresh basil

¼ cup low-fat mayonnaise

¼ cup plain low-fat yoghurt

1½ tablespoons lemon juice

Salt

3 teaspoons vegetable oil

4 chicken thigh fillets (about 125g each)

4 lettuce leaves

4 bread rolls

8 slices tomato

1. Combine the basil, mayonnaise, yoghurt, lemon juice and a pinch of salt in a food processor; purée until smooth.

2. Heat the oil in a medium nonstick frying pan. Cook the chicken for 3 minutes each side or until cooked through.

3. Place the lettuce leaves on the bread rolls. Top each with the tomato slices, a chicken fillet and the lemon and basil mayonnaise.

Nutrients per serving: Kilojoules 1714; Fibre 3g; Protein 28g; Carbohydrate 31g; Saturated Fat 4g; Total Fat 19g; Cholesterol 123mg

Did you know?

Chicken legs and thighs supply more zinc than do chicken breasts. Zinc plays a key role in cell growth and division. In this capacity, zinc helps your body heal itself when you are injured.

Citrus Chicken Skewers

Preparation: 20 minutes / Marinate: 2 hours

Cooking: 5–6 minutes / Serves: 4

500g skinless, boneless, chicken thighs, cut into 3cm cubes

½ cup orange juice

¼ cup lemon juice

2 tablespoons lime juice

¼ cup olive oil

1 teaspoon honey

¼ cup chopped fresh coriander leaves

1 red chilli, seeded and chopped

2 cloves garlic, crushed

½ lemon, cut into thick slices

Mixed salad (optional)

1. Thread the chicken onto 8 small skewers (if using bamboo skewers, soak in water for 30 minutes beforehand, so that they won't burn).

2. Combine the orange juice, lemon juice, lime juice, oil, honey, coriander, chilli and garlic in a medium bowl. Pour over the skewers and leave to marinate for at least 2 hours, turning occasionally.

3. Preheat a ridged, iron grill pan. Cook the chicken skewers for 2 minutes each side or until the chicken is cooked through. Serve with the lemon, and a side salad if liked.

Nutrients per serving: Kilojoules 1428; Fibre 1g; Protein 23g; Carbohydrate 5g; Saturated Fat 5g; Total Fat 26g; Cholesterol 119mg

Citrus Chicken Skewers

Risotto with Chicken & Mushrooms

Risotto with Chicken & Mushrooms

Preparation: 15 minutes / Cooking: 55 minutes / Serves: 4

2 teaspoons olive oil

500g skinless, boneless chicken thigh or leg meat, cut into 3cm cubes

1 small onion, chopped

250g fresh shiitake or oyster mushrooms, trimmed and thinly sliced

250g button mushrooms, sliced

1¼ cups Arborio rice

⅔ cup dry white wine

3 cups boiling chicken stock

Salt

2 tablespoons grated Parmesan cheese

Freshly ground pepper

1. Heat the oil in a large nonstick saucepan over moderate heat. Add the chicken and cook for 5 minutes. Transfer the chicken to a plate and put aside.

2. Add the onion to the saucepan and cook for 5 minutes. Add the shiitake mushrooms and cook for 5 minutes. Add the button mushrooms and cook for 4 minutes.

3. Add the rice, stir to coat, then add the wine. Cook until the wine has been absorbed, about 4 minutes. Add 1 cup stock to the rice along with a pinch of salt and cook, stirring, for 10 minutes or until the liquid has been absorbed. Add 1 cup stock and cook, stirring, for 10 minutes or until the liquid has been absorbed. Repeat with the last cup of stock.

4. Return the chicken to the pan, and cook for 2 minutes or until the rice is creamy but not mushy and the chicken is cooked. Stir in the Parmesan and top with a grinding of pepper.

Nutrients per serving: Kilojoules 2142; Fibre 5g; Protein 34g; Carbohydrate 55g; Saturated Fat 5g; Total Fat 16g; Cholesterol 122mg

Did you know?

• Chicken is almost always a good menu choice, but beware of what fast-food restaurants do to it. Most commercially crumbed chicken nuggets have more than 17 grams of fat per serving.

• Chicken is rich in niacin, which may play a role in cancer protection. Laboratory experiments suggest that niacin may help prevent certain precancerous changes at the cellular level.

Chicken & Cashew Stir-Fry

Preparation: 20 minutes / Cooking: 15 minutes / Serves: 4

3 cups broccoli florets

3 teaspoons reduced-salt soy sauce

3 teaspoons dry sherry

375g skinless, boneless chicken thighs, cut into 2cm cubes

2 teaspoons vegetable oil

3 teaspoons grated fresh ginger

3 cloves garlic, crushed

1 red capsicum, cut into 2cm cubes

½ cup chicken stock

2 tablespoons chilli sauce

2 teaspoons cornflour

2 spring onions, sliced diagonally

¼ cup cashews, chopped

1. Cook the broccoli in a steamer for 3 minutes or until crisp-tender; put aside. Combine the soy sauce and sherry in a medium bowl. Add the chicken and toss.

2. Heat the oil in a large nonstick frying pan. Add the chicken and stir-fry for 3 minutes; transfer to a plate. Add the ginger and garlic and stir-fry for 30 seconds. Add the broccoli and capsicum and stir-fry for 2 minutes.

3. Add the stock and chilli sauce and bring to the boil. Combine the cornflour with 1 tablespoon water; add to the pan and stir for 1 minute or until slightly thickened. Return the chicken to the pan; add the spring onions and cook for 1 minute. Stir in the cashews just before serving.

Nutrients per serving: Kilojoules 1128; Fibre 5g; Protein 23g; Carbohydrate 7g; Saturated Fat 4g; Total Fat 16g; Cholesterol 89mg

Did you know?

The dark meat (legs and thighs) of chicken contains only slightly more cholesterol than the white breast meat.

Chicken & Cashew Stir-Fry

Whole Chicken

Always an impressive dish, a whole bird (eaten without the skin) provides plenty of protein, little saturated fat, and good amounts of B vitamins and zinc.

Healthy Highlights

1 serving*, cooked (125g)		Nutrients % RDI	
Kilojoules	874	Niacin	91%
Fibre	0g	Phosphorus	28%
Protein	30.6g	Zinc	17%
Carbohydrate	0g	Potassium	13%
Saturated Fat	2.8g	Riboflavin	13%
Total Fat	9.5g	Magnesium	11%
Cholesterol	118mg		
Sodium	103mg	*meat only, no skin	

Shopping & Preparation

At the market Whole chickens come in several sizes. Young, tender poussins average 500g each. Roasting chickens are larger – ranging in size from 0.9kg to 2.5kg. The bigger, older birds sold as boilers are best used for soups and stocks.

Look for Choose a chicken with a meaty breast. The skin colour will depend on the chicken's breed and diet, and does not affect nutritional value.

Preparation Rinse the chicken under cold water, then remove any visible fat. Some recipes, especially those using poussins, may call for the bird to be spatchcocked (opened out flat) before cooking. To do this, place the bird breast-side-down on a board and cut along each side of the backbone with poultry shears; discard the bone. Turn the bird breast-side-up and push down sharply to break the breastbone and flatten the bird. To halve a chicken, cut through the breastbone, then along the backbone.

Basic cooking Cook a whole chicken until a thermometer inserted in the thigh reads 80°C (the meat will be white, and juices will run clear – not pink – when the meat is pierced with a skewer or small knife).

Grilled Chicken Diablo

Preparation: 15 minutes / Marinate: 1 hour
Cooking: 15 minutes / Serves: 4

⅓ cup chilli sauce
2 teaspoons olive oil
1 teaspoon Tabasco sauce
1 teaspoon grated lemon zest
3 cloves garlic, crushed
½ teaspoon black pepper
Salt
2 poussins (500g each), halved
1½ tablespoons red wine vinegar
1 red capsicum, diced
1 stalk celery, diced

1. Combine 2 tablespoons of the chilli sauce, the oil, Tabasco sauce, lemon zest, garlic, pepper and a pinch of salt in a shallow bowl. Add the poussins, turn to coat, then cover and refrigerate for 1 hour.

2. Meanwhile, combine the remaining chilli sauce, the vinegar, capsicum and celery in a medium bowl. Put aside.

3. Preheat the griller. Reserving the marinade, grill the birds, breast-side-down, 15 cm from the heat for 8 minutes; brush with the reserved marinade as they cook. Turn the birds over and brush with the marinade. Grill for 6 minutes or until they are just cooked through. Serve with the capsicum and celery relish.

Nutrients per serving: Kilojoules 1344; Fibre 2g; Protein 28g; Carbohydrate 6g; Saturated Fat 6g; Total Fat 21g; Cholesterol 133mg

Did you know?

One American study found that no significant fat is transferred from the skin to the meat when chicken is cooked. So when roasting or grilling chicken, it's okay to leave the skin on during cooking as long as you remove it before eating.

Grilled Chicken Diablo

Roasted Chicken with Garlic Potatoes

Roasted Chicken with Garlic Potatoes

Preparation: 15 minutes / Cooking: 1 hour / Serves: 4

1kg small potatoes, quartered

3 teaspoons olive oil

8 cloves garlic, peeled

Salt

4 sprigs fresh rosemary

1 teaspoon dried oregano

1 teaspoon chilli powder

Freshly ground pepper

2 poussins (500g each)

1 lemon, cut into 8 wedges

1. Preheat the oven to 210°C. Cook the potatoes in a large saucepan of boiling water for 5 minutes, to blanch. Drain.

2. Meanwhile, place the oil and garlic in a large baking dish and heat for 5 minutes. Add the potatoes, sprinkle with salt to taste, and bake for 15 minutes, turning as they brown. Scatter over half the rosemary leaves.

3. Combine the oregano, chilli powder and a grinding of pepper in a small bowl. Rub the poussins with the spice mixture. Place, breast-side-up, on the potatoes and roast for 30 to 35 minutes or until cooked through.

Serve the birds halved, with the lemon, remaining rosemary sprigs and the potatoes.

Nutrients per serving: Kilojoules 1823; Fibre 7g; Protein 30g; Carbohydrate 33g; Saturated Fat 5g; Total Fat 20g; Cholesterol 115mg

Did you know?

• It's best to roast a whole chicken on a rack, which allows the fat to drip off as the bird cooks.

• Remove the skin after cooking and you subtract nearly half the fat from roast chicken.

Greek-Style Roast Chicken

Preparation: 20 minutes / Cooking: 30 minutes / Serves: 4

¼ cup sun-dried tomato halves (not oil-packed)

⅓ cup chopped fresh mint

¼ cup Kalamata or other brine-cured black olives, pitted and chopped

2 cloves garlic, finely chopped

½ teaspoon grated lemon zest

Salt

2 poussins (500g each), halved

Oven-roasted potatoes (optional)

4 sprigs fresh flat-leaf parsley

1. Preheat the oven to 210°C. Bring 1 cup water to a boil in a small saucepan. Add the sun-dried tomatoes and cook for 5 minutes. Drain the tomatoes, reserving 2 tablespoons of the cooking liquid. Place the reserved liquid in a medium bowl. When cool enough to handle, coarsely chop the sun-dried tomatoes and add to the bowl.

2. Add the mint, olives, garlic, lemon zest and a pinch of salt to the sun-dried tomatoes, stirring to combine. Using your fingers, carefully lift the breast skin and as much of the thigh skin as you can on each poussin without tearing it. Place a quarter of the stuffing mixture under the skin of each half.

3. Place the birds, skin-side-up, on a rack in a baking dish, and roast for 25 minutes or until cooked through. Serve with potatoes, if liked, and garnished with the parsley sprigs.

Nutrients per serving: Kilojoules 1141; Fibre 2g; Protein 25g; Carbohydrate 6g; Saturated Fat 5g; Total Fat 17g; Cholesterol 115mg

Herb-Roasted Chicken

Preparation: 10 minutes / Cooking: 1 hour 5 minutes / Serves: 4

1 chicken (1.5 to 1.75kg), trimmed of excess fat

10 sprigs fresh rosemary

1 tablespoon chopped fresh sage leaves

6 large cloves garlic, unpeeled

½ cup chicken stock

2 tablespoons lemon juice

3 teaspoons plain flour

1. Preheat the oven to 210°C. Stuff the cavity of the chicken with the rosemary, reserving 2 teaspoons of the leaves. Place the sage and garlic in the cavity.

2. Place the chicken, breast-side-down, on a rack in a baking dish and roast for 30 minutes. Turn breast-side-up and roast for a further 30 minutes or until cooked through. Transfer to a platter.

3. Add the stock, lemon juice, reserved rosemary leaves and ¼ cup water to the baking dish and stir, scraping up the browned bits. Pour the drippings into a gravy separator, then pour the defatted juices into a small saucepan. Blend the flour with ¼ cup water, add to the saucepan, and cook over medium heat, stirring, until the gravy is thickened. Serve the gravy alongside the chicken.

Nutrients per serving: Kilojoules 1571; Fibre 1g; Protein 36g; Carbohydrate 2g; Saturated Fat 7g; Total Fat 25g; Cholesterol 172mg

Greek-Style Roast Chicken

Turkey

Eaten without the skin, turkey makes a healthy, tasty meal. Turkey breast is the leanest of meats, and its mild flavour makes it a versatile ingredient. It also supplies high-quality protein and B vitamins.

Healthy Highlights

Whole turkey
1 serving*, cooked
(125g)

Nutrients		% RDI	
Kilojoules	1016	Niacin	90%
Fibre	0g	Zinc	29%
Protein	34.5g	Phosphorus	27%
Carbohydrate	0g	Potassium	19%
Saturated Fat	3.3g	Riboflavin	14%
Total Fat	11.6g	Iron	13%
Cholesterol	99mg	Magnesium	11%
Sodium	238mg	Vitamin A	11%

meat only, no skin

Turkey breast*
1 serving, cooked
(125g)

Nutrients		% RDI	
Kilojoules	810	Niacin	100%
Fibre	0g	Phosphorus	30%
Protein	36.8g	Potassium	21%
Carbohydrate	0g	Zinc	20%
Saturated Fat	1.1g	Vitamin A	14%
Total Fat	5g	Magnesium	12%
Cholesterol	81mg		
Sodium	262mg	*skinless*	

Shopping & Preparation

At the market Fresh and frozen whole turkeys are available throughout the year. Turkeys can weigh from 2.2kg to as much as 11kg. Turkey breasts are available as whole, bone-in (turkey buffé), or whole, boneless (halves and quarters, too) and turkey breast steaks and cutlets. Turkey mince is sold in most larger supermarkets.

Look for A fresh turkey should be firm and well shaped, with creamy white skin. Frozen turkeys should be solidly frozen. Turkey breast meat should appear moist and pink.

Preparation Remove the giblets and neck from the cavity of a whole turkey. Rinse the bird under cold running water and remove any pinfeathers. Turkey breasts need no preparation before cooking. For the leanest possible turkey mince, buy a skinless turkey breast portion, cut into 3cm chunks and chop in a food processor, taking care not to turn the meat into a paste.

Teriyaki Turkey

Preparation: 15 minutes / Cooking: 3 hours / Serves: 12

⅓ cup reduced-salt soy sauce

2 tablespoons honey

2 tablespoons sesame oil

1 tablespoon grated orange zest

1 teaspoon ground cinnamon

1 turkey (about 6kg)

2 heads garlic, sliced in half

1 tablespoon plain flour

2 cups chicken or turkey stock

Salt

Freshly ground black pepper

1. Preheat the oven to 180°C. Combine the soy sauce, honey, sesame oil, orange zest and cinnamon in a small bowl. Rub the mixture under the skin of the turkey's breast and drumsticks. Place the garlic in the cavity of the turkey.

2. Place the bird on a rack in a baking dish and pour 2 cups water into the dish. Roast the turkey, covered, for 24 minutes per kilogram, or until the thigh meat registers 75°C. Uncover for the last 40 minutes of cooking.

3. Transfer the turkey to a cutting board; discard the garlic. Pour the pan juices into a gravy separator and then pour the defatted juices into a small saucepan. Whisk together the flour, stock, and salt and pepper to taste, and add to the pan juices. Cook, stirring for 4 minutes or until the gravy is slightly thickened. Remove the turkey skin before carving the bird.

Nutrients per serving: Kilojoules 2051; Fibre 0g; Protein 63g; Carbohydrate 5g; Saturated Fat 6g; Total Fat 24g; Cholesterol 178mg

Ricotta-Stuffed Turkey Breast

Preparation: 25 minutes / Cooking: 1 hour 5 minutes / Serves: 8

1 tablespoon olive oil

4 cloves garlic, crushed

½ packet frozen chopped spinach (300g packet), thawed and well drained

⅔ cup reduced-fat ricotta cheese

1 egg white

2 teaspoons grated orange zest

½ teaspoon pepper

½ teaspoon grated nutmeg

1 skinless, boneless turkey breast half (about 2 kg)

Salt

2 tablespoons fresh rosemary leaves

1. Preheat the oven to 180°C. Heat 2 teaspoons of the oil in a large nonstick frying pan over low heat. Add the garlic and cook for 1 minute. Add the spinach and cook, stirring occasionally, for 4 minutes. Let cool.

2. Combine the ricotta, egg white, orange zest, pepper and nutmeg in a medium bowl. Stir in the spinach mixture. Place the turkey between 2 sheets of greaseproof paper or foil and pound to a 2 cm thickness. Sprinkle with a pinch of salt. Spread the ricotta mixture on the turkey and roll up from one long side. Tie the roast to secure it, then place seam-side-down in a small baking dish.

3. Brush with the remaining oil and sprinkle with the rosemary and salt to taste. Roast for 1 hour or until browned and cooked through.

Nutrients per serving: Kilojoules 1413; Fibre 1g; Protein 57g; Carbohydrate 1g; Saturated Fat 3g; Total Fat 12g; Cholesterol 128mg

Turkey & Garlic Stir-Fry

Turkey & Garlic Stir-Fry

Preparation: 10 minutes / Cooking: 6 minutes / Serves: 4

- 3 teaspoons vegetable oil
- 1 red capsicum, sliced
- 1 yellow capsicum, sliced
- 3 cloves garlic, crushed
- 2 tablespoons lime juice
- 1 tablespoon teriyaki sauce
- 1 tablespoon grated fresh ginger
- 500g skinless, boneless turkey breast, cut into thin strips
- 300g spinach, chopped

1. Heat the oil in a large nonstick frying pan over moderate heat. Add the capsicums, garlic, lime juice, teriyaki sauce and ginger and stir-fry for 3 minutes until the capsicums are crisp-tender. Add the turkey and stir-fry for 2 minutes, then add the spinach and stir-fry for 1 minute or until the spinach is wilted and the turkey is cooked through.

Nutrients per serving: Kilojoules 856; Fibre 5g; Protein 30g; Carbohydrate 4g; Saturated Fat 1g; Total Fat 7g; Cholesterol 59mg

Did you know?

- It's best to cook the stuffing for a whole turkey separately. It will not absorb fat from the turkey – and the bird will cook in far less time.

- If you've been advised to watch your intake of saturated fat (everyone should, but it's especially important for people with high cholesterol), skinless turkey breast should be on the table frequently. It contains less saturated fat than any other meat.

- Skinless turkey breast has about the same amount of protein, vitamin B_6 and niacin as lean beef, but less fat.

Turkey Caesar Salad

Turkey Caesar Salad @

Preparation: 10 minutes / Serves: 4

¼ cup low-fat mayonnaise

1½ tablespoons lemon juice

2 tablespoons grated Parmesan cheese

1 medium cos lettuce, leaves roughly torn

250g cooked turkey breast, diced

1 cup oven-roasted croutons

6 anchovy fillets, finely diced

2 teaspoons capers, rinsed

1. Combine the mayonnaise, lemon juice and Parmesan in a large serving bowl. Toss with the lettuce, turkey, croutons, anchovies and capers.

Nutrients per serving: Kilojoules 836; Fibre 1g; Protein 22g; Carbohydrate 6g; Saturated Fat 3g; Total Fat 9g; Cholesterol 53mg

Did you know?

• With just over 1g of saturated fat, turkey breast is even leaner than many types of fish.

• Turkey breast can be substituted for veal in many recipes.

• Turkey mince made from skinless turkey breast is the perfect lower-fat substitute for beef, lamb or pork mince. Handled lightly, it remains moist – and makes your burgers, meat loaves or pasta sauces far healthier.

Tandoori Turkey Skewers

Preparation: 10 minutes / Marinate: 2 hours / Cooking: 5 minutes / Serves: 4

1½ teaspoons ground cumin

1½ teaspoons ground coriander

1½ teaspoons ground turmeric

1½ teaspoons chilli powder

1 teaspoon ground cardamom

1 teaspoon freshly ground pepper

⅔ cup plain low-fat yoghurt

Salt

500g skinless, boneless turkey breast, cut into 3cm cubes

2 teaspoons vegetable oil

1 tablespoon chopped fresh mint

1. Combine the cumin, coriander, turmeric, chilli powder, cardamom, pepper, half the yoghurt and a pinch of salt in a small bowl. Thread the turkey cubes onto 4 skewers (if using bamboo skewers, soak in water for 30 minutes beforehand, so that they won't burn), then brush the marinade over the turkey, rubbing in well. Leave to marinate for 2 hours.

2. Heat the oil in a medium nonstick frying pan over moderate heat. Cook the turkey skewers for 2 minutes each side or until cooked through. Serve with the remaining yoghurt mixed with the mint.

Nutrients per serving: Kilojoules 788; Fibre 0g; Protein 29g; Carbohydrate 3g; Saturated Fat 1g; Total Fat 6g; Cholesterol 61mg

Tandoori Turkey Skewers

Fruit

Apples & Pears

One of the most popular snack fruits, apples supply vitamin C as well as some potassium. Eat the peel to get the full measure of fibre. Pears are also a good source of fibre.

Healthy Highlights

Apples*
1 medium (155g)

Kilojoules	323	Nutrients % RDI	
Fibre	3.1g	Vitamin C	26%
Protein	0.5g		
Carbohydrate	19.2g	*with skin	
Saturated Fat	0g		
Total Fat	0.2g		
Cholesterol	0mg		
Sodium	2mg		

Pears*
1 medium (185g)

Kilojoules	390	Nutrients % RDI	
Fibre	4.3g	Vitamin C	31%
Protein	0.6g		
Carbohydrate	23.3g	*with skin	
Saturated Fat	0g		
Total Fat	0.2g		
Cholesterol	0mg		
Sodium	4mg		

Shopping & Preparation

At the market Apples and pears are available all year. Many shops now offer less-common apples alongside the familiar varieties. Try Bonza, Fuji, Sundowner, Royal Gala, Pink Lady or Jonagold apples for both cooking and eating fresh. Red Sensation pears, as tasty as their yellow cousins, add colour to dishes when left unpeeled.

Look for Choose hard apples with an unbruised skin. Buy firm, unblemished pears a few days before you'll eat them; pears are sold underripe and need time to ripen at room temperature.

Preparation When you need apple or pear wedges, use a disc-shaped corer-slicer on peeled or unpeeled fruit. To just core apples, use an apple corer – basically a metal tube with a cutting end, set into a handle.

Pork Chops with Fresh Pear Salsa

Preparation: 20 minutes / Cooking: 10 minutes / Serves: 4

375g pears
1 red capsicum, diced
⅓ cup finely chopped red onion
2 tablespoons lemon juice
½ teaspoon Tabasco sauce
Salt
¾ teaspoon dried sage
¼ teaspoon ground ginger
2 cloves garlic, minced
Freshly ground black pepper
4 well-trimmed centre-cut pork chops (185g each)

1. Peel the pears and dice. Transfer to a large bowl. Add the capsicum, onion, lemon juice, Tabasco sauce and salt to taste. Toss to combine. Refrigerate until serving time.

2. Preheat the griller. Combine the sage, ginger, garlic and salt and pepper to taste in a small bowl. Rub the mixture into both sides of the chops. Grill 15 cm from the heat for 3 to 4 minutes each side or until cooked through but still juicy. Serve with the pear salsa.

Nutrients per serving: Kilojoules 1707; Fibre 2g; Protein 57g; Carbohydrate 13g; Saturated Fat 5g; Total Fat 14g; Cholesterol 168mg

Did you know?

• Nashi, also known as Asian pears, are becoming much more common in shops and fruit markets. They are small and apple-shaped but taste like pears. Juicy and very crisp, nashi contain about one-third more fibre than regular pears.

• Canned pears packed in juice or water (not syrup) may be substituted for fresh in many recipes. However, they do contain considerably less vitamin C than fresh pears.

Apple Pear Crisp

Preparation: 15 minutes / Cooking: 40 minutes / Serves: 4

500g apples
500g pears
3 tablespoons lemon juice
2 tablespoons caster sugar
½ teaspoon ground ginger
½ cup light brown sugar
1 teaspoon cinnamon
2 tablespoons cold unsalted butter

1. Preheat the oven to 180°C. Peel and slice the apples and pears. Combine with the lemon juice, caster sugar and ginger in a large bowl, then tip the mixture into a 20 cm square baking dish.

2. Combine the brown sugar and cinnamon in a small bowl. Cut in the butter. Sprinkle the mixture over the fruit and bake for 40 minutes.

Nutrients per serving: Kilojoules 1277; Fibre 5g; Protein 1g; Carbohydrate 58g; Saturated Fat 5g; Total Fat 8g; Cholesterol 24mg

Did you know?

Most of the fibre in pears is insoluble – the kind that helps prevent diverticulosis and colon cancer.

Saffron Pears

Preparation: 5 minutes / Cooking: 1 hour 55 minutes / Serves: 6

1 cup water

1 cup white wine

1 cup sugar

1 vanilla bean, halved

½ cinnamon stick

½ teaspoon saffron threads

2 teaspoons grated orange zest

6 firm pears

1. Combine all the ingredients, except the pears, in a saucepan in which the pears will fit snugly upright. Simmer for 3 to 4 minutes or until the sugar is dissolved.

2. Meanwhile, peel the pears, leaving the stems intact. Add to the saucepan, cover, then simmer until the pears begin to take on a glazed appearance, about 1½ hours.

3. Close to serving time, remove the pears and reduce the syrup for 20 minutes or until it is

almost toffee-like. Pour the syrup over the pears and serve with crisp sweet biscuits on the side.

Nutrients per serving: Kilojoules 1004; Fibre 3g; Protein 0g; Carbohydrate 55g; Saturated Fat 0g; Total Fat 0g; Cholesterol 0mg

Saffron Pears

Baked Apples with Sultanas & Brandy

Preparation: 15 minutes

Cooking: 1 hour / Serves: 4

4 green apples
2½ tablespoons butter, at room temperature
3 tablespoons sultanas
¼ cup raisins
2 teaspoons mixed spice
5 teaspoons julienned orange zest
⅓ cup orange juice
⅓ cup light brown sugar
⅓ cup brandy

1. Preheat the oven to 175°C. Core the apples, score the top in a cross, then make a slit in the skin around the centre of each one with a small knife.

2. Combine the butter, sultanas, raisins, mixed spice and orange zest in a medium bowl. Stuff the centre of each apple with this mixture, then sprinkle with the orange juice and sugar.

3. Arrange the apples in a baking dish, along with ⅔ cup water. Pour 1 tablespoon brandy over each apple and bake for 45 minutes to 1 hour, until the apples are soft and the sugar is caramelised. Pour a little of the sauce over each apple and serve immediately.

Nutrients per serving: Kilojoules 1421; Fibre 6g; Protein 1g; Carbohydrate 51g; Saturated Fat 6g; Total Fat 10g; Cholesterol 31mg

Pumpkin & Apple Soup

Pumpkin & Apple Soup

Preparation: 25 minutes / Cooking: 40 minutes / Serves: 6

3 teapoons olive oil

1 onion, diced

3 cloves garlic, crushed

1 tablespoon minced fresh ginger

750g butternut pumpkin, peeled and thinly sliced

500g green apples, peeled and thinly sliced

2 teaspoons fresh thyme leaves

1½ teaspoons chilli powder

Salt

3 cups chicken stock

1 tablespoon fresh thyme leaves, chopped

1. Heat the oil in a large saucepan over moderate heat. Add the onion, garlic and ginger, and cook for 5 minutes or until the onion is soft. Add the pumpkin and cook for a further 5 minutes or until crisp-tender.

2. Add the apples, thyme leaves, chilli powder and salt to taste, stirring to coat. Add the stock and 1½ cups water, and bring to the boil. Reduce to a simmer, partially cover, then cook for 30 minutes or until the pumpkin is very tender. Transfer to a food processor and purée. If necessary, gently reheat. Serve sprinkled with fresh thyme.

Nutrients per serving: Kilojoules 712; Fibre 3g; Protein 4g; Carbohydrate 16g; Saturated Fat 2g; Total Fat 10g; Cholesterol 0mg

Did you know?

• Some of the fibre in apples is pectin, which may help lower blood cholesterol.

• Apples should be stored in the refrigerator. At room temperature they quickly begin to decline in quality; their flesh becomes mushy and they lose some of their vitamin content.

• Dried apples and pears have concentrated natural sugars, making them a quick source of energy. They are also a good source of potassium.

Apricots

These golden fruits are also as 'good as gold' nutritionally. An outstanding source of beta-carotene, apricots provide considerable vitamin C and a healthy amount of potassium.

Healthy Highlights

Apricots, fresh
1 medium (56g)

		Nutrients	% RDI
Kilojoules	87	Vitamin C	22%
Fibre	1.2g	Vitamin A	15%
Protein	0.4g	Potassium	10%
Carbohydrate	4.1g		
Saturated Fat	0g		
Total Fat	0.1g		
Cholesterol	0mg		
Sodium	1mg		

Apricots, dried
½ cup (70g)

		Nutrients	% RDI
Kilojoules	561	Potassium	53%
Fibre	6.2g	Vitamin A	37%
Protein	2.9g	Iron	18%
Carbohydrate	30.4g	Magnesium	14%
Saturated Fat	0g	Niacin	14%
Total Fat	0.1g		
Cholesterol	0mg		
Sodium	25mg		

Shopping & Preparation

At the market Fresh apricots are at their best in the summer months, from November through to January. Dried apricots are available year round.

Look for Apricots are highly perishable, so they're usually picked underripe. Buy plump fruits that are firm but not rock-hard; the skin should be orange-gold, with no greenish tinge.

Preparation Ripen apricots at home in a paper bag at room temperature; when they are ripe they have a strong apricot fragrance. Eat them immediately or refrigerate for a few days. To peel a fresh apricot, drop into boiling water for about 20 seconds; cool in cold water then peel.

It's easiest to chop or dice dried apricots with kitchen scissors if you spray the blades with cooking spray. Cut the apricots into strips, then cut the strips into bits.

Grilled Chicken with Fresh Apricot Sauce

Preparation: 20 minutes / Marinate: 1 hour
Cooking: 20 minutes / Serves: 4

¾ cup apricot nectar
1½ tablespoons balsamic vinegar
3 teaspoons sesame oil
2 spring onions, chopped
2 teaspoons grated fresh ginger
2 cloves garlic, chopped
4 skinless, boneless chicken breast halves (500g total)
1 teaspoon cornflour blended with 1 tablespoon water
Salt
300g fresh apricots, sliced
2 spring onions, sliced

1. Whisk together the apricot nectar, vinegar, sesame oil, chopped spring onions, ginger and garlic in a medium bowl. Measure out ½ cup, transfer to a medium saucepan and put aside. Add the chicken to the mixture remaining in the bowl, tossing to coat. Marinate at room temperature for 1 hour or in the refrigerator for up to 4 hours.

2. Preheat the oven to 180°C. Heat a nonstick frying pan and cook the chicken breasts for 2 minutes on each side. Transfer to a baking dish and place in the oven; cook for a further 15 minutes, or until cooked through.

3. Meanwhile, add the cornflour mixture and a pinch of salt to the saucepan of reserved apricot nectar mixture. Bring to a simmer over moderate heat, stirring. Add the apricots and cook for 2 minutes or until the sauce is slightly thickened and the apricots are fork-tender. Serve the chicken with the sauce spooned on top, garnished with the sliced spring onions.

Nutrients per serving: Kilojoules 1110; Fibre 2g; Protein 28g; Carbohydrate 11g; Saturated Fat 3g; Total Fat 11g; Cholesterol 89mg

Did you know?

It's a good idea to substitute chopped dried apricots for raisins in some of your favourite cake or biscuit recipes: the apricots contain nearly 100 times more beta-carotene.

Fresh Apricots Poached in Syrup

Preparation: 3 minutes / Cooking: 15 minutes / Serves: 4

½ cup sugar

½ teaspoon ground
   ginger

1 vanilla bean, halved

8 fresh apricots,
   peeled

1. Bring 1 cup water, the sugar, ginger and vanilla bean to the boil in a medium saucepan. Cook for 3 minutes.

2. Add the apricots, cover the saucepan, then cook for 10 minutes or until tender. Remove from the heat and cool the apricots in the syrup. Chill before serving.

Nutrients per serving: Kilojoules 555; Fibre 2g; Protein 1g; Carbohydrate 33g; Saturated Fat 0g; Total Fat 0g; Cholesterol 0mg

Did you know?

Canned apricots may be substituted for fresh in most recipes; juice- or water-packed fruit is the best choice. Apricots packed in syrup have three to four times as many kilojoules as water-packed. The extra kilojoules come from sugar.

Fresh Apricots Poached in Syrup

Apricot Bavarois

Apricot Bavarois

Preparation: 20 minutes / Chill: 4 hours / Cooking: 20 minutes / Serves: 8

I can (375ml) low-fat evaporated milk

2 envelopes gelatine

¼ cup boiling water

I can (825g) apricot halves, drained

2 tablespoons honey

5 tablespoons light brown sugar

¼ cup cream

I tablespoon lemon juice

½ teaspoon cinnamon

Ground nutmeg

8 fresh apricots, halved

1. Pour the evaporated milk into a large metal bowl and put in the freezer for 1 hour or until semi-frozen (slushy).

2. Meanwhile, sprinkle the gelatine over ¼ cup cold water in a small bowl and stand for 5 minutes. Transfer the gelatine to a blender or food processor, add the boiling water, then process for 30 seconds or until dissolved. Add the canned apricots, honey, 3 tablespoons brown sugar, the cream, half the lemon juice, the cinnamon and a pinch of nutmeg, and process until smooth. Refrigerate the apricot purée for 1 to 1½ hours or until it is the texture of raw egg whites. (Or quick-chill in a bowl set in a larger bowl of iced water.)

3. When the evaporated milk is slushy, beat with an electric mixer at high speed until soft peaks form. Fold the milk into the chilled apricot mixture. Pour into individual 1-cup dishes. Chill for at least 3 hours or until set.

4. Preheat the oven to 180°C. Sprinkle the fresh apricot halves with the remaining brown sugar, place on a baking tray, then bake in the oven for 20 minutes.

5. Turn the bavarois out on to serving plates and serve with the baked apricot halves.

Nutrients per serving: Kilojoules 785; Fibre 2g; Protein 6g; Carbohydrate 30g; Saturated Fat 3g; Total Fat 4g; Cholesterol 15mg

Apricot Pound Cake

Preparation: 20 minutes / Cooking: 1 hour 35 minutes / Serves: 16

1⅔ cups dried apricots, chopped

¾ cup unsweetened puréed cooked apple

1½ tablespoons unsalted butter

1½ tablespoons light olive oil

¼ cup buttermilk

3 eggs

2 teaspoons vanilla essence

2 teaspoons grated orange zest

1½ cups sugar

3½ cups plain flour

1 teaspoon baking powder

½ teaspoon bicarbonate of soda

Salt

1. Preheat the oven to 170°C. Spray a 22 cm round cake tin with cooking spray and line with greaseproof paper.

2. Combine ⅓ cup of the apricots, the apple purée and ½ cup water in a medium saucepan. Simmer for 5 minutes or until the apricots are softened. Transfer to a food processor or blender. Add the butter, oil and buttermilk and process until smooth. Put the apricot mixture aside to cool slightly, then beat in the eggs, vanilla essence and orange zest, blending just until smooth. Transfer to a large bowl. Stir in the sugar.

3. Stir together the flour, baking powder, bicarbonate of soda and a pinch of salt in a medium bowl. Fold the flour mixture into the apricot mixture in 3 additions. Fold in the remaining 1⅓ cups apricots and turn into the prepared tin.

4. Bake for 1½ hours or until a skewer inserted halfway between the sides and the centre comes out clean. Cool in the tin on a wire rack for 10 minutes, then turn out of the tin onto the rack to cool completely.

Nutrients per serving: Kilojoules 1046; Fibre 2g; Protein 5g; Carbohydrate 47g; Saturated Fat 2g; Total Fat 5g; Cholesterol 45mg

Did you know?

• Drying concentrates the apricot's impressive nutrient value. Dried apricots make a good cereal topping as well as a healthful addition to breads, cakes and biscuits.

• Dried apricots are often treated with sulphur dioxide to keep their colour bright. This substance may trigger asthma attacks in susceptible people, so look for 'sun-dried' produce without additives.

Apricot Pound Cake

Avocados

Their texture tells you that avocados are high in fat – but it's mostly monounsaturated fat, the type that has a positive effect on blood cholesterol levels.

Healthy Highlights

½ medium (120g)		Nutrients % RDI	
Kilojoules	1064	Vitamin C	36%
Fibre	1.8g	Potassium	29%
Protein	2.3g	Niacin	16%
Carbohydrate	0.5g	Riboflavin	11%
Saturated Fat	5.9g	Magnesium	10%
Total Fat	27.3g		
Cholesterol	0mg		
Sodium	2mg		

Shopping & Preparation

At the market There are many types of avocado, but the main varieties seen in local shops are Fuerte, Haas, Reed, Sharwil and Shepard. Fuerte have a smooth green skin; Haas have dark, pebbly, almost black skin; Reed are almost perfectly spherical with a smooth skins; Sharwil (developed in Australia) look like a Haas–Fuerte cross; and Shepard have a slightly rough skin. Avocados are available all year but are at their best from March to November.

Look for Choose a heavy avocado with unbroken skin. The fruit should yield to gentle pressure. If necessary, leave it at room temperature for a few days to soften.

Preparation Peel and slice avocados close to serving time; their flesh darkens when exposed to air. To halve the fruit, run a knife lengthways around the avocado, sliding it around the stone, then twist the halves. Remove the stone by twisting it out with a knife blade (see below).

To stone an avocado, strike the stone lightly but sharply with the blade of a chef's knife. Then twist the blade to loosen the stone and lift it out (still attached to the blade).

Avocado & Orange Salad

Preparation: 20 minutes / Cooking: 1 minute / Serves: 4–6

¼ cup olive oil

2 tablespoons orange juice

1 teaspoon prepared mustard

Freshly ground pepper

2 oranges

1 bunch asparagus

4 cups mixed salad leaves

2 avocados, halved and sliced

1. Whisk together the oil, orange juice, mustard and some freshly ground pepper in a small bowl to form a vinaigrette.

2. Peel the oranges and remove all the white pith with a sharp knife. Cut in slices and then halve. Blanch the asparagus for 1 minute in boiling water in a large saucepan then refresh under cold running water.

3. Arrange the salad leaves on 4 plates then top with the asparagus spears, the orange slices and the avocado slices. Drizzle with the vinaigrette and add a further grinding of pepper.

Nutrients per serving: Kilojoules 2265; Fibre 4g; Protein 4g; Carbohydrate 7g; Saturated Fat 10g; Total Fat 56g; Cholesterol 0mg

Avocado & Orange Salad

Did you know?

• Avocados are a source of lutein, a carotenoid that seems to help prevent age-related macular degeneration, an eye disease affecting the elderly.

• One medium avocado supplies about a fifth of the daily adult requirement of vitamin E, which is a potent antioxidant.

Guacamole

Preparation: 20 minutes / Serves: 4

3 large cloves garlic

1 small chilli, chopped

2 ripe avocados, peeled, halved and stoned

3 tablespoons fresh lemon juice

2 egg tomatoes, seeded and chopped

2 spring onions, sliced

1 teaspoon Tabasco sauce

2 tablespoons chopped fresh coriander

½ teaspoon ground cumin

Salt

Freshly ground pepper

1. Process the garlic and chilli in a food processor until finely chopped.

2. Add one of the avocados and the lemon juice and process until smooth. Transfer the mixture to a medium bowl.

3. Add the remaining avocado to the bowl and mash with a wooden spoon. Add the tomatoes, spring onions, Tabasco sauce, coriander, cumin, and salt and pepper to taste. Mix thoroughly with a fork. Taste and adjust seasoning if necessary. Serve immediately.

Nutrients per serving: Kilojoules 1122; Fibre 3g; Protein 3g; Carbohydrate 2g; Saturated Fat 6g; Total Fat 27g; Cholesterol 0mg

Guacamole

Bananas

One of nature's sweetest (and virtually fat-free) treats, the banana offers a healthy helping of potassium along with valuable B vitamins and vitamin C.

Healthy Highlights

1 medium (110g)*		Nutrients % RDI	
Kilojoules	419	Vitamin C	51%
Fibre	2.7g	Potassium	19%
Protein	1.7g	Magnesium	10%
Carbohydrate	23.3g		
Saturated Fat	0g	*peeled	
Total Fat	0.1g		
Cholesterol	0mg		
Sodium	1mg		

Shopping & Preparation

At the market You can buy bananas all year: the trick is finding them at the proper stage of ripeness. To be sure, buy them several days before you need them.

Look for Buy firm, unblemished bananas, either green-tipped or fully yellow. Beware of greyish bananas: they've probably been stored at too cool a temperature and will never ripen.

Preparation Store bananas in a paper bag at room temperature if they need ripening. Sliced bananas will darken when exposed to air; to keep them from turning brown, toss the slices with a little citrus juice. To prevent bananas from getting overripe, store in the refrigerator. The skin will turn an alarming black, but the bananas will be fine.

Banana & Pecan Loaf

Preparation: 15 minutes / Cooking: 1 hour 25 minutes / Serves: 8

1 cup rolled oats
⅓ cup pecans or walnuts
3 very ripe bananas (500g)
1 cup buttermilk
2 tablespoons vegetable oil
2 egg whites
1 teaspoon vanilla essence
½ cup white sugar
½ cup firmly packed dark brown sugar
2 cups plain flour
2½ teaspoons baking powder
½ teaspoon bicarbonate of soda
Salt

1. Preheat the oven to 180°C. Spray a 23 x 13 cm loaf tin with cooking spray. Toast the oats in a small baking dish, stirring occasionally, for 10 minutes or until lightly browned. At the same time, toast the pecans in another small baking dish for 7 minutes or until fragrant and lightly browned. When the nuts are cool enough to handle, chop coarsely.

2. Mash the bananas in a large bowl until not quite smooth. Add the buttermilk, oil, egg whites, vanilla essence and both sugars, and mix until well blended; put aside.

3. Combine the flour, baking powder, bicarbonate of soda and and a pinch of salt in a small bowl. Fold the dry ingredients into the banana mixture along with the oats and pecans until just combined. Do not overmix. Spoon the batter into the prepared tin, smoothing the top. Bake for 1 hour and 25 minutes or until a skewer inserted in the centre comes out clean. Cool in the tin on a rack for 10 minutes. Turn out of the tin onto the rack to cool completely.

Nutrients per serving: Kilojoules 1684; Fibre 3g; Protein 8g; Carbohydrate 71g; Saturated Fat 1g; Total Fat 10g; Cholesterol 3mg

Banana & Pecan Loaf

Banana Pancakes

Banana Pancakes

Preparation: 5 minutes / Cooking: 10 minutes / Serves: 4

1½ cups self-raising flour

¾ teaspoon baking powder

2 tablespoons caster sugar

1½ cups buttermilk

2 eggs

2 tablespoons plus 1 teaspoon unsalted butter, melted and cooled

2 bananas, sliced

⅓ cup maple syrup or honey

1. Sift the flour and baking powder into a medium bowl. Stir in the sugar. Combine the buttermilk, eggs and melted butter in a jug. Make a well in the centre of the dry ingredients. Pour in the milk mixture and use a whisk to mix to a smooth batter. Pour into a jug.

2. Lightly spray a small nonstick frying pan with cooking spray and put over a moderately low heat. Pour ¼ cup batter into the pan and cook for about 1 minute until small bubbles appear on the surface. Turn the pancake and cook for a further 1 minute until golden and cooked through. Remove from the pan and keep warm. Repeat with the remaining batter.

3. Place the pancakes on individual serving plates. Layer with the sliced banana (toss the slices with some lemon juice if you want to prepare them in advance) and drizzle a little maple syrup or honey over the top.

Nutrients per serving: Kilojoules 2137; Fibre 3g; Protein 14g; Carbohydrate 82g; Saturated Fat 8g; Total Fat 15g; Cholesterol 143mg

Did you know?

The human body's supply of vitamin B_6 must be replenished daily, and eating bananas is a good way to do this. Vitamin B_6 plays a role in antibody production, but a recent study has revealed that many people – particularly the elderly – don't get enough vitamin B_6.

Blueberries

Blueberries are packed with pectin (a form of soluble fibre) as well as vitamin C, and are also very rich in antioxidants, including anthocyanosides, pigments from which the fruit gets its colour.

Healthy Highlights

1 cup (125g)		Nutrients % RDI	
Kilojoules	255	Vitamin C	54%
Fibre	2.2g		
Protein	0.7g		
Carbohydrate	14.1g		
Saturated Fat	0g		
Total Fat	0.1g		
Cholesterol	0mg		
Sodium	0mg		

Shopping & Preparation

At the market Fresh blueberries are available all year but are best in summer, and are at their peak in January and February. Canned and frozen blueberries are available year round.

Look for Always choose plump berries; those with a waxy 'bloom' on the surface are the freshest. If the punnet is stained with juice, the berries at the bottom may be spoiled or crushed.

Preparation Pick over the blueberries, removing any green, withered or squashed ones. Pull off the stems with your fingers. To store, place the unwashed berries in a single layer on a sheet of paper towel on a plate. Cover, refrigerate, and use within 5 days.

Pat the dough for the Blueberry Wedges (recipe, right) into an 18cm round, then cut the round into six even pieces.

Blueberry Wedges

Preparation: 15 minutes / Cooking: 25 minutes / Serves: 6

⅓ cup buttermilk
1 egg, separated
1½ cups plain flour
2 tablespoons sugar
1½ teaspoons baking powder
¼ teaspoon bicarbonate of soda
Salt
2 tablespoons cold unsalted butter
1½ cups blueberries
1 teaspoon grated lemon zest

1. Preheat the oven to 190°C. Combine the buttermilk and egg yolk in a small bowl; put aside.

2. Combine the flour, sugar, baking powder, bicarbonate of soda and a pinch of salt in a large bowl. With a pastry blender or two knives, cut in the butter until the mixture resembles coarse crumbs. Add the blueberries and lemon zest, stirring until well mixed.

3. Make a well in the centre of the dry ingredients, add the buttermilk mixture and, with a fork, combine until a soft dough is formed. (If the mixture is too dry, add up to 2 tablespoons more buttermilk.)

4. Transfer the dough to a lightly floured surface and knead 4 or 5 times until well mixed. Transfer to an ungreased baking tray and shape into an 18 cm round. Lightly beat the egg white and brush over the dough. Cut the round into 6 wedges. Bake for 25 minutes or until a skewer inserted in the centre comes out clean. Cool on a wire rack.

Nutrients per serving: Kilojoules 992; Fibre 2g; Protein 6g; Carbohydrate 37g; Saturated Fat 4g; Total Fat 7g; Cholesterol 53mg

Did you know?

Blueberries have natural antibacterial properties that can inhibit the growth of bacteria such as *E. coli*, thus guarding against stomach upsets and other digestive problems.

Fresh Blueberry Jam

Preparation: 10 minutes / Cooking: 20 minutes / Makes: 1½ cups

3 cups blueberries
1 cup sugar
2 tablespoons lemon juice
4 strips (7 x 1cm) orange zest
½ teaspoon cinnamon
Salt
1 teaspoon vanilla essence

1. Sterilise 2 x 1-cup glass jars and their lids.

2. Combine the blueberries, sugar, lemon juice, orange zest, cinnamon and a pinch of salt in a medium saucepan and cook over moderate heat, stirring frequently, for 20 minutes or until thick. Remove from the heat. Discard the zest and stir in the vanilla essence. Spoon the jam into the sterilised jars, cover and cool.

Nutrients per tablespoon: Kilojoules 223; Fibre 0g; Protein 0g; Carbohydrate 13g; Saturated Fat 0g; Total Fat 0g; Cholesterol 0mg

Blueberry Semifreddo

Preparation: 10 minutes / Cooking: 10 minutes / Freeze: 4 hours / Stand: 10 minutes / Serves: 8

4 cups blueberries

½ cup sugar

3 teaspoons plain flour

1 cup low-fat milk

500g low-fat ricotta cheese

⅓ cup reduced-fat sour cream

¼ cup honey

1 teaspoon vanilla essence

1. Combine the blueberries and sugar in a medium saucepan and simmer over moderate heat for 5 minutes or until slightly thickened. Cool to room temperature.

2. Meanwhile, whisk the flour into the milk in a small saucepan. Cook, stirring, for 5 minutes or until the mixture is slightly thickened. Cool to room temperature, then transfer to a food processor. Add the ricotta, sour cream, honey and vanilla essence, then process until smooth. Transfer to a bowl and fold in 2 cups of the blueberry sauce. (Refrigerate the remaining sauce until serving time.)

3. Line a 23 x 13 cm glass loaf dish with plastic wrap, leaving a 5 cm overhang. Spoon the berry mixture into the dish, smoothing the top. Cover with plastic wrap and freeze for 4 hours.

4. To serve, let stand for 10 minutes at room temperature, then unmould onto a serving platter. Cut the loaf into slices and serve with the reserved blueberry sauce.

Nutrients per serving: Kilojoules 1095; Fibre 2g; Protein 9g; Carbohydrate 37g; Saturated Fat 6g; Total Fat 9g; Cholesterol 38mg

Cherries

The irresistible cherry is notable for its vitamin C, and sour cherries have even more vitamin C than sweet ones. Both varieties supply beta-carotene as well – and studies show that cherry juice may neutralise the enzymes that cause tooth decay.

Healthy Highlights

10 medium (40g)		Nutrients % RDI	
Kilojoules	85	Vitamin C	23%
Fibre	0.6g		
Protein	0.4g		
Carbohydrate	4.5g		
Total Fat	0.1g		
Saturated Fat	0g		
Cholesterol	0mg		
Sodium	0.4mg		

Shopping & Preparation

At the market Fresh sweet cherries are available from November to January. Most sour cherries are canned or frozen, but fresh sour Morello cherries can be found in January in some specialist fruit shops.

Look for It's worth the extra time to buy loose cherries instead of prepackaged. Fresh cherries should be plump, firm and shiny, with flexible green stems still attached. If the fruit is sticky, it has been damaged and is leaking juice.

Preparation Use cherries as soon as possible after purchase. If you need to stone fresh cherries for a recipe, a cherry stoner (see below) is the best tool. However, a hairpin (not a bobby pin) or even a paper clip can also be used for the job.

This handy little tool quickly pops the stones out of fresh cherries. (It works nicely on olives, too.)

Sour Cherry Pie

Sour Cherry Pie

Preparation: 30 minutes / Chill: 1 hour / Cooking: 45 minutes / Serves: 6

1 cup plain flour

1 tablespoon plus
⅔ cup sugar

Salt

2 tablespoons unsalted
butter

3 teaspoons solid
vegetable shortening

5 cups sour cherries
(packed in light
syrup), drained

2 tablespoons honey

1 tablespoon lemon
juice

¼ cup cornflour

¼ teaspoon ground
allspice

1 tablespoon low-fat
milk

1. Combine the flour, 3 teaspoons of the sugar and a pinch of salt in a medium bowl. With a pastry blender or 2 knives, cut in the butter and shortening until the mixture resembles coarse crumbs. Stir 1½ to 2 tablespoons iced water into the flour mixture until just combined. Flatten the dough into a round, wrap in plastic wrap, and refrigerate for at least 1 hour.

2. Preheat the oven to 190°C. Stir together the cherries, honey, lemon juice, ⅔ cup of the sugar, the cornflour and allspice in a large bowl. Transfer to a 23 cm pie plate.

3. Roll the dough out to a 30 cm round on a lightly floured surface. Place the dough on top of the pie, crimping the edges to seal to the rim of the pie plate. Brush the crust with the milk and sprinkle with the remaining sugar. Cut 3 or 4 slits in the crust with a sharp knife to act as steam vents, and decorate as desired.

4. Place the pie on a baking tray with sides and bake in the oven for 45 to 50 minutes or until bubbly and hot in the centre. Serve warm or at room temperature.

Nutrients per serving: Kilojoules 1800; Fibre 4g; Protein 4g; Carbohydrate 86g; Saturated Fat 6g; Total Fat 8g; Cholesterol 16mg

Fresh Cherry Sundaes

Preparation: 1 hour / Cooking: 5 minutes

Freeze: 1 hour 30 minutes / Serves: 4

500ml reduced-fat
frozen vanilla yoghurt

¾ cup chopped stoned
cherries plus 1 cup
halved stoned cherries
(650g unstoned)

¼ cup chopped toasted
almonds

½ cup cherry or
raspberry jam

2 teaspoons cornflour
mixed with
1 tablespoon water

1 teaspoon vanilla
essence

1. Let the frozen yoghurt stand in the refrigerator for 30 minutes or until softened. Scoop the softened yoghurt into a medium bowl and stir in the chopped cherries and 2 tablespoons of the almonds. Return the bowl to the freezer for 1½ hours or until refrozen.

2. Meanwhile, combine the halved cherries, jam and cornflour mixture in a medium saucepan. Bring to a simmer over moderate heat, stirring, and cook for 1 minute or until thickened. Stir in the vanilla essence.

3. Serve the cherry sauce, either warm or at room temperature, with the yoghurt. Sprinkle with the remaining almonds.

Nutrients per serving: Kilojoules 1408; Fibre 3g; Protein 8g; Carbohydrate 64g; Saturated Fat 1g; Total Fat 6g; Cholesterol 10mg

Figs

The tiny seeds that give figs their unique texture also supply a lot of dietary fibre. Potassium, magnesium and calcium are among the other benefits. And dried figs are just as good for you as fresh.

Healthy Highlights

Figs, fresh
1 medium (40g)

Nutrients		% RDI
Kilojoules	68	*Standard serve has less than 10% of RDI for individual nutrients*
Fibre	1g	
Protein	0.6g	
Carbohydrate	3.2g	
Saturated Fat	0g	
Total Fat	0.1g	
Cholesterol	0mg	
Sodium	1mg	

Figs, dried
3 medium (45g)

		Nutrients % RDI	
Kilojoules	436	Potassium	18%
Fibre	6.4g	Magnesium	12%
Protein	1.6g	Calcium	11%
Carbohydrate	24.5g		
Saturated Fat	0g		
Total Fat	0.3g		
Cholesterol	0mg		
Sodium	18mg		

Shopping & Preparation

At the market Fresh figs come into season in late January and last until the end of February and even into March. Dried figs are, of course, available all year.

Look for Fresh figs have greenish-yellow or dark purple skins; when ripe, the skin should be fully coloured and the fruit should be soft but not mushy. Figs bruise easily, so handle them with care, making sure you do not damage them in your shopping basket. Dried figs should be plump and soft; squeeze the packet to make sure.

Preparation Fresh figs are eaten skin and all; they can also be served halved or sliced. To make chopping dried figs easier, first spray the knife (or the blades of kitchen shears) with cooking spray, or coat lightly with vegetable oil.

Fig & Almond Slices

Fig & Almond Slices

Preparation: 25 minutes / Chill: 1 hour

Cooking: 1 hour 5 minutes / Makes: 2 dozen

2¼ cups plain flour

½ teaspoon baking powder

Salt

3 tablespoons unsalted butter

1½ tablespoons solid vegetable shortening

⅔ cup sugar

1 egg

2 tablespoons low-fat milk

1 teaspoon grated lemon zest

375g dried figs, cut into 5mm bits

¼ cup whole almonds

2 tablespoons honey

2 teaspoons lemon juice

¼ teaspoon ground ginger

1. Combine the flour, baking powder and a pinch of salt in a small bowl. Beat the butter and shortening with an electric mixer in a medium bowl until creamy. Beat in the sugar until light and fluffy. Beat in the egg, milk, and the lemon zest. Stir in the flour mixture just until combined. Halve the dough, wrap in plastic, and refrigerate for at least 1 hour.

2. Combine the figs and 1½ cups water in a medium saucepan. Bring to the boil, reduce to a simmer, cover and cook for 30 minutes. Uncover and cook for 5 minutes more or until no liquid remains. Transfer the figs to a food processor along with the almonds. Process to a smooth purée. Stir in the honey, lemon juice and ginger. Cool to room temperature.

3. Preheat the oven to 180°C. Spray a baking tray with cooking spray. Roll each dough half to a 13 x 23 cm rectangle on a lightly floured surface. Spoon half the filling down the centre of one rectangle, leaving a 5 cm border on the long sides and 1 cm at each end. Fold in the ends then, starting on a long side, roll the dough over the filling. Repeat with the other dough.

4. Place the rolls, seam-side-down and 10 cm apart, on the prepared baking tray. Bake for 30 minutes or until golden brown. Cool for 10 minutes on the tray, then transfer to a wire rack to cool. Cut each roll into 12 slices.

Nutrients per slice: Kilojoules 647; Fibre 3g; Protein 3g; Carbohydrate 26g; Saturated Fat 3g; Total Fat 5g; Cholesterol 15mg

Fresh Fig Tarts

Preparation: 15 minutes / Chill: 30 minutes plus 30 minutes / Cooking: 27 minutes / Serves: 6

2 cups plain flour

¼ cup caster sugar

Salt

2 tablespoons ground almonds

180g unsalted butter, chopped

1 egg

12 ripe figs

1½ tablespoons caster sugar

⅔ cup plain low-fat yoghurt

1. Process the flour, sugar, a pinch of salt and the almonds in a food processor for 10 seconds. Add the butter and process until the mixture resembles coarse crumbs. Add the egg and process to a dough, adding 1 tablespoon cold water if necessary.

2. Form the dough into a round, wrap in plastic wrap and refrigerate for 30 minutes. Preheat the oven to 200°C. Spray 2 baking trays with cooking spray.

3. Roll out the pastry on a lightly floured surface until 5 mm thick. Cut into 13 cm rounds. Lift the pastry onto the baking trays and pinch the edge of each round with your fingertips to give shallow tart shapes. Rest in the refrigerator for 30 minutes then put the trays in the oven. Bake for 12 minutes. Reduce the heat to 180°C.

4. Meanwhile, peel the figs and cut into 5 mm slices. Overlap the slices on the pastry bases. Sprinkle with sugar and return to the oven for a further 15 minutes. Serve the tarts warm, with a little yoghurt on the side.

Nutrients per serving: Kilojoules 2088; Fibre 3g; Protein 9g; Carbohydrate 52g; Saturated Fat 17g; Total Fat 28g; Cholesterol 113mg

Fresh Fig Tarts

Grapefruit

In addition to its rich supply of vitamin C, grapefruit provides potassium, dietary fibre, folate and, if it's ruby or pink grapefruit, some beta-carotene as well.

Healthy Highlights

1 medium (205g)		Nutrients % RDI	
Kilojoules	229	Vitamin C	247%
Fibre	1.2g	Folate	26%
Protein	1.8g	Potassium	13%
Carbohydrate	9.9g		
Saturated Fat	0g		
Total Fat	0.4g		
Cholesterol	0mg		
Sodium	8mg		

Shopping & Preparation

At the market You'll find grapefruit available all year round. The peak periods for white grapefruit are April to November, while pink grapefruit are at their best from late April to early July

Look for Choose nice round fruit that feel heavy in your hand (that means they'll be juicy). The skin should be glossy, but a few dull or brown patches are not a bad sign.

Preparation To cut neat segments from a grapefruit, first peel the fruit, using a sharp knife to remove all the white pith, which is bitter. Also remove the outer layer of membrane that surrounds the fruit. Working over a bowl to catch the juice, free the segments from the membranes (see below).

After peeling, carefully slice between each dividing membrane and the grapefruit pulp to release the segments.

Grapefruit with Spiced Redcurrant Sauce

Preparation: 15 minutes / Cooking: 5 minutes / Chill: 1 hour / Serves: 4

2 pink grapefruit
1 white grapefruit
⅓ cup redcurrant jelly
½ teaspoon ground ginger
⅛ teaspoon ground allspice
White pepper
3 teaspoons lemon juice

1. Peel the grapefruit with a small paring knife. Working over a bowl to catch the juice, separate the grapefruit segments from the membranes; reserve any juice that collects in the bowl.

2. Combine the redcurrant jelly, ginger, allspice and a pinch of pepper in a small frying pan. Bring to a simmer and cook for 1 minute.

3. Pour the mixture into a medium bowl and stir in the lemon juice and 1 tablespoon of the reserved grapefruit juice. Add the grapefruit and toss to combine. Serve chilled.

Nutrients per serving: Kilojoules 518; Fibre 1g; Protein 2g; Carbohydrate 28g; Saturated Fat 0g; Total Fat 0g; Cholesterol 0mg

Crab & Grapefruit Salad

Preparation: 25 minutes / Serves: 4

4 grapefruit

1½ tablespoons low-fat mayonnaise

3 teaspoons finely chopped mango chutney

2 teaspoons Dijon mustard

1 teaspoon sesame oil

Salt and pepper

375g crab meat, picked over to remove any cartilage

2 cups watercress, tough stems trimmed

1 head witlof, cut crossways into 1cm wide strips

1 head mignonette lettuce, separated into leaves

1. Peel the grapefruit with a small paring knife. Working over a bowl to catch the juice, separate the grapefruit segments from the membranes; reserve any juice that collects in the bowl.

2. Whisk together the mayonnaise, chutney, mustard, sesame oil, a pinch of salt and pepper and 3 tablespoons reserved grapefruit juice in a medium bowl.

3. Add the crab, tossing to combine. Add the watercress, witlof and grapefruit segments, and toss. Serve the salad on a bed of mignonette lettuce leaves.

Nutrients per serving: Kilojoules 668; Fibre 3g; Protein 15g; Carbohydrate 15g; Saturated Fat 0g; Total Fat 4g; Cholesterol 80mg

Did you know?

• Researchers have discovered chemical compounds in grapefruit that cause the body to absorb more of certain medications. If you are in the habit of taking medication with grapefruit juice, check with your doctor to be sure this does not pose a problem.

• Grapefruit is rich in pectin, a type of dietary fibre that seems to reduce LDL cholesterol.

Seared Salmon with Grapefruit

Preparation: 20 minutes

Cooking: 4 minutes / Serves: 4

2 grapefruit

1 red capsicum, diced

1 stalk celery, cut into 5mm dice

¼ cup finely chopped red onion

2 tablespoons chopped fresh parsley

1 teaspoon Dijon mustard

1 tablespoon olive oil

Freshly ground black pepper

1 teaspoon sambal oelek (optional)

4 boneless salmon fillets, with skin (185g each)

1. Peel the grapefruit with a small paring knife. Working over a bowl to catch the juice, separate the grapefruit segments from the membranes; reserve any juice that collects in the bowl. Halve the grapefruit sections crossways and transfer to a serving bowl. Add the capsicum, celery, onion, parsley, mustard, half the oil and pepper to taste. Toss to combine and refrigerate until serving time.

2. Preheat a nonstick frying pan. Add the remaining oil. Mix the reserved grapefruit juice with the sambal oelek, if using, and brush onto the salmon fillets.

3. Put the salmon into the frying pan, skin-side-down, and cook over moderately high heat for 2 minutes. Turn the fish over and cook for a further 2 minutes. Serve the salmon with the grapefruit salad alongside.

Nutrients per serving: Kilojoules 1748; Fibre 1g; Protein 48g; Carbohydrate 7g; Saturated Fat 4g; Total Fat 22g; Cholesterol 126mg

Seared Salmon with Grapefruit

Grapes & Raisins

First found in wine, a cholesterol-lowering phytochemical called resveratrol is also present in red grapes. Grapes and raisins also supply some potassium and fibre, and are a good source of boron, which helps keep the bones strong.

Healthy Highlights

Sultana grapes
20 medium (60g)

		Nutrients % RDI	
Kilojoules	149	Vitamin C	10%
Fibre	0.5g		
Protein	0.3g		
Carbohydrate	8.7g		
Saturated Fat	0g		
Total Fat	0.1g		
Cholesterol	0mg		
Sodium	3mg		

Raisins
¼ cup (40g)

		Nutrients % RDI	
Kilojoules	488	Potassium	22%
Fibre	2g	Iron	14%
Protein	0.9g		
Carbohydrate	28.4g		
Saturated Fat	0.1g		
Total Fat	0.4g		
Cholesterol	0mg		
Sodium	23mg		

Shopping & Preparation

At the market Grapes come in seedless and seeded varieties. Among the seedless varieties are green or ruby sultana grapes and Thompson, while seeded varieties include Black Muscatel, Red Globe, Ribiers, Purple Cornichon and Waltham Cross. Available most of the year, grapes are at their best from December to May.

Look for Choose a well-shaped bunch of plump grapes, avoiding any bunches with withered, shrivelled or crushed fruit. Check the colour: green grapes that are yellow-green are the sweetest, while the tastiest red grapes are a warm crimson colour. The grapes should not be pale around the stems, and the stems should be pliable.

Preparation Don't rinse grapes until shortly before serving.

Raisin Bars

Preparation: 10 minutes / Cooking: 25 minutes / Makes: 24 bars

2 cups raisins
2 cups boiling water
1¼ cups plain flour
½ teaspoon baking powder
¼ teaspoon bicarbonate of soda
½ teaspoon cinnamon
¼ teaspoon ground nutmeg
⅛ teaspoon ground cloves
3 tablespoons unsalted butter, at room temperature
½ cup firmly packed dark brown sugar
2 tablespoons molasses
1 egg
1 egg white

1. Preheat the oven to 180°C. Spray a 23 cm square metal baking tin with cooking spray. Dust with flour; put aside. Combine the raisins in a small heatproof bowl with the boiling water. Stand for 5 minutes; drain.

2. Combine the flour, baking powder, bicarbonate of soda, cinnamon, nutmeg and cloves in a small bowl. Beat the butter, brown sugar and molasses with an electric mixer in a large bowl until creamy. Add the whole egg and egg white, one at a time, beating well after each addition. Stir in the dry ingredients.

3. Fold the raisins into the batter. Spread the batter in the prepared tin. Bake for 25 minutes or until the top is springy to the touch and lightly golden. Cool the cake in the dish on a rack, then cut into 24 bars.

Nutrients per bar: Kilojoules 462; Fibre 1g; Protein 1g; Carbohydrate 21g; Saturated Fat 1g; Total Fat 2g; Cholesterol 15mg

Grape & Raisin Cake

Preparation: 15 minutes / Cooking: 55 minutes / Serves: 8

1⅓ cups plain flour
1¼ teaspoons baking powder
½ teaspoon bicarbonate of soda
Salt
3 tablespoons unsalted butter, at room temperature
⅔ cup plus ¼ cup sugar
1 egg
2 egg whites
¾ cup buttermilk
1 teaspoon vanilla essence
½ cup raisins
¼ cup walnuts or pecans
¾ teaspoon cinnamon
2 cups seedless red and/or green grapes

1. Preheat the oven to 180°C. Spray a 23 cm square baking tin with cooking spray; put aside. Combine the flour, baking powder, bicarbonate of soda and a pinch of salt in a small bowl.

2. Cream the butter and ⅔ cup of the sugar with an electric mixer in a large bowl until light and fluffy. Add the whole egg and egg whites, one at a time, beating until well combined. Beat in the buttermilk and vanilla essence. Fold the dry ingredients into the butter mixture. Fold in the raisins.

3. Combine the remaining sugar, the walnuts and cinnamon in a food processor, pulsing until the nuts are coarsely ground. Spoon half the batter into the tin and sprinkle with half the nut mixture. Top with the remaining batter, the grapes and the remaining nut mixture. Bake for 55 minutes or until a skewer inserted in the centre comes out clean.

Nutrients per serving: Kilojoules 1395; Fibre 2g; Protein 6g; Carbohydrate 56g; Saturated Fat 5g; Total Fat 10g; Cholesterol 47mg

Raisin Bars

Kiwifruit

Following its debut as the darling of upscale chefs, the kiwifruit – a great source of vitamin C, fibre and potassium – has become a popular snack fruit.

Healthy Highlights

1 medium (80g)		Nutrients % RDI	
Kilojoules	159	Vitamin C	190%
Fibre	2.6g	Potassium	11%
Protein	1.1g		
Carbohydrate	7.6g		
Saturated Fat	0g		
Total Fat	0.2g		
Cholesterol	0mg		
Sodium	5mg		

Shopping & Preparation

At the market Kiwifruit are generally available year round, but they are at their best from March to June. A large proportion of the kiwifruit sold in Australia from July to December is imported from New Zealand.

Look for Kiwifruit are usually firm when sold, but they readily ripen at room temperature. Choose plump, unbruised fruits; avoid any with shrivelled skin.

Preparation Ripen kiwifruit at room temperature; when ready to eat, a kiwifruit is about as yielding as a ripe peach. Refrigerate when ripe away from other fruit. You can eat a kiwifruit skin and all; though it's a bit furry, the skin is good for you. Or peel and then slice the fruit. Instead of using a peeler, use a spoon (see below).

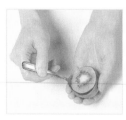

Cut the kiwifruit in half, then use a teaspoon to scoop out the flesh in one piece.

Cooking tip Kiwifruit, like pineapple, contain an enzyme that keeps gelatine from setting, so they should not be used when making jellied desserts.

Chicken Salad with Kiwifruit & Lime-Ginger Dressing

Preparation: 25 minutes / Cooking: 10 minutes / Serves: 4

½ teaspoon dried tarragon

Salt

Freshly ground pepper

4 skinless, boneless chicken breast halves (150g each)

1 teaspoon grated lime zest

2 tablespoons lime juice

2 tablespoons chilli sauce

3 teaspoons honey

1 teaspoon olive oil

¾ teaspoon ground ginger

4 cups mixed lettuce leaves

4 kiwifruit, peeled and cut into 1cm cubes

½ cup canned sliced water chestnuts, rinsed and cut into strips

1. Preheat the griller. Rub the tarragon, a pinch of salt and a good grinding of pepper into the chicken. Grill 15 cm from the heat for 4 minutes each side or until cooked through. Cool to room temperature and cut crossways into 1 cm slices.

2. Meanwhile, whisk together the lime zest, lime juice, chilli sauce, honey, oil and ginger in a large bowl.

3. Add the lettuce leaves, kiwifruit and water chestnuts, tossing to combine. Add the chicken and toss again.

Nutrients per serving: Kilojoules 1547; Fibre 5g; Protein 44g; Carbohydrate 16g; Saturated Fat 4g; Total Fat 14g; Cholesterol 135mg

Did you know?

Kiwifruit contain an enzyme called actinidin, which breaks down protein. Mashed or puréed kiwifruit can serve as a tenderising marinade; leave it on the meat for at least 15 minutes.

Fresh Kiwifruit Salsa

Preparation: 15 minutes / Serves: 4

4 kiwifruit, peeled and cut into 1cm cubes

1 red capsicum, diced

1 small cucumber, peeled and cut into 5mm dice

1 spring onion, thinly sliced

¾ teaspoon ground coriander

¾ teaspoon ground cumin

1 tablespoon lime juice

Dried crushed chilli

1. Combine all the ingredients in a medium bowl. Cover and refrigerate. Serve with grilled fish or chicken.

Nutrients per serving: Kilojoules 217; Fibre 3g; Protein 2g; Carbohydrate 10g; Saturated Fat 0g; Total Fat 0g; Cholesterol 0mg

Kiwifruit with Ricotta Cream

Kiwifruit with Ricotta Cream

Preparation: 15 minutes / Serves: 4

¼ cup plus
   2 tablespoons sugar

¼ cup lime juice

8 kiwifruit, peeled and
   cut into 1cm wedges

½ teaspoon grated lime
   zest

½ cup low-fat ricotta
   cheese

2 tablespoons reduced-
   fat sour cream

2 teaspoons julienned
   lime zest

1. Combine the ¼ cup of sugar and the lime juice in a medium bowl. Add the kiwifruit, tossing to combine. Cover and refrigerate until serving time.

2. In a small bowl, combine the grated lime zest, ricotta, sour cream and the remaining sugar. Serve the kiwifruit with its syrup in dessert bowls, topped with the ricotta cream and the julienned lime zest.

Nutrients per serving: Kilojoules 975; Fibre 5g; Protein 6g; Carbohydrate 38g; Saturated Fat 4g; Total Fat 6g; Cholesterol 23mg

Did you know?

• Two kiwifruit – a healthy snack – supply more potassium than a medium banana.

• One kiwifruit contains more vitamin C than a small orange.

Lemons & Limes

Bursting with vitamin C, these tart fruits serve as fat-free, virtually sodium-free seasonings for many foods and beverages.

Healthy Highlights

Lemons
1 medium (100g)		Nutrients % RDI	
Kilojoules	94	Vitamin C	158%
Fibre	2.5		
Protein	0.6g		
Carbohydrate	1.8g		
Saturated Fat	0g		
Total Fat	0.2g		
Cholesterol	0mg		
Sodium	2mg		

Limes
1 medium (50g)		Nutrients % RDI	
Kilojoules	44	Vitamin C	77%
Fibre	0.1g		
Protein	0.4g		
Carbohydrate	0.6g		
Saturated Fat	0g		
Total Fat	0.1g		
Cholesterol	0mg		
Sodium	1mg		

Shopping & Preparation

At the market Both lemons and limes are available throughout the year.

Look for Pick firm, heavy, brightly coloured lemons and limes that have fine-grained, glossy skins. Large-pored skin can be an indication of very thick pith and less juice.

Preparation If a recipe calls for the zest as well as the juice or pulp of the lemon or lime, be sure to remove the zest first. Rolling the fruit under the palm of your hand (or warming it under hot water) will make it easier to squeeze the juice.

There are two ways to peel off the zest from citrus. You can use a vegetable peeler, then sliver the zest with a knife. Or you can use a zester (pictured), which pulls the zest off in thin strands.

Lime Parfait

Preparation: 1 hour 40 minutes / Cooking: 5 minutes
Chill: 2 hours / Serves: 8

- 1 can (375ml) low-fat evaporated milk
- 1 envelope gelatine
- ½ cup icing sugar
- ½ cup reduced-fat sour cream
- ½ teaspoon grated lime zest
- ½ cup lime juice

1. Pour the evaporated milk into a large mixing bowl and place in the freezer until ice crystals begin to form, about 1 hour.

2. Sprinkle the gelatine over ¼ cup cold water in a glass measuring cup and stand for 5 minutes or until softened. Place the cup in a pan of simmering water and heat for 4 minutes or until the gelatine has dissolved. Cool to room temperature.

3. Beat the partially frozen evaporated milk until soft peaks form. Gradually beat in the icing sugar and continue whipping until stiff peaks form. Beat in the sour cream. Beat in the lime zest and cooled gelatine mixture until well combined. Place the bowl in the refrigerator and chill for 30 minutes or until the mixture begins to mound.

4. Fold the lime juice into the milk mixture. Transfer to parfait glasses and chill for 2 hours.

Nutrients per serving: Kilojoules 552; Fibre 0g; Protein 5g; Carbohydrate 15g; Saturated Fat 4g; Total Fat 6g; Cholesterol 19mg

Did you know?

Citrus fruits contain pectin, a type of dietary fibre that can lower blood cholesterol levels.

Tomato & Vegetable Salad with Lemon Vinaigrette

Preparation: 20 minutes / Cooking: 12 minutes / Serves: 4

- 1 yellow or red capsicum, cut lengthways into flat strips
- 2 lemons
- ¼ cup lemon juice
- 3 teaspoons olive oil
- ¼ teaspoon sugar
- Salt
- Freshly ground pepper
- 3 large tomatoes, cut into 2cm chunks
- 1 stalk celery, thinly sliced
- ¼ cup chopped fresh basil

1. Preheat the griller. Place the capsicum pieces, skin-side-up, on the griller tray and grill for 12 minutes or until the skin is charred. When cool enough to handle, peel and thinly slice.

2. Peel the lemons with a paring knife. Cut the flesh into 5 mm dice, discarding the seeds. Whisk together the lemon juice, oil, sugar and salt and pepper to taste in a large bowl.

3. Add the lemon pieces to the bowl along with the tomatoes, celery, basil and roasted capsicum. Toss well to combine.

Nutrients per serving: Kilojoules 283; Fibre 3g; Protein 2g; Carbohydrate 5g; Saturated Fat 0g; Total Fat 4g; Cholesterol 0mg

Lemon & Saffron Risotto

Preparation: 10 minutes / Cooking: 35 minutes / Serves: 4

1 tablespoon olive oil

1 tablespoon butter

1 onion, peeled and finely chopped

2 cloves garlic, finely chopped

2 cups Arborio rice

4 cups hot chicken stock

1 pinch saffron strands

2 tablespoons lemon juice

1 tablespoon grated lemon zest

Salt

Freshly ground pepper

½ cup shaved Parmesan cheese

1. Heat the oil and butter in a saucepan over moderate heat.

2. Add the onion, garlic and rice and cook for 3 to 4 minutes, stirring with a wooden spoon.

3. Bring the stock to a gentle simmer with the saffron. Add 1 ladleful stock to the rice, stirring for about 3 minutes until the rice has absorbed almost all of the liquid.

4. Continue adding the stock, 1 ladleful at a time, until it has all been absorbed (about 20 to 25 minutes) and the rice is cooked to a creamy al dente stage. (You may need to add a little extra hot water.)

5. Remove from the heat and stir in the lemon juice and lemon zest. Season to taste with salt and pepper. Return the saucepan to the heat for 1 minute, then stir the risotto again before serving. Top each serving with shaved Parmesan cheese and another good grinding of pepper, if liked.

Nutrients per serving: Kilojoules 2121; Fibre 2g; Protein 12g; Carbohydrate 86g; Saturated Fat 5g; Total Fat 12g; Cholesterol 18mg

Lemon & Saffron Risotto

Mangoes

Its golden-orange flesh tips you off to the mango's stellar beta-carotene content. This tropical delight also supplies lots of vitamin C and even some vitamin E.

Healthy Highlights

1 medium (205g)*		Nutrients % RDI	
Kilojoules	488	Vitamin C	193%
Fibre	3.1g	Vitamin A	110%
Protein	2.1g	Potassium	27%
Carbohydrate	26.1g	Niacin	12%
Saturated Fat	0g		
Total Fat	0.4g	*peeled, seeded	
Cholesterol	0mg		
Sodium	2mg		

Shopping & Preparation

At the market Spring and summer (September to March) are the best time for mangoes. Kensington Pride, Bowen Special, Irwin, Kietts and Palmer are among the most common varieties and they are all at their best during this time. Nam doc mai is a green, elongated mango with golden flesh.

Look for Mangoes are picked unripe; choose a smooth, unbruised fruit with a red or orange tint to its skin. The fruit should be firm and bright with a pleasant aroma.

Preparation Ripen mangoes at room temperature until fragrant; black freckles are also a sign of ripeness. To cut, hold the mango stem-end up and make two vertical cuts, one on either side of the large, flat seed. Remove these two side cheeks, then cut off the band of flesh that remains around the edges of the seed. Peel the flesh or cube.

To cube a mango, make crisscross cuts with a small knife down to, but not through, the skin of each of the side pieces. Turn these cheeks inside out and slice off the cubes.

Mango Mousse

Preparation: 20 minutes / Chill: 2 hours / Serves: 4

3 mangoes (1kg total), peeled and sliced
¼ cup lime juice
½ teaspoon ground ginger
1 envelope gelatine
2 tablespoons sugar
½ cup reduced-fat sour cream

1. Reserve 8 small mango slices. Purée the remaining mango slices with the lime juice and ginger in a food processor.

2. Sprinkle the gelatine over ¼ cup water in a small bowl. Let stand for 5 minutes or until softened. Meanwhile, combine the sugar and ¼ cup water in a small saucepan and bring to the boil. Stir the gelatine into the sugar mixture and cook, stirring, for 1 minute or just until the gelatine is dissolved.

3. Add the gelatine mixture to the mango purée and process until well combined. Add the sour cream and process briefly just to blend.

4. Spoon into dessert bowls or glasses, top with the reserved mango slices, cover and refrigerate for 2 hours or until chilled and set.

Nutrients per serving: Kilojoules 939; Fibre 2g; Protein 4g; Carbohydrate 29g; Saturated Fat 6g; Total Fat 10g; Cholesterol 30mg

Did you know?

Much of the dietary fibre in mangoes is pectin, a form of soluble fibre that has been shown to reduce blood cholesterol.

Mango Mousse

Mango & Prawn Salad

Mango & Prawn Salad

Preparation: 25 minutes / Serves: 4

I clove garlic, crushed

I tablespoon chilli sauce

2 tablespoons olive oil

4 tablespoons lime juice

¼ cup chopped fresh mint

4 cups mixed salad leaves

½ telegraph cucumber

I red capsicum, sliced

I punnet cherry tomatoes, quartered

2 large mangoes, peeled and sliced

16 cooked king prawns, peeled with tails left attached

Freshly ground pepper

1. Combine the garlic, chilli sauce, oil, lime juice and mint in a small jug. Stir well.

2. Rinse the salad leaves lightly in cool water, then shake or spin dry. Blot any excess moisture with a paper towel.

3. Slice the half cucumber, leaving the skin on. Combine the cucumber, capsicum, tomatoes, mangoes, prawns and salad leaves in a large bowl, add the dressing and toss well.

4. Pile the salad onto individual serving plates. Season with freshly ground pepper to taste and serve immediately.

Nutrients per serving: Kilojoules 1126; Fibre 5g; Protein 18g; Carbohydrate 24g; Saturated Fat 1g; Total Fat 11g; Cholesterol 120mg

Did you know?

The high content of beta-carotene, an antioxidant, in mangoes helps boost the body's defences against free radicals, which are thought to be responsible for certain cancers.

Melons

These delicious fruits provide plenty of vitamin C. Orange-fleshed melons supply beta-carotene; watermelon has lycopene, another carotenoid.

Healthy Highlights

Rockmelon

1 cup, diced (170g)		Nutrients % RDI	
Kilojoules	154	Vitamin C	192%
Fibre	1.7g	Vitamin A	32%
Protein	0.8g	Potassium	16%
Carbohydrate	7.9g		
Saturated Fat	0g		
Total Fat	0.2g		
Cholesterol	0mg		
Sodium	17mg		

Honeydew

1 cup, diced (180g)		Nutrients % RDI	
Kilojoules	238	Vitamin C	108%
Fibre	1.8g	Potassium	15%
Protein	1.3g		
Carbohydrate	11.7g		
Saturated Fat	0g		
Total Fat	0.5g		
Cholesterol	0mg		
Sodium	77mg		

Watermelon

1 cup, diced (160g)		Nutrients % RDI	
Kilojoules	155	Vitamin C	38%
Fibre	1.2g		
Protein	1g		
Carbohydrate	8.1g		
Saturated Fat	0g		
Total Fat	0.3g		
Cholesterol	0mg		
Sodium	3mg		

Shopping & Preparation

At the market Summer is peak season for all melons, but they are nearly always available.

Look for Rockmelons and honeydews should have a smooth indentation at the stem end (this indicates that the melon was picked ripe). A honeydew should have a velvety skin; the 'netting' on a rockmelon should cover the whole surface, with no breaks. The rind of a watermelon should look somewhat dull and waxy.

Preparation Once a melon is picked, it won't get any sweeter; but if you leave a melon at room temperature for a day or two, it will get softer and juicier. Simply slice, remove the skin and seeds, and enjoy.

Prosciutto & Melon with Parmesan

Prosciutto & Melon with Parmesan

Preparation: 15 minutes / Serves: 6

1 rockmelon (1.2kg)
12 thin slices prosciutto (125g)
½ cup shaved Parmesan cheese
2 tablespoons extra virgin olive oil
Freshly ground black pepper

1. Halve and seed the rockmelon and cut into 12 wedges. Drape each wedge with a thin slice of prosciutto and top with a little Parmesan.

2. Drizzle the oil over the top and serve with a little freshly ground pepper.

Nutrients per serving: Kilojoules 580; Fibre 1g; Protein 7g; Carbohydrate 6g; Saturated Fat 3g; Total Fat 10g; Cholesterol 17mg

Did you know?

Watermelon is rich in lycopene. One large study showed that men who ate ten or more servings per week of lycopene-rich foods had a 45 per cent reduction in prostate cancer risk.

Smoked Turkey & Melon Salad

Preparation: 20 minutes / Serves: 4

3 cups honeydew and/or rockmelon balls
375g smoked turkey breast, cut into 1cm cubes
½ cup thinly sliced celery
2 spring onions, sliced
2 tablespoons chopped fresh basil
2 tablespoons chopped toasted walnuts
1½ tablespoons honey-mustard
3 teaspoon white wine vinegar
2 teaspoons olive oil
½ teaspoon soy sauce

1. Toss together the melon balls, turkey, celery, spring onions, basil and walnuts in a large bowl.

2. Whisk together the mustard, vinegar, oil and soy sauce in a small bowl. Toss the dressing with the melon mixture just before serving.

Nutrients per serving: Kilojoules 969; Fibre 2g; Protein 29g; Carbohydrate 7g; Saturated Fat 1g; Total Fat 9g; Cholesterol 61mg

Orange & Rockmelon Sorbet

Preparation: 15 minutes

Freeze: 2 to 3 hours / Serves: 4

4 cups rockmelon cubes
¾ cup buttermilk
⅓ cup maple syrup
¼ cup orange juice
⅓ cup sugar
1 teaspoon grated orange zest

1. Purée the rockmelon in a food processor. Transfer to a bowl and stir in the buttermilk, maple syrup, orange juice, sugar and orange zest. Combine well.

2. Freeze in an ice cream machine or place in a 23 x 33 x 5 cm cake tin and freeze for 2 to 3 hours or until almost frozen. Cut into chunks and process in a food processor until smooth. If not serving right away, refreeze, but let soften in the refrigerator for 30 minutes before serving.

Nutrients per serving: Kilojoules 877; Fibre 2g; Protein 3g; Carbohydrate 48g; Saturated Fat 1g; Total Fat 1g; Cholesterol 4mg

Did you know?

Rockmelons, also known as cantaloupes, have a particularly high vitamin A content (converted from beta-carotene), which is of major importance to the health of your eyes.

Honeydew Crush

Preparation: 10 minutes / Serves: 2

2 cups honeydew chunks
½ cup orange juice
2 tablespoons lime juice
1 tablespoon honey
2 tablespoons chopped fresh mint
1 cup ice cubes
2 mint sprigs

1. Place all the ingredients, except the mint sprigs, in a blender and purée.

2. Serve in tall glasses, garnished with the mint sprigs.

Nutrients per serving: Kilojoules 536; Fibre 2g; Protein 2g; Carbohydrate 28g; Saturated Fat 0g; Total Fat 1g; Cholesterol 0mg

Orange & Rockmelon Sorbet

Melon Salad with Yoghurt & Lime Sauce

Melon Salad with Yoghurt & Lime Sauce

Preparation: 40 minutes / Serves: 8

¼ small watermelon (1.5kg), cut into cubes

½ rockmelon, cut into cubes (2 cups)

¼ honeydew melon, cut into cubes (1½ cups)

1 cup seedless red or green grapes

1 cup fresh or canned pineapple cubes

1 cup plain low-fat yoghurt

2 tablespoons reduced-fat sour cream

2 tablespoons honey

1 tablespoon lime juice

Ground ginger

1. Combine the watermelon, rockmelon, honeydew melon, grapes and pineapple in a large bowl. Chill the fruit until serving time.

2. Combine the yoghurt, sour cream, honey, lime juice and a pinch of ginger in a small bowl. Chill until serving time.

3. Serve the fruit in individual bowls, with the yoghurt sauce on the side.

Nutrients per serving: Kilojoules 494; Fibre 2g; Protein 3g; Carbohydrate 22g; Saturated Fat 1g; Total Fat 2g; Cholesterol 6mg

Did you know?

Cut watermelons are a tempting purchase because you can more easily judge their ripeness, but keep in mind that melons lose vitamin C when they are cut. If you do buy a half or quarter melon, choose one that's been tightly wrapped in plastic and kept chilled.

Oranges & Mandarins

These popular snack fruits are outstanding sources of vitamin C; they also supply folate and fibre as well as flavonoids, which are cancer-fighting compounds.

Healthy Highlights

Oranges*

1 medium (160g)		Nutrients % RDI	
Kilojoules	253	Vitamin C	279%
Fibre	3.2g	Folate	24%
Protein	1.7g	Thiamin	15%
Carbohydrate	12.8g	Potassium	12%
Saturated Fat	0g		
Total Fat	0.2g	*navel	
Cholesterol	0mg		
Sodium	5mg		

Mandarins

1 medium (60g)		Nutrients % RDI	
Kilojoules	99	Vitamin C	96%
Fibre	1.2g		
Protein	0.5g		
Carbohydrate	4.9g		
Saturated Fat	0g		
Total Fat	0.1g		
Cholesterol	0mg		
Sodium	1mg		

Shopping & Preparation

At the market Oranges are available all year; mandarins are most bountiful in the winter.

Look for Select firm, heavy oranges and mandarins. Choose thin-skinned oranges such as Valencias for juicing; use navel oranges for snacking and cooking (they're seedless and easy to peel).

Preparation Remove all the white pith when peeling an orange. Mandarins are easy to peel but must be seeded: snip the top of each segment and squeeze out the pips.

To segment an orange after peeling, cut along both sides of each dividing membrane.

Mandarin & Lamb Stir-Fry

Preparation: 25 minutes / Cooking: 10 minutes / Serves: 4

- 1½ tablespoons reduced-salt soy sauce
- 1 teaspoon ground coriander
- 2 teaspoons grated mandarin zest
- ½ teaspoon sugar
- Cayenne pepper
- 500g well-trimmed boneless leg of lamb, cut into 1cm strips
- 2 teaspoons vegetable oil
- 1 red capsicum, cut into 1cm squares
- 3 cloves garlic, crushed
- 4 spring onions, thinly sliced
- ½ cup chicken stock
- 2 teaspoons cornflour
- 4 mandarins, peeled, separated into segments, halved and seeded
- 12 fresh coriander leaves
- 4 spring onion spirals

1. Combine the soy sauce, ground coriander, mandarin zest, sugar and a pinch of cayenne pepper in a medium bowl. Add the lamb, tossing well to coat.

2. Heat 1 teaspoon of the oil in a large nonstick frying pan over moderately high heat. Add the lamb and stir-fry for 2 minutes or until lightly browned. Transfer the lamb to a plate with a slotted spoon. Reduce the heat to moderate, add the remaining oil, the capsicum, garlic and spring onions, and stir-fry for 4 minutes or until the capsicum is crisp-tender.

3. Whisk the stock into the cornflour in a small bowl. Add to the pan and bring to the boil. Return the lamb to the pan, add the mandarins and cook for 1 minute or until the sauce is slightly thickened. Garnish with the coriander leaves and spring onion spirals.

Nutrients per serving: Kilojoules 1079; Fibre 2g; Protein 30g; Carbohydrate 11g; Saturated Fat 4g; Total Fat 11g; Cholesterol 85mg

Orange Chicken

Preparation: 15 minutes / Cooking: 20 minutes / Serves: 4

3 teaspoons olive oil

4 skinless, boneless chicken breast halves (125g each)

1 red capsicum, diced

1½ tablespoons sugar

1 tablespoon julienned orange zest

½ cup orange juice

½ cup chicken stock

¼ teaspoon dried rosemary

Salt

Freshly ground black pepper

1 teaspoon cornflour blended with 2 teaspoons water

2 navel oranges

1. Heat 2 teaspoons of the oil in a large frying pan over moderate heat. Cook the chicken for 2 minutes each side or until lightly golden. Transfer to a plate. Add the capsicum and the remaining oil to the frying pan and cook for 3 minutes or until crisp-tender. Add to the plate with the chicken.

2. Add the sugar to the pan and cook for 3 minutes or until caramelised. Add the orange zest, orange juice, stock, rosemary and salt and pepper to taste, and bring to the boil.

3. Return the chicken and capsicum to the pan, reduce to a simmer, cover and cook for 7 minutes or until the chicken is just cooked. Stir in the cornflour mixture and boil for 1 minute, stirring, until slightly thickened.

4. Meanwhile, peel the oranges with a small paring knife. Separate the orange segments from the membranes and stir the segments into the pan to gently heat through. Serve the chicken with the orange sauce.

Nutrients per serving: Kilojoules 1279; Fibre 2g; Protein 32g; Carbohydrate 16g; Saturated Fat 3g; Total Fat 12g; Cholesterol 99mg

Did you know?

• Mandarins and oranges contain compounds called terpenes, which seem to limit the body's production of cholesterol. Terpenes also fight cancer by deactivating carcinogens.

• Oranges contain a phytochemical called limonene, which studies show may have an anticarcinogenic effect in the body. Oranges also contain glucarase, another cancer-fighting agent, as well as plenty of vitamin C, an antioxidant.

Mandarin & Lamb Stir-Fry

Caramelised Orange Compote

Preparation: 15 minutes / Cooking: 3 minutes / Serves: 4

4 navel oranges
¼ cup brown sugar
½ teaspoon cinnamon
1 tablespoon julienned
orange zest

1. Cut the rind off the oranges and cut the oranges into skinless segments, making sure all the pith has been removed.

2. Place in a gratin dish or a shallow baking dish and sprinkle with the brown sugar and cinnamon. Top with the orange zest. Grill for 2 minutes or until the sugar melts.

Nutrients per serving: Kilojoules 373; Fibre 3g; Protein 1g; Carbohydrate 21g; Saturated Fat 0g; Total Fat 0g; Cholesterol 0mg

Middle Eastern Orange Cake

Middle Eastern Orange Cake

Preparation: 2½ hours / Cooking: 1 hour / Serves: 10

5 large oranges

6 eggs, beaten

2¼ cups ground almonds

1¼ cups caster sugar

1 teaspoon baking powder

1 cup plain low-fat yoghurt

1. Wash 2 of the oranges and place in a saucepan with water to cover. Bring to the boil, cover and simmer for 2 hours. Allow the oranges to cool, then cut open, remove the pips and roughly chop the flesh.

2. Preheat the oven to 190°C. Grease and flour a 22 cm springform tin. Process the cooked oranges, eggs, ground almonds, sugar and baking powder in a food processor.

3. Pour the batter into the prepared tin. Bake for 1 hour or until the centre is firm (note that this is a very moist cake). Cool in the tin before gently turning out.

4. Peel the remaining oranges with a small paring knife. Separate the orange segments from the membranes. Serve the cake with the fresh orange segments and some yoghurt on the side.

Nutrients per serving: Kilojoules 1390; Fibre 4g; Protein 11g; Carbohydrate 37g; Saturated Fat 2g; Total Fat 16g; Cholesterol 130mg

Did you know?

If you usually drink orange juice at breakfast, eat a a whole orange instead; you'll get the same amount of vitamin C, but also all the fibre.

Pawpaws

Take your vitamin C in the form of this luscious tropical fruit and you'll replenish potassium and vitamin A, as well. There's a good amount of fibre, too.

Healthy Highlights

1 cup, diced (150g)		Nutrients % RDI	
Kilojoules	185	Vitamin C	300%
Fibre	3.4g	Vitamin A	30%
Protein	0.6g	Potassium	11%
Carbohydrate	10.3g		
Saturated Fat	0g		
Total Fat	0.2g		
Cholesterol	0mg		
Sodium	10mg		

Shopping & Preparation

At the market Yellow-fleshed local pawpaws are at their best in spring and early summer, when you will also find imported pink-fleshed papayas in some specialist fruit shops. A close relative to the pawpaw, the papaya has a more subtle flavour than the larger pawpaw, but they are interchangeable in recipes.

Look for A truly green pawpaw will never ripen, so choose one that's at least half yellow. The fruit should yield slightly to gentle thumb pressure. Sniffing won't help you pick – an uncut pawpaw has no fragrance.

Preparation Ripen a pawpaw by leaving it at room temperature in a paper bag for a few days. When ripe, store it in the refrigerator and use as soon as possible. To serve, just halve the fruit lengthways and spoon out the seeds, which are edible. Scoop out the flesh with a spoon or melon baller, or peel the pawpaw halves with a swivel-bladed vegetable peeler.

Scoop out the pawpaw seeds with a spoon; they are edible, so you can use them as a garnish if you like.

Cooking tip An enzyme in uncooked pawpaw keeps gelatine from setting so you shouldn't use pawpaw when making jellied desserts.

Tropical Fruit Salad ◎

Preparation: 30 minutes / Serves: 4

⅓ cup apricot nectar

2 tablespoons lime juice

¼ cup chopped fresh mint

I large mango (500g), peeled and cut into 2cm chunks

I cup fresh or canned pineapple wedges

I large banana, thickly sliced

2 kiwifruit, peeled and cut into 1cm chunks

I medium pawpaw (500g), peeled and cut into 1cm chunks

1. Whisk together the apricot nectar, lime juice and mint in a large bowl. Add the mango, pineapple, banana and kiwifruit, tossing to combine. Refrigerate until serving time.

2. At serving time, add the pawpaw and toss again. Serve immediately.

Nutrients per serving: Kilojoules 607; Fibre 6g; Protein 3g; Carbohydrate 32g; Saturated Fat 0g; Total Fat 0g; Cholesterol 0mg

Did you know?

Pawpaw leaves and fruit contain papain, an enzyme which breaks down some of the fibres in meat, thus acting as a tenderiser. This is the reason many Pacific Islanders wrap their meat in pawpaw leaves for cooking.

Pawpaw & Raspberry Crisp ◎

Preparation: 10 minutes / Cooking: 15 minutes / Serves: 4

2 small pawpaws (750g total), peeled and cut into 2cm chunks

I teaspoon grated lemon zest

I tablespoon lemon juice

Ground allspice

Pepper

¾ cup raspberries

1½ tablespoons white sugar

1½ tablespoons firmly packed light brown sugar

3 teaspoons unsalted butter

2 tablespoons plain flour

1. Preheat the oven to 220°C. Toss together the pawpaw, lemon zest, lemon juice and a pinch each of allspice and pepper in a 20 cm round ceramic or glass baking dish. Scatter the raspberries on top.

2. Combine both the sugars and the butter in a small bowl. Mix in the flour until the mixture is crumbly. Sprinkle the crumb mixture over the fruit. Bake for 12 to 15 minutes or until the top is lightly browned and set and the fruit is heated through.

Nutrients per serving: Kilojoules 574; Fibre 5g; Protein 1g; Carbohydrate 26g; Saturated Fat 2g; Total Fat 3g; Cholesterol 9mg

Did you know?

Pawpaws are a wise choice for snacking: gram for gram, they contain more than ten times as much vitamin C as apples.

Tropical Fruit Salad

Peaches & Nectarines

These closely related tree fruits are good sources of beta-carotene, vitamin C, niacin and potassium. They also supply some fibre and, gram for gram, contain more potassium than a navel orange.

Healthy Highlights

Peaches

1 medium (145g)		Nutrients % RDI	
Kilojoules	191	Vitamin C	48%
Fibre	2g	Potassium	14%
Protein	1.3g	Niacin	11%
Carbohydrate	9.3g		
Saturated Fat	0g		
Total Fat	0.1g		
Cholesterol	0mg		
Sodium	3mg		

Nectarines

1 medium (150g)		Nutrients % RDI	
Kilojoules	235	Vitamin C	60%
Fibre	3.6g	Potassium	18%
Protein	1.7g	Niacin	14%
Carbohydrate	11.6g		
Saturated Fat	0g		
Total Fat	0.1g		
Cholesterol	0mg		
Sodium	1mg		

Shopping & Preparation

At the market Locally grown peaches are at their best from January to March, while nectarines are also best at around the same time.

Look for Choose firm, plump peaches that yield to gentle pressure. Avoid green, extra-hard, bruised or blemished fruit. Select nectarines that are fragrant, firm, plump and richly coloured with smooth, glossy skin.

Preparation If a recipe requires you to peel peaches, you'll need to blanch them in boiling water for about 2 minutes – not enough to cook them, but just enough to loosen the skin. Cool the fruit in a bowl of iced water, then peel.

Fresh Peach Conserve

Preparation: 20 minutes / Cooking: 25 minutes / Makes: 7 cups

1.5kg peaches
1½ tablespoons lemon juice
1 teaspoon cinnamon
¼ teaspoon ground allspice
3½ cups sugar

1. Add the peaches in batches to a large pot of boiling water and cook for 2 minutes to blanch. Peel and stone the peaches, transfer to a large saucepan, and mash with a potato masher.

2. Stir in the lemon juice, cinnamon and allspice. Bring to the boil over high heat. Add the sugar all at once, stirring constantly. Return to the rolling boil and cook for 5 minutes or until slightly thickened. Skim off the foam.

3. Ladle the conserve into containers rinsed in boiling water; fill to within 1 cm of the top. Cover with tight lids and let stand at room temperature overnight. Store in the refrigerator for up to 3 weeks.

Nutrients per tablespoon: Kilojoules 155; Fibre 0g; Protein 0g; Carbohydrate 9g; Saturated Fat 0g; Total Fat 0g; Cholesterol 0mg

Did you know?

Peaches and nectarines are not only sweeter, softer and more fragrant when they're fully ripe, they also contain more vitamin C.

Peach & Cherry Crumble

Preparation: 15 minutes / Cooking: 25 minutes / Serves: 4

4 cups sliced peaches
2 cups cherries (250g), stoned and halved
½ cup white sugar
3 teaspoons cornflour
1 teaspoon vanilla essence
½ teaspoon grated lemon zest
⅓ cup rolled oats
2 tablespoons firmly packed light brown sugar
2 tablespoons plain flour
1 tablespoon unsalted butter, cut up

1. Preheat the oven to 190°C. Spray a 23 cm glass pie dish with cooking spray.

2. Combine the peaches, cherries, white sugar and cornflour in a medium saucepan and bring to the boil over a moderate heat. Remove from the heat and stir in the vanilla essence and lemon zest. Spoon into the pie dish.

3. Combine the oats, brown sugar and flour in a medium bowl. Cut in the butter with a pastry blender or 2 knives until the mixture is crumbly. Scatter over the fruit, place the pie dish on a baking tray and bake for 20 minutes or until the filling is bubbly and the top is browned. Serve warm or at room temperature.

Nutrients per serving: Kilojoules 1300; Fibre 4g; Protein 4g; Carbohydrate 63g; Saturated Fat 3g; Total Fat 5g; Cholesterol 12mg

Swordfish with Fresh Nectarine Relish

Swordfish with Fresh Nectarine Relish @

Preparation: 20 minutes / Cooking: 10 minutes / Serves: 4

1 small red chilli, seeded and minced

1½ tablespoons red wine vinegar

Salt

500g nectarines, cut into 1cm cubes

1 red capsicum, cut into 1cm squares

2 spring onions, thinly sliced

¼ cup chopped fresh mint

4 swordfish steaks (185g each)

½ teaspoon ground coriander

½ teaspoon ground cumin

2 limes, halved

1. Whisk together the chilli, vinegar and a pinch of salt in a medium bowl. Add the nectarines, capsicum, spring onions and mint, tossing to mix. Refrigerate until serving time.

2. Preheat the griller. Rub the swordfish with the coriander and cumin. Grill 15 cm from the heat for 3 minutes each side or until lightly browned and just cooked through. Serve topped with the nectarine relish and accompany each serving with half a lime.

Nutrients per serving: Kilojoules 1683; Fibre 4g; Protein 59g; Carbohydrate 11g; Saturated Fat 5g; Total Fat 13g; Cholesterol 81mg

Amaretti-Stuffed Peaches

Preparation: 15 minutes / Cooking: 30 minutes / Serves: 6

¾ cup ground almonds

¾ cup ground amaretti biscuits

¼ cup caster sugar

2 egg yolks or I whole egg, beaten

6 freestone peaches, peeled

1½ tablespoons butter

⅔ cup marsala

1. Combine the almonds, amaretti and sugar in a medium bowl. Stir in the beaten egg slowly, a little at a time. Add just enough egg so that the sticky mixture holds together but don't let it become too wet to hold its shape. Form the mixture into 12 balls about the size of whole walnuts.

2. Spray a shallow baking dish with cooking spray. Cut the peaches in half and remove the stones. Place the peach halves close together in the baking dish, cut side up.

3. Press a ball of the almond mixture into the cavity of each peach half. Dot the tops with butter. Pour the marsala over the peaches.

4. Bake at 180°C for approximately 30 minutes or until the almond mixture is crusty and golden. Serve the peaches warm or chilled.

Nutrients per serving: Kilojoules 1229; Fibre 3g; Protein 6g; Carbohydrate 29g; Saturated Fat 4g; Total Fat 14g; Cholesterol 73mg

Did you know?

• Some frozen peaches will have as much as 20 per cent more vitamin C than fresh peaches. That's because ascorbic acid is added to maintain the fruit's colour.

• Cooking has very little effect on beta-carotene.

Nectarine Brûlée

Preparation: 10 minutes / Cooking: 15 minutes / Serves: 4

4 nectarines or peaches

I tablespoon lemon juice

I tablespoon sugar

½ cup reduced-fat sour cream

⅓ cup firmly packed brown sugar

1. Preheat the oven to 180°C. Cut the nectarines into thin wedges and toss with the lemon juice and sugar. Spoon into a 20 cm gratin dish or small baking dish and bake for 10 minutes.

2. Preheat the griller. Top the nectarines with the sour cream and sprinkle with the brown sugar. Grill for 5 minutes or until the sugar is melted and bubbly.

Nutrients per serving: Kilojoules 1001; Fibre 4g; Protein 2g; Carbohydrate 36g; Saturated Fat 6g; Total Fat 10g; Cholesterol 30mg

Amaretti-Stuffed Peaches

Pineapples

Serve luscious pineapple in place of cake or confectionery and you reap the advantages of vitamin C, potassium and manganese, a mineral that helps build strong bones.

Healthy Highlights

1 slice (110g)		Nutrients % RDI	
Kilojoules	174	Vitamin C	77%
Fibre	2.3g	Potassium	10%
Protein	1.1g		
Carbohydrate	8.8g		
Saturated Fat	0g		
Total Fat	0.1g		
Cholesterol	0mg		
Sodium	2mg		

Shopping & Preparation

At the market Fresh pineapples are available all year, with best value being from November to February.

Look for Once picked, a pineapple won't get any sweeter. Choose a large, plump, heavy specimen with fresh green leaves; a ripe pineapple may have a sweet fragrance, but if it's chilled that may not be detectable.

Preparation To cut pineapple, first remove the crown (see below). For slices, first pare off the skin with a sharp knife, then slice the fruit (cut out the woody core after slicing). For chopped fruit, it's simpler to quarter the unpeeled fruit lengthways and then cut the fruit off the skin before chopping.

Cooking tip The bromelain in fresh pineapple will prevent gelatine from setting. So use only cooked (or canned) pineapple when making jellied desserts.

To remove the crown of a pineapple, grasp it in your hand and twist firmly.

Pineapple Brown Betty

Preparation: 10 minutes / Cooking: 30 minutes / Serves: 4

- 125g amaretti biscuits (20 medium)
- ¼ cup walnuts or pecans
- ⅓ cup firmly packed light brown sugar
- 3 teaspoons unsalted butter, cut up
- ½ teaspoon cinnamon
- 1 teaspoon vanilla essence
- 2 cans (450g each) juice-packed pineapple chunks, drained

1. Preheat the oven to 180°C. Combine the amaretti biscuits, walnuts, brown sugar, butter, cinnamon and vanilla essence, and pulse until the biscuits are finely ground.

2. Toss the pineapple with the crumb mixture in a 20 cm square glass baking dish. Bake for 30 minutes or until the pineapple is piping hot and the crumbs are crusty.

Nutrients per serving: Kilojoules 1440; Fibre 4g; Protein 5g; Carbohydrate 55g; Saturated Fat 4g; Total Fat 12g; Cholesterol 12mg

Did you know?

- When buying canned pineapple, opt for the juice-packed type; pineapple packed in heavy syrup has lots of added sugar and about 150 kilojoules more per serving.

- Fresh pineapple can be used as a meat tenderiser as it contains an enzyme, bromelain, that breaks down protein. Bromelain is used to make commercial meat tenderisers.

Grilled Prawns with Pineapple Salsa

Preparation: 30 minutes / Marinate: 30 minutes
Cooking: 5 minutes / Serves: 4

- 1½ tablespoons lime juice
- ¾ teaspoon chilli powder
- ¼ teaspoon dried crushed chilli
- Salt
- 3 cups fresh pineapple chunks (5mm)
- ½ cup diced red capsicum
- ½ cup diced cucumber (5mm)
- ¼ cup diced red onion
- ½ cup pineapple juice
- 2 teaspoons olive oil
- ½ teaspoon dried oregano
- 500g large green prawns, peeled and deveined

1. Whisk together the lime juice, ¼ teaspoon of the chilli powder, the crushed chilli and a pinch of salt in a large bowl. Add the pineapple, capsicum, cucumber and onion, tossing well to combine. Cover the salsa and refrigerate until serving time.

2. Whisk together the pineapple juice, oil, oregano and the remaining chilli powder in a large bowl. Add the prawns and toss well. Marinate for 30 minutes.

3. Preheat the griller. Grill the prawns 15 cm from the heat for 2 minutes each side or until just cooked. Serve with the pineapple salsa.

Nutrients per serving: Kilojoules 668; Fibre 3g; Protein 17g; Carbohydrate 15g; Saturated Fat 1g; Total Fat 3g; Cholesterol 120mg

Pineapple Flambé

Preparation: 15 minutes / Cooking: 10 minutes / Serves: 4

1 tablespoon unsalted butter

2 tablespoons firmly packed light brown sugar

¼ teaspoon ground nutmeg

6 slices (2cm thick) fresh pineapple, cored and cut into thirds

2 tablespoons dark rum

1 tablespoon Grand Marnier or other orange liqueur

1⅓ cups reduced-fat frozen vanilla yoghurt

1. Melt the butter in a large frying pan over moderate heat. When it begins to foam, add the sugar and nutmeg, and heat until the sugar has melted. Add the pineapple and cook, tossing often, for 4 minutes or until the pineapple is warmed through.

2. Remove the pan from the heat, sprinkle the rum and Grand Marnier over the pineapple, and ignite the alcohol with a long match. Return the pan to the heat and shake until all the alcohol burns off.

3. Serve the pineapple slices and sauce with the frozen yoghurt.

Nutrients per serving: Kilojoules 1156; Fibre 5g; Protein 6g; Carbohydrate 44g; Saturated Fat 3g; Total Fat 5g; Cholesterol 19mg

Pineapple Flambé

Plums

Along with vitamin C, beta-carotene, potassium and fibre, plums are a source of lutein, a lesser-known carotenoid that is lacking in many people's diets. Lutein, which is also found in leafy greens, parsley and pumpkin, helps protect your retinas against the damaging effects of free radicals.

Healthy Highlights

2 medium (130g)		Nutrients % RDI	
Kilojoules	193	Vitamin C	22%
Fibre	2.8g	Potassium	10%
Protein	0.8g		
Carbohydrate	9.4g		
Saturated Fat	0g		
Total Fat	0.1g		
Cholesterol	0mg		
Sodium	3mg		

Shopping & Preparation

At the market Plums – both clingstone and freestone – are available from October to May, with February and March the peak months. Red-fleshed varieties have more nutrients than those with yellow flesh, and they also have a higher sugar content so are much sweeter.

Look for Red, yellow, green, purple or 'black' (really blue-black) plums offer many varieties to choose from. Pick firm (but not hard) plums that are full and plump, not shrivelled or bruised. For recipes that require the plums to be pitted, freestone varieties, such as Angelina or President, are the best choice.

Preparation Plums are often cooked with the skin left on; they can also be eaten raw, as is – or they can be peeled.

Spiced Plum Tart

Preparation: 30 minutes / Chill: 1 hour / Cooking: 40 minutes / Serves: 6

- 1 cup plus 1 tablespoon plain flour
- 3 teaspoons white sugar
- Salt
- 2 tablespoons plus 1 teaspoon unsalted butter, cut up
- 1½ tablespoons low-fat cream cheese
- 1½ tablespoons reduced-fat sour cream
- 1 egg white, lightly beaten
- 650g purple plums, cut into 5mm wedges
- ⅓ cup firmly packed light brown sugar
- ¼ teaspoon ground ginger
- Black pepper

1. Combine the cup of flour, the white sugar and a pinch of salt in a large bowl. Cut in the butter and cream cheese with a pastry blender or 2 knives until the mixture resembles coarse crumbs. Combine the sour cream and 1 tablespoon iced water in a small bowl, then stir into the flour mixture until just combined. Flatten the dough into a round, wrap in plastic wrap, and refrigerate for at least 1 hour.

2. Preheat the oven to 190°C. Roll out the dough on a lightly floured surface to a 33 cm round. Place on a baking tray and roll the edges over once to form a neat edge and a 28 cm circle.

3. Brush the dough with the beaten egg white. Arrange the plum wedges on top in overlapping concentric circles. Combine the brown sugar, ginger, a pinch of pepper and the remaining flour in a small bowl. Sprinkle evenly over the plums. Bake for 40 minutes or until the plums are tender and the crust is golden.

Nutrients per serving: Kilojoules 1071; Fibre 3g; Protein 4g; Carbohydrate 39g; Saturated Fat 6g; Total Fat 9g; Cholesterol 25mg

Did you know?

Umeboshi is a Japanese plum pickle that is served with food. While high in salt, it is a traditional remedy for a range of digestive problems.

Plum Clafouti

Preparation: 15 minutes / Cooking: 30 minutes / Serves: 6

- 750g black or red plums, cut into 1cm wedges
- ½ cup sugar
- 2 eggs
- 2 egg whites
- ½ cup plain flour
- 1 cup low-fat milk
- ¼ cup reduced-fat sour cream
- 1 teaspoon vanilla essence
- 1 teaspoon grated orange zest
- 1 tablespoon icing sugar

1. Preheat the oven to 200°C. Toss the plums with 1 tablespoon of the sugar in a medium bowl; put aside.

2. Whisk together the whole eggs, egg whites and the remaining sugar in another medium bowl. Slowly beat in the flour, milk, sour cream, vanilla essence and orange zest. Arrange the plums in a 25 cm quiche dish or pie plate. Gently pour in the egg mixture. Bake for 30 minutes or until the custard is just set. Dust with the icing sugar and serve warm.

Nutrients per serving: Kilojoules 1007; Fibre 3g; Protein 7g; Carbohydrate 39g; Saturated Fat 3g; Total Fat 6g; Cholesterol 85mg

Spiced Plum Tart

Prunes & Dates

Prunes are rich in beta-carotene, potassium, iron and fibre, while dates also provide fibre and iron, as well as folate and nicacin.

Healthy Highlights

Prunes
5 (40g)

		Nutrients	% RDI
Kilojoules	311	Potassium	14%
Fibre	3.1g		
Protein	1g		
Carbohydrate	17.6g		
Saturated Fat	0g		
Total Fat	0.2g		
Cholesterol	0mg		
Sodium	3mg		

Dates, dried
½ cup (95g)

		Nutrients	% RDI
Kilojoules	1062	Potassium	35%
Fibre	9.1g	Iron	20%
Protein	1.9g	Magnesium	17%
Carbohydrate	63.2g	Nicacin	10%
Saturated Fat	0g		
Total Fat	0.2g		
Cholesterol	0mg		
Sodium	13mg		

Dates, fresh
5 (95g)

		Nutrients	% RDI
Kilojoules	506	Vitamin C	44%
Fibre	4.3g	Potassium	17%
Protein	1g	Folate	12%
Carbohydrate	30.1g		
Saturated Fat	0g		
Total Fat	0.1g		
Cholesterol	0mg		
Sodium	2mg		

Shopping & Preparation

At the market Dried prunes are sold whole or stoned, while dried dates are sold already stoned. Fresh dates are available all year, either locally grown or imported from the Middle East.

Look for When buying fresh dates, choose fruit that is plump and shiny, with lighter, smoother skins than the dried ones.

Preparation To remove the stones from prunes, snip with kitchen shears or scissors dipped in hot water (to keep the blades from sticking) and squeeze out the stones.

Dried Fruit Compote

Dried Fruit Compote @

Preparation: 5 minutes / Cooking: 25 minutes / Serves: 6–8

1¼ cups prunes
1 cup dried apricots
¾ cup dried peaches or pears, halved
⅓ cup sultanas
1 vanilla bean, halved
1 tablespoon julienned orange zest
½ cup sugar
2 tablespoons orange flower water or rose water
1 cup plain low-fat yoghurt

1. Rinse the prunes, apricots and peaches and place in a large saucepan with 4 cups water. Add the sultanas, vanilla bean and the orange zest. Partly cover and bring slowly to the boil.

2. Fully cover and simmer for 5 minutes. Add the sugar and stir until dissolved. Cover and simmer over low heat for a further 15 minutes then allow to cool.

3. Add the orange flower water to the fruit. Transfer to a serving bowl, cover and refrigerate. Serve with the yoghurt on the side.

Nutrients per serving: Kilojoules 845; Fibre 4g; Protein 5g; Carbohydrate 45g; Saturated Fat 0g; Total Fat 0g; Cholesterol 2mg

Date Scones

Preparation: 15 minutes / Cooking: 15 minutes / Makes: 10–12

2 cups self-raising flour

½ teaspoon ground nutmeg

Salt

1 tablespoon butter

1¼ cups dried dates, stoned and chopped

2 teaspoons grated orange zest

1 cup skim milk

1. Preheat the oven to 210°C. Sift the flour, nutmeg and a pinch of salt together then rub in the butter. Add the dates and orange zest.

2. Add the milk and mix into the flour to form a soft dough. Knead together quickly, then press out onto a lightly floured surface and cut the dough into rounds with a scone cutter.

3. Bake for 7 minutes, then reduce the heat to 180°C and bake for a further 8 minutes or until the scones are golden.

Nutrients per serving: Kilojoules 758; Fibre 3g; Protein 4g; Carbohydrate 37g; Saturated Fat 1g; Total Fat 2g; Cholesterol 6mg

Did you know?

Prune purée can replace much of the shortening in many baking recipes – a substitution that greatly cuts fat and increases fibre and nutrient content. To make 1 cup prune purée, process 250g stoned prunes with 4½ tablespoons water in a food processor, then use in place of up to half the butter or margarine in your recipe (using the same number of grams of purée).

Date Scones

Raspberries & Blackberries

These luscious berries are loaded with pectin, a type of fibre that can help lower cholesterol; they also contain cancer-fighting ellagic acid and carotenoids.

Healthy Highlights

Raspberries
1 cup (130g)

		Nutrients	% RDI
Kilojoules	199	Vitamin C	113%
Fibre	7g	Folate	21%
Protein	1.6g	Magnesium	10%
Carbohydrate	7.8g		
Saturated Fat	0g		
Total Fat	0.5g		
Cholesterol	0mg		
Sodium	3mg		

Blackberries
1 cup (195g)

		Nutrients	% RDI
Kilojoules	317	Vitamin C	250%
Fibre	12g	Folate	35%
Protein	2.8g	Magnesium	22%
Carbohydrate	14.8g	Vitamin A	14%
Saturated Fat	0g	Potassium	12%
Total Fat	0.6g		
Cholesterol	0mg		
Sodium	2mg		

Shopping & Preparation

At the market The best time of year for berries is summer. You'll find all sorts of varieties – blackberries, boysenberries, gooseberries, mulberries, loganberries and raspberries. Out of season they can be very expensive because they damage easily, which makes transporting them costly. Frozen berries can be used instead of fresh in many recipes.

Look for Be sure that the berries are in good condition. If the bottom of the box is stained, some of them may be crushed.

Preparation Do not wash berries. Remove from the refrigerator 30 minutes before serving.

A seedless raspberry sauce is a delectable luxury that can enhance many desserts. To eliminate the seeds, use a rubber spatula to press the berry purée through a sieve.

Blackberry Fool

Preparation: 5 minutes / Chill: 30 minutes / Serves: 4

- 2 cups fresh or frozen blackberries, plus 8 whole blackberries for garnish
- ½ cup caster sugar
- ½ cup reduced-fat sour cream
- 1 cup low-fat evaporated milk, chilled
- Almond bread (optional)

1. Purée the 2 cups of blackberries and the sugar in a food processor. Stir in the sour cream.
2. Whip the evaporated milk in a medium bowl until stiff peaks form. Fold into the blackberry mix and pour into 4 serving dishes. Chill for 30 minutes, decorate with the reserved whole blackberries, then serve, if liked, with slices of almond bread.

Nutrients per serving: Kilojoules 1261; Fibre 7g; Protein 7g; Carbohydrate 44g; Saturated Fat 7g; Total Fat 12g; Cholesterol 36mg

Blackberry Fool

No-Bake Raspberry Cheesecake

Preparation: 30 minutes / Cooking: 5 minutes Chill: 4 hours / Serves: 8

1 cup low-fat evaporated milk

3 cups fresh or frozen unsweetened raspberries, thawed

1 cup sugar

2 teaspoons cornflour mixed with 1 tablespoon water

2 envelopes gelatine

500g low-fat cream cheese

2 cups low-fat cottage cheese

½ cup reduced-fat sour cream

2 teaspoons grated lemon zest

2 tablespoons lemon or lime juice

1. Pour the evaporated milk into a metal bowl; place in the freezer until ice crystals form. Spray a 23 cm springform tin with cooking spray.

2. Meanwhile, purée 1 cup of the raspberries in a blender or food processor, then strain through a sieve into a small saucepan. Add ¼ cup of the sugar and the cornflour mixture. Bring to a simmer, stirring, and cook for 1 minute or until thickened. Put aside to cool slightly.

3. Place the gelatine in a small bowl and sprinkle on ⅓ cup cold water to soften. Place the bowl over a pan of simmering water and stir to dissolve the gelatine. Combine the cream cheese, cottage cheese, sour cream, lemon zest, lemon juice and the remaining sugar in a food processor and process until smooth. Add the dissolved gelatine and process again until smooth. Scrape into a large bowl and refrigerate until the mixture begins to mound.

4. Whip the partially frozen evaporated milk with an electric mixer until soft peaks form. Fold half of the raspberry sauce into the cheese mixture, then fold in the whipped milk. Fold in the remaining raspberries. Scrape the mixture into the prepared springform tin. Dollop the remaining raspberry sauce on top and swirl with a knife. Chill for 3 to 4 hours or until set. Remove the sides of the tin and serve the cheesecake cut into slices.

Nutrients per serving: Kilojoules 1556; Fibre 3g; Protein 20g; Carbohydrate 37g; Saturated Fat 11g; Total Fat 16g; Cholesterol 55mg

Raspberry Swirl Sorbet

Preparation: 25 minutes / Freeze: 4 hours / Serves: 6

2 mangoes, peeled and seeded

2 tablespoons lime juice

½ cup sugar

¼ cup plus 1 tablespoon honey

2 cups fresh or frozen raspberries

⅓ cup seedless raspberry jam

1. Purée the mangoes with ¾ cup water, the lime juice, sugar and the ¼ cup honey in a food processor. Place in a metal cake tin and freeze for 2 to 3 hours or until almost frozen.

2. Meanwhile, purée the raspberries, jam and the remaining honey in the food processor. Strain through a sieve to remove the seeds. Place in a metal cake tin and freeze for 2 to 3 hours or until almost frozen.

3. Cut the frozen mango purée into chunks and process in a food processor until smooth; transfer to a bowl. Repeat the process with the raspberry purée. Add the raspberry sorbet to the mango sorbet, swirl together, and return to the freezer to refreeze.

Nutrients per serving: Kilojoules 976; Fibre 4g; Protein 1g; Carbohydrate 57g; Saturated Fat 0g; Total Fat 0g; Cholesterol 0mg

Did you know?

The high fibre content of raspberries and blackberries is due in large part to the fact that they are usually eaten seeds and all.

Summer Pudding

Preparation: 25 minutes / Chill: 8 hours / Serves: 8

2 cups blackberries

2 cups raspberries

1 cup blueberries

½ cup seedless raspberry jam

½ cup caster sugar

3 teaspoons lemon juice

10 slices firm-textured white sandwich bread, crusts removed

⅓ cup cream, whipped

1. Combine the blackberries, raspberries, blueberries, raspberry jam and sugar in a medium saucepan. Bring to a simmer and cook for 1 minute. Stir in the lemon juice and put aside to cool.

2. Line a 5-cup soufflé dish or mixing bowl with plastic wrap, leaving a 13 cm overhang all round. Slice the bread in half on the diagonal and arrange the triangular slices on the bottom and sides of the dish (there will be bread left over for the top).

3. Spoon the berries and juices into the bowl. Cover with the remaining bread, trimming all sides. Cover with plastic wrap and fold the overhang over the top. Weight down with a heavy can. Refrigerate for at least 8 hours. Unmould onto a serving plate and remove the plastic. Cut the pudding into wedges and serve with the whipped cream.

Nutrients per serving: Kilojoules 1006; Fibre 6g; Protein 4g; Carbohydrate 49g; Saturated Fat 1g; Total Fat 3g; Cholesterol 7mg

Summer Pudding

Raspberry & Walnut Cake

Raspberry & Walnut Cake

Preparation: 30 minutes / Cooking: 50 minutes / Serves: 8

2½ cups plain flour

¾ cup firmly packed light brown sugar

1 teaspoon cinnamon

1 tablespoon baking powder

Salt

1 cup low-fat milk

1 egg

3 tablespoons unsalted butter, melted

2 tablespoons vegetable oil

¾ cup walnuts, chopped

1 teaspoon grated lemon zest

2 cups fresh raspberries

1. Preheat the oven to 180°C. Spray a 20 cm square baking tin with cooking spray and line with nonstick baking paper.

2. Combine the flour, sugar, cinnamon, baking powder and a pinch of salt in a large bowl. Mix together the milk, egg, butter and oil in a jug, then add to the dry ingredients. Stir the walnuts and lemon zest through the mixture.

3. Pour the batter into the prepared tin. Top the mixture with the raspberries. Bake for 50 minutes or until a skewer inserted in the centre comes out clean.

Nutrients per serving: Kilojoules 1848; Fibre 4g; Protein 9g; Carbohydrate 55g; Saturated Fat 6g; Total Fat 21g; Cholesterol 47mg

Did you know?

• Along with ellagic acid and beta-carotene, blackberries and raspberries contain other cancer-fighting phytochemicals: monoterpenes, catechins and phenolic acids. Monoterpenes also inhibit cholesterol production.

• If you're seeking a good potassium source, consider raspberries, which are superior to blackberries in their potassium content. This vital mineral helps to regulate blood pressure.

Strawberries

Strawberries are a primary source of ellagic acid, a phytochemical that fights carcinogens. Strawberries are also an excellent source of vitamin C and fibre.

Healthy Highlights

1 cup (145g)		Nutrients % RDI	
Kilojoules	117	Vitamin C	218%
Fibre	3.2g	Potassium	10%
Protein	2.5g	Folate	10%
Carbohydrate	3.9g		
Saturated Fat	0g		
Total Fat	0.1g		
Cholesterol	0mg		
Sodium	9mg		

Shopping & Preparation

At the market Strawberries are available all year, but for the ultimate flavour buy strawberries when they are in season: October to March in southern states, May to September in the north, and throughout summer in New Zealand.

Look for Choose strawberries that are plump, colourful and, most important, sweetly fragrant. The leafy caps should look fresh and green. Check the bottom of the punnet – stains suggest that the berries at the bottom may be crushed or spoiled.

Preparation Rinse berries in cold water, then hull them (see below). If you hull the berries before rinsing, they will absorb excess water.

Hulling a strawberry involves more than removing the leafy caps; you also need to remove the white 'core' attached to the cap. Use a small paring knife to dig it out quickly.

Strawberry & Ricotta Crêpes

Preparation: 25 minutes / Stand: 30 minutes
Cooking: 15 minutes / Serves: 4

½ cup milk
⅓ cup plain flour
¼ cup sugar
1 egg
1 egg white
2 teaspoons unsalted butter, melted
1 cup ricotta cheese
1 teaspoon vanilla essence
3 cups strawberries, hulled and thinly sliced, plus 4 whole strawberries for garnish
1 tablespoon icing sugar

1. Combine the milk, flour, 1 teaspoon of the sugar, the whole egg, egg white and melted butter in a blender and process until smooth. Let stand for 30 minutes.

2. Spray a 20 cm nonstick frying pan with cooking spray and heat over moderate heat. Spoon the batter, 2 tablespoons at a time, into the pan and swirl to coat the bottom. Cook for 15 seconds or until lightly browned on the bottom. Lift and turn the crêpe and cook for 5 seconds or until cooked through. Slide the crêpe onto a plate, cover with greaseproof paper, and continue making crêpes and stacking them with sheets of greaseproof paper in between. You will need 8 crêpes (if you are adept at making crêpes, you may get more than 8).

3. Combine the ricotta, vanilla essence and the remaining white sugar in a large bowl. Fold in the sliced strawberries. Spoon the mixture onto the centre of each crêpe, fold the ends over and roll up. Place 2 crêpes on each of 4 dessert plates, sprinkle with the icing sugar and garnish with a whole strawberry.

Nutrients per serving: Kilojoules 1201; Fibre 4g; Protein 14g; Carbohydrate 30g; Saturated Fat 7g; Total Fat 12g; Cholesterol 95mg

Did you know?

• One cup of strawberries supplies more vitamin C than a small orange.

• Strawberries contain respectable amounts of folate – a heart-healthy B vitamin – as well as some potassium.

Strawberries in Balsamic Vinegar

Preparation: 5 minutes / Chill: 1 hour / Serves: 4

1 punnet strawberries, hulled
2 tablespoons balsamic vinegar
2 tablespoons caster sugar

1. Combine the ingredients and leave to macerate in the refrigerator for 1 hour.

Nutrients per serving: Kilojoules 196; Fibre 1g; Protein 1g; Carbohydrate 10g; Saturated Fat 0g; Total Fat 0g; Cholesterol 0mg

Strawberry Pavlova

Preparation: 15 minutes / Cooking: 1¼ hours / Serves: 8

4 egg whites

Salt

1½ cups caster sugar

1 tablespoon cornflour

1 teaspoon vanilla essence

1 teaspoon vinegar

300ml cream, whipped, or 450ml vanilla low-fat yoghurt

1 punnet strawberries, sliced

1 tablespoon caster sugar (optional)

1. Preheat the oven to 150°C. Line a large baking tray with nonstick baking paper.

2. Beat the egg whites and a pinch of salt together in a medium bowl until stiff peaks form. Beat in the sugar, a third at a time, until the meringue is stiff and shiny. Sprinkle over the cornflour, then lightly fold in the vanilla essence and vinegar.

3. Mound the mixture onto the paper-lined tray in a circle about 20 cm round. Cook on the bottom shelf of the oven for 1¼ hours, then turn the heat off and allow the pavlova to cool completely in the oven.

4. Just before serving, peel off the backing paper and transfer the pavlova to a large platter. Pile on the cream, then spoon the strawberries on top. If using the caster sugar, sprinkle over the fruit at the last minute.

Nutrients per serving: Kilojoules 1048; Fibre 1g; Protein 3g; Carbohydrate 45g; Saturated Fat 5g; Total Fat 8g; Cholesterol 24mg

Did you know?

Strawberries rank second after blueberries in their antioxidant power.

Strawberry Pavlova

Q,R

Quick Fixings

All these recipes can be prepared, cooked and served in 30 minutes or less.

S